To G. Blair Laing

(1911–199[illegible])

MORRICE

A Gift to the Nation

THE G. BLAIR LAING COLLECTION

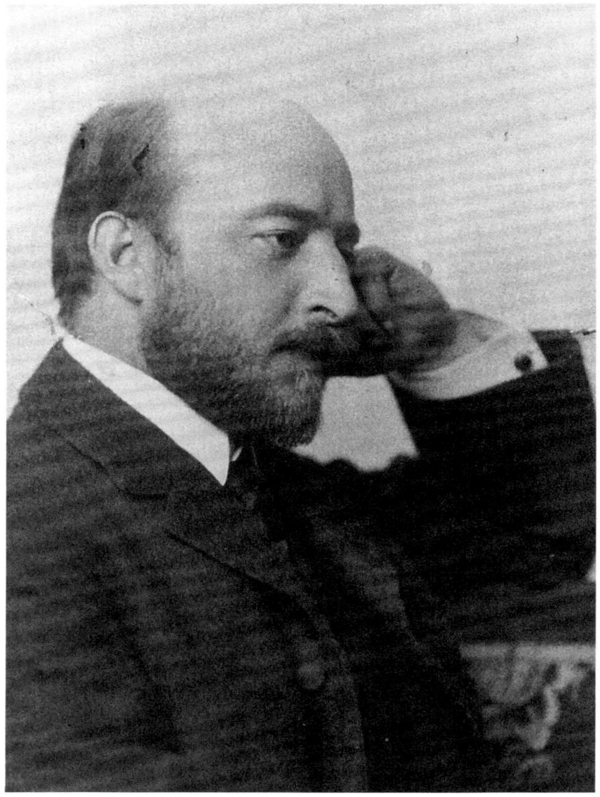

Morrice

A Gift to the Nation

The G. Blair Laing Collection

Charles C. Hill

National Gallery of Canada, Ottawa

Published in conjunction with the exhibition *Morrice – A Gift to the Nation : The G. Blair Laing Collection*, organized by the National Gallery of Canada.

Montreal Museum of Fine Arts
22 May–5 July 1992

Confederation Centre Art Gallery and Museum, Charlottetown
19 July–7 September 1992

Memorial University Art Gallery, St. John's
24 September–1 November 1992

Art Gallery of Nova Scotia, Halifax
28 November 1992–24 January 1993

Mendel Art Gallery, Saskatoon
12 March–2 May 1993

Glenbow Museum, Calgary
26 June–8 August 1993

Art Gallery of Greater Victoria
27 August–17 October 1993

McMichael Canadian Art Collection, Kleinburg
21 November 1993–2 January 1994

Mackenzie Art Gallery, Regina
26 January–20 March 1994

Canadian Cataloguing in Publication Data

Hill, Charles C., 1945–
Morrice – A Gift to the Nation: The G. Blair Laing Collection.
ISBN 0-88884-618-5

Published also in French under the title:
Morrice. Un don à la patrie : La collection G. Blair Laing.

1. Morrice, James Wilson, 1865–1924 – Exhibitions. 2. Laing, G. Blair, 1911–1991 – Art collections – Exhibitions. 3. National Gallery of Canada – Exhibitions.
I. National Gallery of Canada.
II. Title.

ND249 M67 H54 1992 759.11
CIP 92-099202-1

Catalogue produced by the Publications Division of the National Gallery of Canada.

Chief of Publications: Serge Thériault

Translation : Danielle Chaput

Editors: Usher Caplan and Claire Rochon

Picture Editor: Colleen Evans

Assistant Picture Editor: Roxanne Lafleur

Production Manager: Jean-Guy Bergeron

Designed by Associés libres, Montreal.

Printed on Patina paper by Tri-Graphic.

Typeset in Janson by Chromascan, Ottawa.

Film by Chromascan, Ottawa.

Available from your local bookseller or from The Bookstore, National Gallery of Canada
380 Sussex Drive, Box 427, Station A, Ottawa
K1N 9N4

PRINTED IN CANADA

Cover:
James Wilson Morrice
Café el Pasaje, Havana
(cat. no. 76)

Front flap:
G. Blair Laing
19 September 1989

Frontispiece:
James Wilson Morrice

Contents

Foreword

EVERY ART INSTITUTION in Canada owes an important part of its existence and growth to the generous contributions of private individuals. The bequest of Benaiah Gibb in 1877 enabled the fledgling Art Association of Montreal to build its first permanent art gallery and provided the core of its permanent collection. (Among those citizens who would further that institution, now the Montreal Museum of Fine Arts, was David Morrice, the father of the painter whose work we honour here.) In Saint John, New Brunswick, the trustees of the estate of John Owens initiated the art collection and art school now at Mount Allison University in Sackville. Artists and their families have also made vital contributions to the foundation and growth of art museums in Canada. One has only to think of the Blair Bruce collection in Hamilton, the Robert Harris collection in Charlottetown, the works of Napoleon Bourassa in Quebec, and the Emily Carr Trust in Vancouver. The Glenbow Museum in Calgary, the Beaverbrook Art Gallery in Fredericton, and the McMichael Canadian Art Collection in Kleinburg, Ontario, among others, owe their existence to the creative energy of single individuals.

The National Gallery of Canada has been especially favoured by the generosity and public spirit of individual collectors. The MacCallum bequest of paintings by Tom Thomson and the Group of Seven, the Massey gifts of British and Canadian paintings, the Douglas M. Duncan collection, and the Henry Birks collection of Canadian silver have enormously enriched the national collections.

The donation of the G. Blair Laing collection of eighty-three works by the outstanding Canadian artist James Wilson Morrice constitutes a major new landmark in this long history of public acts. The range and quality of the collection are unparalleled, and the National Gallery of Canada is very honoured to have been chosen as its custodian. It is also an honour and a great pleasure to be able to present these paintings to the people of Canada during its extended tour from coast to coast.

This is a collection of the work of one artist, formed over a period of almost forty years, and developed by a man with a keen eye and a passionate love. In his books Blair Laing tells of his first discovery of Morrice in 1934 and of his lively encounters with many collectors and dealers as he sought out and acquired the artist's works. Each individual piece in the collection has its own fascinating story.

On several occasions I had the opportunity to see these works in Blair Laing's home, and I was continually impressed by his great affection for the paintings and his admiration for their creator. His obvious delight in seeing them installed in the National Gallery, and the numerous letters he received from friends and strangers alike congratulating him on his most generous gift, reassured all of us of the wisdom of having kept the collection intact in a public institution.

My first thanks on behalf of the National Gallery would, of course, have gone to Blair Laing himself. I only wish that he might have lived to witness the continuing pleasure that was to be had from his gift. I would also like to thank the family of Blair Laing for their considerate support of the gift; it is a living testimony to the knowledge and public spirit of their father. A special note of thanks to Blair's sister, Mrs. Elizabeth Cowper-Smith, who has been of great assistance and unfailingly kind to the staff of the National Gallery.

The Laing collection will now travel across Canada, as Blair Laing wished it to be a gift to the entire nation. He subtitled his book on Morrice "A Great Canadian Artist Rediscovered," and indeed this collection will be, for many, a first discovery of one of Canada's greatest painters, and will, we hope, provide the same kind of enjoyment it did to Blair Laing for over fifty years.

Dr. Shirley L. Thomson
Director, National Gallery of Canada

Acknowledgments

ANY PROJECT OF THIS SCALE is, by necessity, a collaborative effort, building on the contributions of previous researchers and involving the assistance of people from many different institutions. A photographic catalogue of Morrice's paintings was assembled at the National Gallery of Canada by Donald Buchanan, and he continued to update it until the time of his death in 1966. It was subsequently reorganized by Dennis Reid, formerly Curator of Post-Confederation Canadian Art at the National Gallery, and has since been expanded by me. The acquisition by the National Gallery of the complete photographs of the Morrice sketchbooks and paintings at the Montreal Museum of Fine Arts has greatly facilitated my work, and for their assistance in this I would very much like to thank Suzelle Baudouin and Dominique Gagnon at the Montreal Museum. The staff of many other museums have also been of great service in responding to my numerous questions and to my requests for photographs and slides. I particularly wish to thank Elizabeth Kidd and Bruce Dunbar at the Edmonton Art Gallery; Gary Essar at the Winnipeg Art Gallery; Tom Smart at the Beaverbrook Art Gallery, Fredericton; James Campbell at the Samuel E. Weir Collection and Library of Art, Queenston, Ontario; Faye Van Horne at the Art Gallery of Ontario, Toronto; Barry Fair at the London Regional Art Gallery and Museum; Megan Bice and Sandra Cooke at the McMichael Canadian Art Collection, Kleinburg, Ontario; Jennifer Watson and Agnes Richard at the Art Gallery of Hamilton; and Mark Holton, formerly with the Confederation Centre Art Gallery, Charlottetown. I am indebted to the Dominion Gallery in Montreal for making available to the National Gallery copies of photographs of the Morrice paintings that they have sold over the years. I am also grateful to the Dominion Gallery and to the Walter Klinkhoff Gallery for putting me in touch with private collectors.

My sincere thanks go to those collectors who graciously allowed me to enter their homes and examine their paintings and who patiently answered my questions; to Mrs. Janet LeClair of New York, who granted me permission to consult the Robert Henri diaries; to W.R. Johnston of the Walters Art Gallery, Baltimore, who furnished copies of letters from his research on Morrice for the 1965 exhibition at the Montreal Museum of Fine Arts and who donated to the National Gallery four books from Morrice's library; to Mme Léa Cadoret Lepage of Malmaison, France, who provided information on her grandmother, Léa Cadoret; to Joan Murray, who generously supplied photographs of works in private collections; and to Margaret Bailey of Ottawa, a loyal supporter of the National Gallery who donated to our library Kathleen Fenwick's annotated copy of Buchanan's 1936 biography of Morrice.

Nicole Cloutier (presently at the Château Ramezay, Montreal) and Micheline Moisan, the curators responsible for the superb Morrice collections at the Montreal Museum of Fine Arts, have both been consistently generous over the years in discussing with me many issues related to Morrice and in allowing me access to their research. This catalogue would not have been possible without their assistance. I also thank Juanita Toupin, Archivist at the Montreal Museum, for her ongoing efforts in support of my project.

Lucie Dorais's thesis on the early years of Morrice's career has been of inestimable value to me in the preparation of this catalogue; her rigorous analysis has set a standard for all subsequent research. I am also indebted to Ms. Dorais for correcting a number of errors in my initial cataloguing of the collection.

Victoria Baker, Assistant Curator of Canadian Art at the National Gallery, took on the enormous job of sorting all the documentation on Blair Laing's paintings and assembling the initial files; many of her insights have been incorporated into this catalogue. Susan Guy helped with the first cataloguing of the collection and the assembling of the photographic documentation. Natalie Schlesak, an intern from York University, prepared an index of Morrice collectors, searched for documentation on painting sites, and helped Pierre Landry, Assistant Curator of Canadian Art, in transcribing the inscriptions. I am especially indebted to my secretary, Kathy Stone, who has worked on this project from the beginning and has been an invaluable support.

The staff of the National Gallery's Registration Department,

Technical Services, Protection Services, Financial Services, Restoration and Conservation Laboratory, and Photographic Services worked very hard on the transportation, processing, examination, and photography of this generous gift. Other sections that made major contributions to the initial presentation of the collection in Ottawa and preparation for tour include Exhibitions, Design, Technical Services and Framing, Library, Education, and Communications. Inevitably, to thank specific individuals is to forget the cooperative effort entailed in any project of this scale.

For their work on the preparation of this catalogue, I extend my thanks to Serge Thériault, Chief of Publications; Colleen Evans and her assistant, Roxanne Lafleur, who were responsible for the illustrations; Jean-Guy Bergeron, who supervised production; Danielle Chaput, who translated the manuscript into French; and Usher Caplan and Claire Rochon, who edited the English and French versions respectively.

I would like also to reiterate Dr. Thomson's thanks to the family of Blair Laing, and especially to his sister, Mrs. Elizabeth Cowper-Smith, for their kind support and cooperation.

It is with a sense of gratitude, mixed with sorrow, that I dedicate this book to the memory of a truly extraordinary man, one who will be fondly remembered by the many people who had the pleasure of dealing with him and by the many more who will now know him for his most generous gift.

Charles C. Hill
Curator of Canadian Art,
National Gallery of Canada

Introduction

MY PARTICULAR INTEREST in the work of James Wilson Morrice goes back about fifteen years to the time when I was organizing a small exhibition for the National Gallery of Canada focusing on the various versions of his beach scenes bearing the title *Landscape, Trinidad*. As so often happens, my project began to spread like a weed: enthralled by Morrice's rosy-hued vision of nature, I attempted to track down as many of his works as I could. It was then that Blair Laing very graciously allowed me to visit him and to see for the first time the numerous sketches and paintings by Morrice that hung on the walls of his apartment above his Toronto gallery. We discussed each of the works in turn and shared our keen admiration for them. As a result of the research I had been doing, I was able to point out to him, with all the pretentiousness of a neophyte, that *Fishing Boats, Nantes* (cat. no. 60) had not belonged to Morrice's friend Henri Matisse (as an inscription on the back mistakenly indicated) but had been obtained by his son, the New York art dealer Pierre Matisse, from Morrice's colour man, César Guichardaz.

Soon after, there came up for auction a watercolour of that famous bay in Trinidad, a variant of a canvas that was then in the collection of the artist's nephew David R. Morrice and which was later bequeathed to the National Gallery. I asked Blair Laing if he would bid on the work for the Gallery, and he kindly pointed out *to me* that as a dealer he did not bid for public institutions. He then purchased the watercolour and turned around and offered us first refusal – at a considerable markup. We declined.

This episode did nothing to alter our relationship, and over the years I had the occasional, all-too-infrequent, opportunity to visit Blair Laing and see his expanding collection. Each newly acquired work seemed more beautiful and more evocative than the one before, and at the same time so appropriately selected to complement the collection as a whole.

With colleagues and associates I wondered what would happen to this superb collection, developed with such love and knowledge. As some major canvases by other artists left his apartment, the rumour spread that the Morrices had been sold but that Blair Laing would keep the works at his pleasure. Therefore it was with great astonishment that we learned in March 1989 that he was willing to donate his entire collection of paintings by Morrice to the National Gallery of Canada.

Excited and somewhat apprehensive, I went to Toronto with several of our staff to wrap and prepare the paintings for delivery to Ottawa. Blair Laing had acquired these works with all the passion of a truly committed collector, and they had been a major part of his daily life, hanging on his walls for so many years. As we packed each work, I thought what a heart-wrenching experience this must be for someone who loved the paintings as much as he did. But Blair Laing was determined that his Morrices should be kept together, and that they should belong to a public institution where they could be seen and enjoyed by all.

So it was with great pleasure that we were able to officially present the collection in a joyful celebration at the National Gallery in Ottawa in March 1990.[1] The delight with which Blair Laing examined each painting in its new setting, and the way his face lit up as he observed the results of some minor cleaning carried out on one work, clearly confirmed in him the feeling that he had made the right decision. In the company of his family and friends, we honoured that evening a man who, by his enthusiasm and by his supreme generosity, had contributed enormously to the appreciation of a great Canadian artist.

❖ ❖ ❖ ❖ ❖ ❖ ❖ ❖ ❖ ❖

On the opening page of his 1979 autobiography, *Memoirs of an Art Dealer*, Blair Laing wrote: "My original intent had been to do a book on the Canadian artist James Wilson Morrice, relating particularly the story of my experiences during our long-time and ultimately successful search for his paintings."[2] That project, which had been close to his heart for so long, would be realized five years later in his lavishly illustrated book *Morrice: A Great Canadian Artist Rediscovered*. Its publication marked the high point of an unwavering passion that extended over fifty years.

Blair Laing first discovered Morrice's work in 1934, at the

age of twenty-two. The occasion was an exhibition at Mellors Fine Arts Limited in Toronto, a gallery financed by Blair's father, A.R. Laing. As Blair Laing recounted:

> *I remember when the Morrice collection arrived from his long-time Montreal dealers, William Scott and Sons, and that I was fascinated to glimpse the pictures as they were unpacked. I can recall how the pictures appeared on the walls glowing under the gallery lights. Although this was my first viewing of the artist's work, I realized I was looking at paintings that were produced by an unusually talented and perceptive artist. In addition to* The Ferry Boat, Quebec *canvas, destined to become one of Canada's most famous pictures, we also had its original sketch-panel version. There was his colourful 1915 canvas* Café el Pasaje, Havana, *and two views of the quais and the Seine as seen from his studio windows, one in spring and the other in autumn. The exhibition consisted of thirty canvases and panels, and twenty-one of his late watercolours. The emotional impact on me was such that in the half-century since, I have increasingly pursued works by James Morrice, and have been haunted by visions of the man himself . . .*[3]

Never would Blair Laing have imagined that four of the works in that exhibition – *Study for "The Ferry, Quebec"* (cat. no. 9), *Sugar Bush* (cat. no. 10), *Café el Pasaje, Havana* (cat. no. 76), and *Spring, Quai des Grands-Augustins* (cat. no. 77) – would one day hang on the walls of his home.

Gilbert Blair Laing was born in Montreal in 1911. Like Morrice he was raised in a Scottish Presbyterian family. During his youth he lived at various times in Fredericton, Port Credit, Brantford, and Windsor, finally settling in Toronto in 1930. It was in 1932, while Blair Laing was a student at the University of Toronto, that his father, A.R. Laing, entered into partnership with Robert Mellors, an Englishman who had run the picture department at the T. Eaton Company department store. Mr. Laing agreed to finance the fledgling Mellors Galleries, which was to become Mellors-Laing Galleries in 1940 and then Laing Galleries in 1941. At first the gallery was located on Yonge Street north of Bloor. In 1941 it moved to 60 Bloor Street East, where for a short period during the following year precision instruments for the war effort were machined in the gallery basement. In 1950 Laing Galleries moved to the excellent gallery building designed by Gordon Adamson at 195 Bloor Street West (see fig. 1).[4]

During the 1930s a number of notable shows were held at Mellors Galleries, including the aforementioned Morrice exhibition, as well as shows of works from the estates of Tom Thomson and J.E.H. MacDonald and five exhibitions (financed by Mr. and Mrs. Vincent Massey) of the work of David Milne. Complementing the ambitious exhibition program of the Art Gallery of Toronto and the solo shows of contemporary Canadian art at the Picture Loan Society, Laing Galleries soon specialized in the Canadian "Old Masters," including Cornelius Krieghoff, F.A. Verner, J.W. Beatty, Tom Thomson, J.E.H. MacDonald, Lawren Harris, and Emily Carr. During the 1950s and 1960s there were exhibitions of the work of Paul-Émile Borduas, Jean-Paul Riopelle, Alfred Pellan, Louis Archambault, and Jack Shadbolt, among others, as well as of traditional and contemporary European art organized with P.D. Colnaghi of London and Van Wisselinghe & Co. of Amsterdam. While the tone of the gallery was occasionally modern, it put more emphasis on the tried and sure value, attracting to its doors many leading Canadian collectors from across the country, including Ernest E. Poole and Ray Milner in Edmonton, John MacAulay

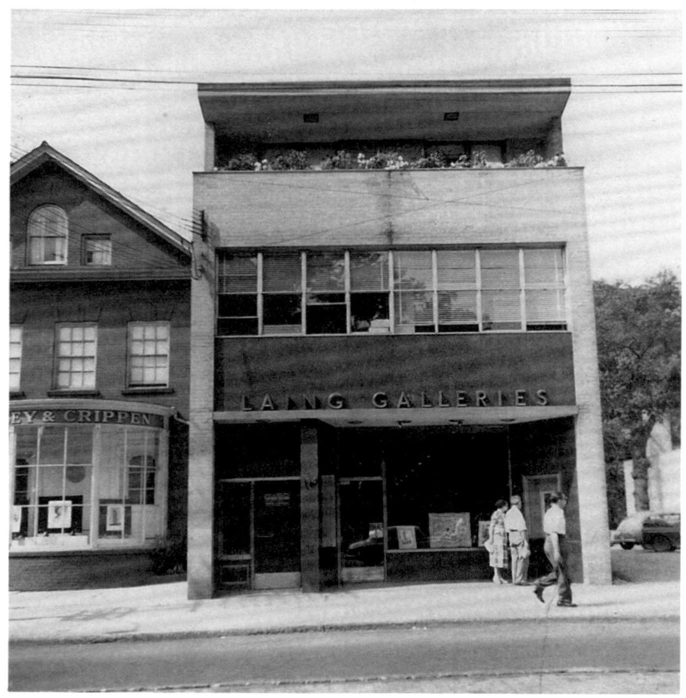

Fig. 1
Laing Galleries, 195 Bloor Street West, Toronto, c. 1950.

in Winnipeg, Lord Beaverbrook in Fredericton, Dr. George Henderson in Halifax, and K.R. Thomson in Toronto. As Blair Laing himself once remarked about a fellow art dealer, he "understood the importance of knowing the prominent individuals in the community who might have the means to buy expensive pictures."[5]

During the 1930s and 1940s art dealing was a slow and difficult business. It was only in the 1950s that Blair Laing was able to acquire the first paintings by Morrice for his own collection – six singular sketches purchased from the dealer John Nicholson of London and New York.

> *One March afternoon in 1952, I met John Nicholson on the premises of Hahn & Son, the London picture restorers. This was an old family business run by two brothers, Charles and Sidney, grandsons of the founder. They were highly experienced restorers who also bought and sold pictures as a side business. . . .*
>
> *On this particular day, John Nicholson was in a jaunty mood, exhilarated over an unexpected purchase. He had just bought another painting by the great English landscape painter John Constable. In a cheery voice, he also informed me that he had found six marvellous little paintings by the Canadian artist James Morrice. "Would you like to take a look at them?" he asked. My answer was a simple "Yes," but he cautioned me: "I will sell you only four because my wife is also fond of them."*
>
> *We picked up a cab at the Ritz Hotel on Piccadilly and within ten minutes had arrived at John's flat, tastefully furnished in good English antiques. "How much do you want for the Morrice's?" I asked, thunderstruck by their superb quality. Then he said: "You can have your choice of four of them at a hundred pounds each, but the other two I shall give to my wife." Before leaving his flat, I extracted his promise that if he ever decided to sell the remaining two I would be the first to know about it.*
>
> *Possibly two years passed by when, one day in New York, I looked up John Nicholson at his gallery. He had recently obtained yet another divorce from one of his charming English wives and, once again, was on his own. He recalled his promise to me about the two remaining Morrice panels and, to his credit, then and there said I could have them for $500 each.*[6]

The quality of these works – *Fishing Boats* (cat. no. 7), *Café, Paris* (cat. no. 20), *The Ramparts, St-Malo* (cat. no. 27), *Café, Venice*

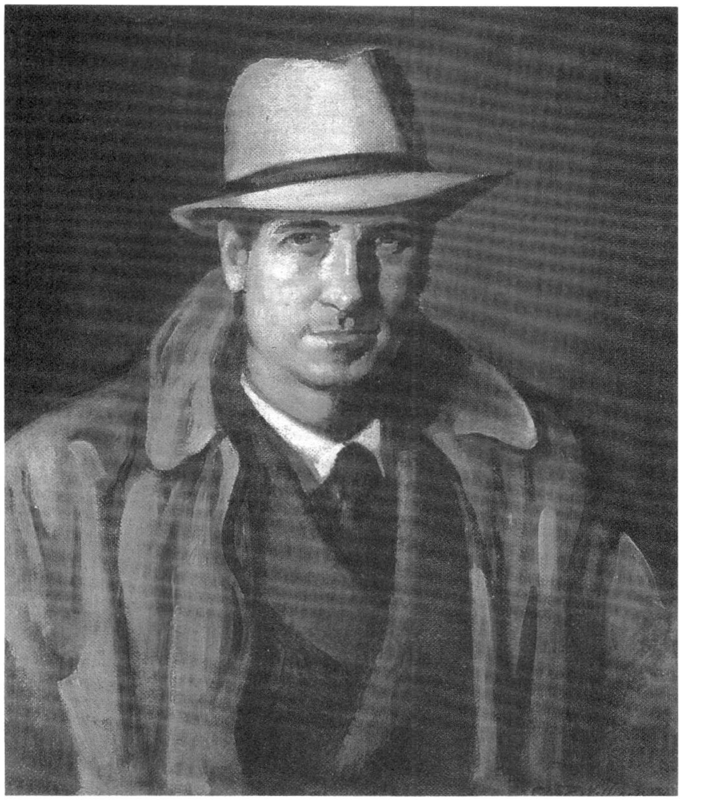

Fig. 2
A. Curtis Williamson (1867–1944), *Portrait of G. Blair Laing*, 1936–37, oil on masonite, 60.1 × 50.7 cm. National Gallery of Canada, Gift of G. Blair Laing, 1989 (30485).

(cat. no. 31), *Study for "At a Country Fair"* (cat. no. 46), and *Beach and Parasols* (cat. no. 54) – set the standard for the growth of a collection that would eventually include a total of fifteen canvases, sixty-six large and small oil sketches, one watercolour, and one drawing.

Certainly many works by Morrice came to Laing Galleries through normal business, and an equal number were sold, but Blair Laing seriously studied the literature on Morrice as he developed his own collection. He analyzed the catalogues of the various Morrice exhibitions held in the 1920s and 1930s. He gathered information on the various owners and visited them to familiarize himself with their paintings, in the hope of a possible purchase. In 1948 he visited the Montreal home of Mrs. Ethel Morrice, the widow of James's brother Arthur. In 1957 he had the rare opportunity of seeing the excellent collection of paintings by Morrice and by Albert Marquet hanging in the family home of Jacques Rouché, the director of the Paris Opera and one of Morrice's most important collectors. In 1970, while on a trip to England he visited the widow of the collector Lieut. Col. A. Hamilton Gault of Montreal. The latter two visits resulted eventually in the acquistion of paintings by Morrice.

Blair Laing's steadily growing interest in the work of Morrice was fuelled by his friendships with the painter Curtis Williamson (who painted his portrait in 1936; see fig. 2)[7] and with the writer Newton MacTavish, each of whom had been closely acquainted with the artist (see fig. 3). It was from MacTavish that Mellors Gallery had purchased the charming St-Malo sketch (cat. no. 26) in 1939, a work Blair Laing later repurchased from Mrs. G.H. Henderson of Halifax. The fortuitous acquisition of the six superb sketches from John Nicholson was followed by the purchase of *Dieppe* (cat. no. 50) from A.B. Fisher of Toronto, an old friend of MacTavish who, on the latter's advice, had purchased it from the Patriotic Fund sale organized by the Royal Canadian Academy in 1914. In 1965 Blair Laing acquired two excellent small canvases, *Barge on the Seine* (cat. no. 1) and *Prow of a Gondola, Venice* (cat. no. 12), from J.J. Vaughan, a colleague of Mr. Fisher's at the T. Eaton Company in Toronto. Further

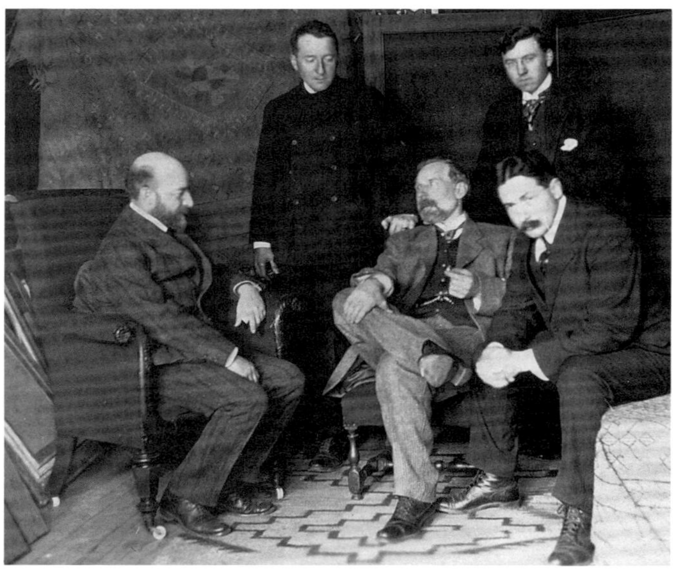

Fig. 3
Members of the Canadian Art Club, Toronto, February 1909. From left to right: James W. Morrice, Edmund Morris, Homer Watson, Newton MacTavish, Curtis Williamson.

purchases were made, some by chance and some by design, but increasingly Blair Laing sought out works that would, taken together, reveal the full scope and development of Morrice's art – major canvases if possible, or else sketches that related to well-known canvases or were especially beautiful in themselves.

Thus, by conscious design, Blair Laing assembled a wide-ranging and remarkably representative collection of works by this great artist. Among the outstanding paintings in the collection are *Prow of a Gondola, Venice*; *Femme au lit (Jane)*; *The Juggler*; *On the Cliff, Normandy*; and *Café el Pasaje, Havana*, to name just a few. There are also sketches for such well-known canvases as *Bullring, Marseilles*; *Venice, Looking out over the Lagoon*; *The Communicant*; *Houses, Cuba*; and *The Ferry, Quebec*.

From the 1893 study of a barge on the Seine to the 1922 sketch of Algiers, the collection spans the entirety of Morrice's career. There are views of Parisian streets, cafés, and quays, Breton and Norman ports, Venetian, Canadian, West Indian, and North African scenes, as well as three important war sketches. The collection evokes the names of Morrice's friends, dealers, and early collectors – Newton MacTavish, Dr. Francis Shepherd, Daniel Wilkie, F.R. Heaton and his son John, Jacques Rouché, Charles Pacquement, Jacques Dubourg, fellow-artists Frits Thaulow, Robert Henri, Sir Gerald Kelly, Percyval Tudor-Hart, Clarence Gagnon, and Edwin Holgate, and Morrice's lifelong friend Léa Cadoret. These former owners of Blair Laing's paintings had loaned them to the major exhibitions of Morrice's work, including the memorial exhibition at the Art Association of Montreal in 1925, the exhibition at Galeries Simonson in Paris in 1926, the inaugural exhibition at the Art Gallery of Toronto that same year, the "Exposition d'art canadien" at the Jeu de Paume in Paris in 1927, the major retrospective at the National Gallery in 1937, and the display organized by the Royal Canadian Academy in 1953.[8]

After many years of collecting Blair Laing determined to write a book on Morrice. He commissioned a historian in Paris to assist him with his research, and he travelled to Dennemont, St-Malo, Dieppe, and other Breton and Norman towns and villages where Morrice had painted. He visited Morrice's studio in Paris, and went also to Cagnes, where Morrice had purchased a house for Léa Cadoret.[9] It was one of Blair Laing's great regrets that he had never had the opportunity of meeting Morrice's friend before she died in November 1973; clearly, their relationship fascinated him, and he touches on it quite frequently in his book.

One of the great delights of Blair Laing's book is the way in which he brings to life the many fascinating stories of his search for Morrice's paintings. He tells of the collectors and dealers he encountered over the years and of his travels to many of the artist's sketching sites. At the same time, he deftly weaves in details of Morrice's biography and quotes extensively from Morrice's correspondence with the painter Edmund Morris and with Newton MacTavish. His infectious love of his subject and his extensive knowledge, acquired over a lifetime, make his book an essential tool for the study of Morrice and a necessary companion to the present volume.

Blair Laing was always very generous in showing his Morrices to other interested collectors, students, and curators. He loaned his paintings and drawings to all the major Morrice exhibitions of recent decades – the Montreal Museum's in 1965, the National Gallery's exhibition shown in England and France in 1968, the Vancouver Art Gallery's in 1977, and the Montreal Museum's again in 1985. Morrices from his collection were included in the Art Gallery of Ontario's *Impressionism in Canada* in 1973, the exhibition *OKanada* organized by the Canada Council and shown in Berlin in 1982, the Agnes Etherington Art Centre's *Canadian Artists in Venice 1830–1930* in 1984, and the exhibition of Canadian painting at the Norton Gallery in West Palm Beach, Florida, also in 1984.[10] Blair Laing's entire Morrice collection was hung at his gallery for a public viewing on the occasion of the launching of his book in 1984 (see fig. 4).

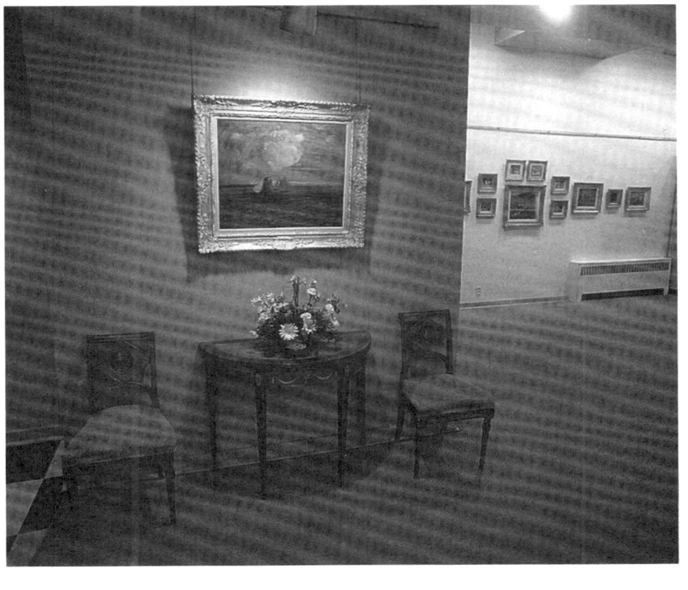

Fig. 4
Exhibition of the Laing collection of paintings by James W. Morrice at G. Blair Laing Ltd., Toronto, December 1984.

Who was this person whose paintings so attracted Blair Laing? James Wilson Morrice was born in Montreal in 1865, into a wealthy Scottish and Presbyterian merchant family, supporters of education and the arts. He studied law in Toronto, but upon completing his bar requirements in 1889 he left for Europe to become a painter. In Paris he befriended the Australian artist Charles Conder,[11] and also the American Maurice Prendergast, with whose work his paintings have many affinities. However, his real reason for staying in France was to see and study French art. The painters he admired most were Camille Corot, Henri Harpignies (with whom Morrice studied briefly), Puvis de Chavannes, Camille Pissarro, Alfred Sisley, Édouard Manet, Claude Monet, the Anglo-American James McNeill Whistler, Paul Gauguin, and Pierre Bonnard, and one can see in his own paintings the lessons acquired from his studies of their work.

But from his earliest works there emanates a very distinctive personality, a subtle rhythm, a mood of calm, quiet pleasures. Like many artists of his generation, he had rejected the classical mythologies and historical narratives of academic art for the pleasures of contemporary life, but his was a very selective immersion in the world. His paintings show elegantly dressed women walking in the streets or seated in cafés, horse-drawn carriages and sleighs, and the glittering night lights of Paris, but there is hardly a glimpse of those scientific innovations that would, in his lifetime, so radically alter the urban environment – trains, automobiles, electrical and telephone wires, or even bicycles. Increasingly Morrice himself would flee from the noise and traffic of Paris to paint in Concarneau or in some other quiet spot.[12]

Like his friend Charles Conder, Morrice was attracted to the world of eighteenth-century *fêtes galantes*, of Watteau's *Voyage to Cythera* reenacted in contemporary dress. No doubt with memories of Seurat's famous painting of the Grande Jatte, the critic Marius-Ary Leblond wrote in 1909, "One has the impression always that he is painting on a Sunday afternoon."[13] Whether seated in a café in Paris or Tangiers, or relaxing on a beach in Brittany or the Côte d'Azur or Trinidad, or walking along the banks of the Seine or a Venice quay, his figures invariably exude a sense of perfect tranquillity. Even the children on his beaches scurry in animated silence. Without haste, they watch and flow with a quiet grace. A lover of poetry and music, and an accomplished flautist, Morrice perceived the world as the expression of harmonious and evocative rhythms.

Morrice himself was a very affable person, friend of some and acquaintance of many. In his letters he would often keep his transatlantic correspondents informed of the comings and goings of their mutual friends. Younger artists were encouraged to look him up when they arrived in Paris, for advice and for an introduction to the city and its art.[14] It was from Morrice that the young Clive Bell learned much about paintings, as well as about the cafés and bars of Paris,[15] and Bell reinforces Arnold Bennett's description of Morrice found in the latter's 1905 journal:

> *He has the joy of life in a high degree, and he likes living alone. "I enjoy everything," he said. "I got up this morning, and I saw an old woman walking along, and she was the finest old woman I ever did see. She was a magnificent old woman, and I was obliged to make a sketch of her. Then there was the* marchand de quatre saisons. *His cry is so beautiful. I began to enjoy myself immediately I got out of bed. It is a privilege to be alive."*[16]

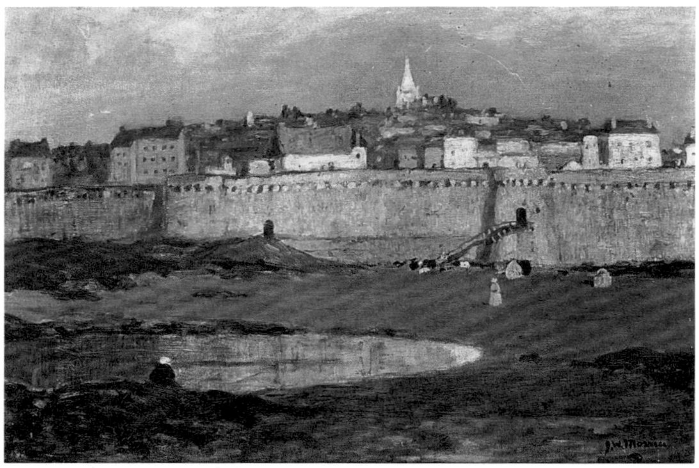

Fig. 5
View of St-Malo, c. 1901–02, oil on canvas, 50.5 × 73.5 cm. Musée de Picardie, Amiens. Bequest of Charles Dumont, 1926 (P.1068).

Morrice was a sensualist, a man who appreciated the pleasures of the flesh,[17] a man with a sense of humour, who saw beauty in all things and took great delight in living. As he wrote to his friend the Toronto painter Edmund Morris: "What prevents me going back to the Ontario Bar is the love I have of paint!! the privilege of gloating over things."[18]

But there was also an opposite side to Morrice's personality. The scholar John O'Brian describes him aptly as "this artist at the centre of the world yet hidden from the world."[19] He would up and leave on the slightest whim, without telling anyone. He kept his mistress, Léa Cadoret, at a distance, and even she might not know if he had left Paris.[20] His constant travels reflect an independence of spirit and an openness to discovery, but also a lack of attachment, an isolation from the world. And then there was his drinking, which undoubtedly softened some spiritual pain, while at the same time abetting the rosy glow of his perception.

Bennett's description of a visit to Morrice's studio is extremely telling:

> *Last night I walked down to the Quai des Grands Augustins to find Morrice. He opened his door for me, flute in hand. It was curious to come in from the noisy quay, from the vast communal life of the city, to this one little personal interior, and discover a bald-headed man playing the air from the slow movement of the D major symphony, perfectly content with himself, perfectly self-contained and self-sufficing. The music was propped up on the mantlepiece near to an old lamp with a shade. The studio was untidy, uncomfortable, shabby and dirty as usual: an awful hole. Morrice wanted me to hear the tone of his new flute, and I heard it and praised it. Then he showed me his sketches, made in Brittany – many of them exquisite things, and so original,* seen *with such a finely organized synthetic eye: also the beginnings of some pictures. We went to the Place St. Michel and he had something poisonous. Then we took the tram to the boulevard (the idea of taking a cab did not seem to occur to him, even), and he told me with the utmost simplicity how he had quite lost his self-control in regard to certain drinks. It was touching, almost pathetic, to see him genuinely concerned, grieved, because of his conviction that the beautiful and the picturesque were passing out of existence. "*You *can look to the future without quaking," he said in a sad tone, "because you don't believe that. But I believe it." We dined at the old Restaurant Viennois, exquisitely, for 6½ francs the two;*

> *and then took tea and coffee on the terrace of the Café Riche, where Morrice had five* verres *of brandy with his coffee.*[21]

In Morrice's paintings there frequently appears a figure alone, confronting the viewer (see, for example, cat. nos. 28, 29, 30, and 33). These figures keep us at a distance, inhibiting our involvement, watching us as we examine them and their surroundings. There also appear figures who are simply observing the activity or scene Morrice is depicting (see cat. nos. 26, 36, and 41), as if insisting that we too take time to see and delight in the world around us. Be it at the bullring in Marseilles, along the quays of Venice, amidst the bustling activity of a market in North Africa, or in a café in Havana, the experience presented to us is essentially neutral, devoid of any brusque emotion. These isolated, watching people are Morrice himself, the outsider, the painter who cannot but see the world through his own personality, a world of visual pleasure bathed in a sensual glow and, on occasion, tinged with a sweet and tender melancholy.

Morrice met with considerable international success during his lifetime. In 1903 he was elected sociétaire of the Société Nationale des Beaux-Arts in Paris. He was elected to the Salon d'Automne and Société Nouvelle in 1908, and to the London-based International Society of Sculptors, Painters and Gravers by 1903. In Canada he was a charter member of the Canadian Art Club in 1907 and was elected honorary non-resident academician by the Royal Canadian Academy of Arts in 1913. Two of his paintings were bought by the French government from the annual Salons,[22] and by the time of his death he was represented in the collections of the Musée National du Luxembourg and the Musée des Arts Décoratifs in Paris, the Musée des Beaux-Arts in Lyons, the Hermitage in St. Petersburg, the Museum of Western and Oriental Art in Odessa, the Contemporary Art Society in London, the Carnegie Institute in Pittsburgh, the Philadelphia Museum's Wilstach Collection, the Barnes Foundation in Merion, Pennsylvania,[23] as well as the Art Association of Montreal and the National Gallery of Canada. Two additional paintings were acquired by French museums in 1926, including *View of St-Malo* (fig. 5), bequeathed by Charles Dumont to the Musée de Picardie.[24]

Especially important to Morrice was the high esteem in which he was held by his fellow artists. In Paris in the late 1890s, Robert Henri repeatedly expressed his great admiration for Morrice's work.[25] Walter Sickert described him as "charming & gifted . . . intelligent & modest & I admire in him that he comes off & he *does*, & doesn't, like me, eternally *prate* of doing."[26] Henri Matisse, in a frequently quoted letter, referred to Morrice as an "artist with a sensitive eye, who with a moving tenderness took delight in rendering landscapes in closely related values . . . On a personal level, he was a real gentleman, a great companion, brimming with liveliness and wit."[27]

In spite of his repute Morrice remains a somewhat mysterious figure. Few of his letters and no personal papers have survived, and the other remaining records of his comings and goings, his friendships, and his associations are scant for an artist who was so active and productive. But as John Lyman, who knew Morrice in France, wrote: "Is there anything more mysterious than a man who hides himself? Not that it was something wilful on his part, for he did not have it in him to strike a pose or call attention to himself. The only recognition he sought was that which stems from the excellence of one's work."[28] It is in Morrice's paintings, then, that we perceive the man, and Blair Laing's collection provides us a rare opportunity to follow him through the entire thirty-year span of his artistic career.

❖ ❖ ❖ ❖ ❖ ❖ ❖ ❖ ❖ ❖

The Laing collection also provides us an opportunity to examine Morrice's working methods, as we can document related drawings, oil sketches, canvases, and variant studies, as well as changes Morrice made to his works over the years. The components of Morrice's working procedures were the standard ones of nineteenth-century landscape painters: sketchbook drawings, studies in watercolour or oil, and canvases. In most instances (figure studies being the main exception), initial sketches in graphite and/or oil preceded a larger canvas.

Thirty of Morrice's sketchbooks are known to exist.[29] Two of them were purchased by the National Gallery in 1936 from Léa Cadoret through Morrice's biographer Donald Buchanan. One early sketchbook is in a private collection. Twenty-four are in the Montreal Museum of Fine Arts, a gift of the artist's nephew David R. Morrice, who had acquired them from Léa Cadoret in 1952. Three sketchbooks were formerly in the collection of Vincent Massey, most likely acquired through Donald Buchanan in the 1930s, and were sold at auction in London in 1960.[30] Blair Laing purchased them and subsequently sold (and in at least one case donated) individual pages from them to public institutions and private collectors. Some of the pages were included with the limited edition of his 1984 book on Morrice. The remnants of these three sketchbooks were given to the National Gallery in 1989, together with his collection of paintings.[31] It is almost certain that other sketchbooks existed, now either destroyed or lost, as the chronology of the known sketchbooks leaves large, inexplicable gaps in Morrice's career.

The sketchbooks are a mine of information on the artist – he filled them with addresses, train schedules, titles of works submitted to exhibitions, lists of paintings in his studio, notes on music and books, bad jokes, and occasionally the dates of his travels. But most important are the drawings themselves. In the early sketchbooks one can find a number of composed studies, framed in the centre of the page (fig. 6), but most of the time his drawings fill the page, still equally arranged, but looser – the first, rapid definition of an idea. On one page he might include several studies of figures walking, a detail of the structure of a lamp post (see fig. 11), or the tracery of a window, or figures sketched at a café table. Now and then he might add colour notes.

Morrice did not use his sketchbooks in a consistently ordered manner. A winter landscape might appear right next to a summer sketch. One of the sketchbooks contains drawings for a canvas exhibited in January 1903 as well as drawings dating from a winter 1906 visit to Canada.[32] Date ranges have been attributed to all the sketchbooks, but the dating of many of the individual drawings remains problematic and disputed.

There are a few other drawings by Morrice, some of which clearly were removed from sketchbooks.[33] Two charcoal drawings are known, one of which is after a drawing in a sketchbook and is on the back of a cut-down drawing of a male model (fig. 7).[34] There are also two drawings after paintings, one having been used to illustrate a review of a salon exhibit.[35] A drawing of Léa Cadoret (cat. no. 18) is a rare example of a more finished work in graphite on drawing paper. Morrice did not do finished, preparatory drawings for his canvases, squaring them off for enlargement.

In his early sketchbooks Morrice would, on occasion, use watercolours to enhance a drawing, and in his 1897 Paris–Quebec Sketchbook in the National Gallery of Canada, washes in blue ink suggest the values and mood. It was only on his trip to Cuba and Jamaica in 1915 that he appears to have returned to the use of watercolour for preparatory studies (see cat. no. 75), possibly due to the heat and the difficulty of working in oil. After 1918, he would produce some of his finest works in watercolour, developed from sketchbook drawings or (in at least one instance) after an oil sketch (see cat. no. 74 and fig. 74a).[36]

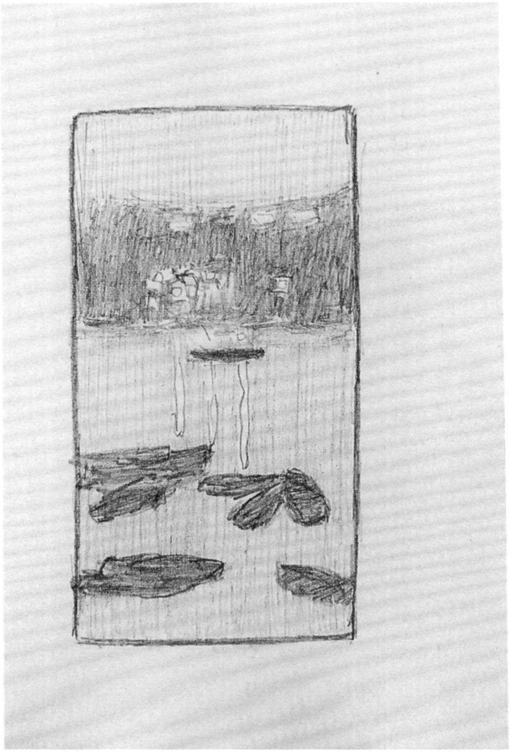

Fig. 6
Sketchbook 9, p. 84r, c. 1896, graphite on wove paper, 16.4 × 10.7 cm. Montreal Museum of Fine Arts. Gift of David R. Morrice, 1973 (Dr.1973.32).

A friend of Morrice's, Muriel Ciolkowska, has described his oil sketching methods:

> *Morrice, so far as I know, was never seen to carry visible painting kit, his complete outfit consisting of a small box which could fit like a cigar case into one of the pockets of his dapper tweed suit, and which held his panels, his brushes and a made-out palette.*
>
> *I once had the good luck to attend the production of one of these little preparations for his bigger pictures. He spent three afternoons on a surface hardly bigger than a medium-sized envelope. He would look long at his subject, mix his tone, look again, then dab on a tiny morsel of color, lay down his little brush, take a puff of smoke, and so on between every minute touch; for the severest precision in the sketch – precision of form*

and tone – was the secret of that lovely looseness and laxness in the enlargement.[37]

A similar description is given by Somerset Maugham in *The Magician*, in his character Warren, based on Morrice.

He has the most fascinating sense of colour in the world, and the more intoxicated he is, the more delicate and beautiful is his painting. Sometimes, after more than the usual number of apéritifs, he will sit down in a café to do a sketch, with his hand so shaky he can hardly hold a brush, he has to wait for a favourable moment, and then he makes a jab at the panel. And the immoral thing is that each of these little jabs is lovely. He's the most delightful interpreter of Paris I know, and when you've seen his sketches – he's done hundreds, of unimaginable grace and feeling and distinction – you can never see Paris in the same way again.[38]

John O'Brian has quite justifiably questioned whether Morrice could actually have spent three afternoons on a single sketch measuring approximately 12.5 by 15.5 centimetres,[39] but what both observers testify to most convincingly is the directness of the touch – the dab or jab – and the spontaneity of the response in paint. Yet how does one account for the fact that so many of the sketches are derived from drawings in the sketchbooks? For it is clear that in many instances the composition was first determined in the drawing and then reworked in the sketch. Even in cases where Morrice may have conceived the composition on paper, the early sketches would appear to have been painted directly on the panel, though a preliminary drawing on the panel itself is evident in some oil sketches from as early as 1897 (see fig. 9b). It is not clear whether Morrice worked consecutively at one sitting from drawing to oil sketch, or returned to the site of the drawing to paint the sketch, or painted the sketches in his studio, from memory. One can assume that, due to the lack of proper lighting, the night sketches were not painted outside.

In his drawings Morrice determines the composition; in the oil sketches he establishes the colours and the lights and darks, synthesizing the elements of the composition with a palette that is relatively strong in contrasts when compared to the more unified tones evident in his canvases. John Lyman observed that the drawings and oil sketches were Morrice's means of defining the "material elements."[40] Yet they are not merely documentary studies – in them the artist's personality, his habitual manner of composing a scene or arranging figures within the frame, are immediately evident. The oil sketches are complete in themselves, and only a few were ever used in the preparation of a larger canvas. Morrice prized them highly, regularly exhibiting them and selling them.

His first oil sketches were painted on irregularly cut pieces of canvas.[41] Tack holes, surrounded by unpainted areas, are often evident in the corners of these sketches where Morrice would have attached them to a support for painting (see fig. 8).

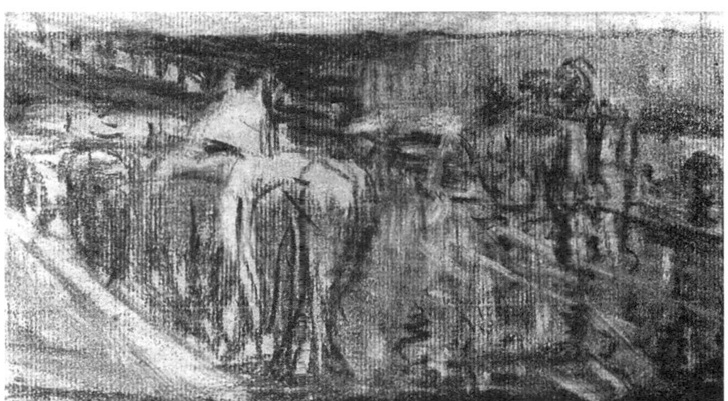

Fig. 7
Street Scene, c. 1897, charcoal on laid paper, 11.7 × 21.8 cm.
Musée du Québec, Quebec City (A53.150D).

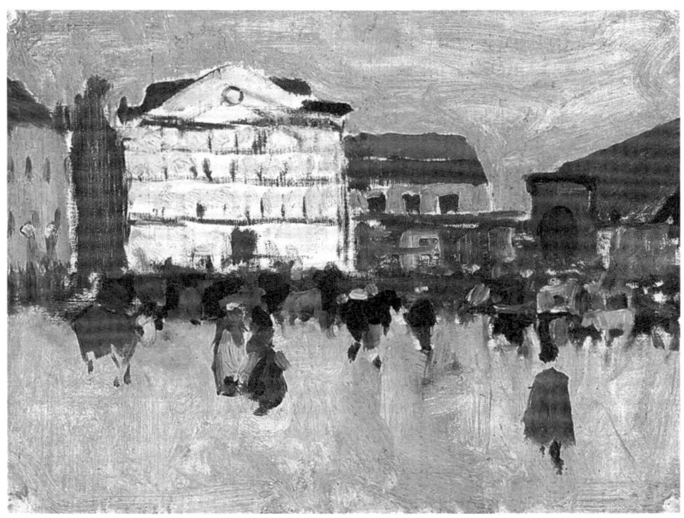

Fig. 8
View of a Square, Dieppe, c. 1894, oil on canvas, 23.3 × 31.6 cm.
National Gallery of Canada (3335).

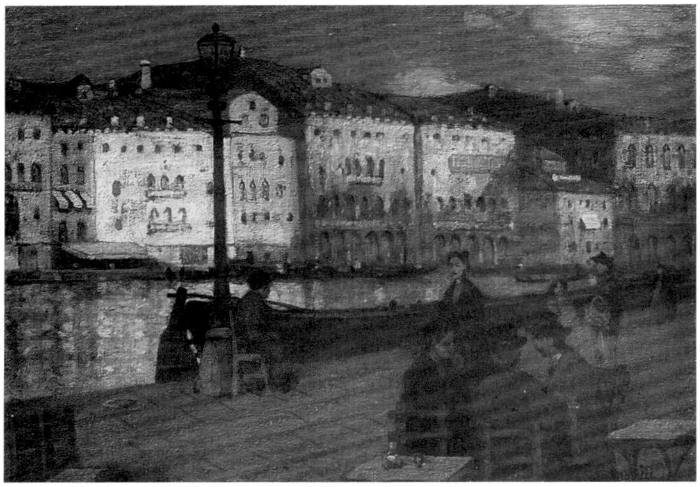

Fig. 9
Venice, the Grand Canal, 1901, oil on canvas, 59 × 82 cm. Private collection. Photograph by E. Crevaux, Paris.

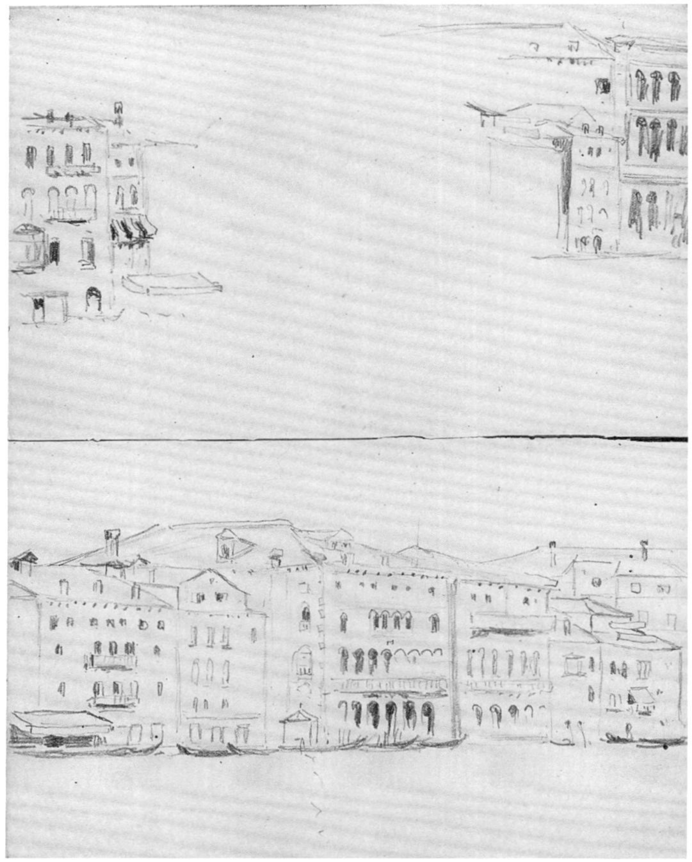

Fig. 10
Paris–Venice Sketchbook, pp. 20v–21r, 1901, graphite on wove paper, 21.7 × 17.2 cm (overall). National Gallery of Canada (7419).

At some later date they were mounted on a wood-pulp board and the edges were trimmed.[42]

Several sketches are painted on wood panels measuring about 17.5 by 25 cm (cat. nos. 9, 28, 30), on larger panels of about 23.5 by 33 cm (cat. nos. 3, 19, 29, 40, 43, 67, 78, 80), or on smaller panels of about 9.7 by 15.5 cm (cat. nos. 11, 14, 22, 23, 24). Morrice's preferred size, though, was about 12.5 by 15.5 cm. From about 1909 one also finds panels of about 13.3 by 17 cm. He purchased his supplies from various colourmen in Paris as well as on his travels in London, Capri, and Venice (see cat. nos. 19 and 29).

From his earliest sketches, Morrice tended to leave part of the support visible, contrasting the unpainted or thinly painted areas with the more worked areas. The canvas or wood becomes a tonal element in the work (see, for example, cat. nos. 6, 26, 47, and 48), to the point where certain sketches are almost coloured drawings (cat. no. 55). The bare wood can also be used to affirm a colour break (cat. nos. 37 and 41). In his sketches Morrice usually paints the figures and the main compositional elements first, filling in the sky and ground after (see cat. nos. 11, 21, 43, and 53). From about 1901 he adopts the technique of rubbing the paint onto the wood, creating glowing surfaces, and then highlighting them with touches of paint for details (cat. no. 40). Graphite is also used to add detail or emphasize a line or form (cat. nos. 41 and 61), but increasingly the graphite becomes an expressive element in itself, sometimes quite independent of colour and form (cat. nos. 67, 69, and 80). Morrice also uses scratching as a graphic device (cat. nos. 16, 39, and 65), or sometimes he draws with a blunt instrument in the wet paint (cat. no. 80).

In all his oil sketches Morrice shows an innate sensibility to subtle colour effects. Often one finds contrasting colours that draw the viewer into the composition but which usually also respond to other touches of the same colours elsewhere in the work, uniting the extremities of the composition. In *Pont d'Austerlitz* (cat. no. 21) the green, orange, and red on the kiosk respond to the same colours on the coach at the left. In *A Brittany Town* (cat. no. 56) a touch of red jumps out from the far end of the square. In *Street, Brittany* (cat. no. 55) the woman's dress is dotted in green.

San Marco Square, Venice (cat. no. 40) is composed of a

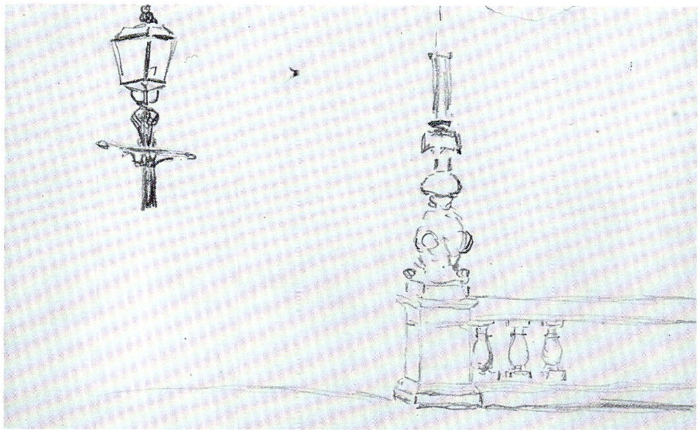

Fig. 11
Paris–Venice Sketchbook, p. 19r, 1901, graphite on wove paper, 11.4 × 17.2 cm. National Gallery of Canada (7419).

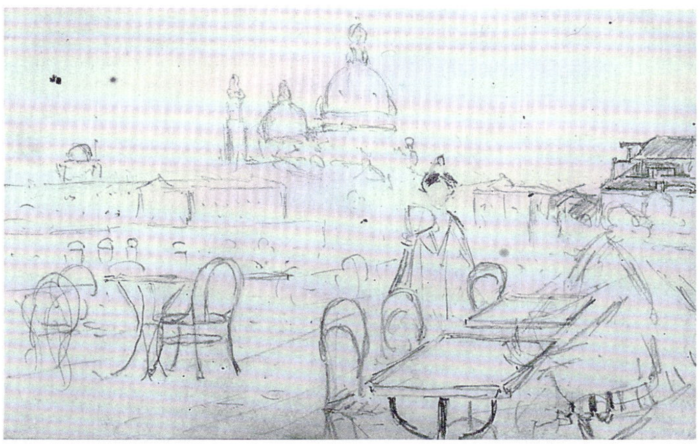

Fig. 12
Paris–Venice Sketchbook, p. 41r, 1901, graphite on wove paper, 11.4 × 17.2 cm. National Gallery of Canada (7419).

variety of surfaces – the thinly rubbed, deep-blue sky, the more thickly rubbed grey foreground, both contrasting with the dense central part of the composition and highlighted central facade of the building. As Morrice's work develops there is an increasing synthesis of techniques as he brushes, rubs, and draws, contrasting the dense, rich, fluid paint with graphite on bare wood, and with paint rubbed and dotted. The vivacity of line and colour combinations, the simplicity and complexity, create dazzling effects.

As for his canvases, there is no reason to believe that Morrice

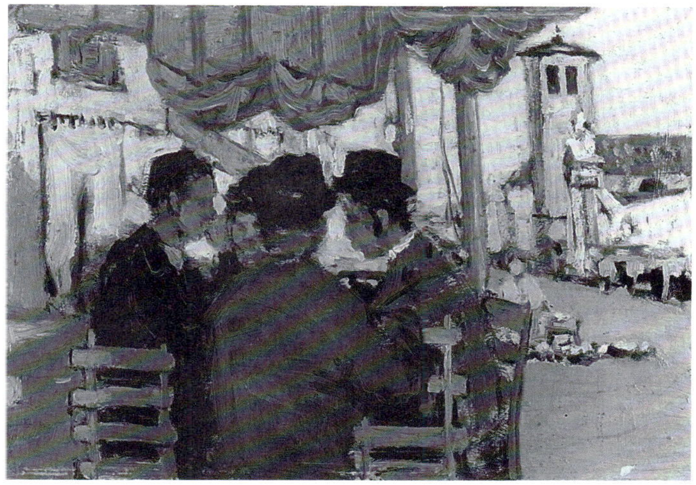

Fig. 13
Cardplayers, c. 1897–1901, oil on wood, 17.8 × 25.2 cm. McMichael Canadian Art Collection, Kleinburg. Bequest of David R. Morrice, 1979 (1979.3.3).

painted them out of doors, at least nothing larger than a canvas sketch. His landscape canvases were almost certainly painted in a studio from studies, either drawings or oil sketches, and he favoured small to medium sizes.[43] But the canvases were not simply enlarged from the sketches. Some of his earlier paintings are in fact composed from several studies. *Venice, the Grand Canal* (fig. 9) was worked up from at least two drawings (figs. 10 and 11 and possibly also fig. 12 for the figure of the woman in the foreground) and an oil sketch (fig. 13). *Notre-Dame, Paris* (cat. no. 36) was based on two drawings and possibly an unlocated oil sketch. The later canvases appear to be based more consistently on a single oil sketch, but even in the case of *Dieppe* (cat. no. 50) there are significant modifications from the oil study (cat. no. 49). In several instances additional figures are included in the canvas (see cat. nos. 41 and 73). A canvas might be painted from a sketch done over a decade earlier (cat. nos. 2 and 9). A finished canvas might be rejected entirely and completely painted over (cat. no. 10), or reworked (cat. nos. 10 and 32),[44] as was the case also with certain sketches (cat. nos. 13 and 40).

Within the same year there can be significant variations in Morrice's methods and style, as evidenced by his war sketches (see cat. nos. 78–80), all surely datable to 1918, and in his 1897 Quebec landscapes (see figs. 14 and 15 and cat. no. 10). *Village in Winter* and *Quebec Citadel by Moonlight* are both based on

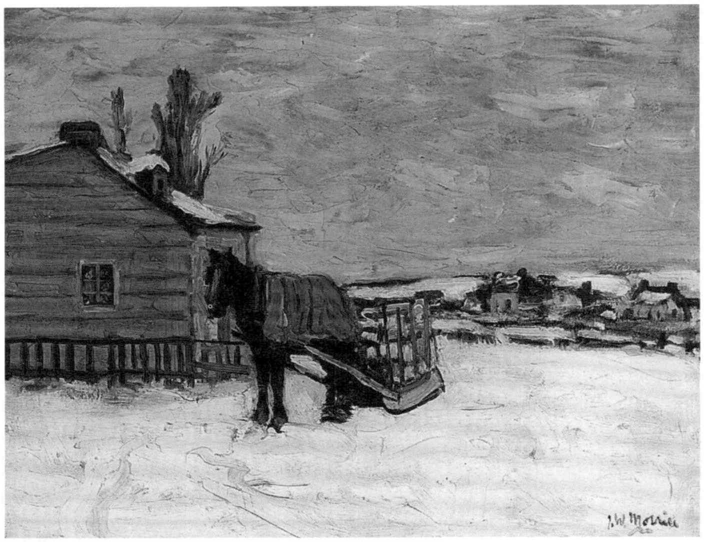

Fig. 14
Village in Winter, 1897, oil on canvas, 41.2 × 51.1 cm. Montreal Museum of Fine Arts. Bequest of Mrs. R. MacD. Paterson, 1949 (949.1007).

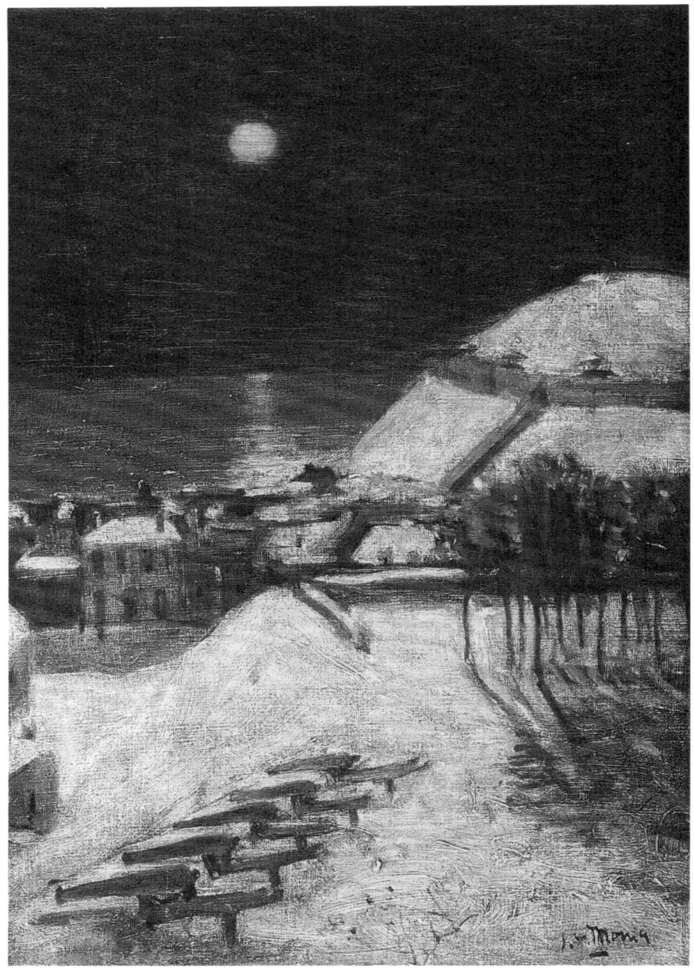

Fig. 15
Quebec Citadel by Moonlight, c. 1897, oil on canvas, 55.7 × 38.5 cm. Musée du Québec, Quebec City. Bequest of F. Eleanore Morrice, 1981 (MQ.81.53).

drawings found in the sketchbook Morrice used during a visit to Quebec City and Ste-Anne-de-Beaupré in 1897.[45] In the former he has applied the paint with a wide brush or palette knife, creating a highly textured surface that contrasts with the thinner drawing of the houses at the right. The Quebec nocturne, on the other hand, is painted thinly, in a Whistlerian mode. The tension between thicker, more material painting and thinner, lighter effects is a constant throughout Morrice's work, one he would exploit in a very original manner.

Over the years there is an increasing synthesis of process and expression in Morrice's work. He used scratching for highlights in an early canvas study (see cat. no. 16) and he does it in his larger canvases from around 1905 (fig. 43b). The bare wood of the sketch is translated into canvas covered with a thin ground in the larger paintings (cat. no. 57 and fig. 57a). The use of graphite as an accent or as an expressive element in the sketch is translated into scratching in the canvas of *The Ferry, Quebec* (fig. 9c). In *Café el Pasaje, Havana* (cat. no. 76) Morrice contrasts flat colour areas, thinly painted areas, canvas merely covered with ground, drawing in charcoal or black paint, and scratching in a perfect unity of expression.

"Synthesis" is the term Arnold Bennett used in describing Morrice's 1906 Breton sketches, and it is this synthetic vision that is so characteristic of all of Morrice's work. Be it in Paris or Brittany, in North Africa or the West Indies, he realizes a poetic vision of a world where humanity and nature operate in a harmonious rhythm, and where they play complementary roles in a world of visual delight.

NOTES

1. A pamphlet containing a checklist of the collection was published on that occasion. The present catalogue incorporates many corrections to the information given there.
2. Laing 1979, p. 9.
3. Laing 1984, pp. 186–88.
4. Laing 1979, pp. 10–14, 27–29, 127–30, 165.
5. Laing 1984, p. 154.
6. Ibid., pp. 198–200.
7. See Laing 1979, pp. 38–40.
8. Montreal 1925, nos. 48, 53, and 101; Paris 1926, nos. 8, 12, 33, and 44; Toronto 1926, nos. 266, 269, and 273; Ottawa 1937, nos. 32, 35, 38, 49, 50, 51, 52, 55, 77, 113, 116, and 125; Toronto 1953, nos. 28 and 32.
9. Laing 1979, pp. 229–32; Laing 1984, pp. 14, 60–68, 138–42.
10. Montreal 1965, nos. 32, 35, 41, 66, 71, 75, 76, 97, 126, and 133; Reid 1968, nos. 1, 2, 12, and 31; Malkin 1977, unnumbered (present cat. nos. 12, 17, 32, 43, 63, and 76); Montreal 1985, nos. 16, 17, 18, 21, 22, 36, 40, and 85; Murray 1973, nos. 27, 33, 34, 36, and 40; O'Brian 1982b, nos. 34, 35, 36, 37, 42, 44, and 45; McTavish 1984, nos. 12, 16, 19, 20, and 27; Hunter 1984, unnumbered (present cat. nos. 9 and 36).
11. Buchanan 1936a, p. 15, 77–79; Bell 1956, p. 157. The friendship is essentially undocumented save for these posthumous references from first-hand accounts. A caricature in Sketchbook 3 (Montreal Museum of Fine Arts, Dr 1973.26), p. 45r, may be of Conder. See also Morrice's letter to MacTavish, 24 March [1909], MacTavish Papers.
12. Letter from Morrice to Newton MacTavish, 3 December 1909, MacTavish Papers; letter from Morrice to Edmund Morris, 1 April 1913, Morris Papers.
13. Leblond 1909, p. 204.
14. Letter from William Brymner (in Montreal) to Clarence Gagnon (in Paris), 28 April 1904, Clarence Gagnon Papers, Archives, McCord Museum of Canadian History, Montreal. See also W.C. Agee and Barbara Rose, *Patrick Henry Bruce: American Modernist* (Houston: Museum of Fine Arts, 1979), pp. 44, 135, 214.
15. Bell 1956, pp. 156–68.
16. Bennett 1933, pp. 217–18, entry for 16 May 1905. This description was used by Bennett in his 1908 novel *Buried Alive* (New York: George H. Doran Co., n.d.), p. 109.
17. See Bennett 1971, p. 156, entry for 18 October 1906, regarding Morrice's visit to a brothel at Lorient.
18. Letter from Morrice to Morris, 11 April 1913, Morris Papers.
19. O'Brian 1982b, p. 58.
20. Buchanan 1936a, p. 41.
21. Bennett 1971, p. 157, entry for 21 October 1906. This passage was the basis for the characterization of the artist in Bennett 1913, pp. 26–29. See also Laing 1984, pp. 112–14.
22. *Quai des Grands-Augustins* in 1904 (see Cloutier 1985, p. 165) and *Au bord de la mer, Saint-Malo* in 1905 (see Maurice Hamel, *Salons of 1905* [Paris/New York: Goupil & Co., 1905], p. 83). Dorais (1985b, p. 14) identifies the latter work as being in the Musée de Picardie, Amiens, but that work was bequeathed in 1926.
23. Cloutier 1985, pp. 24, 30, 106, 134–35, 149, 164–65, 175 and 226; Cloutier 1986. In the Museum of Western and Oriental Art in Odessa is a painting titled *Au bord de la mer*, c. 1904, oil on canvas, 50 × 61 cm. According to the curator of the Odessa museum (in a letter to Nicole Cloutier), the painting was in the collection of Mme Boukovetsky from 1930 to 1961 and was acquired by the museum in 1961. A painting by Morrice had in fact been identified as being in Odessa as early as 1921 (letter from W. Scott & Sons to J.W. Beatty, Carnegie Institute, Pittsburgh, 28 September 1921, Carnegie Institute Papers, Archives of American Art, Washington, D.C., microfilm 38, file 405). See also "Canadian Artist Died in Tunis," *The Gazette* (Montreal), 26 January 1924. My thanks to Nicole Cloutier for providing information on the painting in Odessa. In the Barnes Foundation are two works: *Snow Scene*, c. 1897, oil on canvas, 23 × 30 cm, and *Market Scene*, c. 1901, oil on wood (?), 23.6 × 30 cm.
24. For the other, *Bords de la Seine*, now in the Musée d'Orsay, see Cloutier 1985, pp. 134–35.
25. Letters from Henri to his family, 16 December 1898 and 24 January 1900, Henri Papers.
26. Letter from Sickert to Miss Ethel Sands [c. 15–16 August 1913], quoted in Wendy Baron, *Miss Ethel Sands and Her Circle* (London: Peter Owen, 1977), p. 116, n. 42. My thanks to Dr. Wendy Baron and Col. M.C. Sands for permission to quote from this letter.
27. Letter from Matisse to Armand Dayot, quoted in Paris 1926, pp. 6–7.
28. Lyman 1945, p. 18.
29. Most of Morrice's sketchbooks were supplied to him by the Papeterie des Étudiants, at 10 Galerie de l'Odéon and 16 Rue de Vaugirard in Paris. For discussions of the sketchbooks, see Buchanan 1936a, pp. 145–47; Buchanan 1947, pp. 34–36; Buchanan 1953; Ostiguy 1976; Dorais 1978; and Moisan 1983. Dorais 1980 and Cloutier 1985 also contain numerous references to the sketchbooks.
30. Christie, Manson & Woods Ltd., London, 8 December 1960, lots 29–31.
31. See "Morrice," *Toronto Star*, 27 January 1962, and Robert Ayre, "Morrice Exhibition at Montreal Museum," *Montreal Star*, 9 October 1965 (drawings on consignment to Walter Klinkhoff Galleries, Montreal, from Blair Laing). Blair Laing donated a drawing to the Confederation Centre Art Gallery, Charlottetown. Other drawings from these sketchbooks are in the Art Gallery of Ontario, the Art Gallery of Windsor, the Art Gallery of Hamilton, the London Regional Art and Historical Museums, the Rodman Hall Arts Centre, St. Catharines, the National Library, Ottawa, and the National Gallery of Canada (see fig. 2d), as well as in numerous private collections.
32. Sketchbook 16 (Montreal Museum of Fine Arts, Dr.1973.39). See Cloutier 1985, p. 148.
33. In the Montreal Museum of Fine Arts, the National Gallery of Canada, the Art Gallery of Ontario, Toronto, the Art Gallery of Hamilton, and private collections.
34. The charcoal drawing is after p. 65r in Sketchbook 14 (Montreal Museum of Fine Arts, Dr.1973.37). For the other charcoal drawing, see Jerrold Morris, *100 Years of Canadian Drawings* (Toronto: Methuen, 1980), pp. 52–53.
35. *Sur la plage* (Art Gallery of Hamilton, 84.STI.2874), after *The Beach, St-Malo*, reproduced in Ingram 1907, p. 219; and *Le port à Saint-Servan* (Art Gallery of Hamilton, 84.STI.2887), reproduced in

Maurice Hamel, "Les Salons de 1902," *Gazette des Beaux-Arts*, XXVII (June 1902), p. 473.
36. For a discussion of Morrice's watercolours see Szylinger 1985. Drawings for many of the late finished watercolours can be found in Sketchbook 21 (Montreal Museum of Fine Arts, Dr.1973.44).
37. Ciolkowska 1925b, p. 52.
38. Maugham 1956, pp. 20–21.
39. O'Brian 1985, p. 92.
40. Lyman 1980, p. 40. See cat. no. 60.
41. These were possibly cut down from larger pieces of canvas by the artist. *The Harbour, Dieppe I* of about 1894, in the National Gallery of Canada (3331), has the stamp of Paul Foinet, 54 Rue Notre-Dame-des-Champs, Paris, stencilled on the back of the canvas (the stamp was visible before the canvas was lined). See also Cloutier 1985, p. 127, for another canvas purchased from Foinet.
42. Some oil sketches have the artist's studio stamp on the back of the canvas, and so could not have been glued to a secondary support before his death. See, for example, *Untitled (Beach Scene)*, oil on canvas mounted on plexiglas, 15.9 × 27.3 cm, in the Collection of the Gertrude Poole Estate at the Edmonton Art Gallery.
43. In his sketchbooks Morrice notes the French codes for standard prepared canvases. For a compilation of these sizes, see David Bonford, Jo Kirby, John Leighton, and Ashok Roy, *Art in the Making: Impressionism* (London: National Gallery and Yale University Press, 1990), p. 46. The largest canvases painted by Morrice are No. 50 P (130 × 89 cm) – *La Communiante* (Musée du Québec) and *The Beach, St-Malo* (private collection, ex collection Jacques Rouché, Paris).
44. *On the Beach, Dinard*, in the Vancouver Art Gallery (32.7), was also reworked, as the painting has been signed twice. My thanks to Ian Thom for bringing this to my attention.
45. See Dorais 1978. The drawings are to be found in the Paris–Quebec Sketchbook in the National Gallery of Canada (7420), pp. 47r and 20r respectively.

Note to the Reader

In cataloguing Blair Laing's collection I have attempted to confront and correct a number of problems regarding titles and dates, and also to bring a greater precision to the transcribing of inscriptions and labels. For each work, I have provided as full a provenance as possible but have not included the complete exhibition history or bibliographic references.

Titles

In 1925, a year after Morrice's death, his Montreal agent, W. Scott & Sons, wrote to the National Gallery of Canada: "The pictures, sketches and panels, which we are handling for the Morrice Estate have no titles."[1] Over the years, most of the artist's works (and not only those sold from his estate) have acquired varying and often contradictory titles, depending on the knowledge, wishful thinking, or literary aspirations of the individual owner. Therefore, in cataloguing Blair Laing's collection I have reverted wherever possible to Morrice's own original title. Where no original title is known, I have retained the earliest documented or most frequently cited title. Furthermore, if a place-name in a title could not be confirmed with certainty and did not originate with the artist, I have in most instances removed it from the title.

Dating

In dating the works in the collection I have referred principally to related drawings in the sketchbooks and to paintings whose dates are reasonably well established. I have also relied on records of exhibitions held during the artist's lifetime, provided that there is supporting evidence from other sources, as Morrice did not always exhibit his most recent work. In making use of his correspondence, and also the correspondence and diaries of his friends and acquaintances, I have tried (less successfully than I would have liked) to avoid associating all of Morrice's works with the relatively few documented moments in his life.

Inscriptions

The inscriptions on the work, including those on labels, have been transcribed as they appear, except in the case of the following exhibition-related labels which are recorded in abbreviated form:

Art Gallery of Ontario crating label, Norton Gallery exhibition: a temporary Art Gallery of Ontario crating label put on the works loaned by Blair Laing to the exhibition *Masterpieces of Twentieth-Century Canadian Painting* at the Norton Gallery, West Palm Beach, Florida, in 1984 (for catalogue, see Hunter 1984).

MMFA 1965: a label for the exhibition *James Wilson Morrice 1865–1924*, organized by the Montreal Museum of Fine Arts in 1965 (for catalogue, see Johnston 1965).

MMFA 1985: a label for the exhibition *James Wilson Morrice 1865–1924*, organized by the Montreal Museum of Fine Arts in 1985 (for catalogue, see Cloutier 1985).

OKanada: a label for the exhibition *OKanada*, organized by the Canada Council and shown at the Akademie der Künste, Berlin, in 1982 (for catalogue, see under O'Brian 1982b).

Wildenstein 1968: a label for the exhibition *James Wilson Morrice 1865–1924*, organized by the National Gallery of Canada in 1968 and shown at the Holburne of Menstrie Museum, Bath, at Wildenstein & Company, London, and at Bordeaux and Paris (for catalogue, see Reid 1968).

Parts of inscriptions or labels that are illegible or torn away are supplied in brackets where possible or else shown simply as a bracketed dash.

Typed or written matter on a label is presented in italic type. Printed portions of labels are shown in roman type.

Provenance

Unless otherwise noted, the information in the provenance is derived from inscriptions and labels on the works themselves, and from Blair Laing's cataloguing notes and conversations with the author.

In the account of the provenance of each work, a semicolon between two owners indicates that the work is known to have passed directly from one party to the other. When a direct transfer is not know to have occurred, a period separates the names.

During his lifetime Morrice sold a good number of canvases and oil sketches in France, England, Canada, the United States, and elsewhere. In Canada his agent was the Montreal firm of W. Scott & Sons, founded in 1859. William Scott's daughter married Frank R. Heaton, who continued to run the firm with his son, John C. Heaton. It was John Heaton who arranged the 1934 Morrice exhibition at Mellors Fine Arts Limited in Toronto.

After Morrice's death the works in his studio were stamped "STUDIO / J.W. MORRICE" in order to authenticate them, as many were unsigned and some unfinished. Works by other artists found in his studio also bear this stamp.[2] Often the stamp is inscribed with a number in graphite or is accompanied by an inventory number preceded by the letter *M*. Some works by Morrice that do not bear a studio stamp are inscribed "From the studio of J.W. Morrice / W. Scott & Sons" or "From the studio of J.W. Morrice / J.C. Heaton." It can be assumed that paintings or watercolours bearing such authentications were not sold prior to 1924 and that they indeed came from Morrice's estate.

The firm of W. Scott & Sons held an auction of the bulk of their stock in 1938 and reopened in new premises for one year, closing in May 1939. Frank R. Heaton died in October 1939,[3] and the Morrice paintings from his collection were stamped "ESTATE / F.R. HEATON" and were sold by the Continental Galleries of Fine Art in Montreal from 1949.[4] Continental Galleries was run by Joseph Shima and his wife Vilma Shima, and they became the prime vendors of Morrice paintings in Montreal for many years. Many of the titles on the backs of works that were sold by Continental Galleries are inscribed in Joseph Shima's hand, but the source of his titles is unknown. After Joseph Shima's death, Vilma Shima married Paul Lafontaine. Blair Laing acquired a number of his Morrices from Vilma Lafontaine.[5]

Notes

1. Letter from W. Scott & Sons to the National Gallery of Canada, 23 March 1925, Archives, National Gallery of Canada, file 1.12–Morrice.
2. Moisan 1983, pp. 55–56, 66, no. 58.
3. "Frank R. Heaton Dies in 74th Year," *The Gazette* (Montreal), 23 October 1939.
4. "Fine Paintings Shown in Heaton Collection," *The Gazette* (Montreal), 22 October 1949.
5. For accounts of the galleries and dealers, see Laing 1984, pp. 150–56, and Laing 1979, pp. 33, 43.

Chronology

1865
10 August - James Wilson Morrice born in Montreal, son of David Morrice and Annie Stephenson Anderson.

1886
June - Graduates with Bachelor of Arts degree from the University of Toronto.
Fall - Begins studies at Osgoode Hall law school, Toronto.

1888
Exhibits for the first time at the joint exhibition of the Ontario Society of Artists and the Royal Canadian Academy of Arts, Toronto.

1889
April - Exhibits for the first time at the Art Association of Montreal.
Fall - Called to the Ontario Bar.

1889–?
Studies at the Julian Academy, Paris, and with Henri Harpignies.

1890
Paints at St-Malo.

1891
January - Maurice Prendergast in France to September 1894.
April - Address: 87 Gloucester Road, Regent's Park, London.

1892
April - Exhibits *Evening, Barbizon* in Montreal. Address: 9 Rue Campagne-Première, Paris.

1893
February - Exhibits *Entrance to Dieppe* and *Early Morning Effect on the Conway, Wales* in Montreal. Both works subsequently shown at the World's Columbian Exposition, Chicago.

1892–96
Living in Paris. Travels in France, Belgium, the Netherlands, and Italy; visits Concarneau, Cancale, Mers, Dieppe, Venice, and Capri.

1895
June - Robert Henri in France to autumn 1897.
9 November - Brother, David Morrice, Jr., marries Mabel Lorne Gault.

1896
January or February - Paints at Brolles near Fontainebleau with Curtis Williamson.
April - Exhibits for first time with the Société Nationale des Beaux-Arts, Paris. Address: 34 Rue Notre-Dame-des-Champs, Paris.
June, July - Paints at Cancale and St-Malo.
August - With sister, Annie Mather Morrice, in Paris.
November - To Montreal.

1897
January, April - Paints at Beaupré and Quebec City with Maurice Cullen. Returns to Paris via New York, where he visits William Glackens.
Paints in Venice.
Exhibits for the first time with the Royal Glasgow Institute of the Fine Arts.

1898
Paints at Dieppe and in Belgium and the Netherlands (?).
May - Address: 41 Rue St-Georges, Montmartre, Paris.
June - Robert and Linda Henri in Paris to July 1900.
August, September - At St-Malo.
November - Visits Robert Henri and Edward Redfield at Brolles.
December - Robert Henri paints Morrice's portrait in Paris.
25 December - Brother, Edward McDougall Morrice (born 1875), dies in Augusta, Georgia.

1899
March - Visits Charenton with Robert and Linda Henri.
Submissions to the Société Nationale des Beaux-Arts receive favourable notices.
August, September - At St-Malo.
September - Morrice and Henri invited to exhibit in Berlin.
18 September - Brother, George Sheriff Morrice (born 1871), dies at Saranac Lake, New York.
2 October - Moves to 45 Quai des Grands-Augustins, Paris.
October - Alexander Jamieson paints portrait of Morrice.
December - To Montreal.

1900
January, February - Visits Quebec City. Returns to Paris via New York.
March - Exhibits for the first time with La libre esthétique, Brussels, the Society of American Artists, New York and the Pennsylvania Academy of Fine Arts, Philadelphia. Henri paints new portrait of Morrice.
July - Morrice joins his parents in Hamburg.
5 December - Brother, Arthur Anderson Morrice (1873–1931), marries Florence Ethel Rousseaux of Hamilton, Ontario.

1901
Spring - Morrice elected associate of the Société Nationale des Beaux-Arts.
Summer - *The Beach of Saint Malo*

awarded silver medal at the Pan American Exposition, Buffalo.
Paints at St-Malo, St-Servan, and Paramé. In Venice with Joseph Pennell.
OCTOBER - Exhibits for the first time with the International Society of Sculptors, Painters and Gravers, London.
Gerald Kelly in Paris from 1901 to March 1908.

1902
JUNE, JULY - Visits Madrid and possibly also Gibraltar. In Venice with Edmund Morris, Maurice Cullen, William Brymner, and Charles Fromuth. Visits Florence, Sienna, and Padua.

1903
MARCH - Arnold Bennett in France to February 1913.
APRIL - Exhibits with the Société Nationale des Beaux-Arts as sociétaire. Exhibits for the first time at the Venice International Exposition.
JUNE - Visits New York, Philadelphia, Montreal, Quebec City, and Île d'Orléans.
JULY - Exhibits for the first time with the Munich *Secession*.
AUTUMN - Visits Madrid and possibly also Gibraltar.

1904
JANUARY - Clive Bell in Paris to summer 1905.
APRIL - *Le quai des Grands-Augustins* bought by the French Government. *Fête foraine, Montmartre* purchased by Ivan Morozov, Moscow.
JULY, AUGUST - At Avignon, Martigues, Marseilles, Venice.
AUGUST - Somerset Maugham in Paris to February 1906.
Aleister Crowley publishes *Snowdrops from a Curate's Garden*.
The Shore at Paramé purchased for the Wilstach Collection, Philadelphia.

1905
APRIL - *Au bord de la mer (Saint-Malo)* purchased by the French Government.
FALL - Exhibits for the first time at the Walker Art Gallery, Liverpool.
OCTOBER - Exhibits for the first time with the Salon d'Automne, Paris.
NOVEMBER - Exhibits for the first time at the Carnegie Institute, Pittsburgh.
DECEMBER - To Montreal.

1906
JANUARY, FEBRUARY - In Montreal and Quebec City. Returns to Paris via New York and Liverpool.
SPRING - *Effet de neige (traineau)* purchased by the Musée des Beaux-Arts in Lyons.
JUNE, SEPTEMBER - At Dieppe, Concarneau, Lorient, and Le Pouldu with Robert Henry Logan, Gabriel Thompson, and Mela Muter.
DECEMBER - Exhibits for the first time at the Goupil Gallery, London.

1907
APRIL - *Le Bac* purchased by Ivan Morozov. David Morrice presents *La place Chateaubriand, St-Malo* to the Mount Royal Club, Montreal.
JUNE - At St-Malo.
JULY - At Venice, Perugia, and Sienna.
NOVEMBER - In hospital with measles.

1908
FEBRUARY - Charter member of the Canadian Art Club. *On the Cliff* purchased by the Club's president, Daniel R. Wilkie. Elected member of the Société Nouvelle, Paris. Exhibits with them for first time at Galerie Georges Petit, Paris.
JULY - Visits William Brymner in Martigues (?).
OCTOBER - Serves as vice-president of the jury for the Salon d'Automne with Albert Marquet, Henri Matisse, and Georges Rouault.
DECEMBER - To Montreal via New York.
Buried Alive by Arnold Bennett and *The Magician* by Somerset Maugham published.

1909
JANUARY, FEBRUARY - In Montreal, Quebec City, and Toronto. Returns to Paris via New York.
Quai des Grands-Augustins purchased by the National Gallery of Canada.
MARCH - Louis Vauxcelles writes article on Morrice for *The Canadian Magazine* (published December 1909). Death of Charles Conder.
APRIL - Awarded Jessie Dow Prize for *Regatta, St. Malo* at the Art Association of Montreal.
Essay on Morrice included in Marius-Ary Leblond's *Peintres de races*.
SEPTEMBER - At Dieppe.
NOVEMBER - At Concarneau with Milner Kite and Alexander Harrison.

1910
JANUARY, MAY - At Concarneau and Paris.
JUNE - To Montreal via New York. Visits Quebec City.
14 JUNE - Golden wedding anniversary of parents.
FALL - Returns to Paris.

1911
JUNE - At Boulogne.
DECEMBER - To Montreal for Christmas. Visits Quebec City and Île d'Orléans.

1912
FEBRUARY - *Dieppe, the Beach, Grey Effect* purchased by the National Gallery of Canada.
FEBRUARY, APRIL - At Gibraltar and Tangiers.
MARCH - Awarded Jessie Dow prize for *Palazzo Dario, Venice* at the Art Association of Montreal.
JUNE - *Circus, Montmartre* purchased by the National Gallery of Canada.
DECEMBER - In Tangiers to March 1913.

1913
MARCH - Visits Gibraltar and Toledo.
19 MARCH - Sister, Annie Mather Morrice, marries Alan Gilmour Law in Montreal.
MARCH - *The Beach near Pouldu* purchased by the Art Association of Montreal.
APRIL - At Concarneau (?).
JUNE - Visits Walter Sickert at Envermeu near Dieppe.
SEPTEMBER - Article on Morrice by Muriel Ciolkowska published in *The Studio*.
OCTOBER - At Concarneau.

1914
March - Solo exhibition at The Arts Club, Montreal. J.R. Wilson presents *The Beach, Le Pouldu* and *The Terrace, Quebec* to the Mount Royal Club, Montreal. Visits Cagnes, Grasse, Marseilles, and Tunis.
11 August - Leaves Paris for London as World War erupts. Visits Geneva (?).
November - In Paris.
26 November - Mother, Annie Stephenson Anderson, dies.
19 December - Father, David Morrice, dies.
December - Donates *Dieppe* to the exhibition of Canadian artists in aid of the Patriotic Fund organized by the Royal Canadian Academy; purchased by A.B. Fisher.

1915
January, February - In Montreal.
February, April - To Cuba via New York, Washington, and New Orleans. Paints in Havana and Santiago de Cuba, and briefly in Jamaica.
18 April - Sails from Havana to St-Nazaire.
May - Roger Fry visits Morrice in Paris. *The Old Holton House, Montreal* and *Afternoon, Tunis* purchased by the Art Association of Montreal in exchange for *The Beach near Pouldu.*
August - At Bayonne, Toulouse, Carcasson.

1916
House in Santiago purchased by the Contemporary Art Society, London.
14 November - Brother, David Morrice, Jr., dies in Montreal.

1916 or **1917**
Moves to 23 Quai de la Tournelle, Paris.

1917
November - Receives commission from Canadian War Records Office.

1918
February - Sketches at the front in Picardy.
Paints in studio at Concarneau. Donates *Winter in France (Troops Marching)* to the Canadian War Memorials.

1920
The Beach, Le Pouldu purchased by the Carnegie Institute, Pittsburgh.
December - In Montreal and Quebec City.

1921
22 January - To Trinidad via New York.
3 March - Leaves Trinidad.
6 December - Writes his will in Paris

1922
Buys house for Léa Cadoret in Cagnes.
January - At Monte Carlo and Nice.
February - Visits Carqueiranne, France, and Bastia, Corsica.
30 March - To Algiers and Biskra.
April, July - In Paris.
At Évian-les-Bains and in hospital at Montreux.

1923
At Montreux, Nice, and Cagnes.
28 December - Arrives in Tunis.

1924
14 January - At Palermo.
23 January - Dies in Tunis.

Catalogue

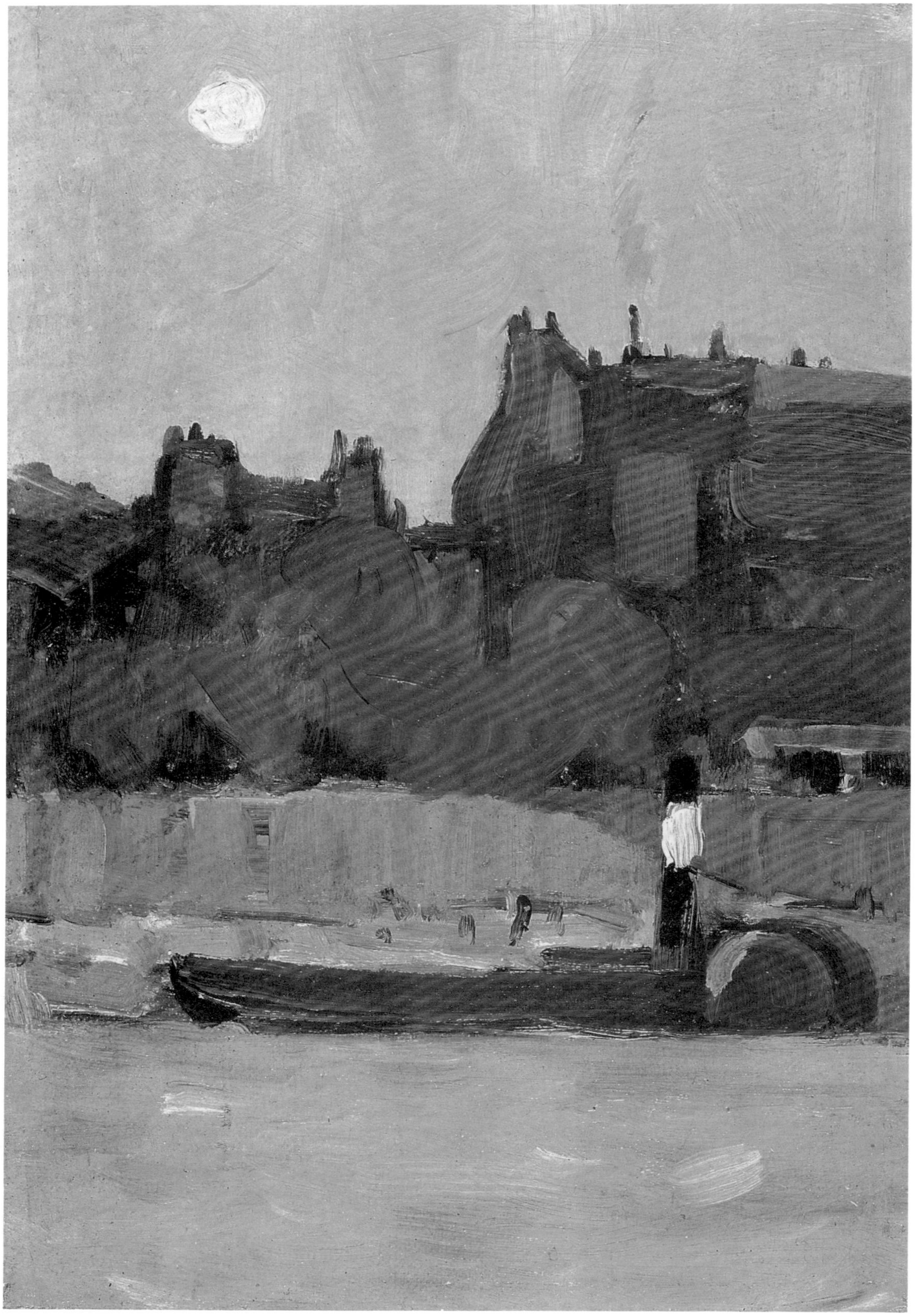

1

Barge on the Seine

c. 1892–93

Oil on canvas mounted on wood-pulp board, 23.3 × 16.2 cm

Inscriptions: verso: t. in brown ink, *From the studio of J W Morrice / J C Heaton*, c. in brown ink (Joseph Shima's hand?), *24 / ISLE DE LA CITÉ – PARIS*, c. stamped, *ESTATE / F.R. HEATON*, c. in graphite, *Steamer on the Seine*

Labels: in blue ballpoint pen, *K / 224*; OKanada, no. 34

Provenance: Estate of the artist; W. Scott & Sons, Montreal; F.R. Heaton, Montreal; Continental Galleries of Fine Art, Montreal (?). J.J. Vaughan, Toronto, by 1959;[1] G. Blair Laing, Toronto, 1965.

30446

Morrice graduated from Osgoode Hall law school in Toronto and was admitted to the Ontario Bar in the fall of 1889 at the age of twenty-four. Having decided that his true vocation lay elsewhere (he had already participated in art exhibitions in Toronto and Montreal), he immediately abandoned the legal profession for a career in art. He appears to have been based in London by the spring of 1891 and Paris by early 1892.[2] In Paris, he was enrolled for a time at the Académie Julian[3] and studied briefly with the landscape painter Henri Harpignies.[4]

From these early years there is a watercolour of St-Malo, dated 1890, and a canvas of the port of Dieppe, dated 1892.[5] In addition there are a number of oil sketches on pieces of canvas which, from their subject matter, can be identified as having been painted in England, Wales, Brittany, Normandy, and Paris.

This broadly painted view of a river barge on the Seine passing Île de la Cité is comparable to the dated sketches *Île St-Louis and Bridge, Paris* and *On the Banks of the Seine* (figs. 1a and 1b). Morrice's superb colour sense is already evident in the range of colours used to depict the water and buildings. As in the 1892 Dieppe canvas, the buildings are composed of broad vertical and horizontal strokes of black, browns, dark terracottas, and blues. The pink sun, responding to the bright white on the funnel, adds a lyrical note to this glowing sketch of Morrice's new abode.

1. Loaned by Mr. and Mrs. J.J. Vaughan to the *Exhibition of Loans from Private Toronto Collections*, Art Gallery of Toronto, 2–18 October 1959, as *Île de la Cité, Paris*.
2. Cloutier 1985, pp. 17, 19; Dorais 1985b, pp. 7–8.
3. From records in the archives of the men's atelier (now at the Archives Nationales de France, Paris), Catherine Fehrer, in *The Julian Academy, Paris, 1868–1939* (New York: Shepherd Gallery, 1989, n.p.), lists Morrice as a pupil of Bouguereau at Julian's from 1888 to 1890. Dorais (1985b, p. 8) and Cloutier (1985, p. 45) state that Morrice enrolled at the Académie Julian in the fall of 1891.
4. "National Gallery of Canada Information Form for the Purpose of Making a Record of Canadian Artists and Their Works," completed by Morrice and received at the National Gallery 31 May 1920 (Library, National Gallery of Canada).
5. Cloutier 1985, nos. 5 and 8.

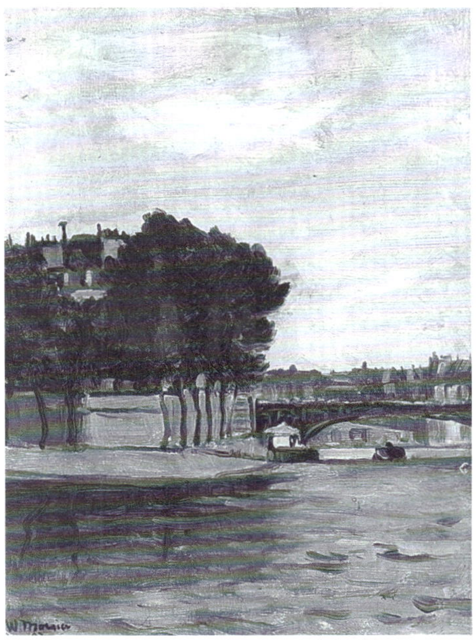

Fig. 1a
Île St-Louis and Bridge, Paris, 1892, oil on canvas mounted on cardboard, 29.2 × 21.5 cm. Montreal General Hospital.

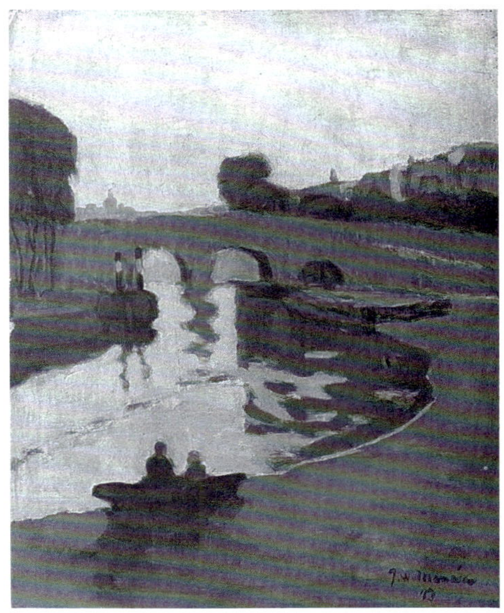

Fig. 1b
On the Banks of the Seine, 1893, oil on canvas mounted on wood-pulp board, 33 × 26.6 cm. Montreal Museum of Fine Arts. Gift of Mrs. R.E. MacDougall, 1965 (66.1526).

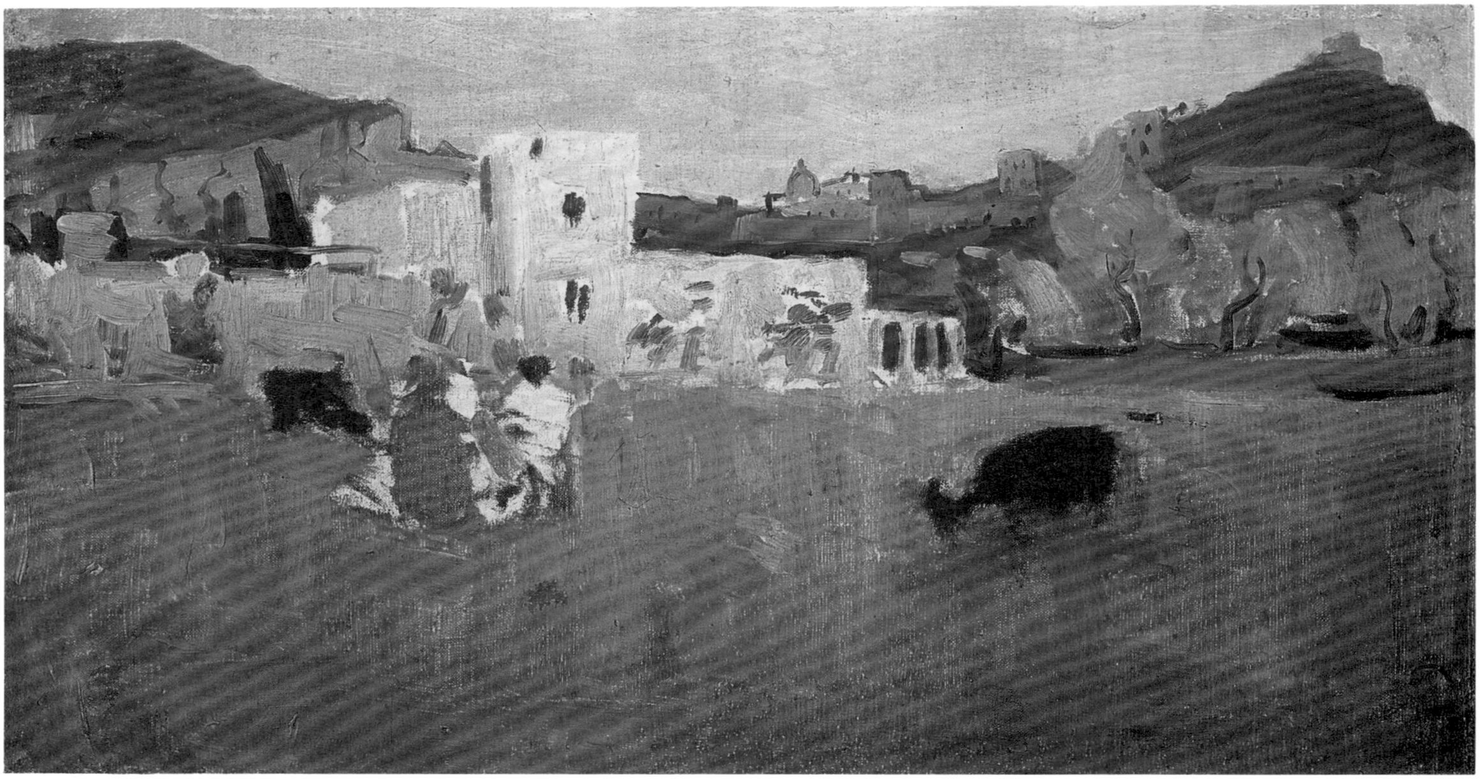

2

The Black Goat (Capri)

c. 1894

Oil on canvas mounted on wood-pulp board on wood, 23.5 × 42.8 cm

Inscriptions: verso: c. stamped, *STUDIO / J.W. MORRICE*

Labels: in blue ballpoint pen, *ALGIERS / BLACK GOAT / 79-11*

Provenance: Estate of the artist; Watson Art Galleries, Montreal (?); Mrs. Howard W. Pillow, Montreal, March 1951 (?);[1] J. Murray Vaughan, Montreal, by 1953;[2] G. Blair Laing Ltd., Toronto, 1979.

30415

In 1892 Morrice exhibited in Montreal a painting titled *Evening, Barbizon*, and the following year his 1892 Dieppe canvas and a Welsh landscape. Apart from these meagre references, there is no further contemporary documentation concerning Morrice's activities until the fall of 1895. However, through a rigorous analysis of his paintings and sketchbooks, scholars studying his work have proposed a chronology of his travels and interests during these years.[3]

In one sketchbook – now identified as Sketchbook 12, in the Montreal Museum of Fine Arts – we can follow Morrice across the island of Capri as he draws the cliffs and streets, trees, buildings, and shepherds. In view of its stylistic similarities to three other sketchbooks, a date of about 1894 can be assigned to this book, which includes three drawings related to the oil sketch *The Black Goat (Capri)*.[4] On one page Morrice has drawn the outline of the crenellated building and the domed church on the hill with a quick sketch of a priest (fig. 2a). In another drawing (fig. 2b) he has included the goats in the foreground and has altered the proportions of the building, adjusting the silhouette with a dark line. On the next page of the sketchbook (fig. 2c) the shepherds herd the goats in front of the walls of the building.

A related drawing (fig. 2d), detached from another sketchbook,[5] more closely approximates the general arrangement of the building and landscape in the oil study. Morrice may have done this particular drawing not from observation but rather as a clarification of the composition.

The oil sketch shows strong stylistic links to *View of a Square, Dieppe* (fig. 8, Introduction). Common to both are the open foreground, the schematic and somewhat angular treatment of the figures, and the dry, textured application of paint. The treatment of the trees is similar to that in *Barge on the Seine* (cat. no. 1).

Capri (fig. 2e), the canvas realized from this oil sketch some fifteen to twenty years later, retains all the essential elements. Thinly painted, it glows with a pale-rose light characteristic of Morrice's work of the pre-war years. The sand-coloured building has become citron yellow, the pink wing by the tower paler and more transparent. The building at the left is now green instead of grey, and the blue sky has turned to glowing rose and white. The curve of the hills and the horizontal lines of the building and field become the dominant design elements.

1. Watson Papers, stock no. 13705, sold to Mrs. Howard W. Pillow, Montreal, 22 March 1951. The entry is unclear and may not refer to this work.
2. Loaned by J. Murray Vaughan to Toronto 1953, no. 32, as *The Black Goat*. The painting was offered for sale at Christie, Manson & Woods (Canada) Ltd., Montreal, 29 October 1969, lot 66, but was bought in.
3. Dorais 1980; Cloutier 1985, pp. 19–21, 104–07.
4. Dorais 1980, pp. 51–52, 85–86, 88–89. See also Cloutier 1985, p. 207.
5. This drawing was purchased in 1965 from Walter Klinkhoff Galleries, Montreal, and comes from one of the three sketchbooks sold by Vincent Massey and acquired by Blair Laing (see Introduction, p. 25, n. 31). One sketchbook (sold as lot 31) contains a number of inscriptions concerning Italy, and this drawing is probably from that book. A drawing in the Art Gallery of Ontario in Toronto (63/10), a study for the sketch *Venetian Canal Scene* in the Montreal Museum of Fine Arts (1981.68; see Cloutier 1985, p. 106), may also be from the same book, which suggests that both drawings, and indeed the entire sketchbook, may date from this same Italian trip, about 1894.

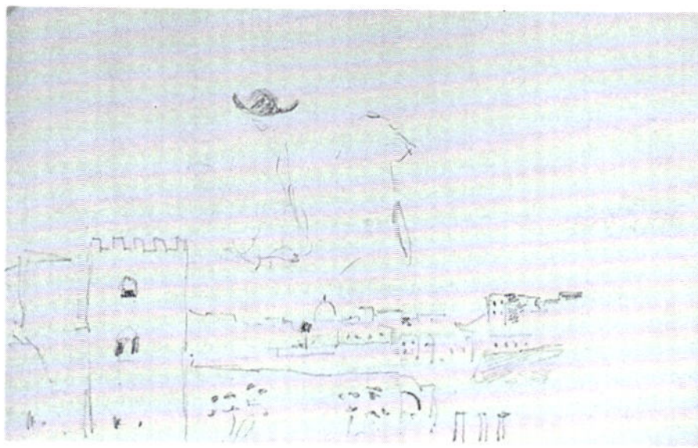

Fig. 2a
Sketchbook 12, p. 97v, c. 1894, graphite on wove paper, 10.8 × 16.6 cm. Montreal Museum of Fine Arts. Gift of David R. Morrice, 1973 (Dr.1973.35).

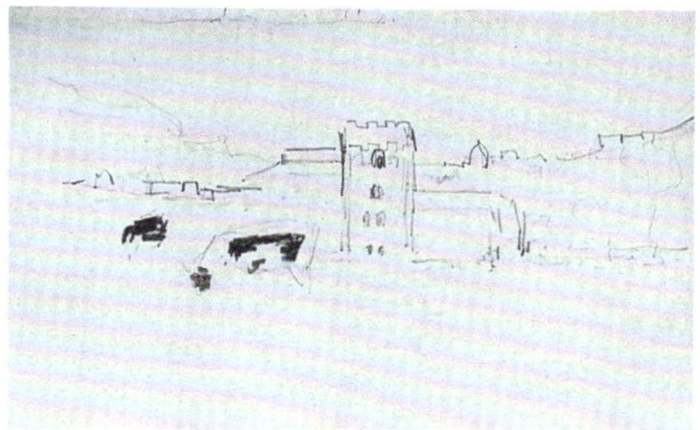

Fig. 2b
Sketchbook 12, p. 98r, c. 1894, graphite on wove paper, 10.8 × 16.6 cm. Montreal Museum of Fine Arts. Gift of David R. Morrice, 1973 (Dr.1973.35).

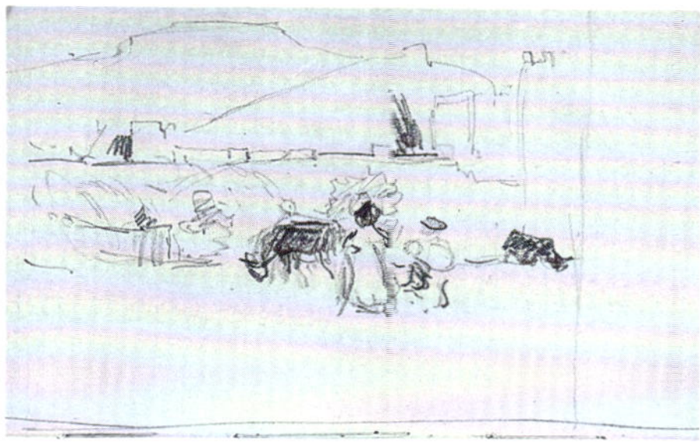

Fig. 2c
Sketchbook 12, p. 99v, c. 1894, graphite on wove paper, 10.8 × 16.6 cm. Montreal Museum of Fine Arts. Gift of David R. Morrice, 1973 (Dr.1973.35).

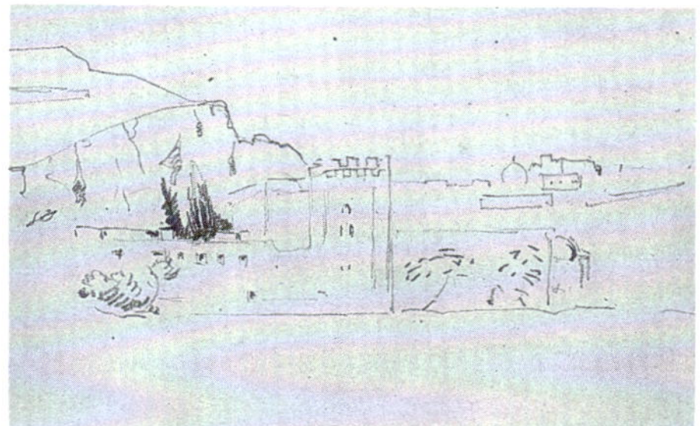

Fig. 2d
Capri, c. 1894, graphite on wove paper, 10.7 × 16.6 cm. National Gallery of Canada (14850).

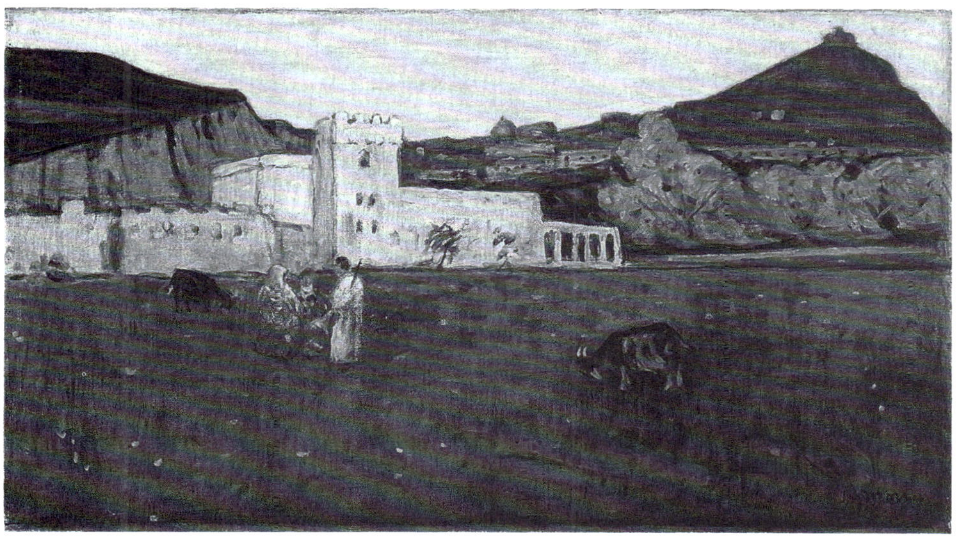

Fig. 2e
Capri, c. 1911–12, oil on canvas, 46 × 81.3 cm. National Gallery of Canada (6670).

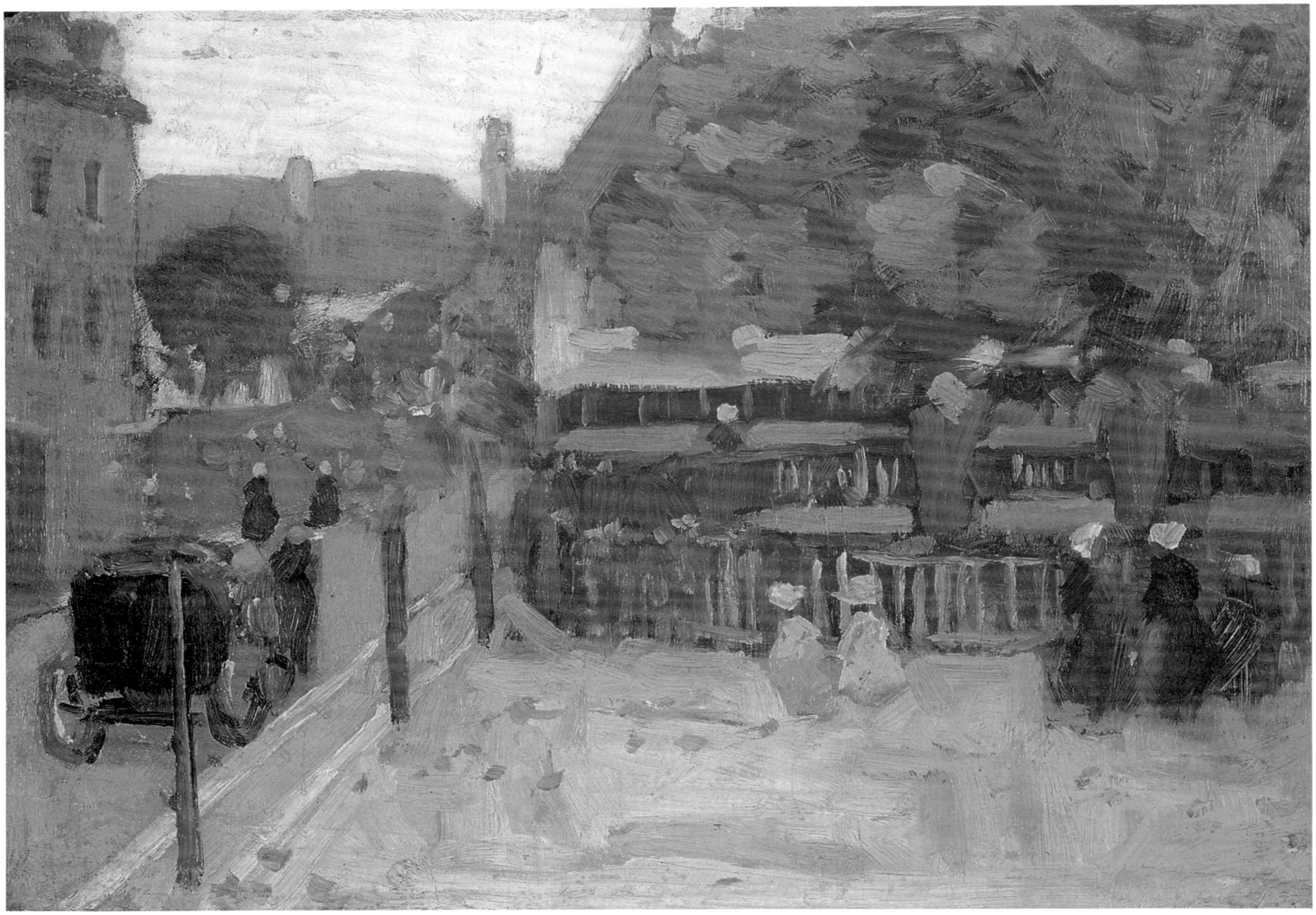

3
Street Scene in Brittany

1896

Oil on wood, 23.5 × 33 cm

Inscriptions: verso: u.l. in brown ink, *Painted by / James Wilson Morrice / Paris 1896*, c. in graphite, *Painted by / James Wilson Morrice / about 1896 / Paris / RH*, l.r. in black ink, *From Estate of / Robert Henri*, l.r. stamped, *LECHERTIER*, c.r. stamped, *PHOTO-D*

Labels: printed, *2872*; in blue ink, *G. Blair Laing / Toronto / –Paris–*, in graphite, *#27*; MMFA 1985, no. 18

Provenance: Robert Henri, New York; Estate of Robert Henri; Hirschl & Adler Galleries Inc., New York (?); G. Blair Laing, Toronto, 1960.[1]

30464

The original owner of this oil sketch, the American painter Robert Henri, was among Morrice's closest friends during the late 1890s. Henri had studied in France from 1888 to 1891, and after several years in Philadelphia he returned in June 1895. That summer he bicycled in Belgium and the Netherlands, and in the fall he set up a studio at 49 Boulevard de Montparnasse in Paris. We do not know whether Henri had met Morrice during his first stay in France, but in any event it was during this latter period, beginning in 1895, that their friendship flourished. Henri settled in New York in 1900, and he later went on to become an influential teacher and active proponent of American art.[2]

The inscriptions on the back of the panel, in Henri's hand, state that the work was painted either in 1896 or about 1896. Henri's uncertainty indicates that he probably wrote these inscriptions at a later date, though in fact 1896 is probably correct. The "Paris" in the inscriptions must refer to where Henri acquired the sketch, not where it was painted, as the coifs of the women suggest rather Brittany or Normandy, not Paris.

The oil sketch, on a moderate-sized wood panel stamped *LECHERTIER* (possibly the supplier), is painted in beiges, browns, greens, and blacks, accented by the pale-blue dresses of the young women in the centre, the russet tones of the trees, and the orange and yellow wheels of the carriage at the left.

Henri owned several works by Morrice, most notably his own portrait, dated 1896 by Henri, an oil sketch (fig. 30b) for the 1901 painting *Venice, Night* in the National

Gallery of Canada (fig. 30c), and Morrice's only known lithograph, in the Art Gallery of Hamilton, depicting boats at Dordrecht and dated on the back 1898.[3] A drawing of Henri can be found in one of Morrice's sketchbooks,[4] and drawings of Morrice by Henri are in the National Gallery of Canada (fig. 3a) and the Montreal Museum of Fine Arts.[5]

1. Laing 1979, p. 228. Blair Laing writes: "The dealer said a compatriot of mine, an art critic and writer, was interested in it but had made no decision, so I bought the picture then and there." The "compatriot" was probably Paul Duval, of Toronto, who bought Morrice's portrait of Henri from Hirschl & Adler; see Cloutier 1985, p. 115.
2. Homer 1988, pp. 40–57, 85–88, 92–98.
3. Johnston 1965, nos. 51, 80, and 127; Cloutier 1985, pp. 113–15.
4. Sketchbook 7 (Montreal Museum of Fine Arts, Dr.1973.30), p. 33r.
5. *Robert Henri* (Wilmington: Delaware Art Museum, 1984), pp. 33, 160; Moisan 1983, p. 75. The drawing in the National Gallery is inscribed on the back by Henri, "sketch of James / Wilson Morrice / 1907 / RH," but it closely matches his own description of a portrait of Morrice that he painted in 1899: "His portrait is standing long overcoat, open showing brownish clothes underneath hands gloved and in one of them soft hat and cane" (letter from Henri to his family, 4 January 1899, Henri Papers).

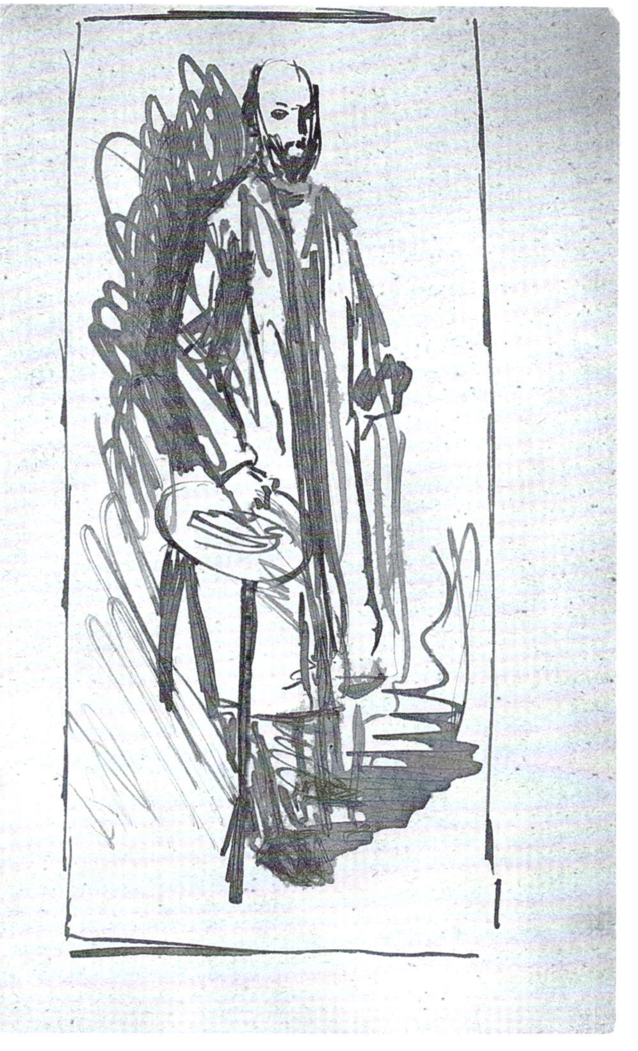

Fig. 3a
Robert Henri (1865–1929), *James Wilson Morrice*, 1907, pen and brown ink on wove paper, 16.2 × 9.7 cm. National Gallery of Canada (28625).

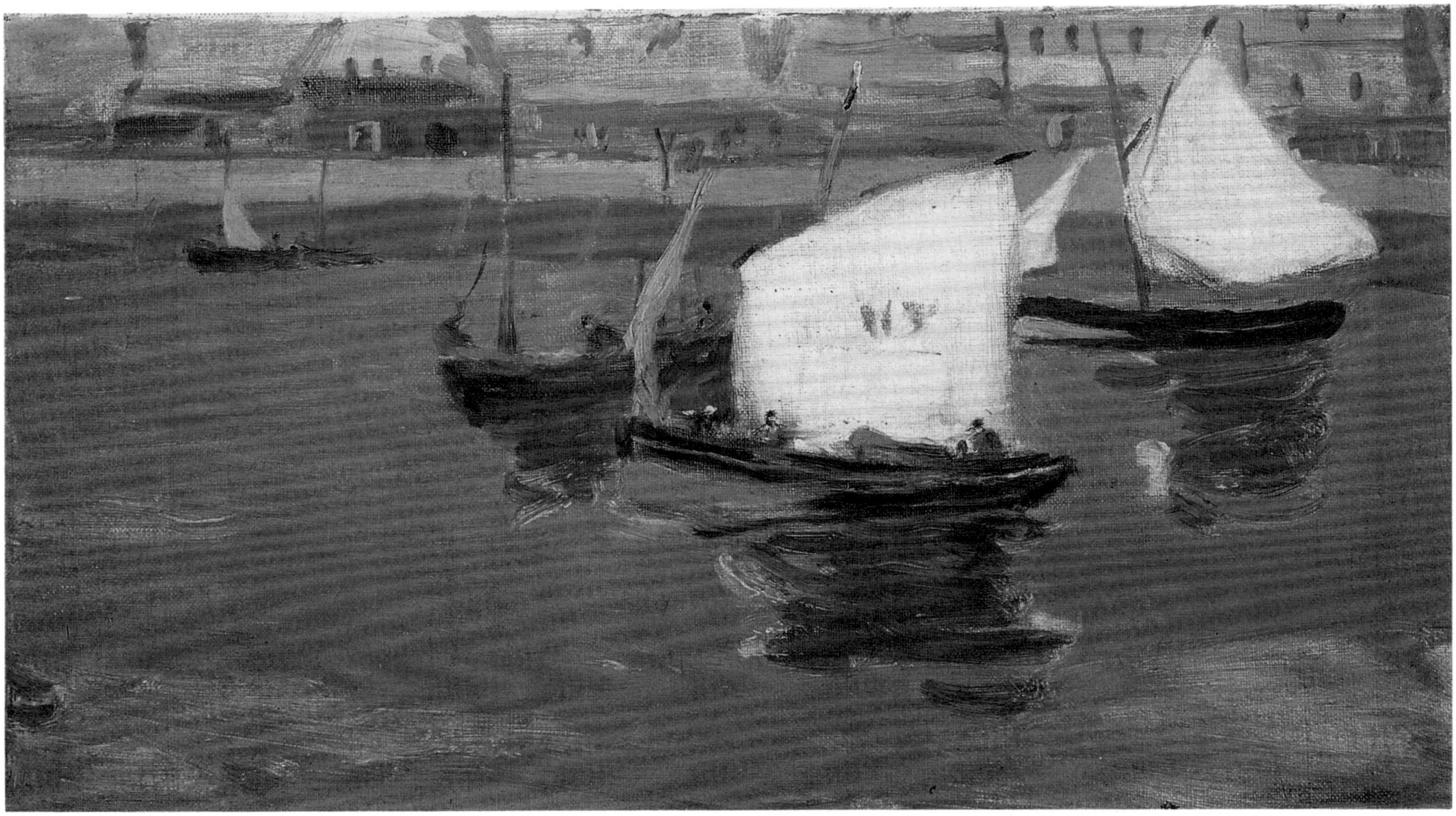

4

Fishing Boats, Cancale

1896

Oil on canvas mounted on wood-pulp board, 23.5 × 40.8 cm

Inscriptions: verso: c.r. stamped, *STUDIO / J.W. MORRICE*, in brown ink, *W. Scott Sons / F.R. Heaton*, c. in yellow chalk, *18*

Labels: in blue ballpoint pen, *G.B.L. / CONCARNEAU*, in graphite, *#10*

Provenance: Estate of the artist; W. Scott & Sons, Montreal. W.R. Watson, Montreal.[1] G. Blair Laing, Toronto, 1971.

30449

In June 1896 Morrice was working in Cancale in Brittany and tried to encourage Robert Henri to come from Paris and join him there. He noted in his letter to Henri that "the people here are not so frightfully picturesque as they are at Concarneau."[2]

Situated just sixteen kilometres east of St-Malo, Cancale was best known for its oyster beds, and Morrice found the town, its harbour, and its inhabitants so attractive that he stayed for over a month. Several of the drawings and small oils that he did in Cancale depict the oyster beds, beach scenes with houses lining the seashore road, or boats in the harbour, their sails inscribed with the port identification "CAN" (see fig. 4a). *Fishing Boats, Cancale* is painted in muted greens, yellows, and beiges, with the red of the house (upper left) echoing the red shirts of the fishermen. In its restrained tonality and brushwork it shows certain similarities to *Street Scene in Brittany* (cat. no. 3).

1. In his cataloguing notes (now in the archives of the National Gallery of Canada) Blair Laing gives the provenance as William R. Watson, and he identifies the port as Concarneau. My identification of it as Cancale derives from the related drawings in Sketchbook 2 in the Montreal Museum of Fine Arts (Dr.1973.25).
2. Letters from Morrice to Henri, 6 June 1896 and "Tuesday," Henri Papers. It is evident that Morrice had already been to Concarneau in Brittany. He had also been to Cancale before, as drawings of boats marked "CAN" appear in a sketchbook containing drawings related to the 1892 Dieppe canvas and the 1893 Seine sketch (fig. 1b); see Sketchbook 4 (Montreal Museum of Fine Arts, Dr.1973.27), pp. 42r, 73r (fig. 4b), and 83r.

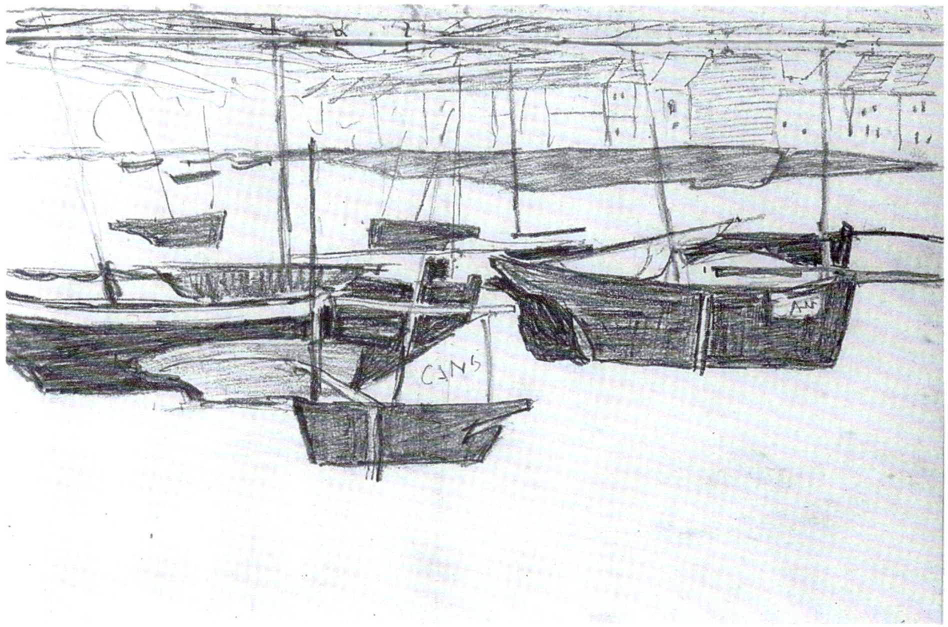

Fig. 4a
Sketchbook 2, p. 8r, 1896, graphite on wove paper, 11 × 16.7 cm. Montreal Museum of Fine Arts. Gift of David R. Morrice, 1973 (Dr.1973.25).

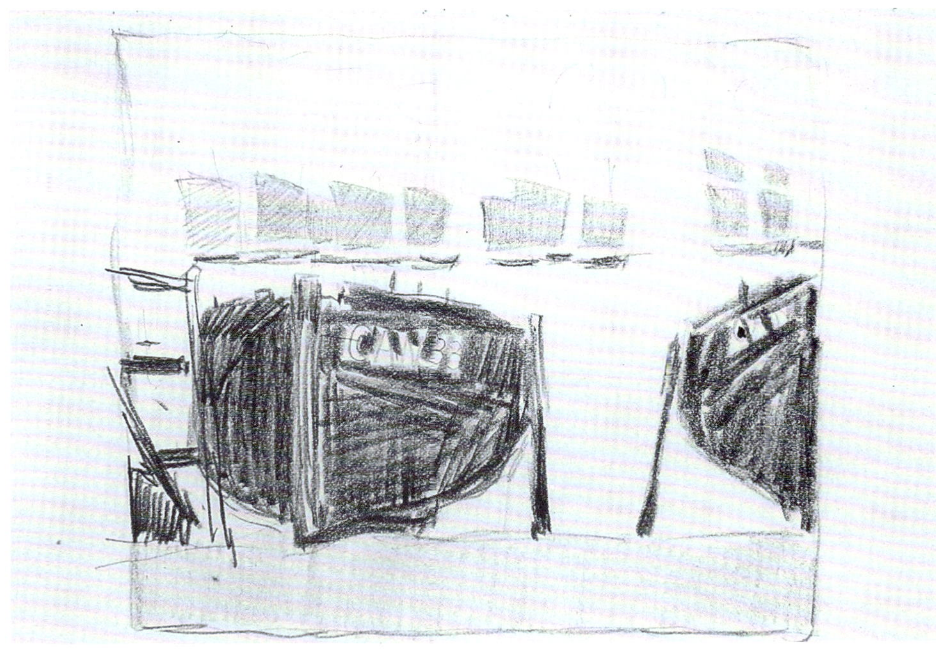

Fig. 4b
Sketchbook 4, p. 73r, c. 1892–93, graphite on wove paper, 10.6 × 16.7 cm. Montreal Museum of Fine Arts. Gift of F. Eleanore and David R. Morrice, 1973 (Dr.1973.27).

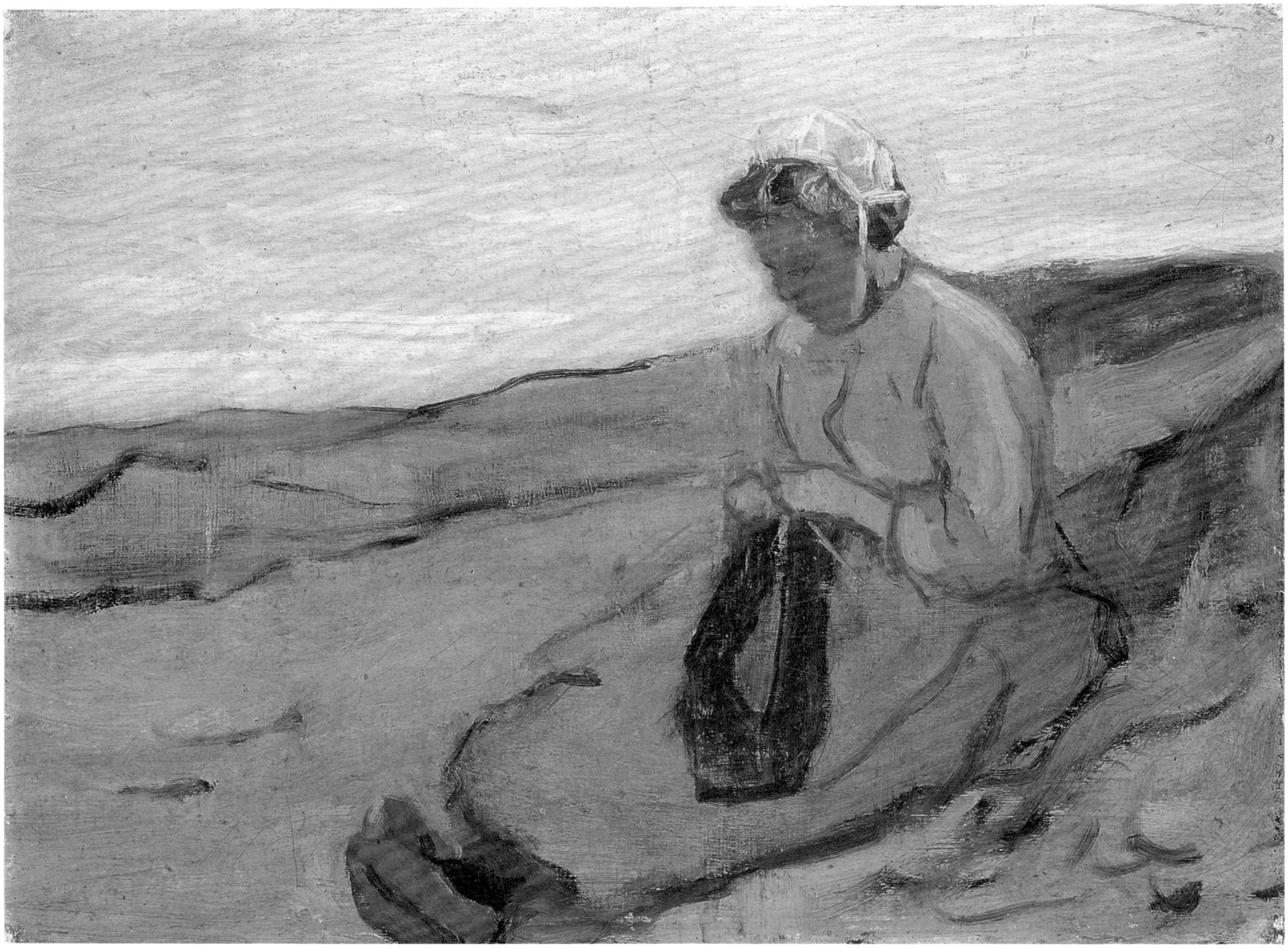

5

Girl Knitting (near St-Malo, Brittany)

c. 1896

Oil on canvas mounted on wood-pulp board, 22.7 × 29.9 cm

Inscriptions: verso: u.c. in brown ink (Joseph Shima's hand), –*GIRL KNITTING (NEAR ST. MALO; BRITTANY)*–, in black ink, *From the studio of J.W. Morrice / J.C. Heaton*, c. in brown ink, *32*, c.l. in brown ink, [—], l.c. stamped, *ESTATE / F.R. HEATON*

Labels: in blue ballpoint pen, *GBL / GIRL KNITTING / BRITTANY*, in graphite, *#18*

Provenance: Estate of the artist; W. Scott & Sons, Montreal; F.R. Heaton, Montreal; Continental Galleries of Fine Art, Montreal; Vilma Lafontaine, Montreal; G. Blair Laing, Toronto, 1960.

30457

In this subtle study of a young blond-haired Breton woman knitting on the beach, Morrice has confined himself to low-toned pinks, greys, blues, and browns, with the red clogs providing a bright accent note. He has used a thin brush with black paint to delineate the folds of the blouse and skirt, the arms and hands, and the curves of the sand.

The bonnet the woman is wearing is characteristic of the area around Cancale and can be seen in another portrait of a young blond girl painted in 1896 (fig. 5a). In the latter work Morrice has silhouetted the figure against the weirs and oyster beds, and dark paint outlines the stones of the wall.

The curved design framing the figure is seen in yet another canvas of a young woman on a beach (fig. 5b), derived from studies made at Cancale or nearby Dinard.[1] Possibly the same blond-haired model as in the other two works, the figure here is enveloped by the prow of the boat and its shadow, while other boats progress across the horizon like musical notes.

1. Sketchbook 2 (Montreal Museum of Fine Arts, Dr.1973.25), p. 47r.

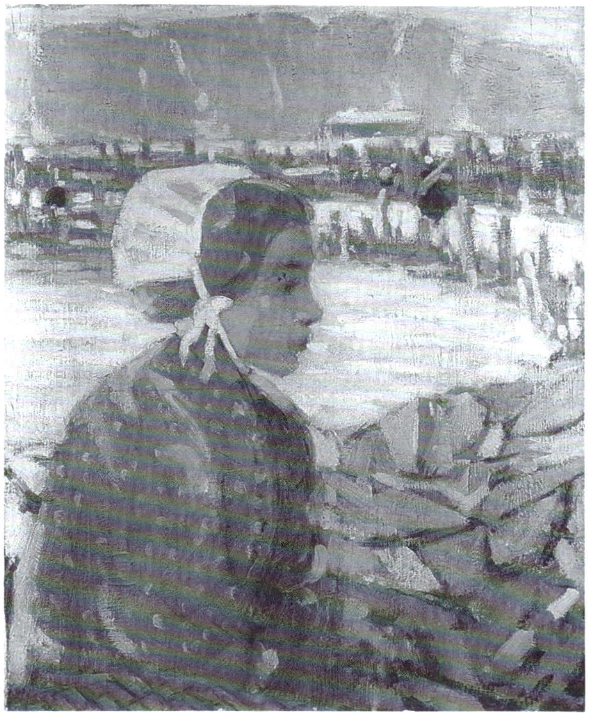

Fig. 5a
La Bretonne, c. 1896, oil on canvas, 47.3 × 35.4 cm. National Gallery of Canada (3186).

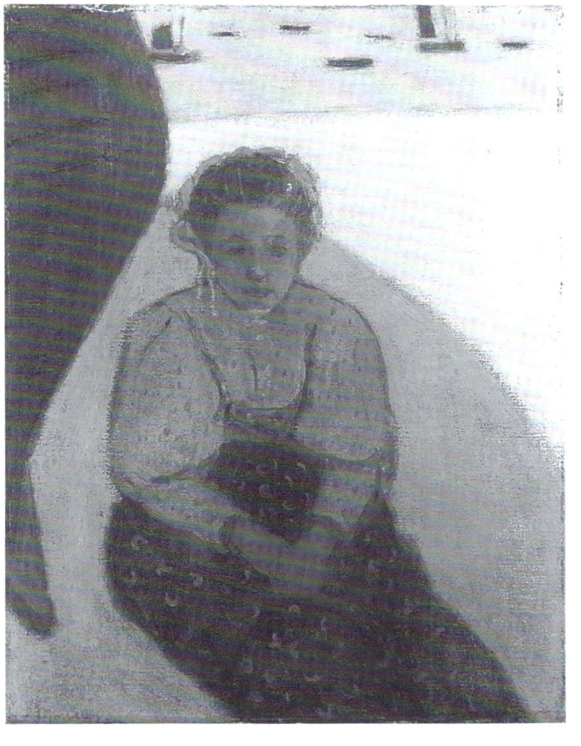

Fig. 5b
Woman on a Beach, c. 1896, oil on canvas laid down on masonite, 45.2 × 34.5 cm. National Gallery of Canada. Gift of Mrs. Ann J. Rosengarten, Montreal, 1982 (28141).

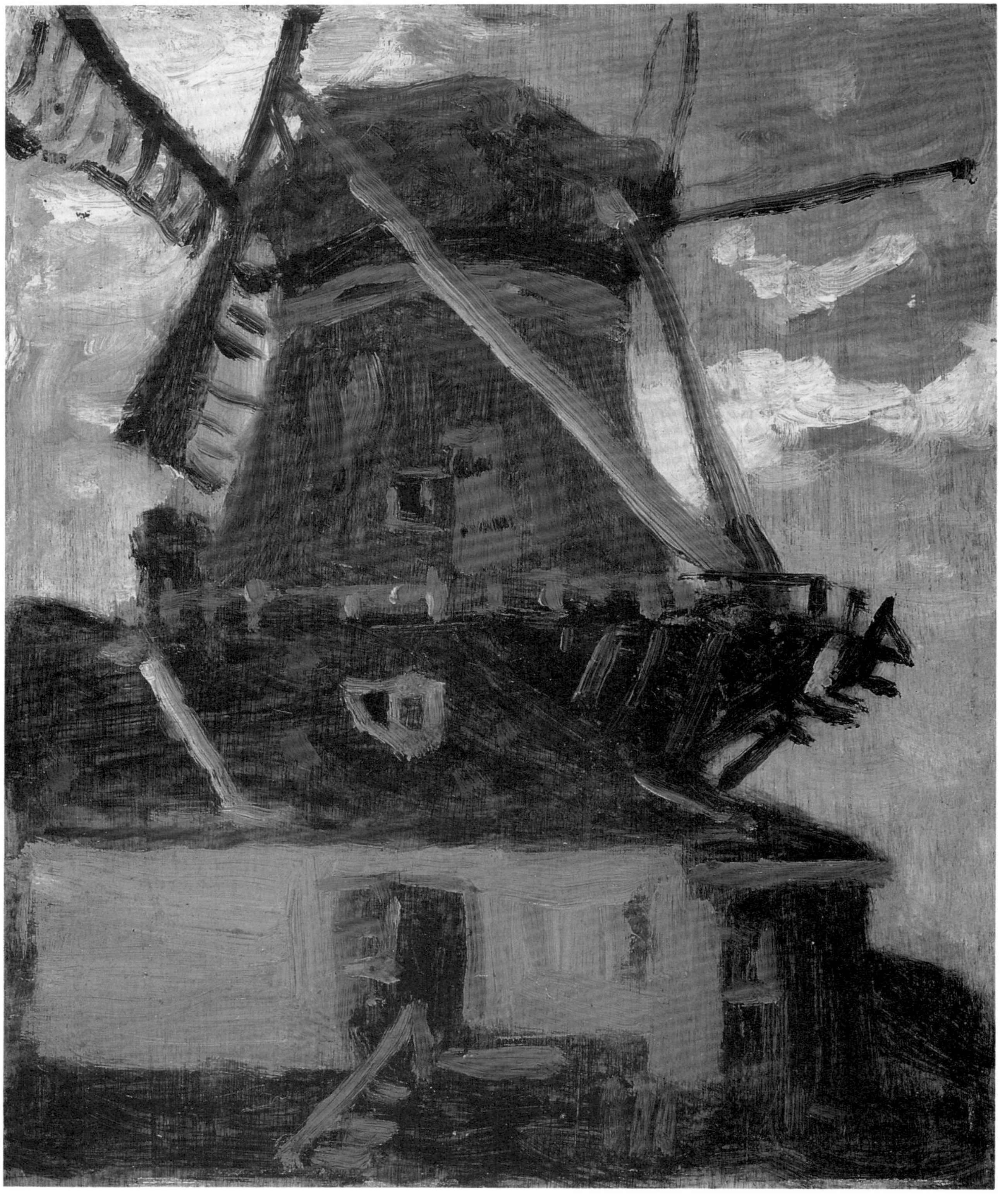

6

Flour Mill at Old Dordrecht, Holland

c. 1896–98

Oil on wood, 15.4 × 12.7 cm

Inscriptions: verso: t. in black ink, *Sketch by James Morrice / Flour Mill / at old Dordrecht / Holland*, b. in black ink, [—]

Labels: in blue ballpoint pen, *79-3 /* "*DORDRECHT*"; typed, Laing Galleries 194 Bloor Street West Toronto 5 Canada / *FLOUR MILL AT OLD DORDRECHT / BY / J.W. MORRICE*

Provenance: Acquired by G. Blair Laing Ltd., Toronto, 1979.

30414

In November 1895 the Toronto artist Edmund Morris visited the Dutch town of Dordrecht and noted in his diary that his friend and colleague James Morrice (their surnames are pronounced the same way) sometimes worked there.[1] We do not know when Morrice first visited the Netherlands, but certainly its picturesque countryside, its museums, and above all its great artistic heritage were well known to British, American, and Canadian artists.

Sketchbooks 7 and 8 in the Montreal Museum of Fine Arts both contain drawings of sailboats, windmills, cows, and Belgian and Dutch landscapes, including views of Dordrecht and detailed studies of the Grote Kerk in that city. Sketchbook 7 has a portrait of Robert Henri and, on the following page, a drawing of a woman who may be Linda Henri, his wife (with whom he lived in Paris from June 1898 to the summer of 1900).[2] In Sketchbook 8 Morrice has inscribed his address at 34 Rue Notre-Dame-des-Champs (where we know he lived in 1896)[3] and that of William Glackens at 13 West 30th Street in New York (he was at that address from 1900).[4] One of the sketchbooks contains a more finished rendering of a drawing in the other, confirming the close relationship between the two books.[5] An extended date range of about 1896 to 1900 can thus be ascribed to them.

In Sketchbook 7 there is a drawing of a windmill (fig. 6a) that is a study for a canvas sketch in the Sobey collection (fig. 6b). In the latter the mill is set on the edge of a field adjacent to the town of Dordrecht, with cows grazing in the foreground. The schematic painting of the buildings at the left, their windows merely thin vertical strokes, is characteristic of other sketches from 1896, such as *Fishing Boats, Cancale* (cat. no. 4).[6]

In *Flour Mill at Old Dordrecht* the windmill is viewed from closer up, filling the composition. The sky is rubbed with touches of turquoise and mauve, echoed in the house whose roof is enlivened with touches of red. In several places Morrice allows the wood of the panel to show through. Given the similarity of treatment in the sky and the blades of the windmill, it is likely that this oil sketch was painted about the same time as the Sobey sketch.

1. Quoted in Cloutier 1985, p. 111, n. 1.
2. Sketchbook 7 (Montreal Museum of Fine Arts, Dr.1973.30), pp. 33r and 34r; Homer 1988, pp. 92–98; Peter Morse, *John Sloan's Prints* (New Haven: Yale University Press, 1969), pp. 146–47.
3. Sketchbook 8 (Montreal Museum of Fine Arts, Dr.1973.31), inside back cover. This address is given for Morrice in the 1896 catalogue of the annual Salon of the Société Nationale des Beaux-Arts, opening 25 April. In the 1898 catalogue of the same Salon, opening 1 May, he is listed at 41 Rue St-Georges in Montmartre.
4. Sketchbook 8, p. 66v; Ira Glackens, *William Glackens and the Ashcan Group* (New York: Crown Publishers, 1957), p. 27. See also Sketchbook 1 (Montreal Museum of Fine Arts, Dr.1973.24), p. 36r, where Glackens is noted as being at the same address.
5. Sketchbook 7, p. 55r, and Sketchbook 8, p. 37r. Both drawings are studies for a sketch that was in the collection of Gérard Beaulieu in 1965, reproduced in *Vie des Arts* 40 (Autumn 1965), p. 6.
6. See also *Cancale* (oil on canvas, 45.7 × 25.4 cm), reproduced in Cloutier 1985, p. 116.

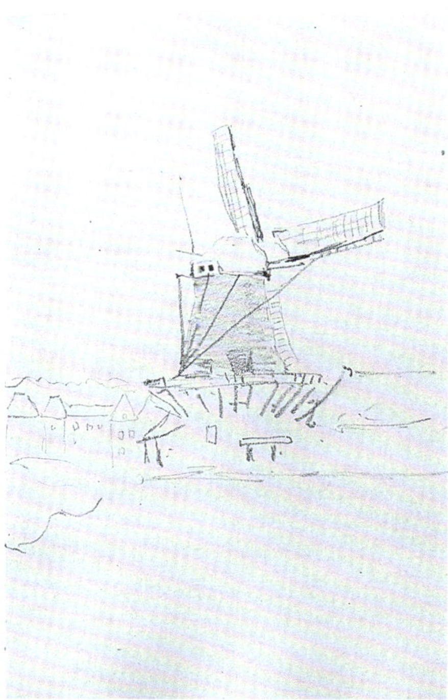

Fig. 6a
Sketchbook 7, p. 50r, c. 1896–98, graphite on wove paper, 16.7 × 10.8 cm. Montreal Museum of Fine Arts. Gift of David R. Morrice, 1973 (Dr.1973.30).

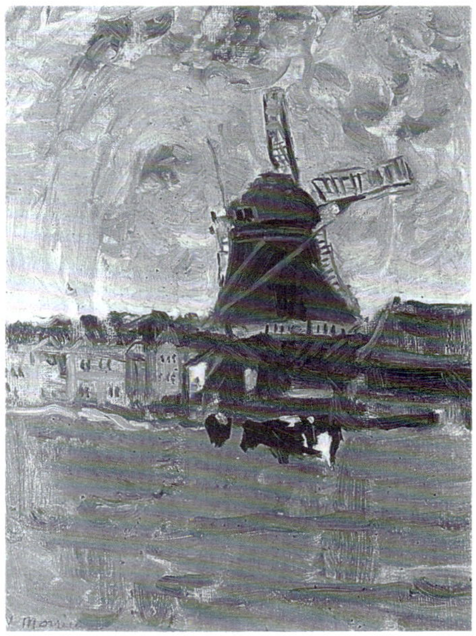

Fig. 6b
Untitled (Windmill and Cows), c. 1896–98, oil on canvas mounted on wood-pulp board, 30.2 × 22.6 cm. The Sobey Art Foundation.

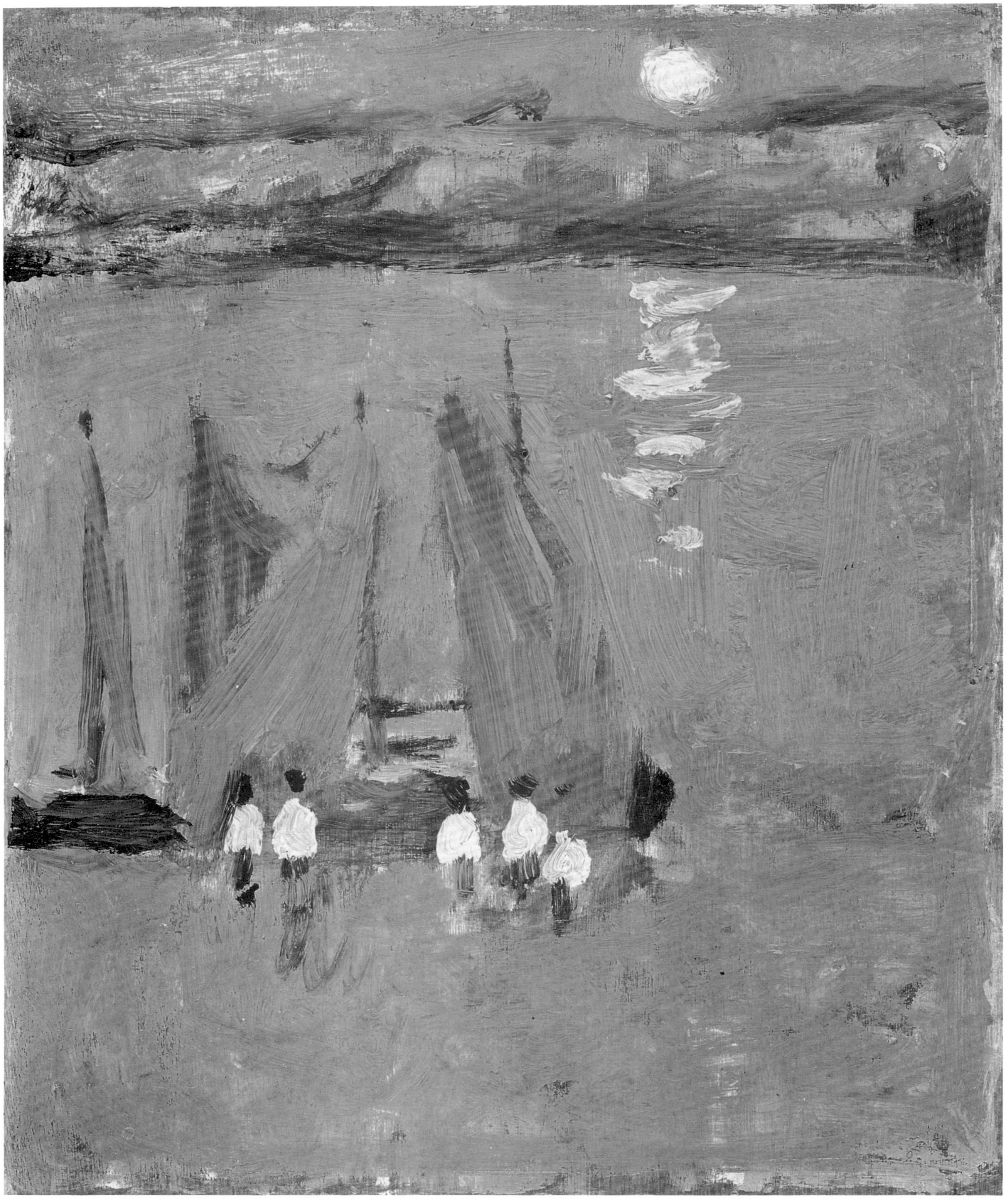

7

Fishing Boats

c. 1896–98

Oil on wood, 15.4 × 12.7 cm

Inscriptions: verso: c. in graphite, *6* (crossed out), in graphite, *6*; back of frame: u.c. in graphite, *Boats on Beach / 10/33*, l.r. in graphite, NICHOLSON

Labels: newspaper clipping, in brown ink, *Truth apl 24 02*; in blue ballpoint pen, BOATS ON / BEACH; in graphite, M2; in graphite, *24*

Provenance: Private collection, England(?); John Nicholson, London and New York; G. Blair Laing, Toronto, c. 1952–56.[1]

30451

Fishing Boats and *Study for "At a Country Fair"* (cat. no. 46) both have clippings from the London newspaper *Truth* pasted on the back of the panel, which suggests that they probably originally belonged to the same owner. Both works were acquired by Blair Laing from John Nicholson in the 1950s.

The clipping on *Fishing Boats*, from a review of the 1902 Salon of the Société Nationale des Beaux-Arts, reads: "Room 12. – A young Canadian, Mr. Morrice (of Montreal), sends four pictures which may not attract much notice among the general public, but which are the best things in this room – two views of St-Malo and an evening and a night at Venice. This is, indeed, painting combining taste and workmanship of the highest order." The four works that Morrice exhibited were *À Venise, le soir*; *À Venise, la nuit*; *La plage à Saint-Malo*; and *Le port à Saint-Servan*.[2] All were undoubtedly canvases, for prior to his becoming a full member of the Société Nationale in 1903 he would still have had to submit his works to a jury and would not yet have had the right to make his own selection.[3] The clipping most likely reflects the date of acquisition of the sketch by a previous owner rather than the date of execution of the work itself.

Two of Morrice's sketchbooks from the mid-1890s contain drawings of fishing boats and studies of sunset or reflections of the moon on water (see fig. 6, Introduction).[4] While none of the drawings are directly related to this work, they reveal Morrice's interests at the time, which are seen also in this oil sketch. The manner of depicting figures with a vertical stroke for the trousers and a large dab of the brush for the head is seen in other studies of this period, including *View of a Square, Dieppe* (fig. 8, Introduction) and *The Black Goat (Capri)* (cat. no. 2). The painting of the light on the water recalls *Fishing Boats, Cancale* (cat. no. 4). The brushwork with which Morrice has delineated the far shore is seen again in his treatment of the forms at the base of the walls in *Beneath the Ramparts, St-Malo* (fig. 27a).

The left foreground in this sketch is painted in brown over blue, and the right side in brown over maroon. The reflections in the aquamarine water are brushed in pinky cream and green and the far hills in aquamarine and royal blue, with the bare wood showing through. The composition consists of four horizontal bands of colour, with the sails and the reflections in the water being the dominant verticals. The serenity and calm of this evening scene is underscored by the simplicity of the structure and the glowing colour.

A very close variant of this sketch (fig. 7a) is in a private collection. In that work the sails and the reflections of the setting sun play a greater role. As a result of the reduced foreground the composition is more vertical and the central grouping is brought forward. One would have thought that in painting a close variant of a sketch Morrice was modifying and perfecting the composition as a study for a canvas, but, unlike the other instance in which he followed this procedure (see cat. no. 46), we know of no canvas based on these sketches.

1. In Laing 1979, pp. 48 and 227, Blair Laing gives 1956 and 1957 as the dates of his purchases of six sketches from Nicholson. In Laing 1984, pp. 198 and 200, he gives the dates as 1952 and c. 1954. In his cataloguing notes (now in the archives of the National Gallery of Canada) he gives the date of acquisition of all six as 1955.
2. The first two are reproduced here as figures 31a and 30c. *Le port à Saint-Servan* is reproduced in Dorais 1985b, p. 44. *La plage à Saint-Malo* may be the painting currently titled *View of Paramé from the Beach* reproduced in Laing 1984, p. 63.
3. C.C. Hungerford, "Meissonier and the Founding of the Société Nationale des Beaux-Arts," *Art Journal* XLVIII:1 (Spring 1989), p. 74.
4. Sketchbooks 9 and 2 (Montreal Museum of Fine Arts, Dr.1973.32 and Dr.1973.25).

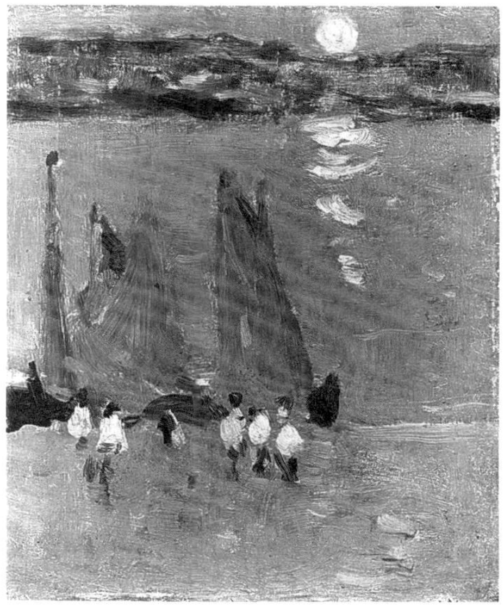

Fig. 7a
Fishing Boats, c. 1896–98, oil on wood, 14.6 × 11.4 cm. Private collection.

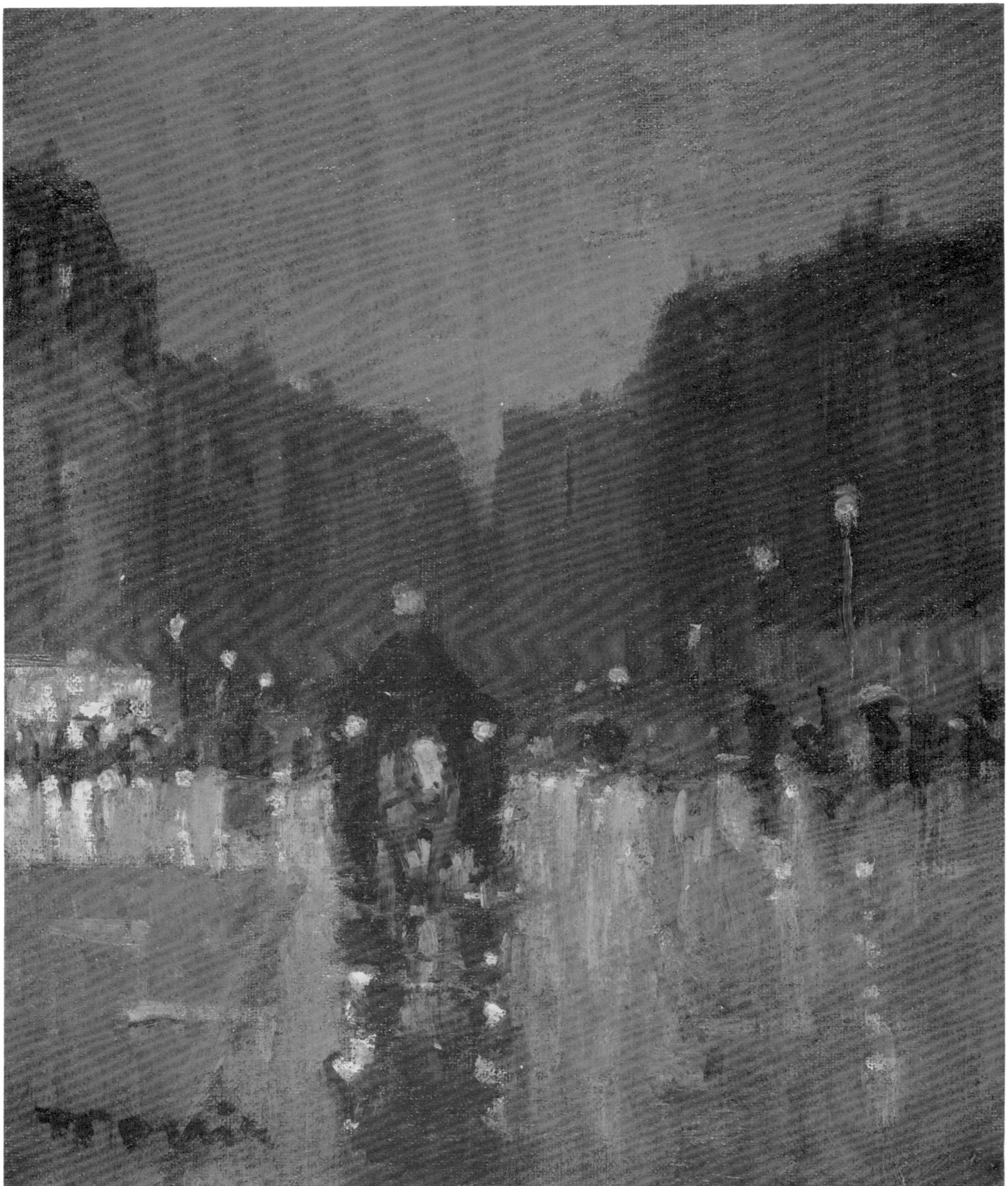

8

A Wet Night on the Boulevard St-Germain, Paris

c. 1895–96

Oil on canvas mounted on wood-pulp board, 22.9 × 19.1 cm

Inscriptions: signed l.l., *Morrice*; verso: l.r. in graphite, *7¼ × 8¾* (crossed out)

Labels: partly torn, in black pencil, No. *1015*(?) *1914*; in black ink, PRICE *RCA* / ARTIST *J.W. Morrice* / DESCRIPTION *A wet night / on the Boulvd / St. Germain / Paris* / FRAME / W. SCOTT & SONS / MONTREAL; in blue ink, *G. Blair Laing, Toronto. / A wet night on the Boulevard / St Germain, Paris.*, in graphite, *#34*; in blue ballpoint pen, *G.B.L. / "A WET NIGHT / "ON THE / BOULEVARD"*

Provenance: W. Scott & Sons, Montreal, by 1914. Walter Klinkhoff Gallery, Montreal. (Sold, Frank Waddington, Toronto, 17 May 1967, lot 74); G. Blair Laing, Toronto, 1967.

30465

Paris at the turn of the century was enormously attractive to North American artists. Though the city was rich in the visible manifestations of history and tradition, it was not this that attracted them so much as the bustle of modern life – the cafés, the streets, the parks, and the public spaces where the dynamism of the great metropolis was most evident.

The streets of Paris appear repeatedly in Morrice's early sketchbooks as well as in one charcoal drawing (fig. 7, Introduction).[1] One notices his special fascination with the horse-drawn carriages, the reflections of city lights on the wet streets, women walking with umbrellas, and fiacres lining up in front of the Gare Montparnasse, close to where Morrice would meet his friends at the Café de Versailles. Among his oil sketches there are other studies of horse-drawn carriages in city streets.[2]

In *A Wet Night on the Boulevard St-Germain* Morrice is primarily concerned with the reflections of the lights. The fiacre is placed off centre in the middle of the boulevard, with the buildings fanning out behind and beside the driver. The surface of the canvas is rough, painted in blacks, greys, and blues, with the reflections in cool yellow-green.

In a related canvas (fig. 8a) one omnibus with a green lamp approaches as a second with a red lamp recedes from the viewer. The surface is richer and more fluidly brushed in predominantly brown tones, while the horses are painted in the jagged planar strokes of the drawings. A woman in a black dress hurries by the orange light of a shop window at the right and two women with umbrellas are seen near the bare young tree at the left.

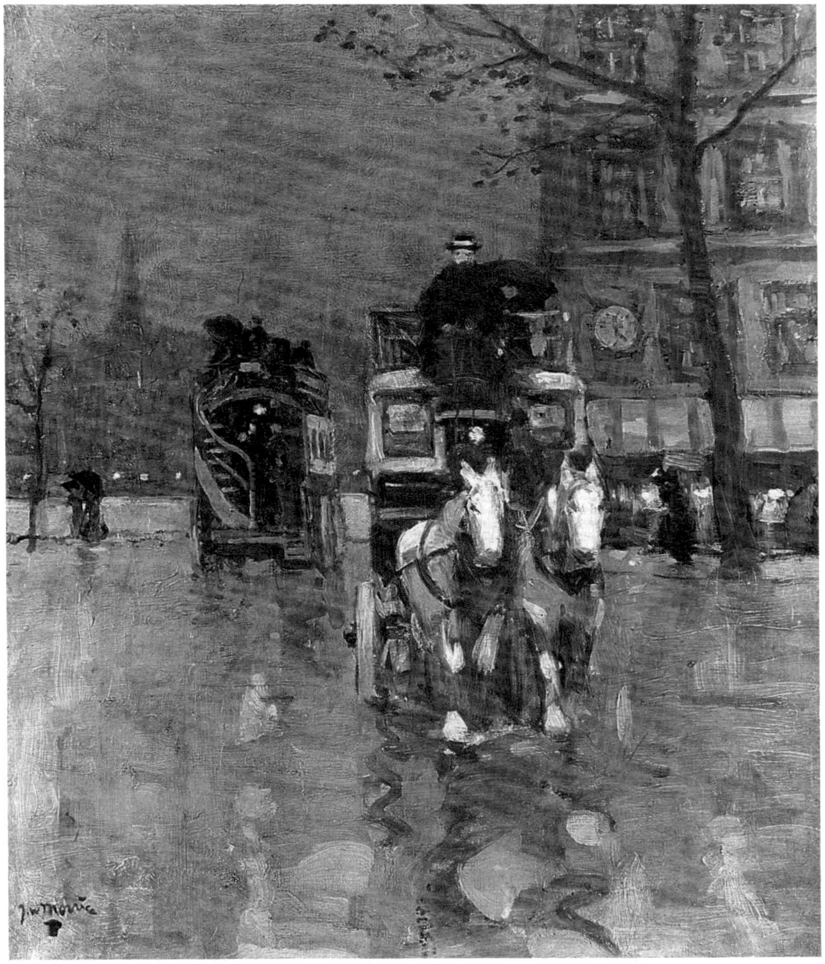

Fig. 8a
The Omnibus, c. 1895–96, oil on canvas, 60.8 × 50 cm. National Gallery of Canada (9509).

1. See Sketchbooks 11, 14, and 3 (Montreal Museum of Fine Arts, Dr.1973.34, Dr.1973.37, and Dr.1973.26), dating from 1894 to 1898.
2. One titled *Paris Street Scene at Dusk* (oil on canvas, 21 × 29.9 cm), formerly in the Doig Collection in Brandon, Manitoba, was sold at Christie, Manson & Woods (Canada) Ltd., Montreal, 2 May 1973, lot 92 (repr.).

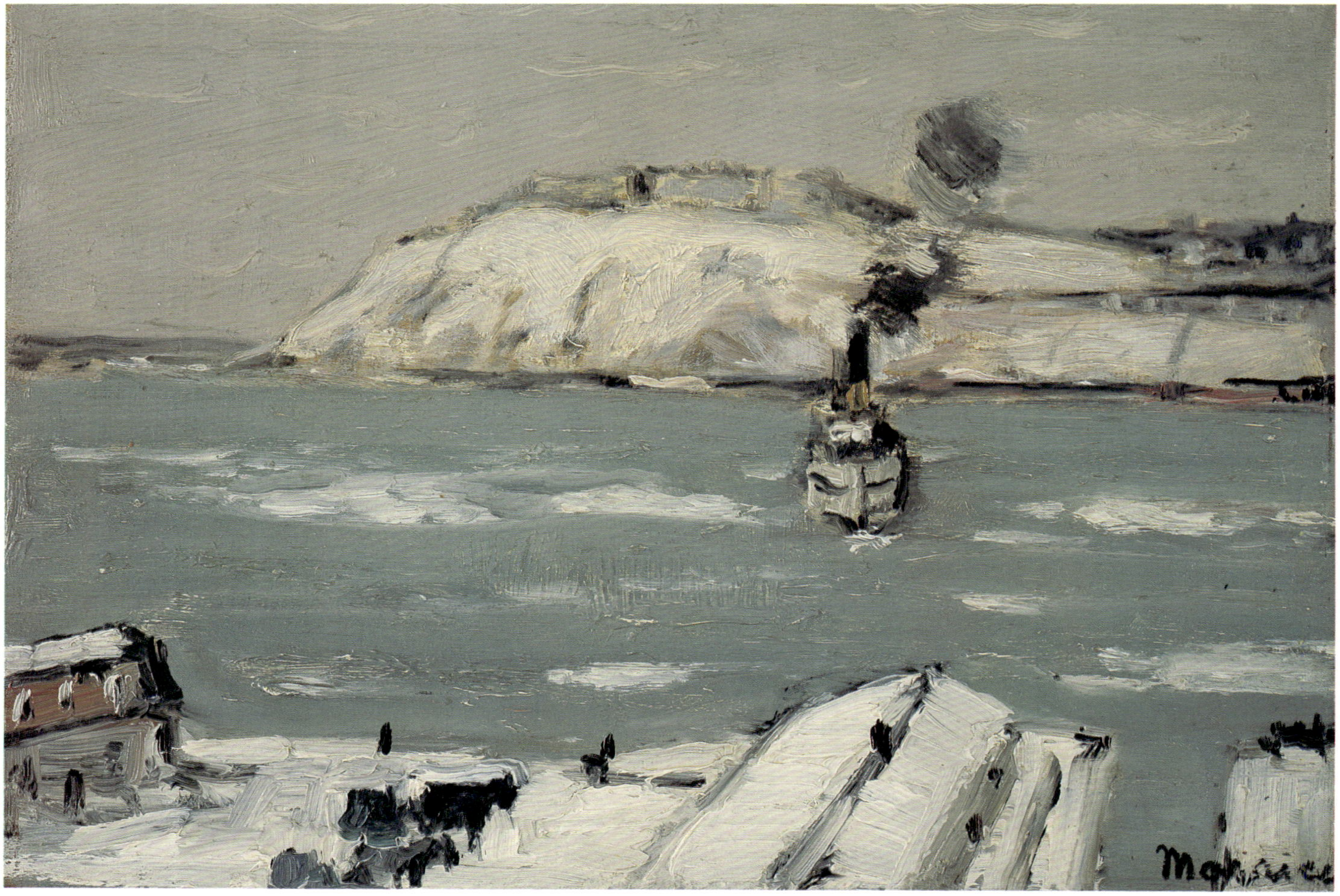

9

Study for "The Ferry, Quebec"

1897

Oil on wood, 17.5 × 25.1 cm

Inscriptions: signed l.r., *Morrice*; verso: u.l. in black ink, *0/2985*

Labels: typed, *"Quebec-Levis, Ferry" / by / J.W. Morrice, R.C.A.*; Art Gallery of Ontario crating label, Norton Gallery exhibition, no. 19

Provenance: W. Scott & Sons, Montreal, by 1934;[1] Dr. G.H. Henderson, Halifax, by 1936;[2] Mrs. G.H. Henderson, Halifax, by 1951;[3] G. Blair Laing, Toronto, by 1978.[4]

30468

The Ferry, Quebec (fig. 9c), one of Morrice's best-loved images, was acquired by the National Gallery of Canada from the 1937 Morrice retrospective exhibition. A key image among his Canadian works, it was first shown at the 1907 Salon of the Société Nationale des Beaux Arts, where it was admired by the young John Lyman, who had recently arrived in Paris.[5]

Though the painting dates from 1907, the sketch was realized during a visit to Canada in 1896–97. Morrice spent the Christmas holidays with his family and then accompanied Maurice Cullen to Quebec City and Ste-Anne-de-Beaupré, where he would remain into March. From Beaupré he wrote to his friend Edmund Morris: "Am painting a picture for the [Paris] Salon, Quebec, floating ice &c."[6] What became of this canvas is unknown, but there are two sketches of similar subjects, the present *Study for "The Ferry, Quebec"* and the Edmonton Art Gallery's *View of Quebec from the River* (fig. 9b). While the bare wood is more evident in the latter, the two sketches are painted in similar tones, the water a pearly blue-grey, the ferry sheds grey and maroon, and the sky a warm grey. In both, a touch of red on the far shore is echoed in the roofs of the sheds. Morrice's fascination with the ferry between Quebec City on the north shore of the St. Lawrence and Lévis on the south shore is also evidenced in a sketchbook he used on this trip that includes studies of the horse-drawn sleighs on the bow of the ferry as well as one graphite drawing (fig. 9a) that served as the basis for the Edmonton sketch. The graphite drawing has been worked over in blue ink, which Morrice also used as a wash on several other drawings in this book. As he noted in his letter to Morris: "We have had cold weather 30 below zero. Difficult to work out of doors – paint gets stiff."[7] The sketches may in fact have been painted indoors.

Study for "The Ferry, Quebec" does not have the studio stamp, so it must have been sold by Morrice prior to 1924 and acquired by W. Scott & Sons before 1934, at which time it was included in the exhibition of Morrice's paintings organized by Scott's at Mellors Fine Arts Limited in Toronto – the exhibition that did so much to spark Blair Laing's passion for Morrice's work.

1. Toronto 1934, no. 17 (an annotated copy of the catalogue in the library of the Art Gallery of Ontario, Toronto, gives the measurements as "8 × 10"). See also Laing 1984, p. 186.
2. Buchanan 1936a, p. 157.
3. Loaned by Mrs. G.H. Henderson to the exhibition *The Development of Canadian Painting*, Halifax Memorial Library, 12 November 1951, no. 20.
4. Author's notes, from visit to G. Blair Laing, 21 October 1978.
5. Lyman 1937b; Lyman 1937c; Lyman 1945, p. 9; Cloutier 1985, p. 173. Cloutier (1986, pp. 84–85) identifies the 1907 Salon painting *Le bac* (no. 900) as one of the Morrices now in the Hermitage, St. Petersburg; if so, *The Ferry, Quebec* must have been the work exhibited as no. 902, *Effet de neige (Québec)*.
6. Letter from Morrice to Morris, "Sunday" [after 23 January 1897], Morris Papers. See also Dorais 1978.
7. Letter from Morrice to Morris, ibid.

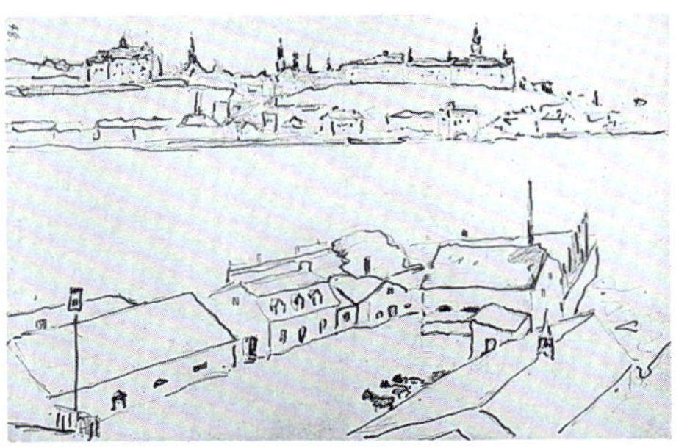

Fig. 9a
Paris–Quebec Sketchbook, p. 48r, 1897, pen and blue ink and graphite on wove paper, 10.8 × 16.7 cm. National Gallery of Canada (7420).

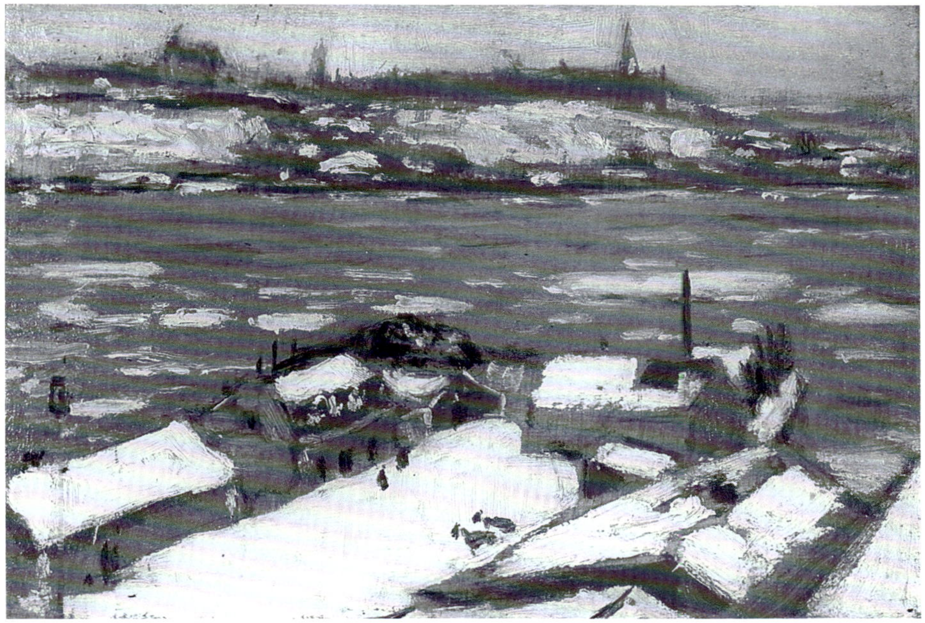

Fig. 9b
View of Quebec from the River, 1897, oil and graphite on wood, 17.7 × 25.2 cm. Edmonton Art Gallery. Bequest of F. Eleanore Morrice, 1981 (81.29.1).

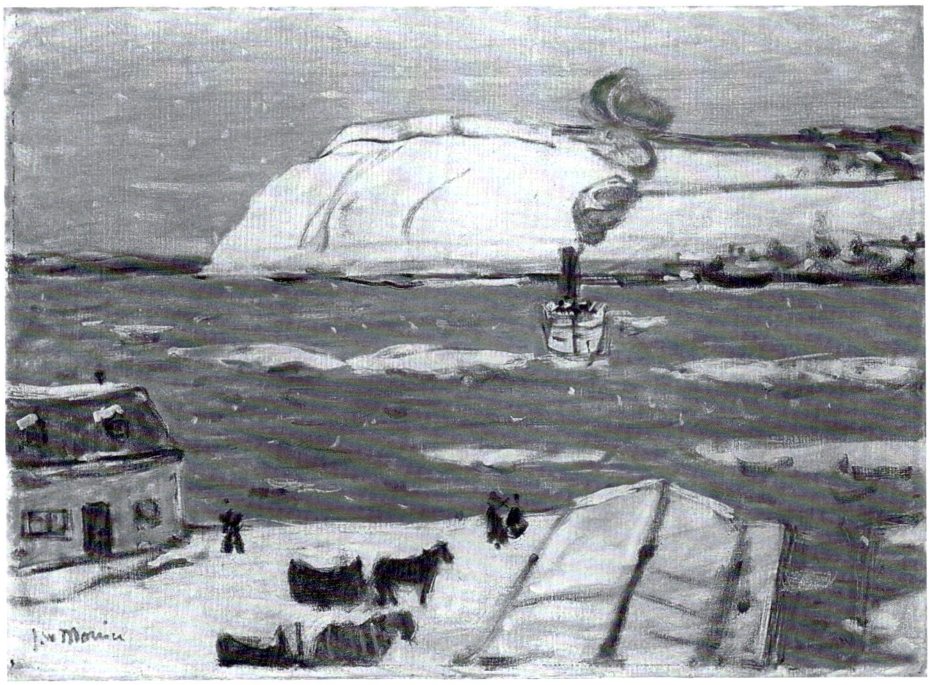

Fig. 9c
The Ferry, Quebec, 1907, oil on canvas, 62 × 81.7 cm. National Gallery of Canada (4301).

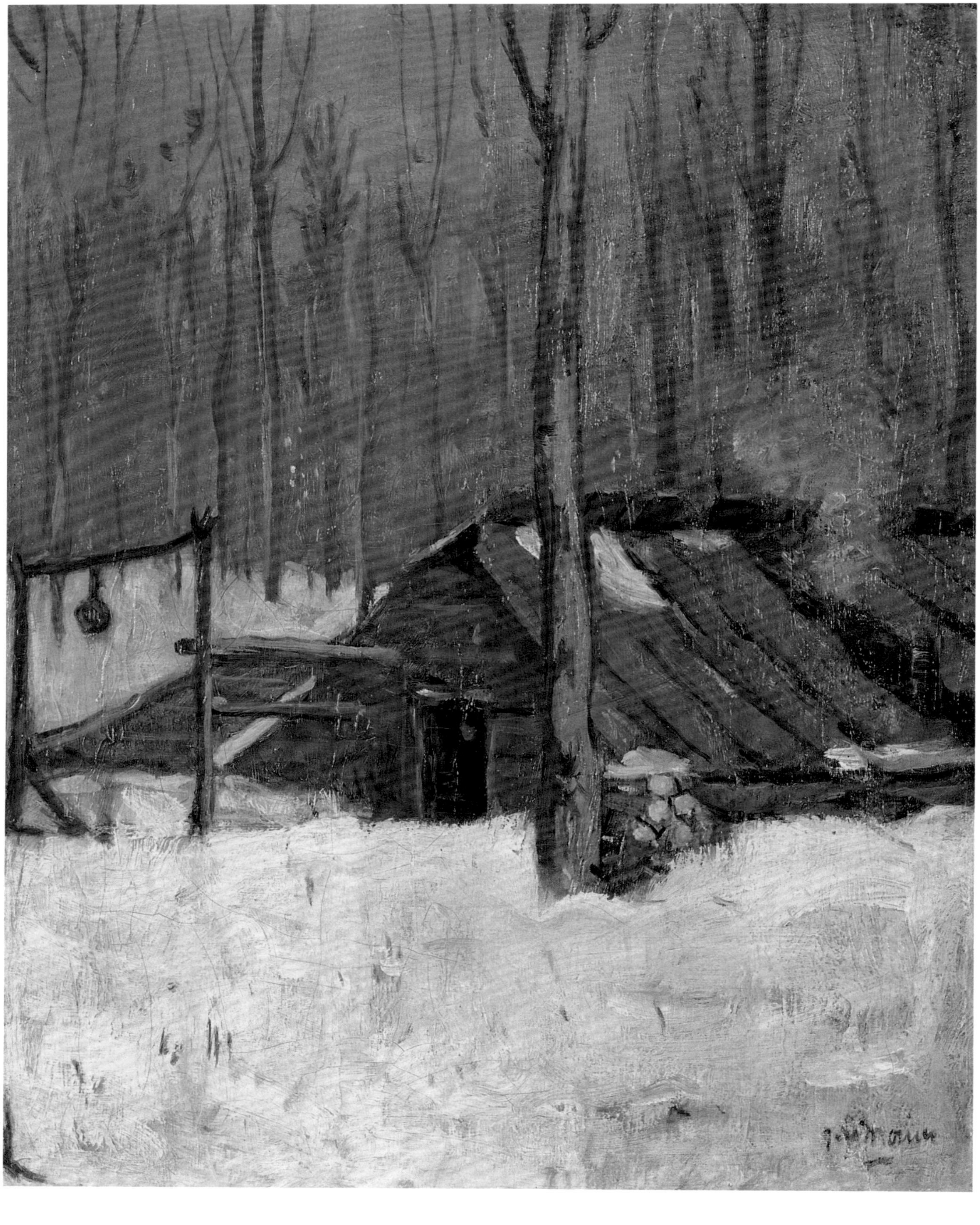

10

Sugar Bush

c. 1897–98

Oil on canvas, 51.6 × 41.1 cm

Inscriptions: signed l.r., *Morrice*; verso: u.l. in graphite (?), 1254, c. stamped, *C. ROWNEY & C° / LONDON, W. / QUALITY E.*; back of frame: c.l. in blue pencil, *L14 4 14 CCC*; in black ballpoint pen, *600*

Labels: MMFA 1985, no. 22; in blue ink, *MAPLE / SUGAR / CAMP / 80-15*

Provenance: W. Scott & Sons, Montreal, by 1932[1] (sold, Fraser Bros. Ltd, Montreal, 1–9 April 1938, lot 159). Private collection, Montreal (sold, Christie, Manson & Woods [Canada] Ltd., Montreal, 12 May 1976, lot 105); Denise Delrue, Montreal.[2] G. Blair Laing Ltd., Toronto, by 1984.[3]

30417

Morrice's 1897 Quebec sketchbook (in the National Gallery of Canada) contains no drawings for this painting, and so it would appear that he worked directly in oil to paint the initial studies. In one related oil sketch (fig. 10a) the shack is depicted from a slightly different viewpoint and a young boy is standing in the foreground. The shadows of the trees at the right are a clear, transparent blue, touches of red animate the smoke from the shack, and the sky is light blue. Another sketch has been identified[4] that more clearly approximates the final canvas, in which a diminutive figure is depicted in the doorway of the shack. In the canvas the colouring is also more unified, the soft, grey tones extending into the trees and sky.

The canvas itself came from C. Rowney & Company, London, as did the canvas for another 1897 painting, *Village in Winter* (fig. 14, Introduction). Morrice had at some earlier time painted a marine on this canvas (see fig. 10b) but then scraped it down and reused it for a painting of the sugar bush in which he initially included a larger figure in silhouette in the foreground (see fig. 10c). Traces of the darker figure are now becoming visible through the lighter overpaints, even under normal viewing conditions. Morrice applied the paint generously and then rubbed it to create a smooth-textured surface.

The canvases realized from Morrice's 1897 trip to Quebec City and Ste-Anne-de-Beaupré differ considerably one from the other. *Village in Winter* is painted thickly with a wide brush or palette knife, creating a rough-textured surface that contrasts with the thin drawing in black of the houses (centre right). *Quebec Citadel by Moonlight* (fig. 15, Introduction) is thinly painted in greys and green with subtle touches of red and pink. In *Sugar Bush* Morrice's use of thick paint (the same technique seen in the work of his sketching companion Maurice Cullen) is combined with his growing interest in Whistlerian tonalities to realize a subtly coloured impression of late winter in Canada.

1. Montreal 1932, no. 21, as *Sugar Camp, Quebec*.
2. Note by Dennis Reid, formerly Curator of Post-Confederation Canadian Art, National Gallery of Canada, undated (probably 1976), now in the National Gallery's curatorial file for *Sugar Bush*.
3. Cloutier (1985, p. 119) states that this painting was with the William Watson Gallery about 1965, but the Watson Art Galleries closed in 1958. I have been unable to document that Blair Laing acquired this painting prior to 1984, the year it was reproduced in his book on Morrice (Laing 1984, p. 105).
4. Documented by Dorais (1980, p. 242) as oil on wood, 28 × 20 cm, private collection, Westmount, Quebec, in 1980.

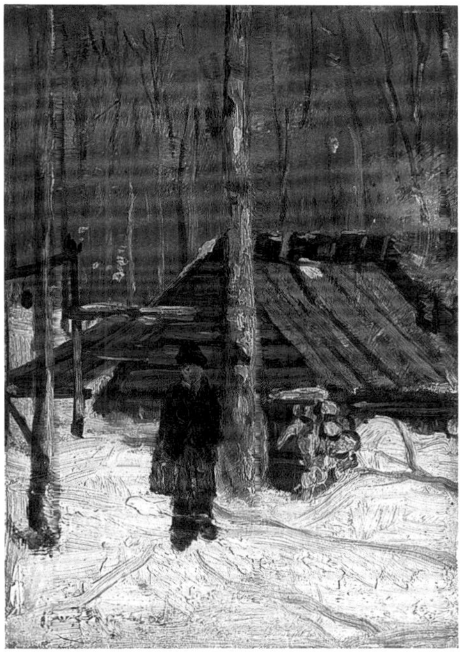

Fig. 10a
Study for "Sugar Bush", 1897, oil on wood, 25.4 × 17.9 cm. Private collection.

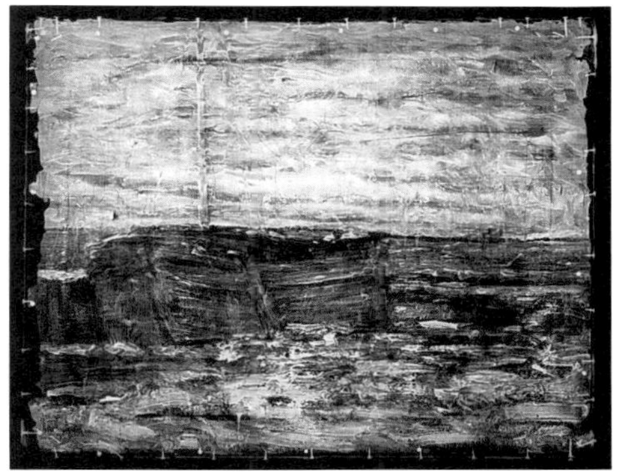

Fig. 10b
X-radiograph of *Sugar Bush*.

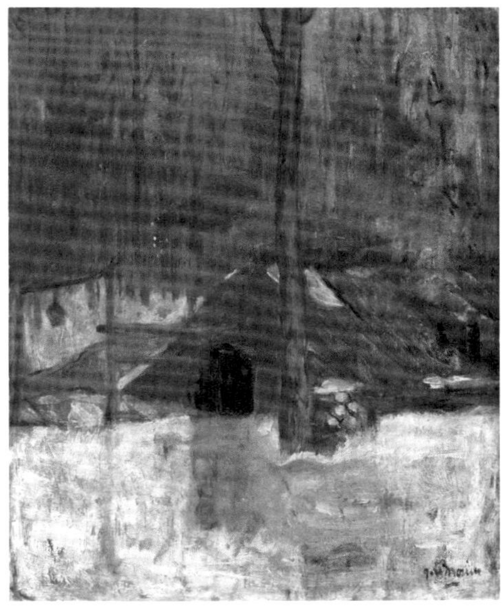

Fig. 10c
Infrared photograph of *Sugar Bush*.

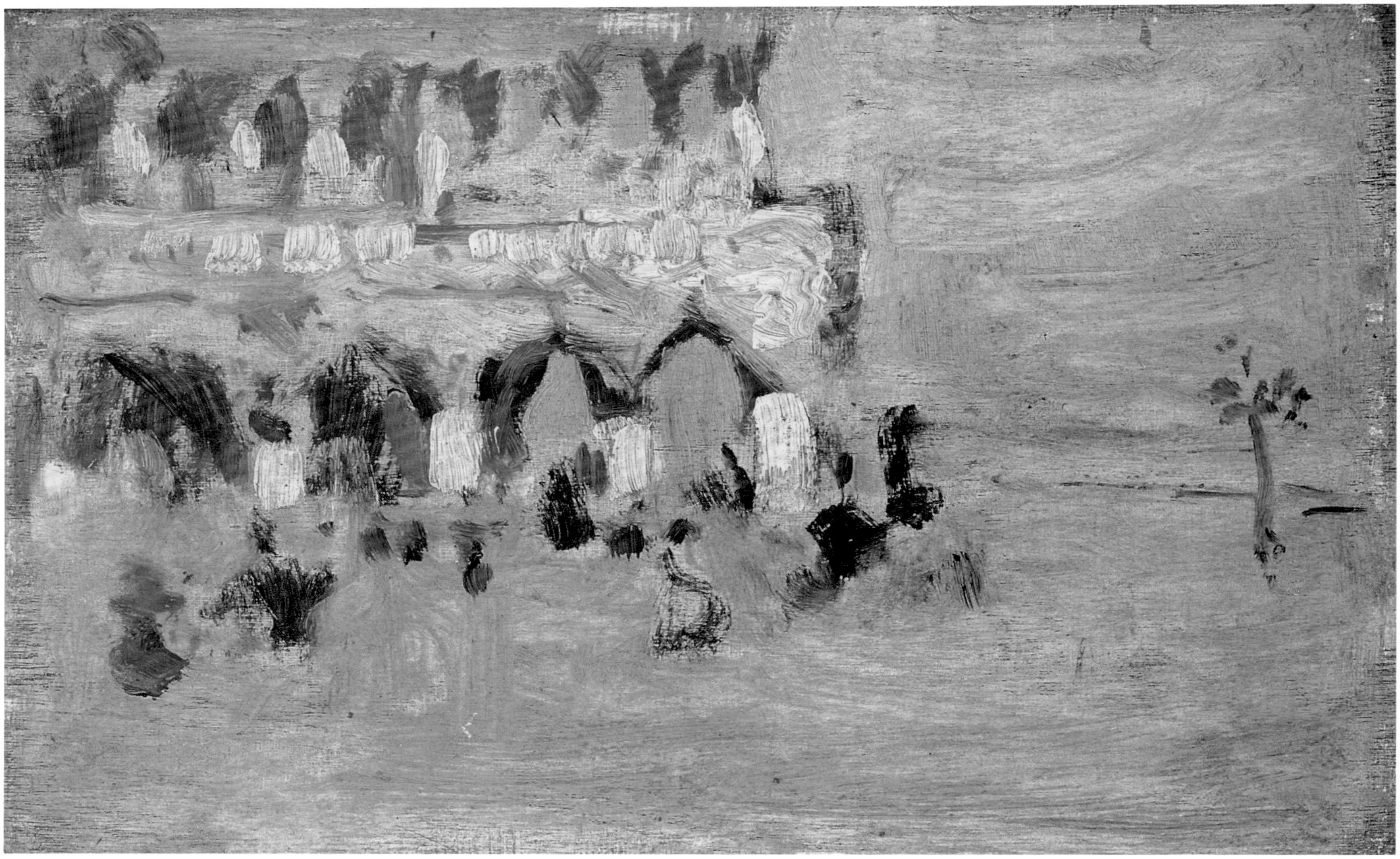

11

Doge's Palace, Venice

c. 1897

Oil on wood, 9.7 × 15.5 cm

Inscriptions: verso: t. in graphite, *St Marks & Doges Palace, Venice*, c.l. in brown ink, *1*, c. stamped, *STUDIO / J.W. MORRICE*, in stamp in graphite, *336*

Labels: in black ink, CONTINENTAL GALLERIES OF FINE ART / 1310 ST. CATHERINE ST. WEST, MONTREAL / PHONE PLATEAU 1072 / ARTIST: *Jas. W. Morrice, R.C.A.* / TITLE OF PICTURE: *St. Marks & Doges Palace Venice* / DESCRIPTION: *Original Sketch on wood panel*; in blue ballpoint pen, *78-27* / *ST MARKS* / *& Doges / Palace*

Provenance: Estate of the artist. Continental Galleries of Fine Art, Montreal; Vilma Lafontaine, Montreal; G. Blair Laing Ltd., Toronto, 1964.

30413

Writing to Robert Henri from Beaupré in March 1897, Morrice commented: "I am getting sick of snow . . . [and] this monstrous virtuous existence . . . After spending a couple of weeks with my people in Montreal I will go to New York and then to Italy to Venice for a month or so."[1] He would exhibit a Venice canvas the following spring at the Salon of the Société Nationale des Beaux-Arts.[2]

We know for certain of six trips that Morrice made to Venice, and it is quite likely that he visited the city on other occasions as well.[3] The lack of precise documentation and the dispersal of a number of his Venetian drawings make it difficult to say which works belong to which trips. Several authors have dated some of his most Whistlerian paintings to his 1897 stay in that city.[4] Yet how can one explain the radical change from the thickly painted, rough-textured studies done in Quebec that same year to this thinly brushed, fleeting sketch? Related works can be found, such as the thinly brushed nocturnal view of the citadel of Quebec (fig. 15, Introduction), done from an 1897 study (possibly in Paris after a visit to Venice), or *Roadside and Beach* (fig. 11a),[5] painted in Brittany or Normandy by 1896.

This view of the Doge's Palace is one Morrice would repeat in several sketches over the years (see cat. no. 44) and in at least one canvas.[6] Rarely, however, did he use such economy of means: on a small panel, the bare wood showing through the thinly brushed pink-mauves and blues, he has produced an ethereal, light-filled impression of the skeletal palace, lamp standard, public square, water, sky, and moving people.

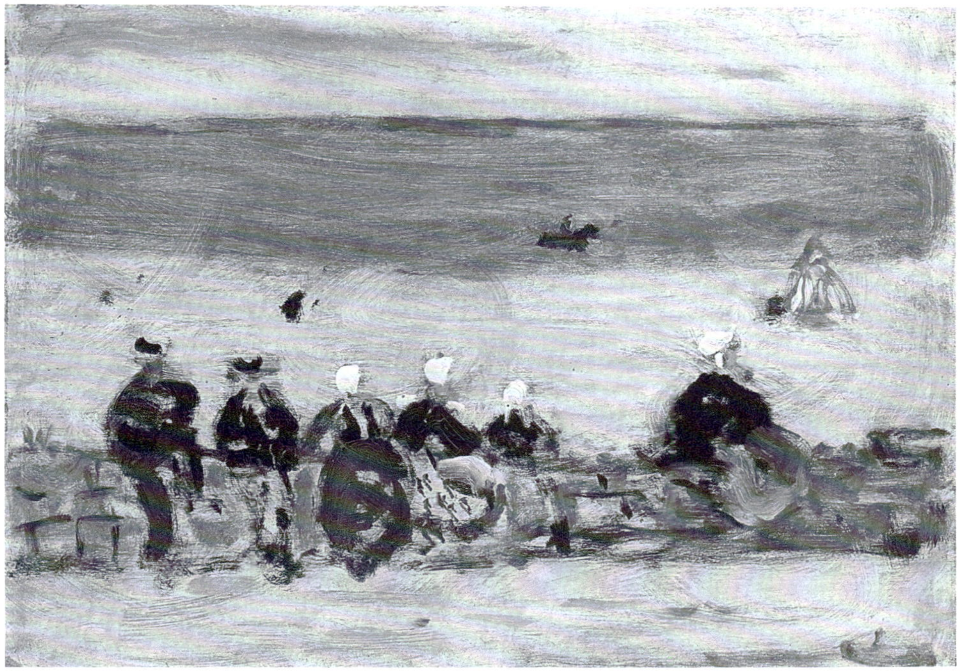

Fig. 11a
Roadside and Beach, c. 1896, oil on wood, 23.5 × 33 cm. National Gallery of Canada (3329).

1. Letter from Morrice to Henri, 17 March [1897], Henri Papers.
2. Cloutier 1985, p. 46. The work, titled *Venise*, is currently unidentified.
3. Trips have been dated to 1894, 1897, 1901, 1902, 1904, and 1907. Ghislain Clermont (quoted in McTavish 1984, p. 19) states that Morrice also visited Venice in 1906.
4. Reid 1968, p. 17; Dorais 1980, pp. 143–47, 216–34; Cloutier 1985, p. 124.
5. This oil sketch is painted on a larger wood panel, of the same size as *Street Scene in Brittany* (cat. no. 3).
6. See the entry for the canvas *The Doge's Palace, Venice* (private collection) in Cloutier 1985, p. 141.

12

Prow of a Gondola, Venice

c. 1897

Oil on canvas mounted on wood-pulp board, 32.1 × 23.2 cm

Inscriptions: verso: c. in black ink, *Guaranteed by W. Scott & Sons*, u.c. in graphite, *28951 / Venice / 9¼ × 12½ / 1*, u.l. in black ink, *M145*, c. stamped, *STUDIO / J.W. MORRICE*

Labels: Wildenstein 1968, no. 2; typed, *MORRICE EXHIBITION / TITLE / PROW OF A GONDOLA / FROM: LAING GALLERY, TORONTO*; typed, Laing Galleries 194 Bloor Street West Toronto 5 Canada / *"Prow of a Gondola, Venice" / c.1896 / By / JAMES WILSON MORRICE / (1865–1924)*; typed, NATIONAL GALLERY OF CANADA / Title of Exhibition / *J W MORRICE / RETROSPECTIVE EX* / Catalogue No. *2#* / Box No. *3*

Provenance: Estate of the artist; W. Scott & Sons, Montreal. J.J. Vaughan, Toronto, by 1959;[1] G. Blair Laing, Toronto, 1965.

30448

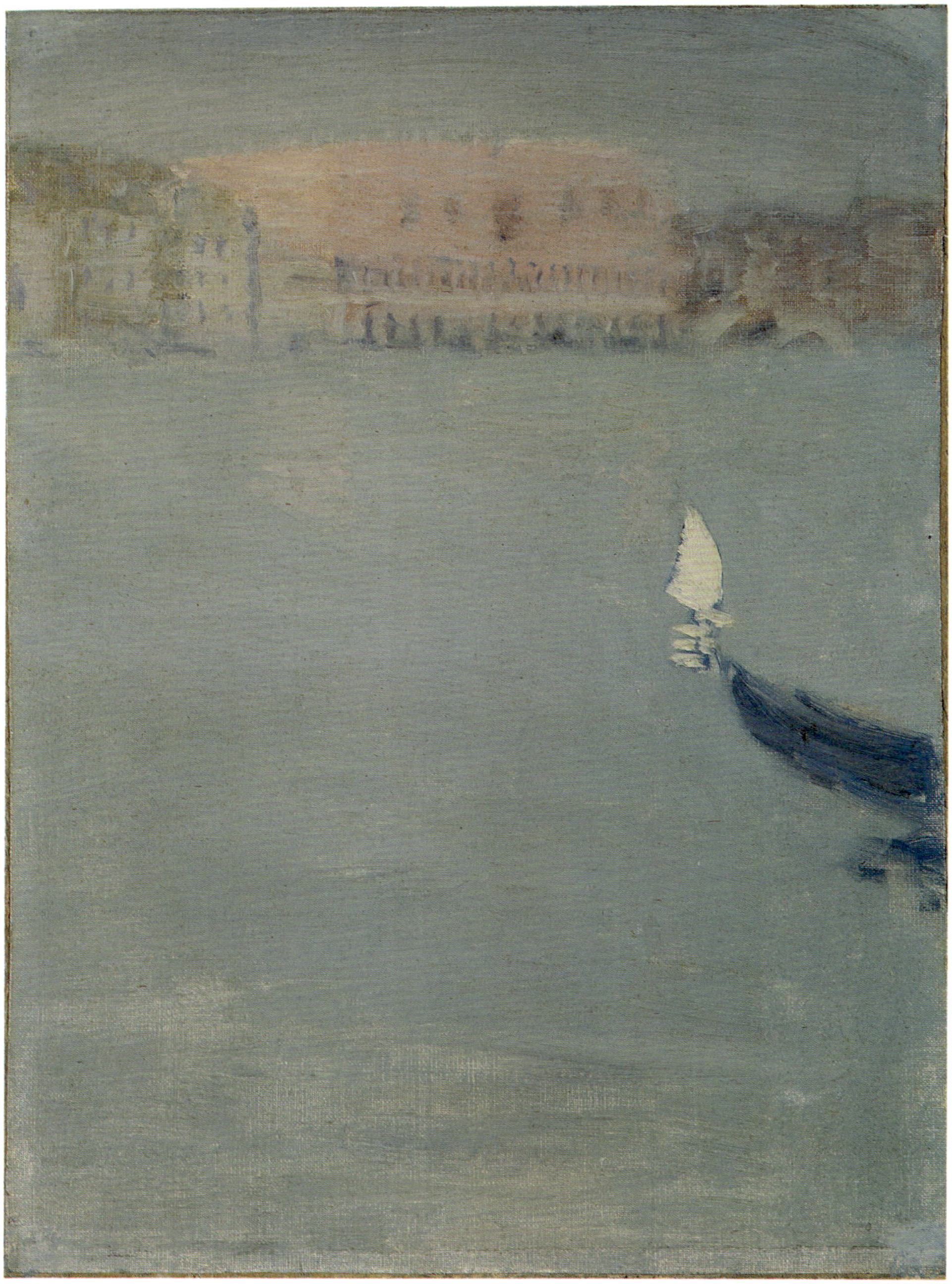

This small canvas is one of the most radical works of Morrice's early years. Two-thirds of the image is of delicate blue water, with the black prow of a gondola sharply cut off at the right. The glowing pink of the Doge's Palace dominates the top of the composition, and the sky above is the same colour as the water. The artist has dragged a thin coat of pale blue-white over the entire painting save for the bright white crest on the tip of the gondola, unifying the tones and overall composition.

A subtle tension is created between the thin and rubbed paint at the bottom and the more evenly covered surfaces above, and also between the bright white ornament and the more atmospheric treatment of the rest of the canvas. While the bow of the gondola thrusts into the composition, suggesting movement, the work remains evocatively contemplative, glowing with a soft light – a light that Morrice undoubtedly admired in the work of the Anglo-American artist James McNeill Whistler, who similarly found Venice to be such an attractive subject.

1. Loaned by Mr. and Mrs. J.J. Vaughan to the *Exhibition of Loans from Private Toronto Collections*, Art Gallery of Toronto, 2–18 October 1959, as *Black Gondola on Canal, Venice.*

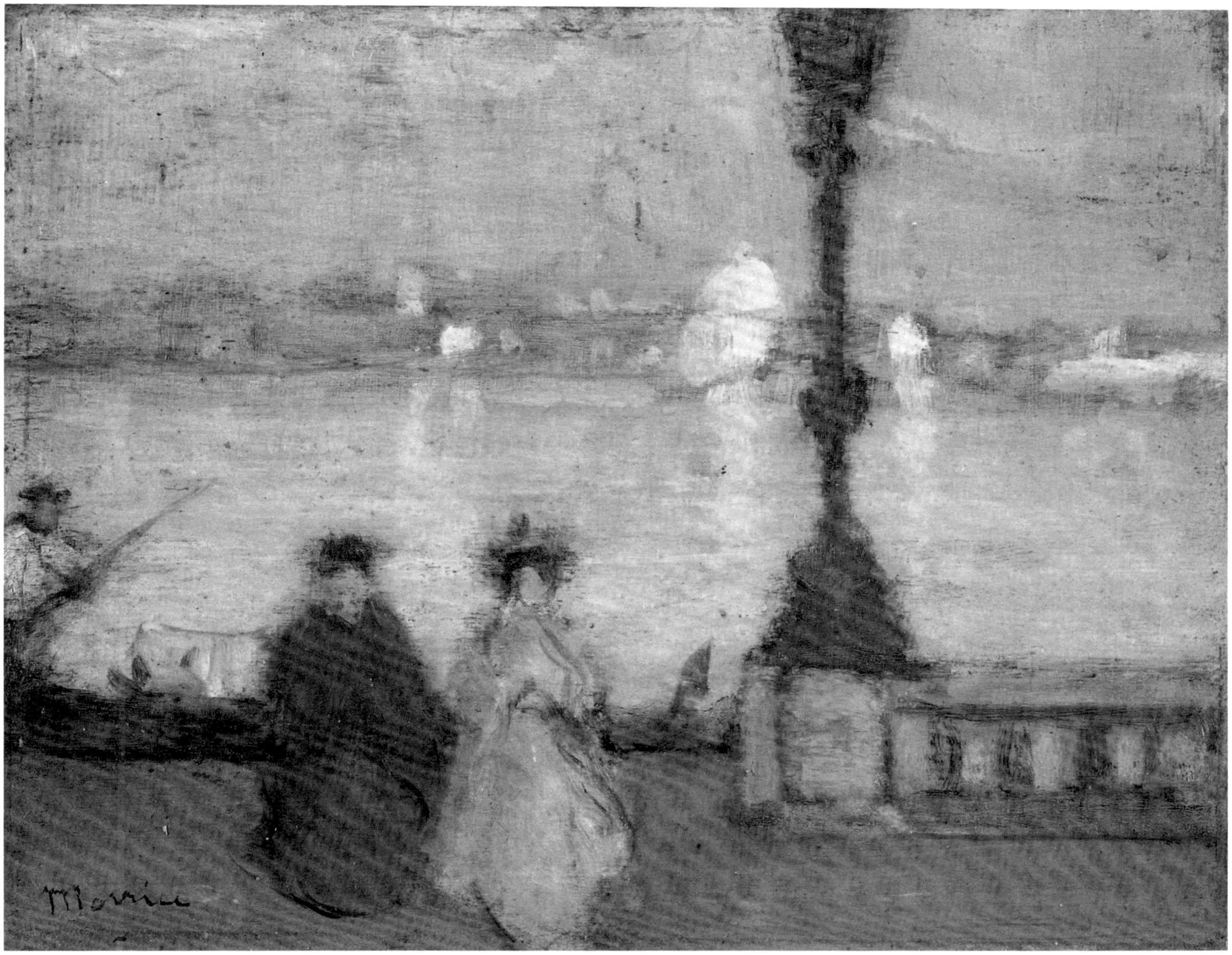

13

Venice

c. 1897

Oil on wood, 12.2 × 15.3 cm

Inscriptions: signed l.l., *Morrice*; back of frame: c.l. in graphite, *12/49 Laing*, u.r. in graphite, K.T., r. in graphite T.D. / *#76*, l.c. in green ink, *#39*

Labels: in blue ballpoint pen, G.B.L. / VENICE

Provenance: (Sold, Sotheby & Co. [Canada] Ltd., Toronto, 21 October 1974, lot 96); G. Blair Laing, Toronto, 1974.

30478

This sketch of two women in the Public Gardens in Venice combines the elegance of *Prow of a Gondola* (cat. no. 12) with the colour of *Doge's Palace* (cat. no. 11). The foreground figure is drawn in black paint in a manner that recalls *Girl Knitting* (cat. no. 5). Yet the actual dating of the sketch is problematic, as Morrice reworked the composition. Originally he had depicted the combined silhouettes of Santa Maria della Salute and San Giorgio Maggiore across the water, but he then overpainted the tower of San Giorgio and the two domes (now visible through the lighter overpaints) and added a white, domed church near the lamp standard. Whether these changes were made when he first painted the sketch or at some later date is uncertain.[1]

Other aspects of Morrice's working procedure are also evident in this sketch. First he painted the lamp standard, the railing, the figure at the right, and the gondola. Next came the darker figure at the left (the gondola, painted first, creates a colour change in her dress). The sky, water, and buildings on the far shore were added last, and finally the aforementioned alterations to the composition were made.

1. A faint drawing of a similar composition can be found in the Paris–Venice Sketchbook (National Gallery of Canada, 7419, p. 39r), which dates from about 1901, but it is unclear whether it relates to the initial conception or to the modification of the sketch.

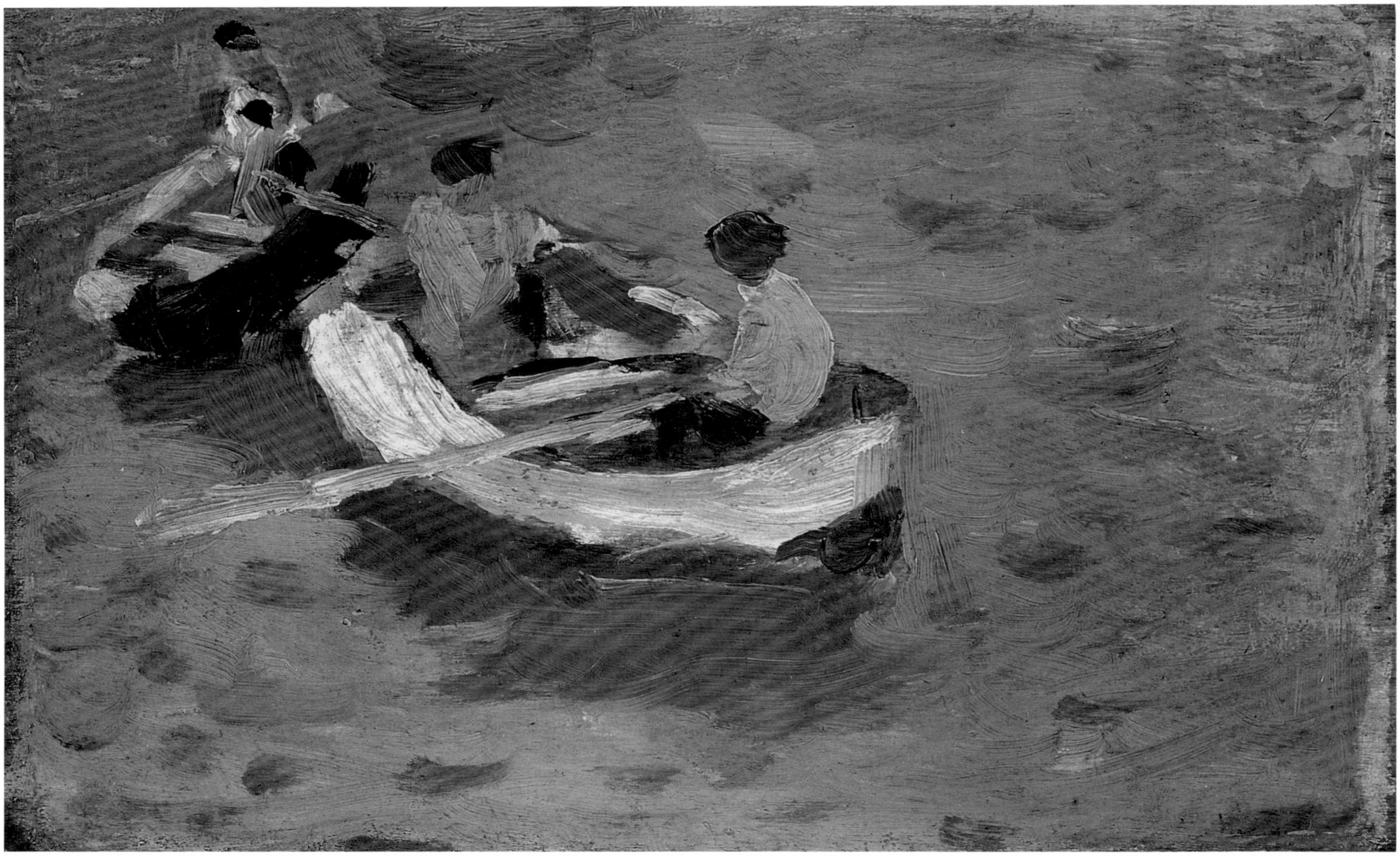

14

Boats on the Seine

c. 1894–97

Oil on wood, 9.7 × 15.5 cm

Inscriptions: verso: u.r. in graphite, *#33*, c. stamped, *STUDIO / J.W. MORRICE*

Labels: typed, *G. Blair Laing, / Toronto, Ontario. / "Boats on the Seine"*; MMFA 1965, no. 41; OKanada, no. 35; in blue ballpoint pen, *78-5 / BOATS ON / THE SEINE*, in blue ballpoint pen, *78-5*

Provenance: Estate of the artist. Vilma Lafontaine, Montreal; G. Blair Laing Ltd., Toronto, by 1965.[1]

30411

Executed with the greatest economy of means, this charming small work is one of those deceptively simple sketches that are difficult to situate within Morrice's oeuvre. It is painted on a small panel of approximately the same size as catalogue numbers 11, 23, and 24.

The two boats and just the hull of the third are viewed from a high vantage point. The water is painted in a thin coat of blue over pink, dabbed with highlights of darker blue and mauve. The boats are rendered in simple, broad strokes, as are the figures, including the young blond-haired girl who pulls on the oars as she glances to her right.

Two other sketches of boats on small wood panels are in the Montreal Museum of Fine Arts. In one (fig. 14a), the boat and reflections in the water are painted in broad strokes of pink, dark green, and cream yellow. This work can be related to a drawing in the sketchbook identified as having been used by Morrice on his trip to Capri around 1894 (fig. 14b).[2] In the other sketch, *Evening, the Lagoon, Venice* (fig. 14c), closer in colour to *Prow of a Gondola* (cat. no. 12), the treatment of the highlights in the water is similar to that in *Boats on the Seine* though the colour is more suffused and the forms less defined.

1. Loaned by Blair Laing to the exhibition *James Wilson Morrice 1865–1924* (Johnston 1965), no. 41.
2. From about the same period there is also a sketch of fishermen in a boat (oil on wood, 10 × 15 cm), sold at Joyner Fine Art Inc., Toronto, 25–26 November 1987, lot 269, as *Boating on the Seine*.

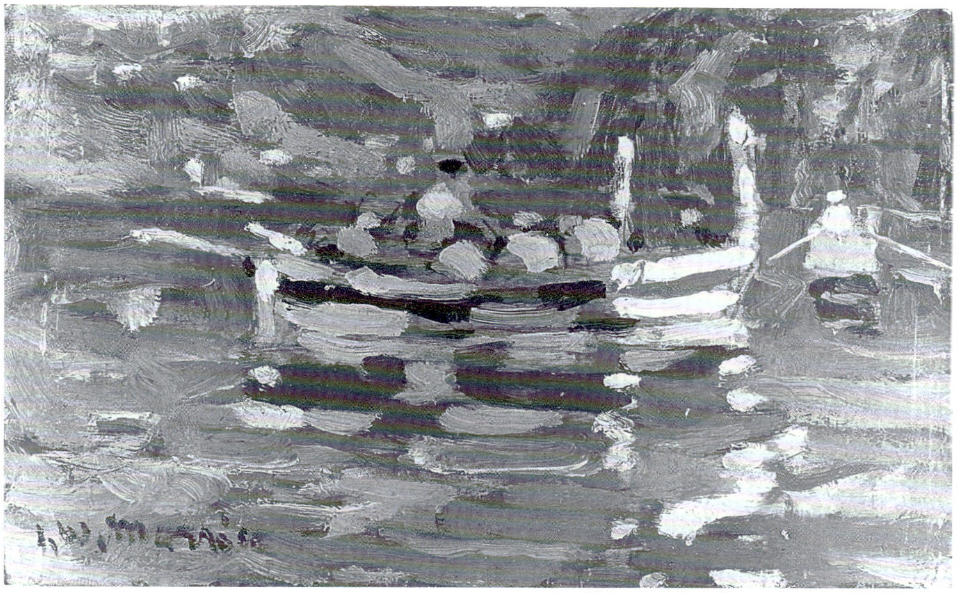

Fig. 14a
Fishermen in a Boat, c. 1894–97, oil on wood, 10 × 16 cm. Montreal Museum of Fine Arts. Bequest of F. Eleanore Morrice, 1981 (1981.79).

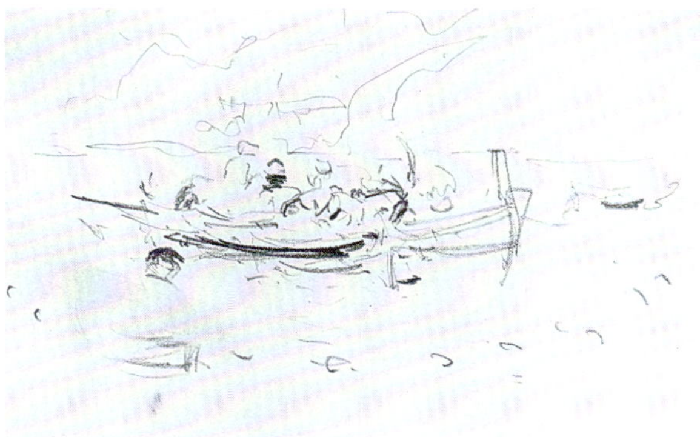

Fig. 14b
Sketchbook 12, p. 58r, c. 1894, graphite on wove paper, 10.8 × 16.6 cm. Montreal Museum of Fine Arts. Gift of David R. Morrice, 1973 (Dr.1973.35).

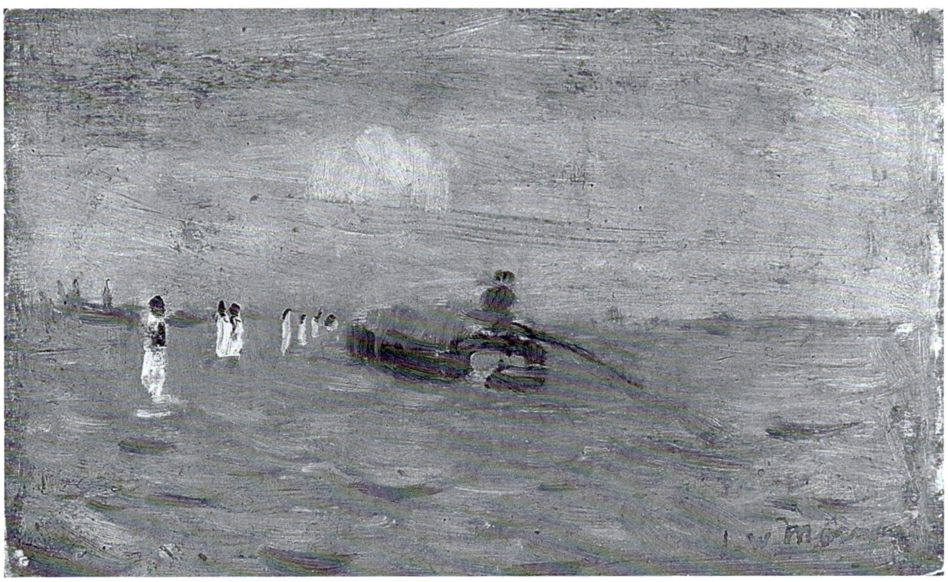

Fig. 14c
Evening, the Lagoon, Venice, c. 1897, oil on wood, 10 × 16.2 cm. Montreal Museum of Fine Arts. Bequest of F. Eleanore Morrice, 1981 (1981.78).

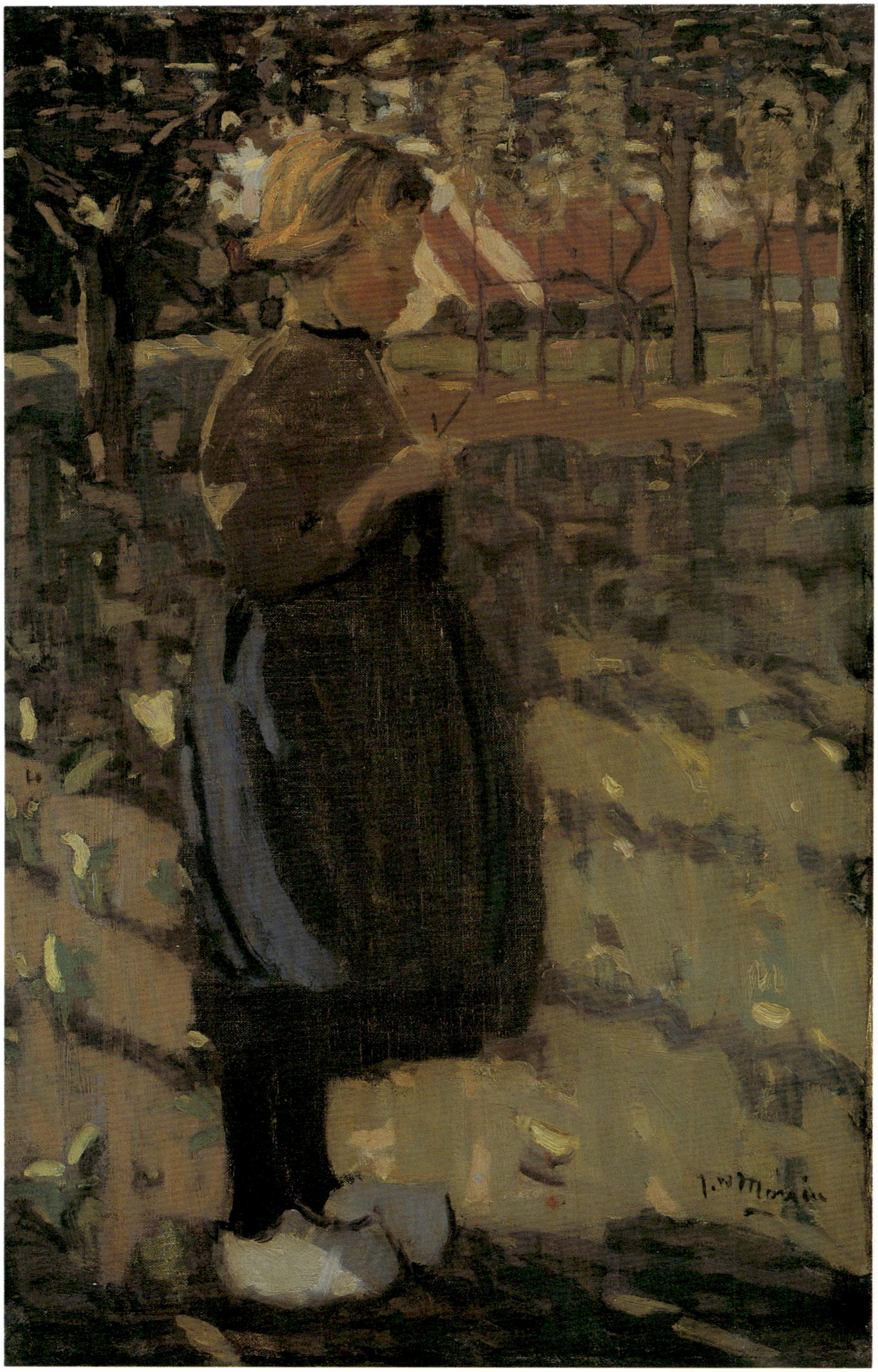

15

Girl Wearing Clogs

c. 1896–98

Oil on canvas, 55.5 × 35.5 cm

Inscriptions: signed l.r., *J.W. Morrice*; stretcher: u.l. in graphite, *750–*

Labels: typed, *G. BLAIR LAING / 194 Bloor St. W., / Toronto, Ontario.*; MMFA 1985, no. 21

Provenance: Estate of the artist; Léa Cadoret, Juan-les-Pins and Paris;[1] Jacques Dubourg, Paris (?). G. Blair Laing, Toronto, by 1978.[2]

30470

There are a number of figure studies dating from the 1890s that bear evidence not only of Morrice's attraction to young women but also of his continuing exploration of a variety of pictorial treatments. In this charming study he has returned to the subject of a girl knitting – a suitable way to keep a young model preoccupied. Morrice exhibited this painting in 1913 under the title *Dutch Girl*,[3] so one can assume that it resulted from one of his visits to the Netherlands. For some time it hung in the home of his parents in Montreal, where it was photographed in 1899 (see fig. 15a).

The figure is placed to the left of centre. A row of trees recedes at an angle in the upper part of the composition. Red-roofed houses behind the trees enhance the red cheeks of the young girl. The furrows of the field recede from the lower right to the upper left, intersecting with the screen of trees and the vertical of the girl's figure. On the left the field is painted over a pink ground and on the right over a lovely yellow-green, with both sides highlighted by green and yellow leaves. The front of the figure is painted thinly, leaving the texture of the canvas visible, while the back is more broadly rendered in contrasting colours. The painting of the foliage recalls that in *Street Scene in Brittany* (cat. no. 3), but the texture, subtlety, variety of colouring, and overall treatment show a greater sophistication and sense of assurance.

1. Buchanan 1936a, p. 181.
2. Author's notes, from visit to G. Blair Laing, 21 October 1978.
3. Buchanan 1936a, p. 181; Cloutier 1985, p. 48.

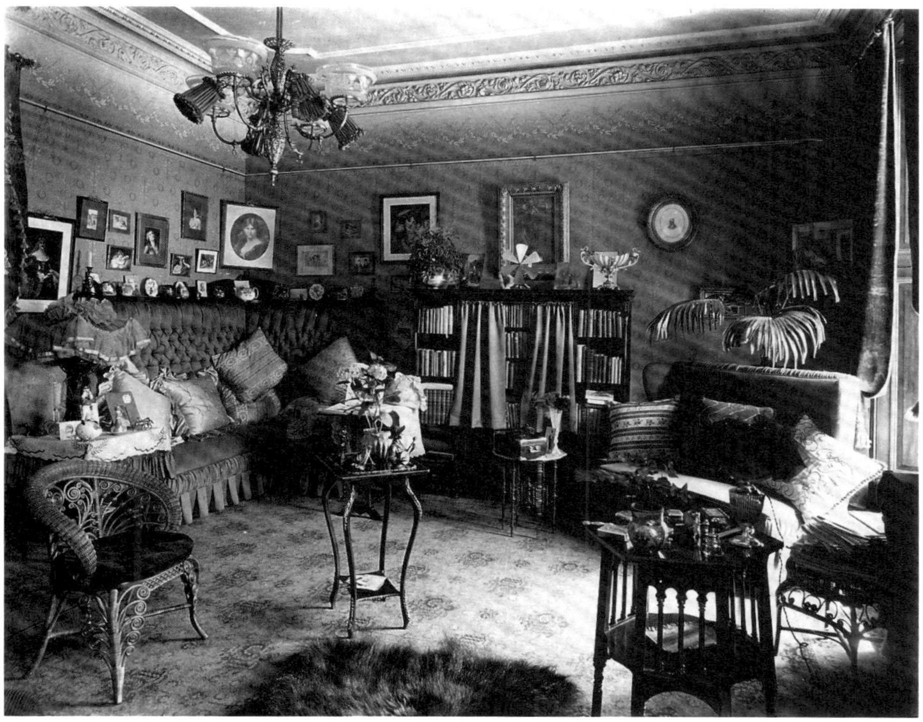

Fig. 15a
W. Notman & Sons photograph of the library in the home of David Morrice (10 Redpath Street, Montreal), 1899. Notman Photographic Archives, McCord Museum of Canadian History, Montreal (128,256-II).

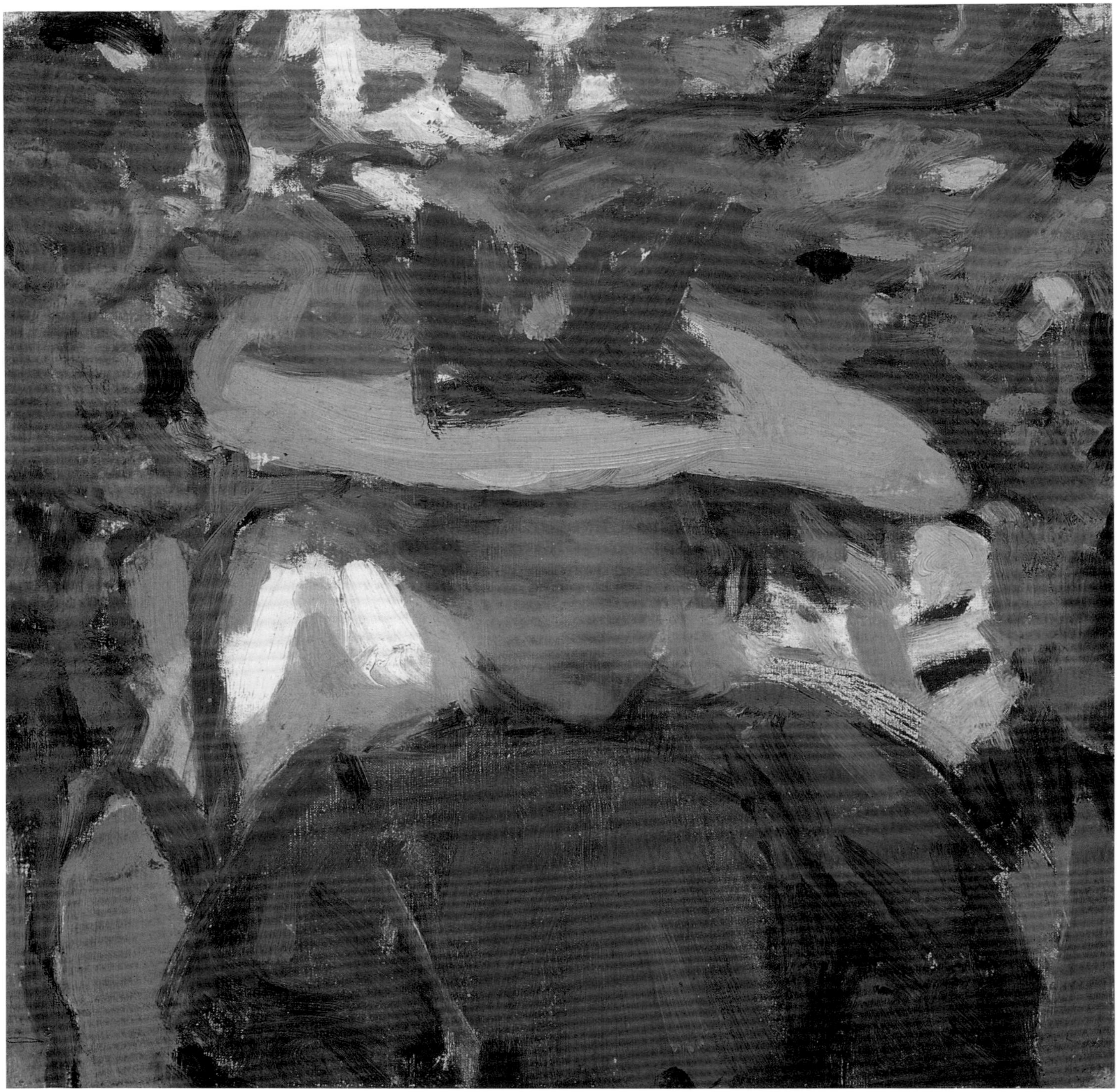

16

Under the Trees

c. 1897–98

Oil on canvas mounted on wood-pulp board, 23.3 × 23.5 cm

Inscriptions: verso: u.l. in green pencil, *M130*, u.c. in blue ballpoint pen, *Frame 4265*, c. in graphite, *2361 / Not for Sale*

Labels: in black ink, Watson Art Galleries, 1434 SHERBROOKE STREET WEST / MONTREAL / The undersigned hereby guarantees this picture to be a / genuine and authenticated *Oil Painting* / by *James Wilson Morrice R.C.A.* / Signed *William R Watson* / For Watson Art Galleries / Title of Picture *Under the Trees* / Size *9⅜* × *9⅜*, Reg. No. 2916 / *March 1939* / *From the Studio J.W. Morrice.*; in blue ink, *J.W. MORRICE* / [L]*a Jeunesse* / *Property of Dr Echlin*; in blue ballpoint pen, *80-32* / *"Le JEUNESSE"*

Provenance: Watson Art Galleries, Montreal; Dr. F.A. Echlin, Montreal, 1939.[1] G. Blair Laing Ltd., Toronto, 1980.

30418

Several studies of young women that Morrice painted in the 1890s depict a half-length or three-quarter-length figure, close to the picture plane, surrounded by a schematic treatment of foliage. In *Under the Trees* and *Seated Girl in a Brown Blouse* (fig. 16a) the stalks of the vines are the main structuring elements in the background. Morrice has scratched into the paint to reinforce the silhouette of both figures, and the green of the foliage is reflected in the sitters' cheeks. In *Under the Trees* the paint is less linear and is applied more thickly. The veil of colour across the model's face is similar to that in *Prow of a Gondola* (cat. no. 12), in this instance denying the specificity of the sitter and affirming the essentially decorative nature of the painting.

1. Watson Papers, stock no. 2361, sold to Dr. Echlin, 4 March 1939, as *Under the Trees*.

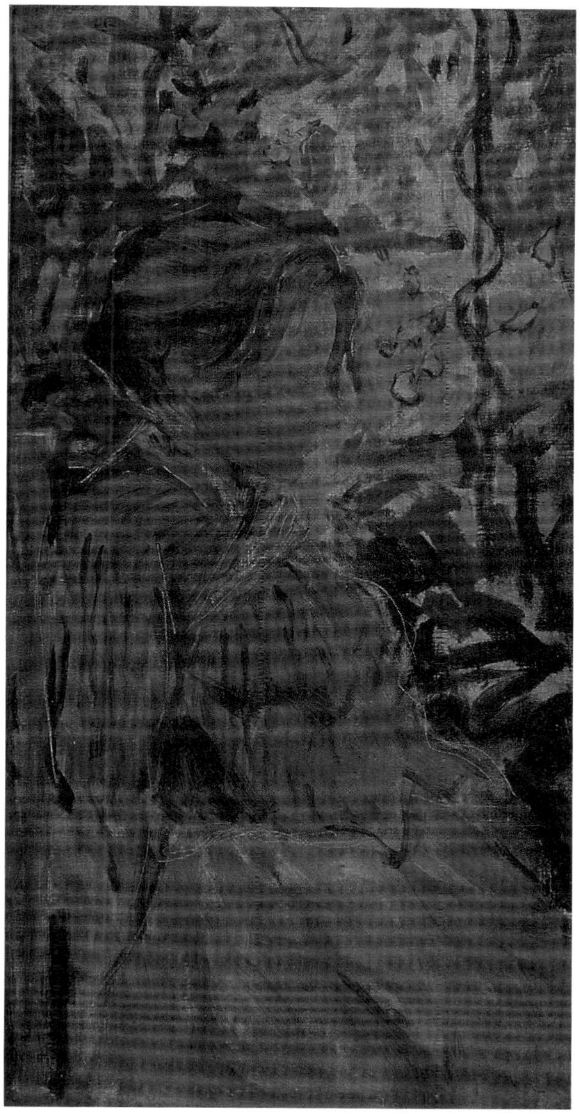

Fig. 16a
Seated Girl in a Brown Blouse, c. 1897–98, oil on canvas laid down on board, 40.6 × 20 cm. Private collection.

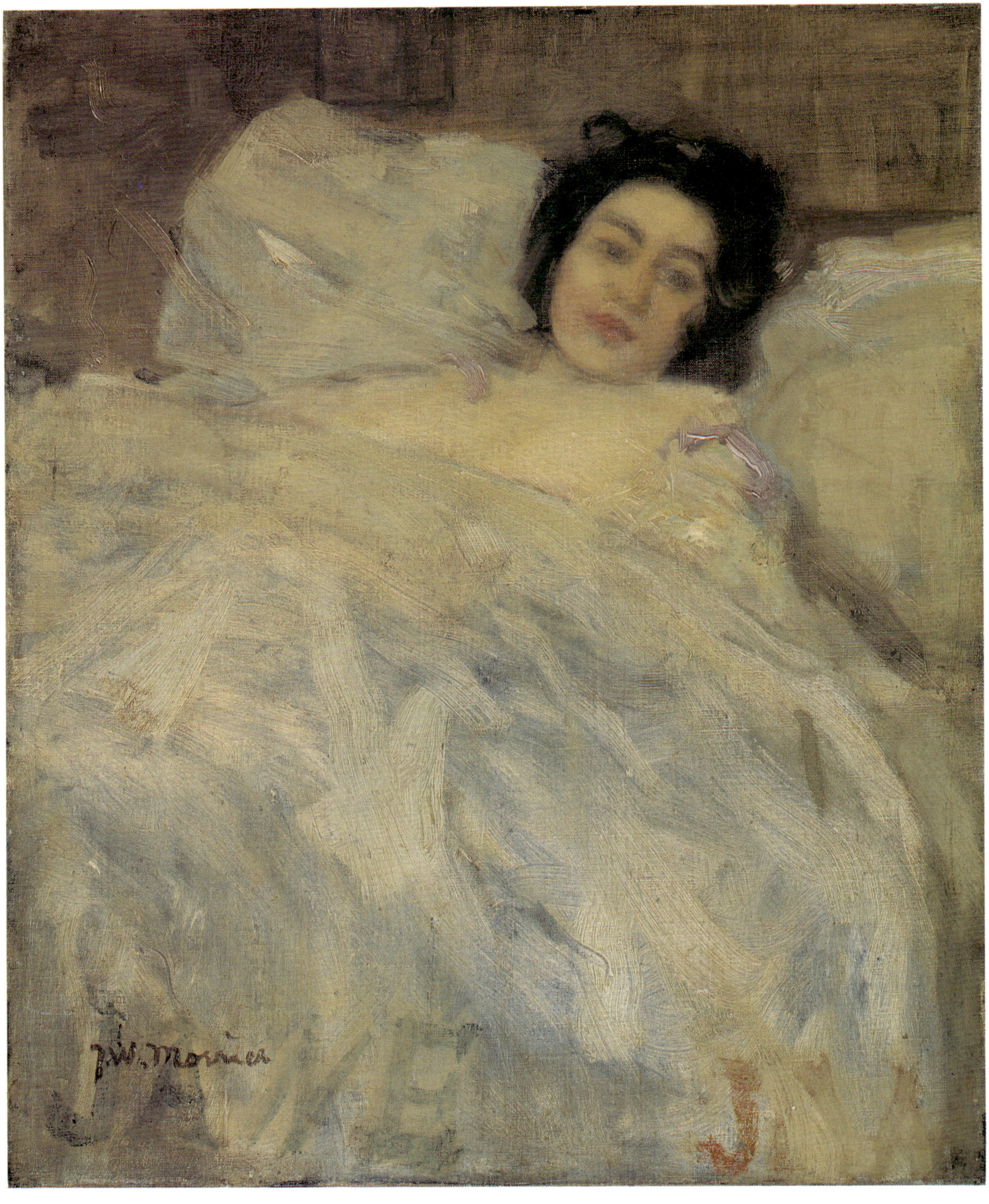
J.W. Morrice

17

Femme au lit (Jane)

c. 1897

Oil on canvas, 40.9 × 33.3 cm

Inscriptions: signed l.l., *J.W. Morrice*; l.l., *JANE*, l.r., *JW* or *JM*; stretcher: on crossbar, partly covered by label, in black ink, *Fe*[—]

Labels: MMFA 1965, no. 126; Wildenstein 1968, no. 1; MMFA 1985, no. 16; typed, NATIONAL GALLERY OF CANADA / Title of Exhibition / *J W MORRICE / RETROSPECTIVE EX* / Catalogue No. *1#* / Box No. *10*; typed, *G. BLAIR LAING / 194 Bloor St. W. / Toronto, Ontario*, in graphite *#11 / PERSONAL / 13 × 16*; typed, "*FEMME AU LIT*" / *c. 1895 / BY / JAMES W. MORRICE*; partly torn, [—] 6 PARIS F[—] / 41 × 33; partly torn, typed, [—]EUM of / [—]*ings*; typed, *MORRICE EXHIBITION / FEMME AU LIT / FROM: LAING GALLERY, TORONTO*; typed, *G. BLAIR LAING, TORONTO*, in black ink, "*Femme au lit*"; in graphite, *37*

Provenance: Samuel W. Livingston, San Francisco, by 1936.[1] The Isaacs Gallery Ltd., Toronto, 1965; Paul Duval, Toronto, 1965;[2] P.G. McCready, Toronto, 1965;[3] G. Blair Laing, Toronto, 1965.

30450

This superb study of a woman in bed is one of the most charming images in the Laing collection. The sheeting, loosely and suggestively brushed, occupies two thirds of the canvas, tenderly enfolding the figure, with a subtle touch of pink at her left shoulder. The model's head and upper chest occupy the top-right corner, and behind her the brown background is thinly painted in horizontal and vertical strokes.

The inscription of the name "Jane" at the lower left is not emblazoned in the academic manner of late-nineteenth-century portrait painters, but is half-hidden and incorporated in the bedding. We have no further knowledge of who Jane was, but writing to Robert Henri in 1906 Morrice closes: "Abraham is sitting next to me & sends regards. also Jane. Remember me to Glackens and all."[4]

A related painting, titled *Nude Reclining* (fig. 17a), may be a study of the very same model; according to Donald Buchanan, it hung in the artist's studio during Morrice's lifetime.[5] Though there is a similarity in the treatment of the foreground sheeting, the two works differ considerably. In *Nude Reclining* the silhouette of the figure is reinforced with a dark line, recalling *Girl Knitting* (cat. no. 5). She is brought aggressively forward, the upper sheeting is more assertively brushed in white over black, and the background is a rich chocolate brown. *Nude Reclining* is all directness and frontality, reminiscent of Manet's *Olympia* in its boldness, while *Jane* is all subtlety and recession, holding back and playing with the nuances of colour and brushwork. *Nude Reclining* relates to the black drawing in the winter paintings of 1897 (see, for example, fig. 14, Introduction), while *Jane* recalls the subtle tonalities of the nocturne of the Quebec citadel (fig. 15, Introduction) and *Sugar Bush* (cat. no. 10).

Nicole Cloutier has noted that a work titled *Femme au lit* is listed in Morrice's 1901 sketchbook. On the following page Morrice lists a painting, "41 × 33 Jane."[6] It is possible that the painting now called *Nude Reclining* is in fact *Femme au lit* and that the present work should simply bear the name of the model.

1. Buchanan 1936a, p. 179.
2. Letter from Av Isaacs to the author, 30 August 1991, Archives, National Gallery of Canada.
3. Letter from Blair Laing to W.R. Johnston, 14 September 1965, Archives, Montreal Museum of Fine Arts, Morrice 1965 exhibition file.
4. Letter from Morrice to Henri, 22 December [1906], Henri Papers.
5. Buchanan 1936a, pp. 84, 179.
6. Cloutier 1985, p. 112; Paris–Venice Sketchbook (National Gallery of Canada, 7419), pp. 62r and 63r.

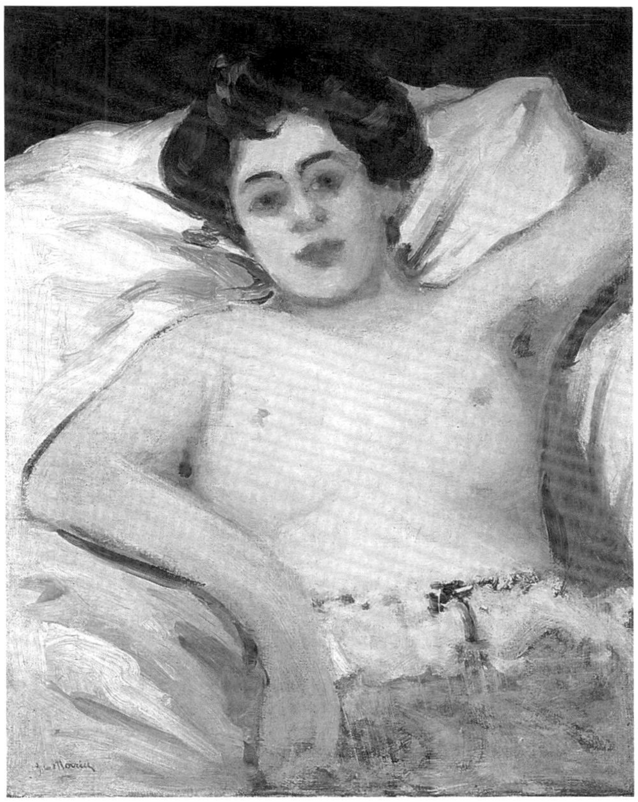

Fig. 17a
Nude Reclining, c. 1897–98, oil on canvas, 48.8 × 39 cm. Private collection.

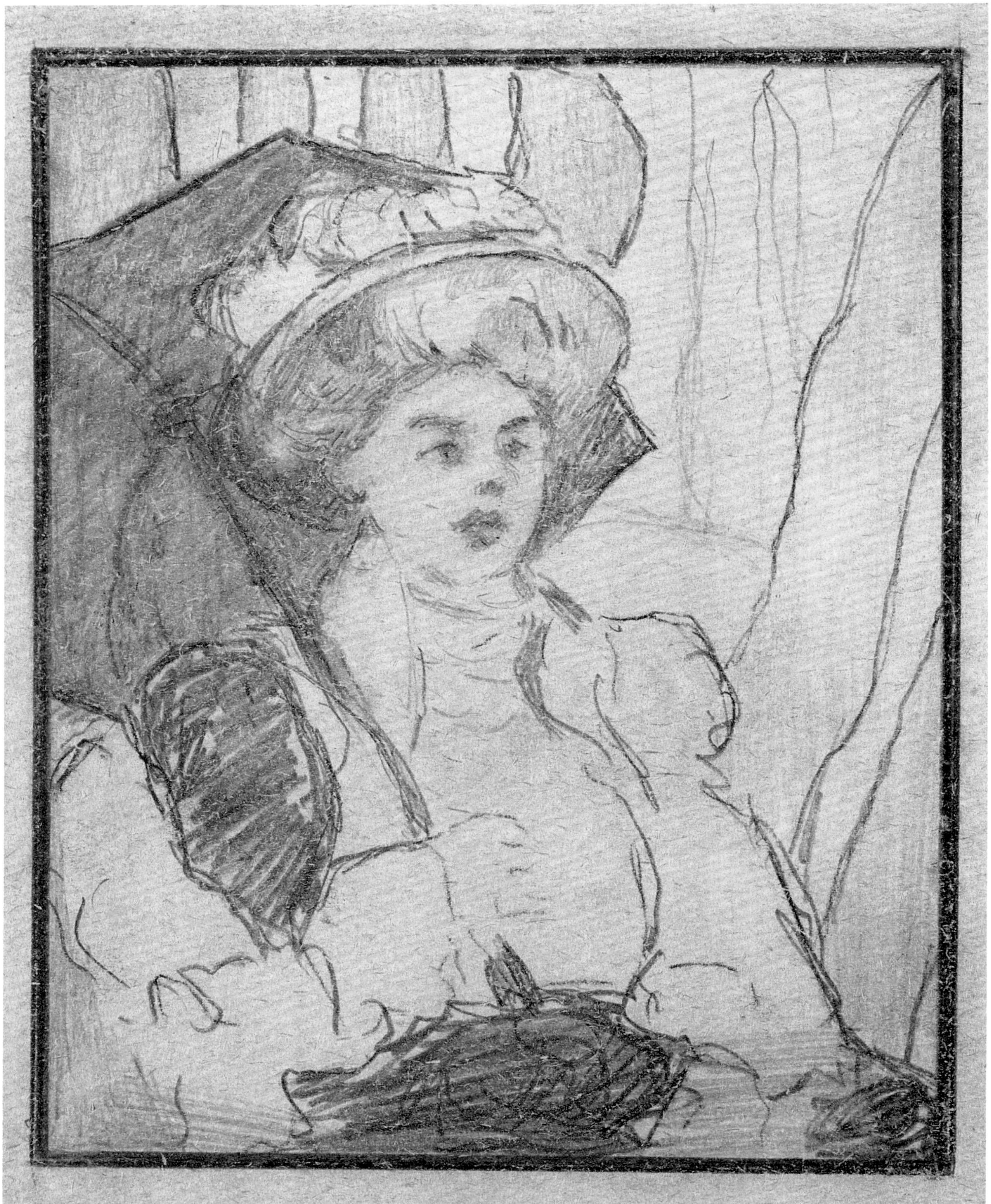

18

Léa Cadoret

c. 1898

Graphite and brown crayon on wove paper, 24.8 × 21.8 cm

Provenance: F.R. Heaton, Montreal;[1] Continental Galleries of Fine Art, Montreal (?); Maurice Corbeil, Montreal, by 1965;[2] G. Blair Laing, Toronto, by 1984.

30473

Not included in exhibition

Marie-Louise-Angèle (Léa) Cadoret was born on 11 September 1877 in Lamballe, Côtes-du-Nord, in Brittany. Orphaned at an early age, she attended a convent near Lamballe to finish her schooling, worked for a time in Brest, and then went to Paris to live with an aunt who had a patisserie on the Boulevard St-Germain. It is not certain when Léa first met Morrice, though it was most likely around 1898.[3] A photograph of Léa taken at Boulogne-sur-Mer (see fig. 18b) shows her to be a very beautiful and coquettish young woman. She soon became Morrice's mistress, and though they never lived together, their liaison would continue until his death.[4] She was to die in Antibes in 1973.

Léa was evidently still quite young when this drawing was made. Its irregular format suggests that it had a special significance. The oil sketch painted from it (fig. 18a) was, as far as we know, the only sketch Morrice ever arranged to have photographed[5] – further proof of its importance to him as a token of his feelings for Léa.

The drawing was executed on a single sheet of wove paper of a size unique in Morrice's oeuvre; at some point it was removed from its original backing and trimmed and laid down on paperboard. It is not a rapid sketch but a composed drawing, centred on the sheet, clearly intended as a formal study. The brown crayon border, though possibly a later addition, underscores this sense of a finished work.

Lucie Dorais has suggested that the drawing is in fact *after* the oil sketch, which she dates about 1905, based on the style of the hat.[6] However, the differences between the drawing and the oil sketch suggest rather the translation of a drawing into paint. One notices, for example, that on the panel Morrice has drawn the sitter's right sleeve in the same proportions as in the drawing, but in painting over it he has reduced the proportions. Also, there are traces of yellow paint on the sheet, indicating that it may have been used as a model for the sketch. The colouring and paint application of the oil sketch recall *Pont d'Austerlitz* (cat. no. 21) and *Sugar Bush* (cat. no. 10), and given the apparent youth of the sitter it is more probable that the drawing and oil sketch are from the late 1890s.

1. Among Blair Laing's notes on Morrice (now in the archives of the National Gallery of Canada) is a typed card: "Sketch for the portrait of Lea Cadoret. pencil on board, comp[osition] 15.7 × 12.3 cm., board 28 × 22.3 cm, inscribed verso l.l. pencil '9264', stamp verso centre 'Estate / F.R. Heaton'."
2. Johnston 1965, p. 78.
3. Buchanan 1936a, p. 75. Dorais (1980, p. 62), proposes a date of about 1901, based on the earliest sketchbook reference to Léa Cadoret's name – in Sketchbook 1 (Montreal Museum of Fine Arts, Dr.1973.24, back endpaper, verso), datable to about 1901–03.
4. Léa Cadoret gave birth to a son in Paris on 4 February 1898. On the birth certificate no father is identified. The son, Gaston Maurice Cadoret, was handed over to a social welfare agency and was raised by a family in Brittany. Only after 1924 would his mother try to locate him. (Conversation with Gaston Maurice Cadoret's daughter, Mme Léa Cadoret Lepage, in Montreal, 18 December 1990. Mme Lepage also gave me photocopies of the birth certificates of Léa Cadoret and Gaston Maurice Cadoret.)
5. Fifty glass negatives of photographs of Morrice's paintings, commissioned by the artist from the firm of E. Crevaux, were located by Donald Buchanan in Paris in 1935 and were purchased by the National Gallery of Canada; forty-nine are extant. See Buchanan 1936a, p. 153.
6. Dorais 1985a, pp. 63, 71, n. 8.

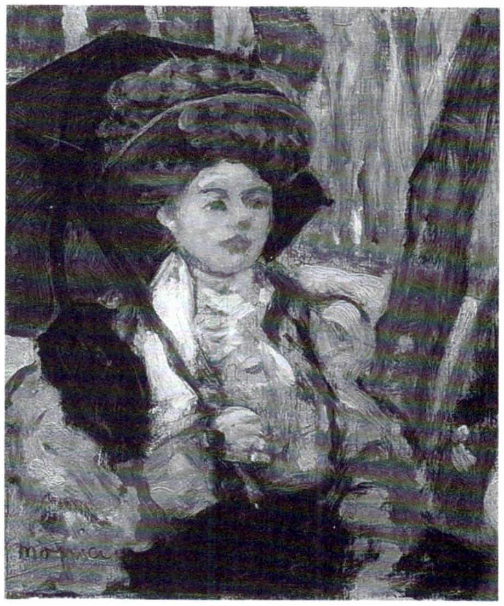

Fig. 18a
Léa Cadoret, c. 1898, oil and graphite on wood, 15.4 × 12.8 cm. Montreal Museum of Fine Arts. Bequest of F. Eleanore Morrice, 1981 (1981.49). Photograph by E. Crevaux, Paris.

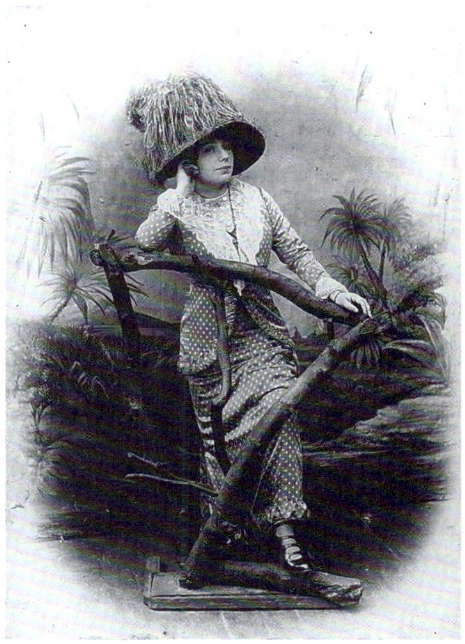

Fig. 18b
Photograph of Léa Cadoret by A. Ebert, Boulogne-sur-Mer and Nice, c. 1900. Collection of Mme Léa Cadoret Lepage, Malmaison, France.

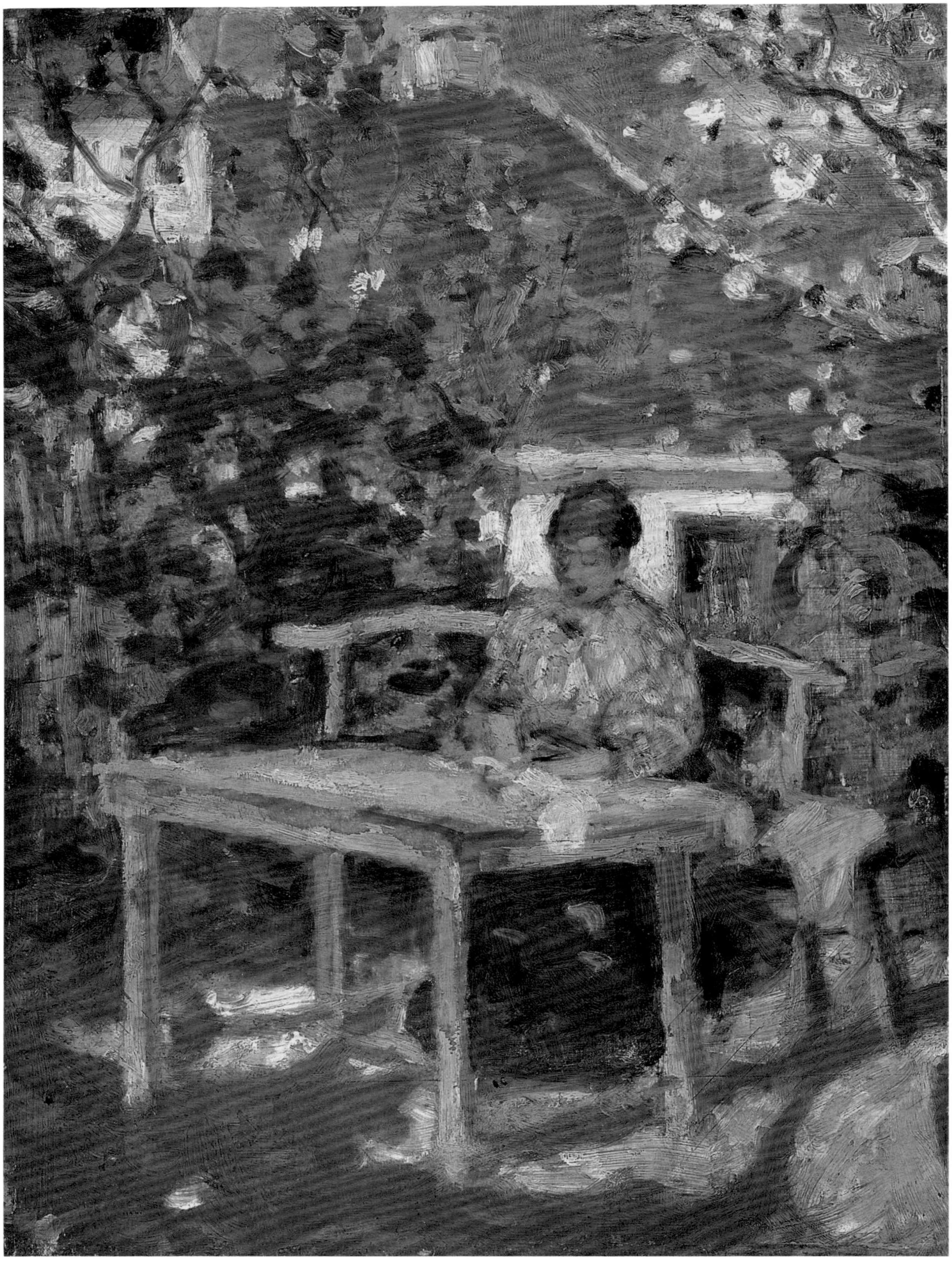

19

Garden

c. 1898

Oil on wood, 32.6 × 24.3 cm

Inscriptions: verso: t. in blue pencil, *M 2711[—]*, in black pencil, *No 7 Jardin*, c. stamped, *STUDIO / J.W. MORRICE*, t. blind stamp, *NEWMAN*, b. blind stamp, *SOHO SQUARE*

Labels: typed, *We certify that this is an original painting / by J.W. Morrice R.C.A. / It was No. 334 in our Exhibition and Sale / held in March 1925.*, in brown ink, *W Scott & Sons*, typed, *W. Scott & Sons. / Montreal, Canada.*; in blue ballpoint pen, *LEA / AU JARDIN / 80-34*

Provenance: Estate of the artist; W. Scott & Sons, Montreal. (Sold, Phillips, Montreal, 26 June 1980, lot 130); G. Blair Laing Ltd., Toronto, 1980.

30419

This charming oil study of a young woman in a pale-blue blouse and dark-blue skirt writing at a table in a garden amidst flowering trees has all the freshness of a spring day. The purple shadows in the foreground are heightened with touches of blue and yellow, the sunlit areas with yellow over white. The foliage is brushed in shades of green and yellow dotted with red. Morrice has allowed the wood to show through at the right and on the legs of the table, contrasting the open, thinner surfaces with the denser areas. The generalized treatment of the dark-green foliage to the left of the table suggests a date similar to that of *Under the Trees* (cat. no. 16).

Garden bears a number of similarities to the canvas *The Blue Umbrella* (fig. 19a), which probably dates from about 1898. The treatment of the trees in *The Blue Umbrella* is similar to that in *Sugar Bush* (cat no. 10), and the sketchy, somewhat unresolved handling of the foreground foliage, the arm, and the skin tones suggests in many ways an early effort to paint a large figure piece out of doors. It is a canvas that has none of the resolve of Morrice's paintings of 1905 to 1909, the period traditionally assigned to this work.[1]

Blair Laing proposed that *Garden* may be a portrait of Léa Cadoret painted at the Hôtel du Moulin at Dennemont.[2] Donald Buchanan described the inn as having a roof of red tile, walls of plaster-covered stone, and tables set out under the trees. We know that Léa visited Dennemont in 1898, where her portrait was painted by an English artist by the name of Curtis. However, the features of the woman in Morrice's painting are too indistinct to allow us to identify her.[3]

Garden is painted on an English panel manufactured by Newman of Soho Square, London, who was also the supplier of one of Morrice's earliest sketchbooks.[4] A work by Morrice titled *Jardin* was exhibited at the Salon d'Automne in 1909 but we do not know if it was this sketch. The typed label on the back of the panel, from the firm of W. Scott & Sons, is the only known documentation of a major exhibition and sale from the estate, held the same month as the memorial exhibition at the Art Association of Montreal. The number "334" gives some idea of the quantity of works found in the artist's studio when he died.

1. Buchanan 1936a, p. 76; Reid 1968, p. 27; Cloutier 1983, p. 28.
2. Laing 1984, pp. 62, 64, 138.
3. Buchanan 1936a, pp. 76–78. A photograph of the portrait, in the collection of Mme Léa Cadoret Lepage, Malmaison, France, corrects the dating to 1898, not 1900 as given in Buchanan. It is inscribed, "à Léa / Souvenir de Dennemont / S. Curtis '98."
4. Sketchbook 24 (Montreal Museum of Fine Arts, Dr.1979.10).

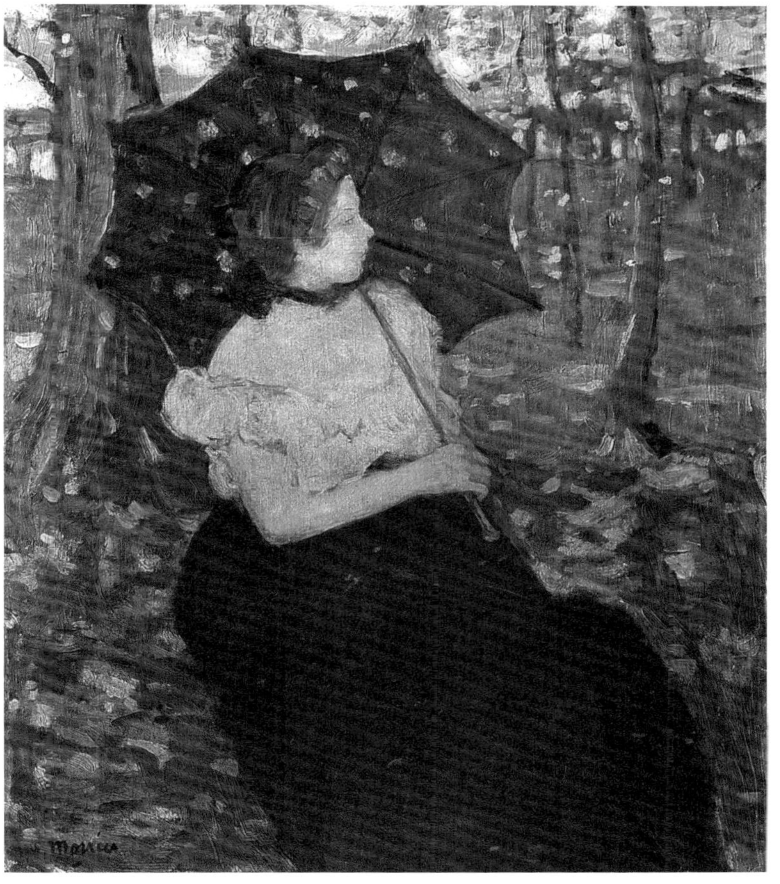

Fig. 19a
The Blue Umbrella, c. 1898, oil on canvas, 55.2 × 46.4 cm. Montreal Museum of Fine Arts. Bequest of F. Eleanore Morrice, 1981 (1981.89).

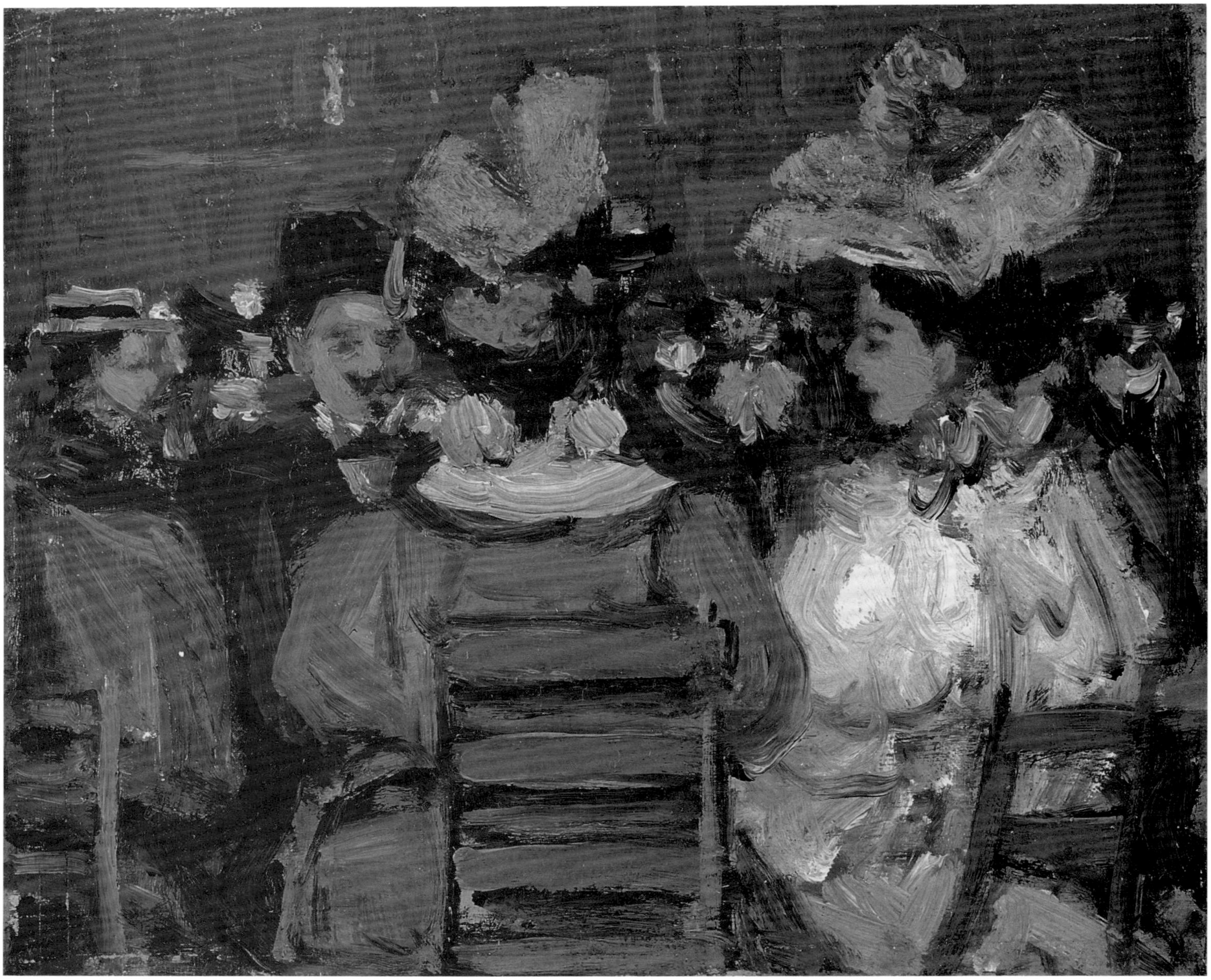

20

Café, Paris

c. 1896–97

Oil on wood, 12.8 × 15.4 cm

Inscriptions: verso: c.r. in graphite, *3*; back of frame: l. in graphite, *NICHOLSON (N° 4) / NICHOLSON*

Labels: MMFA 1965, no. 35; MMFA 1985, no. 17

Provenance: Private collection, England(?); John Nicholson, London and New York; G. Blair Laing, Toronto, c. 1952–56.[1]

30443

Cafés and restaurants were the routine haunts of young artists in Paris. Living as most of them did in bachelor apartments, their meals were most often eaten out, followed by drinks in one of the many cafés frequented by Parisians. The biographies and memoirs of Morrice's friends tell of stimulating evenings spent at the Closerie des Lilas or the Café de Versailles, and later at the Chat Blanc, the Café de la Paix, La Pérouse on the Quai des Grands-Augustins, or the more boisterous Concert Rouge.[2] Morrice's sketchbooks of the mid-1890s (see, for example, fig. 20a) contain numerous drawings of charming young women, with elaborate coifs and hats and capes, seated at café tables, often in the company of men.[3]

This sketch is characterized by the density of the composition (the figures filling the panel), and by the contrasting, brilliant accents of broadly brushed colour, recalling the larger painting *Omnibus* (fig. 8a). The women, seated in brown chairs that are highlighted in orange, wear dresses with billowing mutton sleeves and elaborate citron-yellow hats decorated with pink and mauve ribbons. The application of a lighter over a darker brown in the face of the woman at the right gives her the appearance of an overly made-up habituée of the cafés. The somewhat lecherous male companion contrasts with the youthful innocent behind him. Morrice has cropped the figure seated at the left in a manner recalling *Prow of a Gondola* (cat. no. 12), and the vertical and horizontal patterning of the background recalls *Femme au lit (Jane)* (cat. no. 17).

This sketch was acquired by Blair Laing from the British dealer John Nicholson of London and was among the first Morrices to enter his personal collection.

1. See cat. no. 7, n. 1.
2. Homer 1988, p. 86; Bell 1956, pp. 160–62; Crowley 1971, pp. 360–62.
3. Sketchbooks 2, 11, and 3 (Montreal Museum of Fine Arts, Dr.1973.25, Dr.1973.34, and Dr.1973.26), and Paris–Quebec Sketchbook (National Gallery of Canada, 7420).

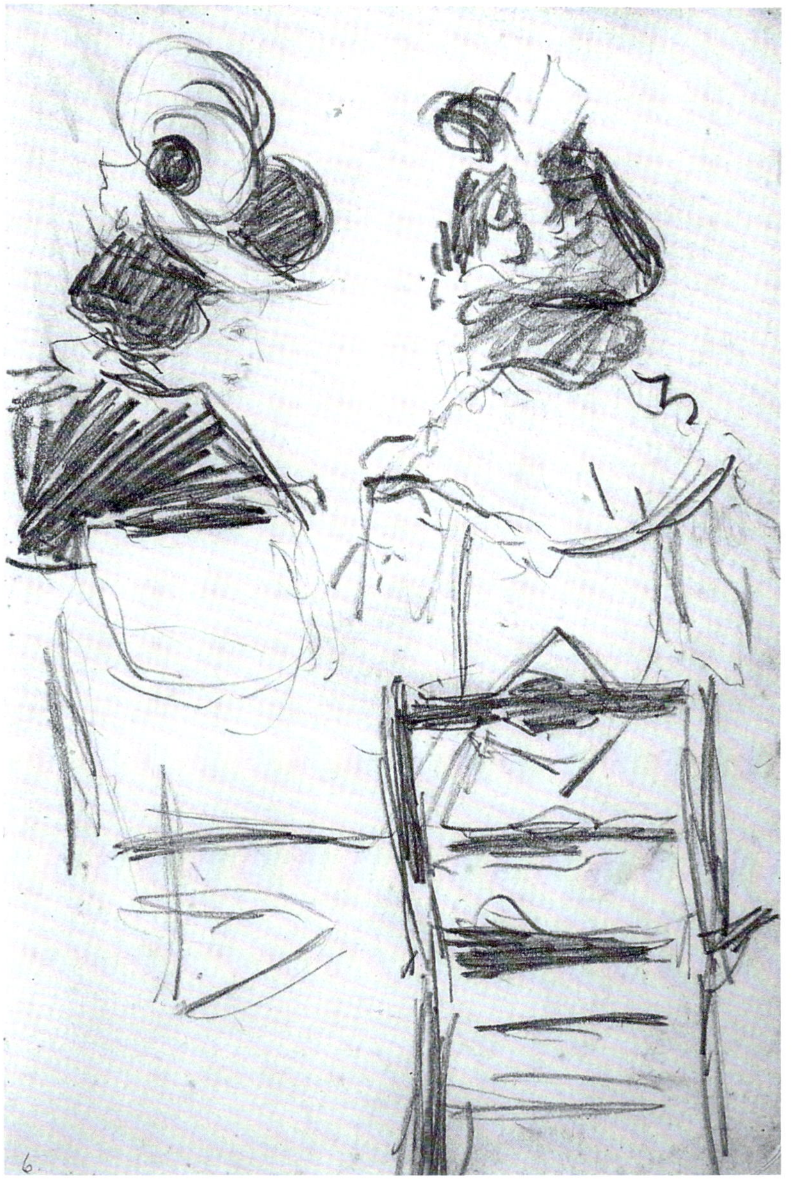

Fig. 20a
Paris–Quebec Sketchbook, p. 6r, c. 1896–97, graphite on wove paper, 16.7 × 10.8 cm. National Gallery of Canada (7420).

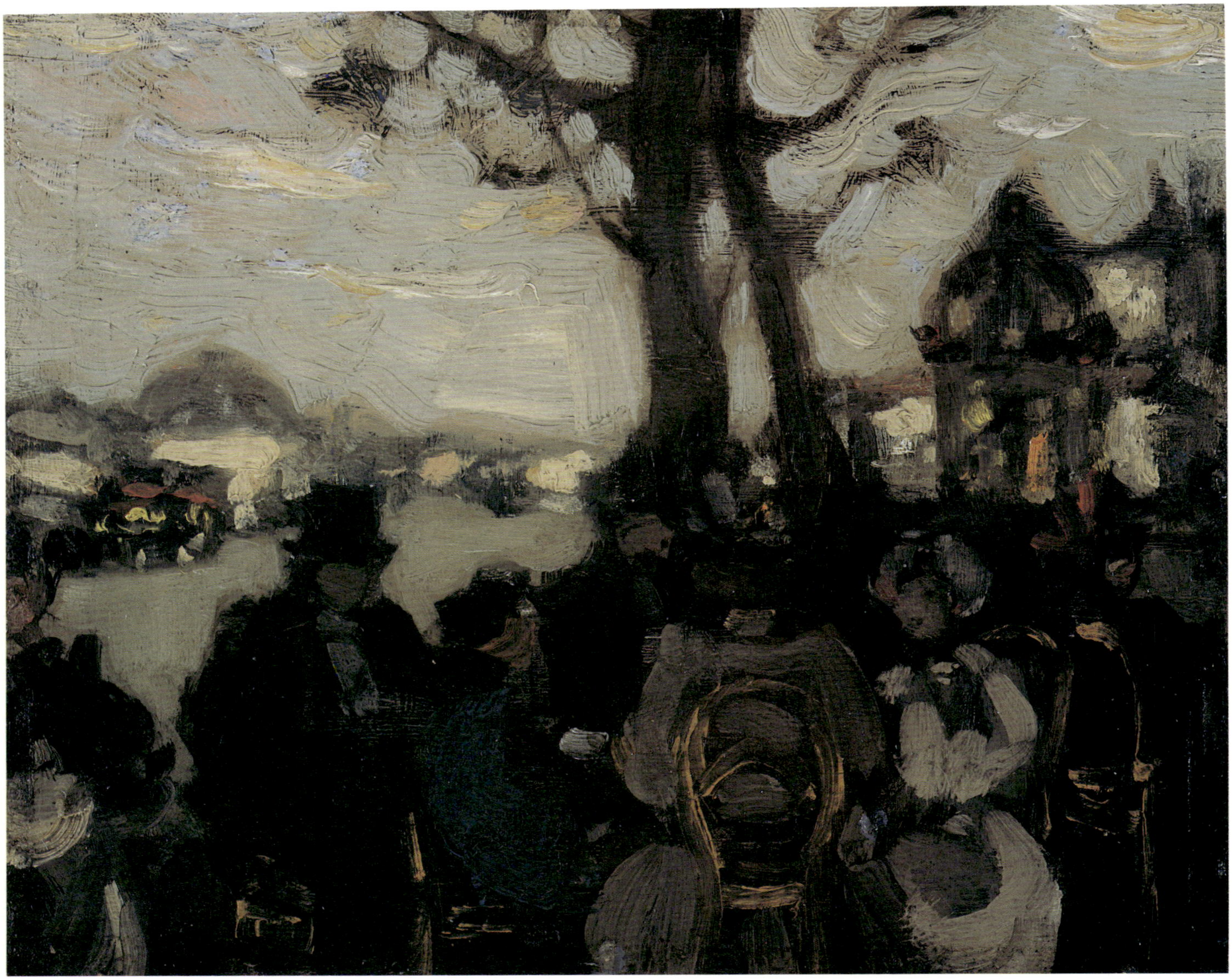

21

Pont d'Austerlitz

c. 1898–99

Oil on wood, 12.1 × 15.4 cm

Inscriptions: verso: t. in graphite (artist's hand), *J.W. Morrice / 45 Quai des G^{ds} Augustins / Le Pont d'Austerliz*, l.c. stamped, *STUDIO / J.W. MORRICE*

Labels: in blue ballpoint pen, *86-1 / LE PONT / AUSTERLITZ*

Provenance: Estate of the artist. (Sold, Joyner Fine Art Inc., Toronto, 27 May 1986, lot 89); G. Blair Laing Ltd., Toronto, 1986.

30430

Morrice's inscription on the back of this panel gives the address of the studio that he occupied from October 1899.[1] His titling of the work bears no apparent relation to the subject – a scene of men and women at a café table by a Paris boulevard, with the often-seen kiosk at the right. The generally sombre blacks, greys, and browns are enlivened by vivid touches of green, orange, and red on the pillar, responding to similar highlights on the carriage at the left. The sky is freely brushed in blues, creams, and pinks around the thinly brushed branches of the trees, allowing some of the wood of the panel to show through. The cropped figure at the left extends the space beyond the limits of the picture frame, creating a vivid impression of a Paris street scene glimpsed while walking along the quays.

1. Letter from Robert Henri to his family, 2 October 1899, Henri Papers.

22

Figures in a Café

c. 1898–99

Oil on wood, 15.6 × 9.9 cm

Inscriptions: signed l.l., *Morrice*; verso: u.l. in graphite, *1406*, b. in blue pencil, *B5964/32*, l. in brown ink, *Fr*[—] / *Thaulow*

Labels: partly torn, in brown ink, *B.Nr. 5964. Morris* / [—], in graphite, *(Frū Thaūlow)*

Provenance: F. Thaulow, Dieppe. (Sold, Sotheby Parke Bernet, London, 4 April 1979, lot 122, as *Place à Paris* and from the collection of Frits Thaulow, Oslo); G. Blair Laing, Toronto, 1979.

30469

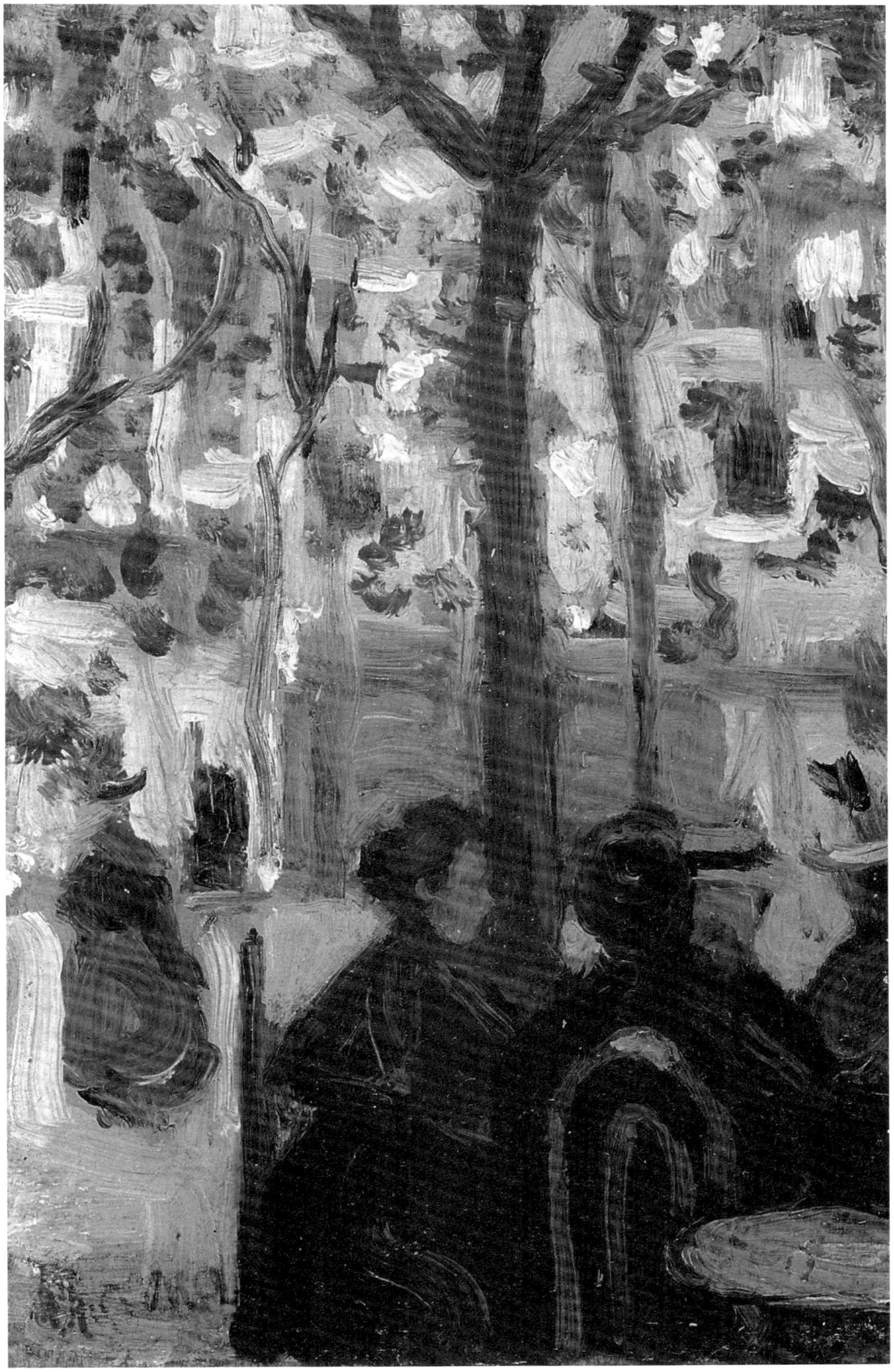

Inscriptions on the back of this small panel give the surname of the Norwegian painter Frits Thaulow and a phonetic spelling of Morrice's name. From the inscriptions one can suppose that it belonged either to Frits Thaulow or to his wife ("Fru" is Norwegian for "Mrs."), the sister-in-law of the painter Paul Gauguin. Blair Laing suggested that the café depicted here may be in Dieppe, where Thaulow lived with his family, travelling regularly to and from Paris.[1]

As in so many of Morrice's café sketches, the foreground table and side figure are cropped. The tree, slightly off centre, and the horizon line structure the composition in verticals and horizontals. The seated figures are arranged at the base of this vertical panel and the space opens at the left to allow us a glimpse of a walking figure. The background is brushed in a mosaic of vertical and horizontal strokes, and the whole is painted in muted tones of cream, pale green, black, and flesh colour.

1. Laing 1984, p. 96. Hardly anything is known of Morrice's acquaintance with Thaulow. Thaulow's address in Burgos, Spain, is in Sketchbook 1 (Montreal Museum of Fine Arts, Dr.1973.24, p. 50r), which by its inscriptions and lists of exhibited works dates from about 1901–03. Morrice was in Spain in June 1902 (letter from Morrice to Joseph Pennell, 1 June [1902], Pennell Papers). Thaulow was a good friend of Charles Conder from 1895; see John Rothenstein, *The Life and Death of Conder* (London: Dent, 1938), p. 117 and passim.

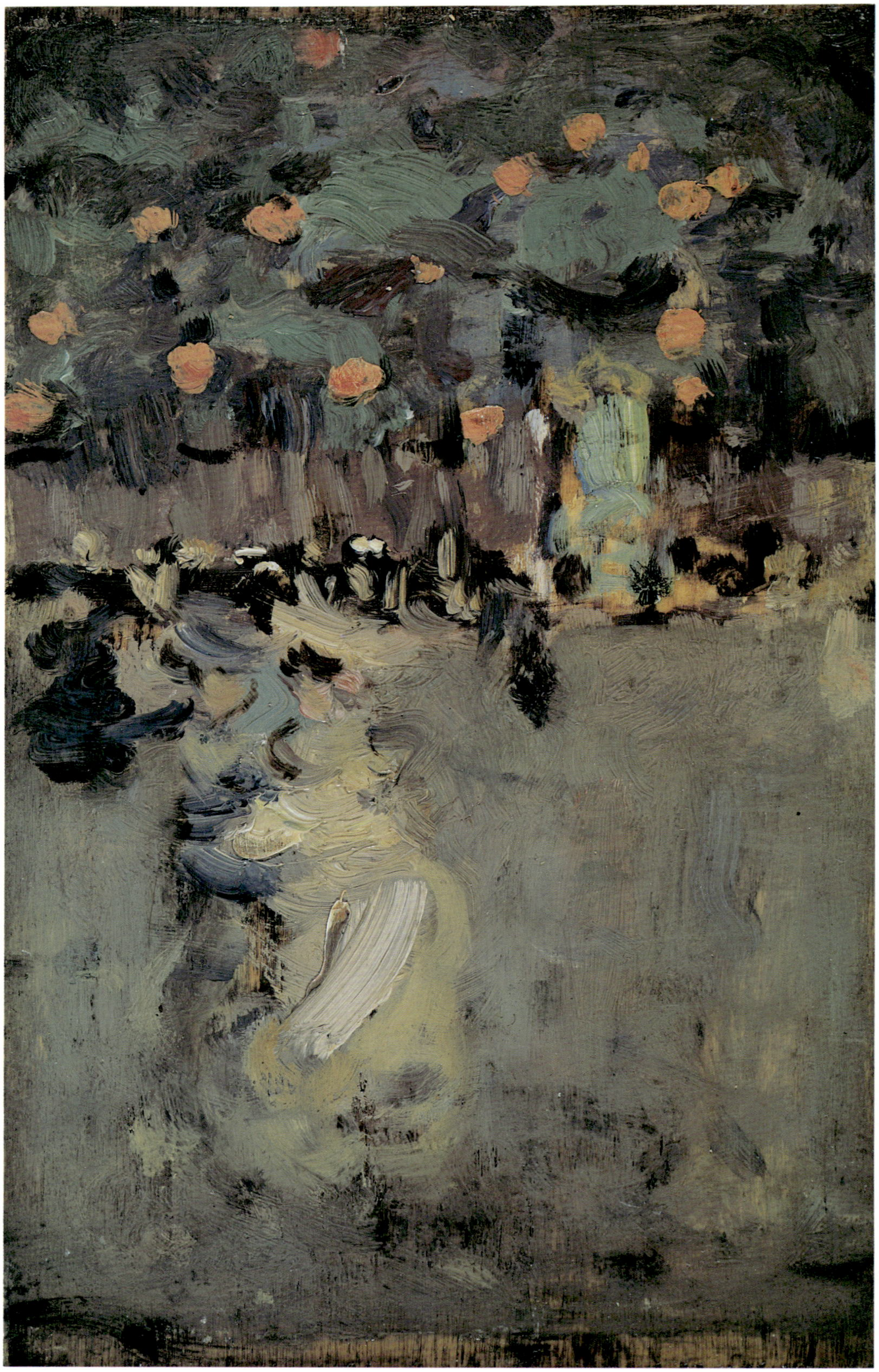

23

Garden Scene with Chinese Lanterns

c. 1897–98

Oil on wood, 15.4 × 9.6 cm

Inscriptions: verso: u.l. in brown ink, *3*, l.l. in blue ballpoint pen, *P12149*, l.c. stamped, *STUDIO / J.W. MORRICE*

Labels: partly torn, in black ink, CONTINENTAL GALLERIES OF FINE ART / 1310 ST. CATHERINE ST. WEST, MONTREAL / PHONE PLATEAU [—] / ARTIST: *James W. Morrice, R.C.A.* / TITLE OF PICTURE: *Garden Scene W. Chinese Lanterns,* / DESCRIPTION: *orig. oil on wood panel*; in blue ballpoint pen, *84-11* / *"GARDEN, / CHINESE / LANTERNS"*

Provenance: Estate of the artist. Continental Galleries of Fine Art, Montreal. (Sold, Sotheby Parke Bernet [Canada] Inc., Toronto, 14 May 1984, lot 126); G. Blair Laing Ltd., Toronto, 1984.

30427

Morrice very early developed a rhythmic shorthand for the depiction of moving people, and his sketchbooks contain numerous drawings of animated walking women (see, for example, fig. 23a) who also appear in a number of early canvas sketches.[1]

Morrice's small wood panels are among his most elegant works. Most of them can be dated to the period around his 1897 trip to Venice. Here, in a few rapidly brushed strokes, two women walk brusquely across an open square painted in greys over a pink ground and bordered by a fence and kiosk surmounted by leafy trees decorated with pink and orange lanterns. The site depicted may be the same as in his watercolour *Paris Street* (fig. 23b), identified by Léa Cadoret as the Place Maubert in Paris.[2]

This decorative treatment of a silhouetted figure, animated by energetic lines or brushstrokes and set against a neutral ground, derives from Japanese prints – examples of which Morrice collected[3] – but the composition recalls above all the work of his American friend Maurice Prendergast, whom he had known in Paris from 1891 to 1894 and six of whose watercolours he owned.[4]

1. See, for example, Reid 1968, nos. 16 and 17.
2. Johnston 1965, p. 63.
3. Ibid., p. 8.
4. Carol Clark, et al., *Maurice Brazil Prendergast, Charles Prendergast: A Catalogue Raisonné* (Williamstown: Williams College Museum of Art / Munich: Prestel, 1990), nos. 555, 564, 576, 578, 594, and 595.

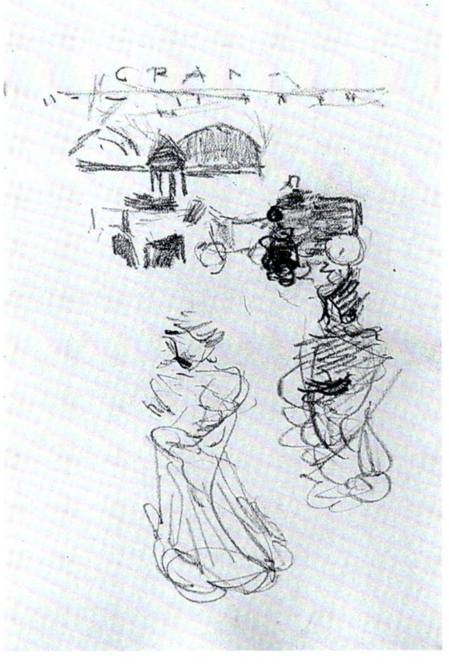

Fig. 23a
Sketchbook 9, p. 25r, c. 1896, graphite on wove paper, 16.4 × 10.7 cm. Montreal Museum of Fine Arts. Gift of David R. Morrice, 1973 (Dr.1973.32).

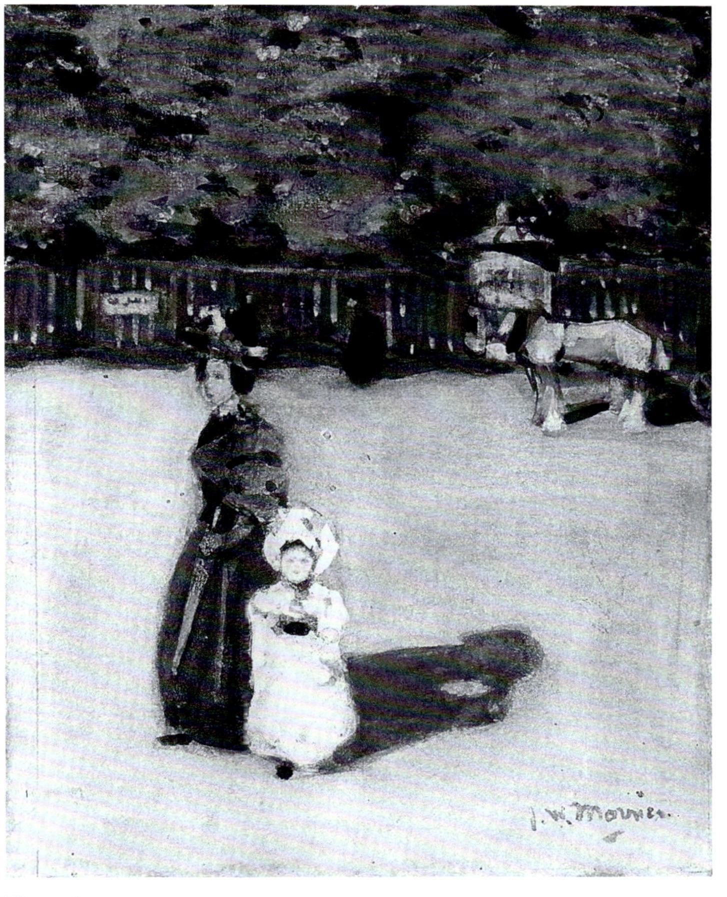

Fig. 23b
Paris Street, c. 1900, watercolour on paper, 28.7 × 22.7 cm. Montreal Museum of Fine Arts. Bequest of David R. Morrice, 1981 (Dr.1981.4).

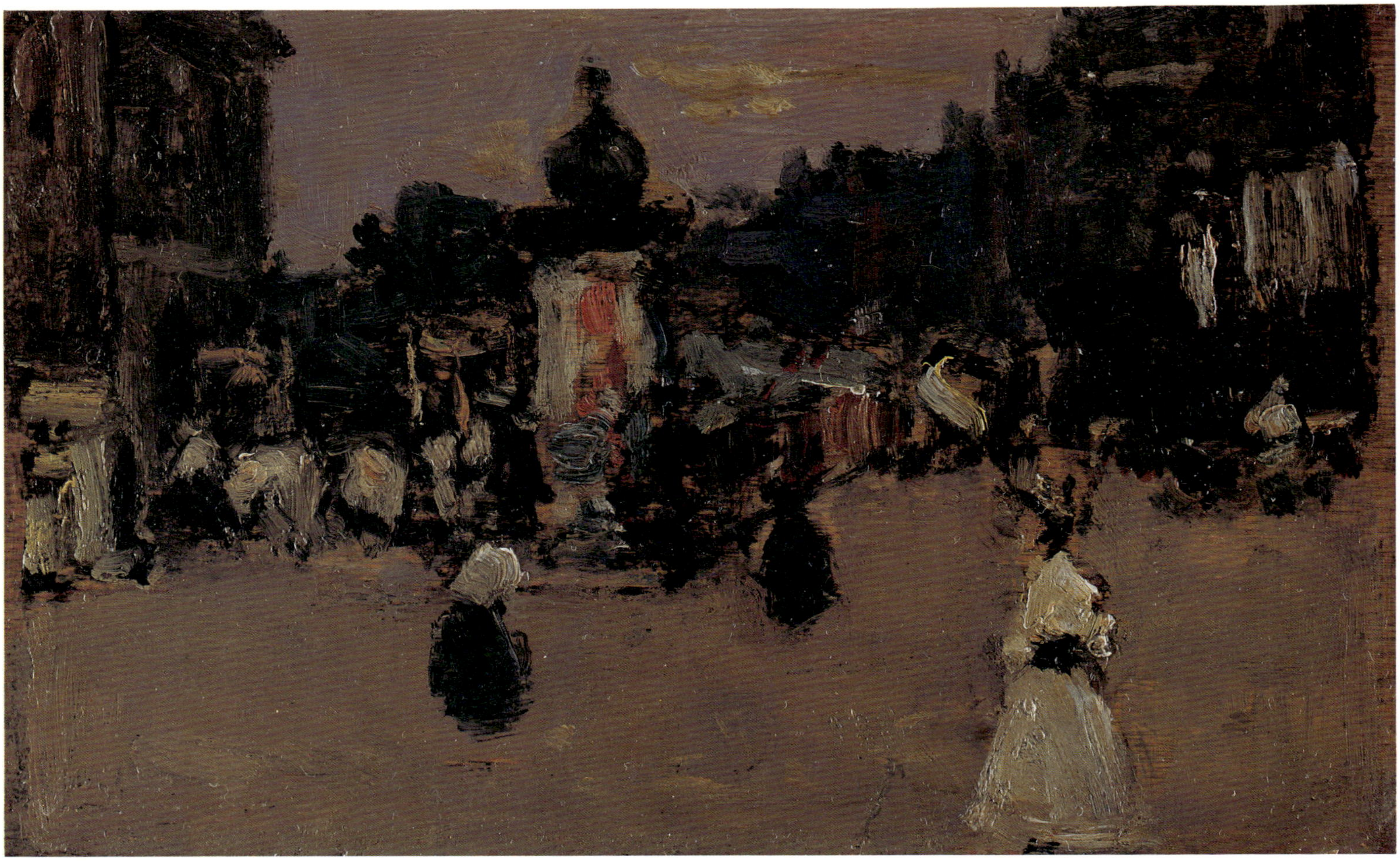

24

Paris Street with Kiosk

c. 1897–98

Oil on wood, 9.8 × 15.5 cm

Inscriptions: verso: c. stamped, *STUDIO / J.W. MORRICE*

Labels: OKanada, no. 36; MMFA 1965, no. 32; in blue ballpoint pen, *76-104 / PARIS / KIOSK*; in blue ballpoint pen, *76-104*

Provenance: Estate of the artist. Jacques Dubourg, Paris; G. Blair Laing Ltd., Toronto, 1976.

30408

A woman in a white dress occupies the foreground of this delightful little sketch, glancing toward a kiosk that anchors the curving line of the background buildings, horses, and figures. The mauve tonality is accented with the reds of the posters on the kiosk and the citron yellow clouds in the sky.

The horizontal composition with an open foreground and a curving central form that closes off the recession to the background is somewhat unusual in Morrice's oeuvre and seems to be most characteristic of his canvases painted in 1898, such as *Autumn Effect*[1] and *Street Fair, Montmartre* (fig. 24a).[2]

Although there is a Montreal Museum of Fine Arts label on the back of the frame, this oil sketch was in fact not loaned to the 1965 Morrice exhibition. Blair Laing at one time removed the frame from a drawing that he had loaned to the exhibition and used it to frame this oil sketch.[3]

1. Reproduced in Dorais 1985b, p. 40. *Effet d'automne* is the original title in the 1898 catalogue of the Salon of the Société Nationale des Beaux-Arts. It is catalogued in Buchanan 1936a, p. 161, as *In the Tuileries Garden, Paris*, but it is clearly a depiction of the Jardin du Luxembourg.
2. On the dating of this painting, see Cloutier 1986, p. 84.
3. See Johnston 1965, pp. 31, 63. The drawing is now in a private collection in Toronto.

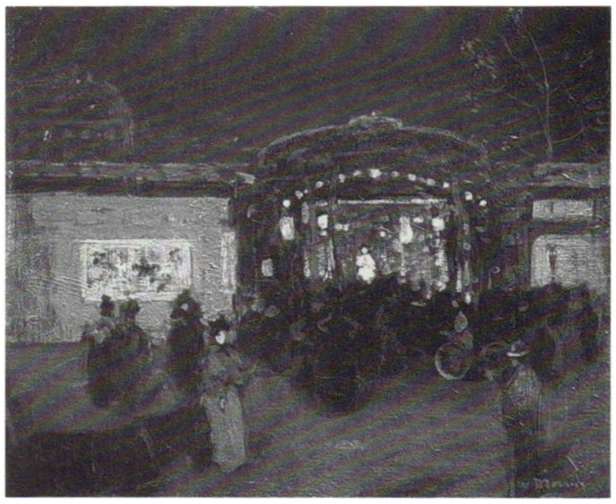

Fig. 24a
Street Fair, Montmartre, 1898–99, oil on canvas, 46 × 56 cm. Hermitage, St. Petersburg (8968). Photograph by E. Crevaux, Paris.

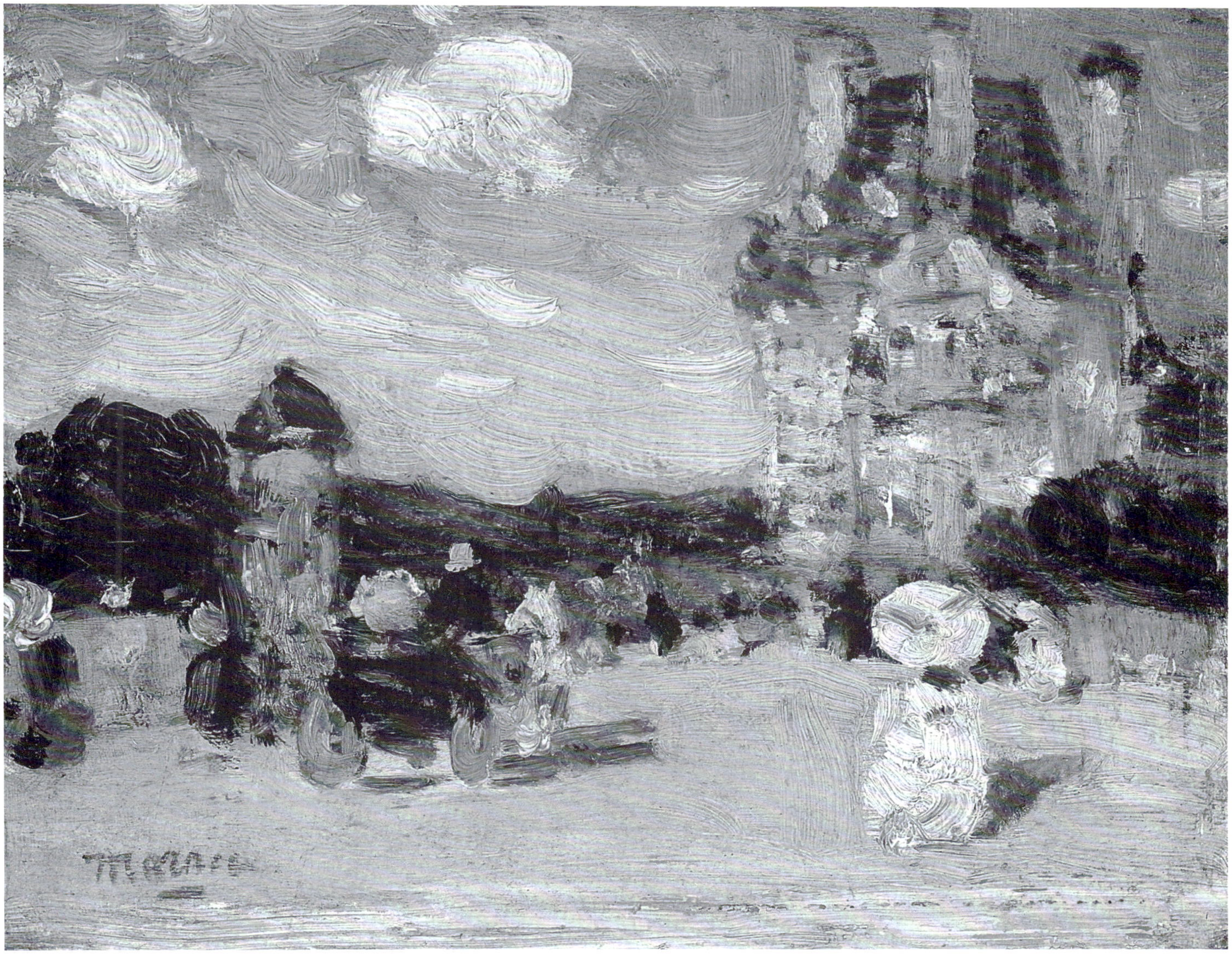

25

Pavillon de Flore, Palais des Tuileries, Paris

c. 1898–99

Oil on wood, 12.4 × 15.4 cm

Inscriptions: signed l.l., *Morrice*; back of frame: c.l. in graphite, *Blair Laing*, l.l. in green ink, *#37*, c.r. in graphite, *B*

Labels: typed, Artist *JAMES W. MORRICE, R.C.A.* / Title *LE PAVILLON DE FLORE, PALAIS DES* / *TUILERIES, PARIS* / Property of *M. JACQUES DUBOURG* / Return Address *PARIS, FRANCE.* / Insurance Value $, in graphite, *51* / *Cat 51*; stamped, *DOUANES PARIS EXPOSITIONS*; in blue ballpoint pen, *GBL* / *PAILLION* / *de FLORE* / *PARIS*

Provenance: Jacques Dubourg, Paris, by 1937;[1] G. Blair Laing, Toronto, 1976.

30476

This view of the Louvre as seen from the Jardin du Luxembourg was formerly in the collection of the Paris dealer Jacques Dubourg and was included in the 1937 Morrice retrospective exhibition organized by the National Gallery of Canada.

As in *Paris Street with Kiosk* (cat. no. 24), a wide open foreground is occupied by the walking figure of a woman at the lower right. A diagonal line leads from her to the yellow-wheeled carriage and the kiosk at the left, and from there another diagonal recedes to the Pavillon de Flore. The kiosk and pavilion do not close off the recession toward the background but rather frame an opening to the landscape and sky beyond. The composition is dominated by the billowing clouds, the flowing brush strokes also animating the walking figures and foliage.

1. Loaned by Jacques Dubourg to Ottawa 1937, no. 51.

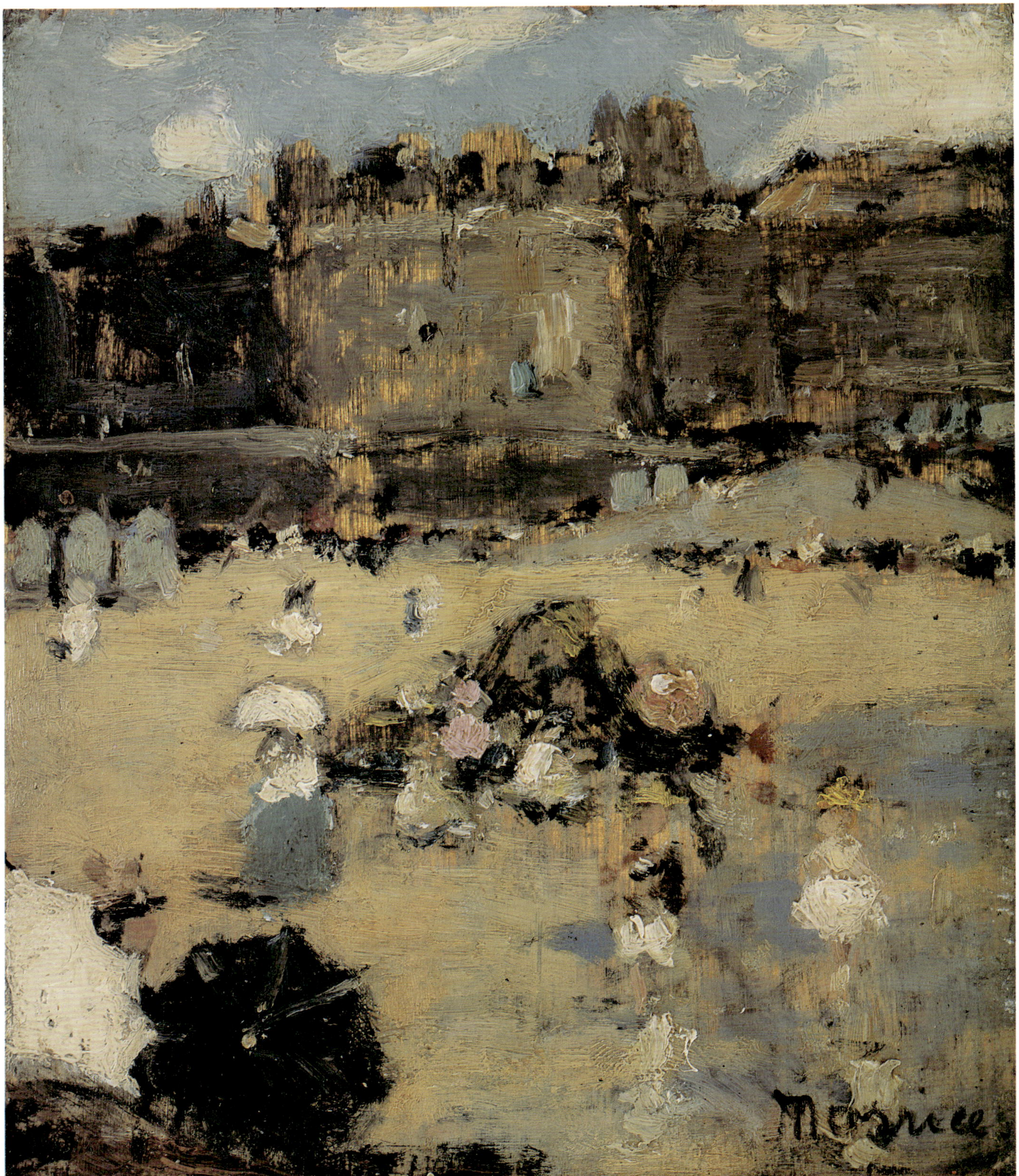

26

The Beach, St-Malo

c. 1898

Oil on wood, 15.4 × 12.7 cm

Inscriptions: signed l.r., *Morrice*; verso: c. in graphite, *4915*

Labels: in blue ballpoint pen, GBL1 / VIEW OF THE / BEACH AND / RAMPARTS / ST. MALO

Provenance: Newton MacTavish, Toronto, by 1909; Mellors Fine Arts Ltd., Toronto, 1939;[1] Dr. G.H. Henderson, Halifax, 1939; Mrs. G.H. Henderson, Halifax, by 1951;[2] G. Blair Laing, Toronto, by 1978.[3]

30440

Morrice painted a watercolour view of St-Malo as early as 1890.[4] A popular bathing resort on the coast of Brittany, it was also a favourite sketching spot of his friend Maurice Prendergast, and it provided easy access to adjacent villages and resorts such as Cancale, Paramé, Dinard, and St-Servan. The crenellated walls of the old town and the picturesque scenes of bathing huts, umbrellas, and bathers would attract Morrice well into the next decade. We know that he visited St-Malo briefly in 1895 and that he spent longer periods there in August 1898 and again in August 1899.[5] From the sketches painted on those trips he would produce some of his best-known canvases.

In this little sketch Morrice has placed a woman in silhouette with white and black umbrellas in the lower-left corner, directing us into the composition on a diagonal to the pile of sand and the children painted in pink, lime green, white, and brown. The children on the right are merely suggested with short touches of the brush. The turret of the fort is defined by a few brush strokes, the bare wood showing through so that the massive form recedes and does not loom over the playful scene on the beach.

In a related, larger sketch in the Art Gallery of Nova Scotia (fig. 26a), Morrice painted a horizontal composition with a figure at the lower right and a shadow at the lower left framing a central grouping of women seated under umbrellas. The characteristic shape of umbrellas is one Morrice used frequently as both a decorative and structuring element.

This sketch was owned by the Toronto editor of *The Canadian Magazine*, Newton MacTavish, who was an active supporter of the Canadian Art Club, of which Morrice was a member. The sketch was loaned by MacTavish to the second exhibition of the club in February 1909 and was reproduced as the frontispiece of his 1925 book *The Fine Arts in Canada*. It was through his friendship with such figures as MacTavish and the painter Curtis Williamson,[6] those of the generation of the Canadian Art Club, that Blair Laing first discovered Canadian art. The inclusion of MacTavish's sketch in the Laing collection provides a link between these early associates and friends of Morrice and the collector who so admired his paintings.

1. Laing 1979, p. 46.
2. Loaned by Mrs. G.H. Henderson to the exhibition *The Development of Canadian Painting*, Halifax Memorial Library, 12 November 1951, no. 21.
3. Author's notes, from visit to G. Blair Laing, 21 October 1978.
4. See Cloutier 1985, p. 102.
5. Letters from Morrice to Henri, July 1896, Henri to his family, 1 August 1899, and Henri to his family, 8 August 1899, Henri Papers; Henri Diaries, p. 124, entry for 26 August 1898.
6. See Williamson's portrait of Blair Laing, fig. 2, Introduction.

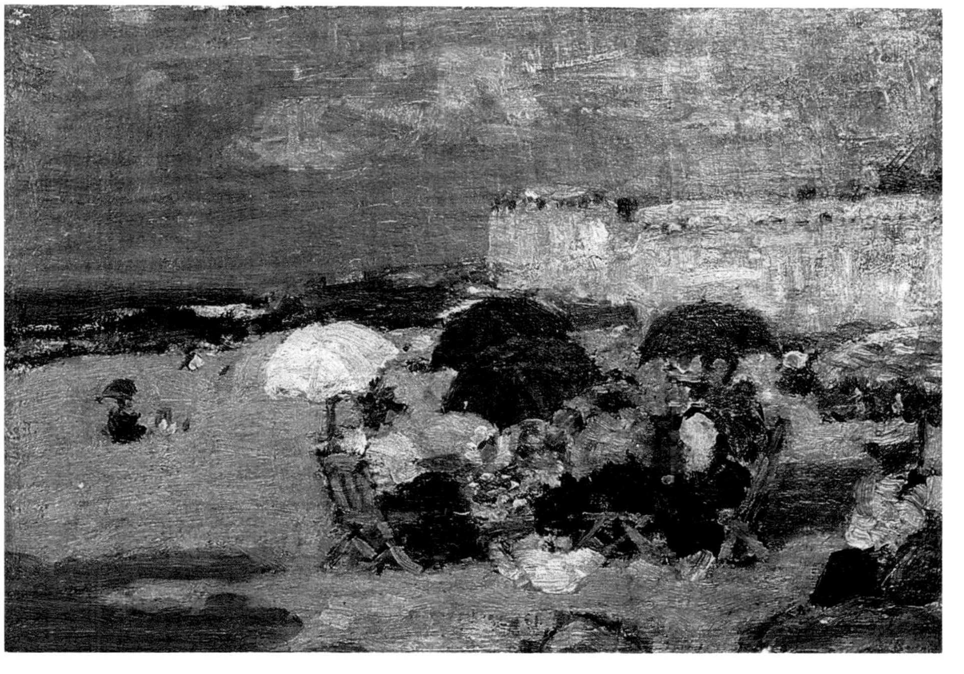

Fig. 26a
The Beach of St-Malo, c. 1898, oil on wood, 17.9 × 25.7 cm. Art Gallery of Nova Scotia, Halifax. Bequest of F. Eleanore Morrice, 1981 (81.12).

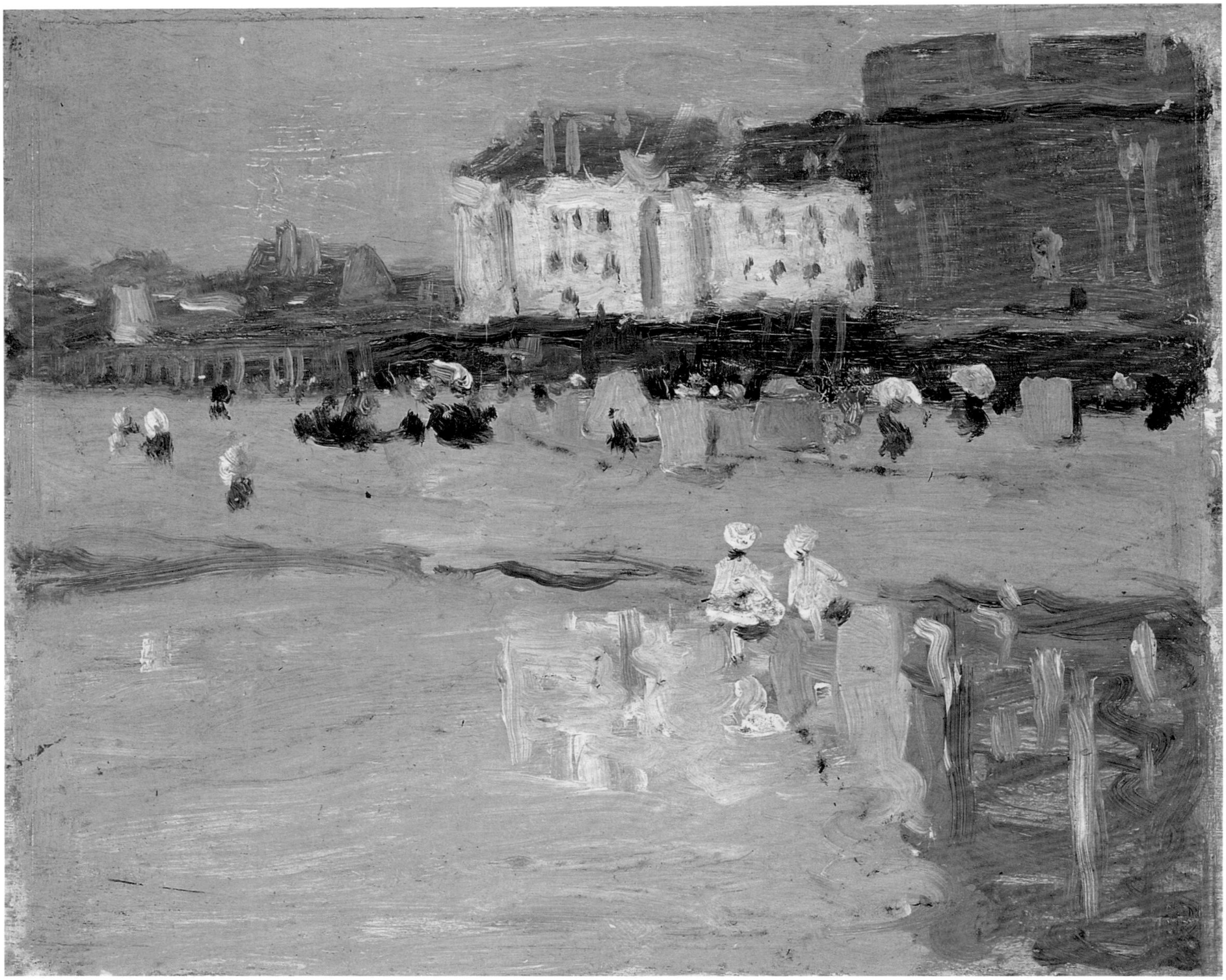

27

The Ramparts, St-Malo

c. 1898–99

Oil on wood, 12.6 × 15.4 cm

Inscriptions: back of frame: l.r. in black ink, *Cat. 66*, l.l. in graphite, *992*

Labels: newspaper clipping (removed), in black ink, *Sept. 1899*; THE HOUSE OF HEYDENRYK, 141 WEST 54TH STREET / New York 19, N.Y.; VICARS BROTHERS / DEALERS IN / HIGH CLASS PAINTINGS & DRAWINGS, / PRINTSELLERS & PUBLISHERS, / 12, OLD BOND ST.; in blue ballpoint pen, *GBL / BATHERS / ST. MALO / 2*; MMFA 1965, no. 66

Provenance: Vicars Brothers, London (?); private collection, England (?); John Nicholson, London and New York; G. Blair Laing, Toronto, c. 1952–56.[1]

30441

This panel showing a view of the ramparts of St-Malo retained its original backing board from Vicars Brothers, London.[2] A previous owner pasted onto the back a clipping from an unidentified newspaper quoting a review of Morrice's submissions to the 1899 spring Salon of the Société Nationale des Beaux-Arts in Paris. Titled "A Canadian Artist," it reads:

> Mr. James Wilson Morrice, son of Mr. David Morrice of Montreal, is this year exhibiting four landscapes at the Paris Salon. His work is very highly praised by the critics, and being a new-comer, he is extended a hearty welcome. One critic in "Les Droits de l'Homme," says "We have this time the happy surprise to find at the Champs de Mars Salon, the work of a new-comer of great talent, Mr. Morrice, four landscapes, full of [—], of truth, of harmony. First of all, the best constructed and most solidly painted, a snow effect, so effective with the severe blacks of the houses, next a beach of gray sand at the foot of the sombre granite of a rampart, with the bright note of umbrellas and of the dresses of children playing in the water; and also pretty studies of trees and of people passing by in the gray atmosphere of the city. Mr. Morrice is certainly a painter with a new and powerful way of seeing nature, and whose next efforts are sure to be eagerly followed.
>
> Mr. Morrice has received invitations to exhibit at Berlin, Honfleur, the Continental Gallery, and New Bond Street, London.

Could it be that this sketch is the work described in the review as "a beach of gray sand at the foot of the sombre granite of a rampart, with the bright note of umbrellas and of the dresses of children playing in the water"? The clipping does indeed provide a good description of this painting, with its subtle reflections of pinks, blues, whites, and greens. However, as Morrice was a relatively new exhibitor and not a full member of the Société, it is more probable that the jury of the Salon would have accepted a finished canvas rather than a sketch. Morrice exhibited four paintings at the 1899 Salon: number 1079, *La communiante* (fig. 57b); number 1080, *La plage*; number 1081, *Effet de neige*; and number 1082, *Paysage* (fig. 33a). The painting described in the review is most likely number 1080, which may be the canvas *Beneath the Ramparts, St-Malo* (fig. 27a).[3]

After seeing their works at the 1899 Salon, Adolf Paulus, representing the firm of Edouard Shulte of Berlin, contacted both Henri and Morrice about the possibility of exhibiting some of their paintings. The two artists gladly agreed to the suggestion, but the proposed show evidently did not materialize.[4]

1. See cat. no. 7, n. 1.
2. On Vicars, see Watson 1974, pp. 19–21.
3. See also Cloutier 1985, p. 131.
4. See letters from Henri to his family, 5 and 26 September 1899, Henri Papers.

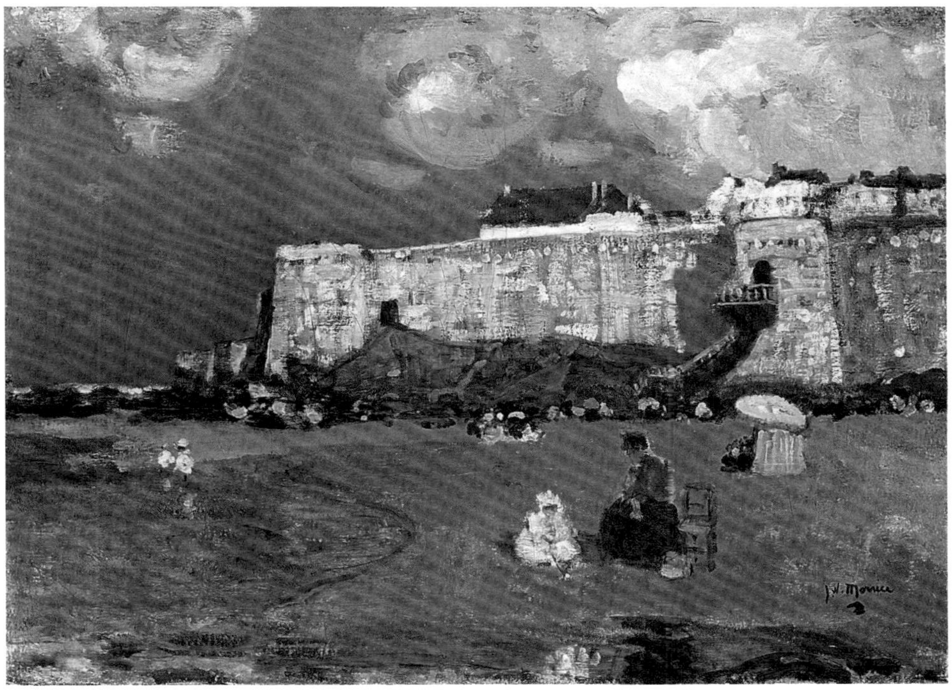

Fig. 27a
Beneath the Ramparts, St-Malo, c. 1898–99, oil on canvas, 61 × 83.5 cm. Montreal Museum of Fine Arts. Bequest of William J. Morrice, 1943 (943.788).

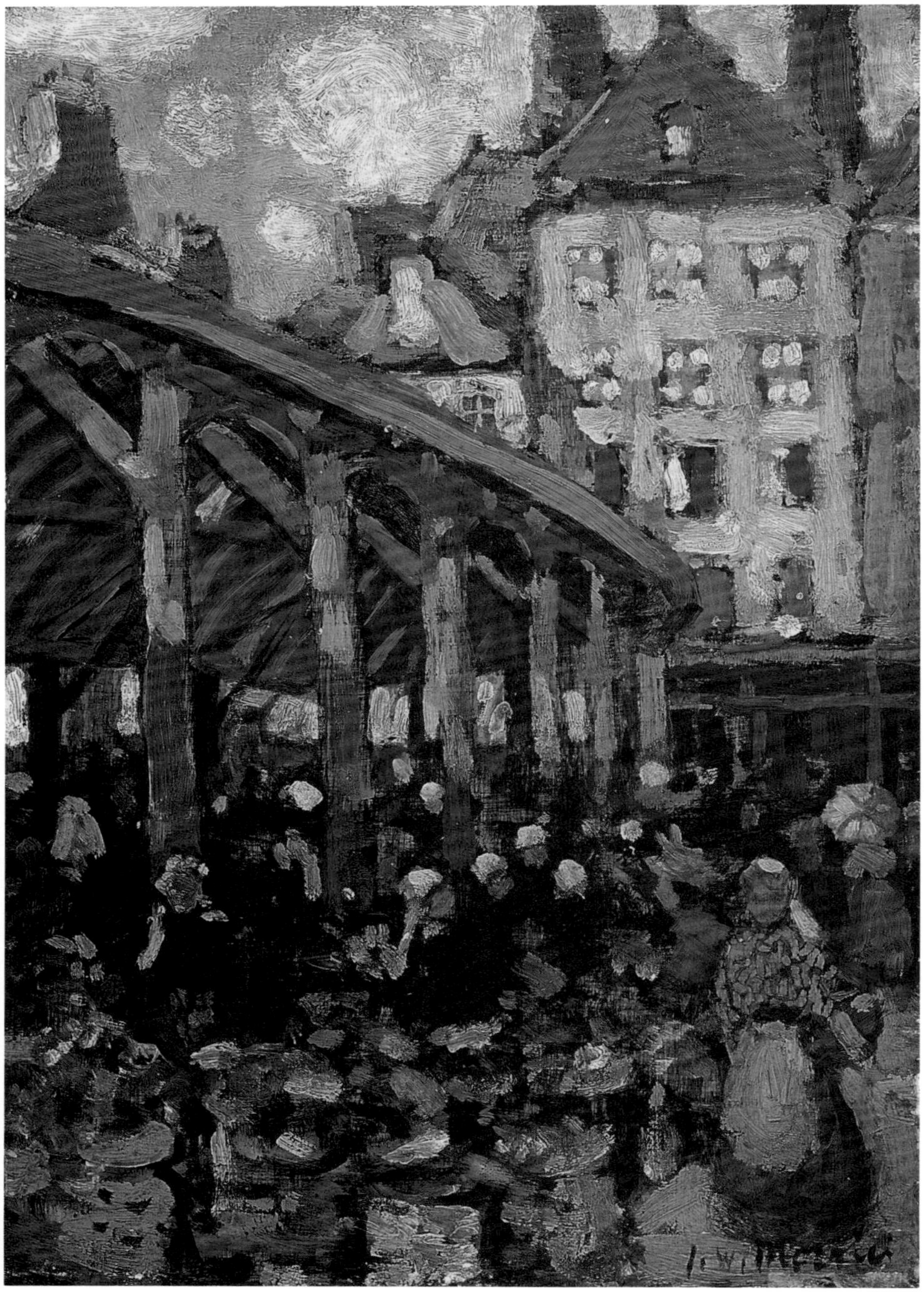

28

Market Place, St-Malo

c. 1898–99

Oil on wood, 25.2 × 17.8 cm

Inscriptions: signed l.r., *J.W. Morrice*; verso: u.c. in graphite, *#7201*, in brown ink, *Market Place, St. Malo, France–*, u.l. in graphite, *14*

Labels: typed, *G. BLAIR LAING, / 194 Bloor St. W., / Toronto, Ontario.*; MMFA 1985, no. 36

Provenance: W. Scott & Sons, Montreal. Continental Galleries of Fine Art, Montreal;[1] Vilma Lafontaine, Montreal; G. Blair Laing Ltd., Toronto, 1976.

30406

In *Market Place, St-Malo* Morrice builds up a dense surface of smoothly textured strokes to compose the buildings and sky, with delightful accents of red, green, and white animating the market scene under the sheds. As in so many of Morrice's works of the late 1890s, a woman in the foreground addresses the viewer, enhancing the immediacy of the subject and at the same time distancing our experience of the scene depicted.

The larger-sized panel, the more finished treatment of the surface, and the complexity of the composition are more characteristic of a small painting than of a sketch. This work was exhibited in 1915 at the last exhibition of the Canadian Art Club and was reproduced in *The Studio* the following year.[2]

1. A photograph of the painting with a Continental Galleries label was with Continental Galleries, Montreal, in 1977, confirming that the work was with the gallery before being acquired by Mrs. Lafontaine.
2. Cloutier 1985, p. 140; Dorais 1985b, p. 12.

29

The Juggler

c. 1899–1900

Oil on wood, 32.6 × 23.2 cm

Inscriptions: signed l.r., *J.W. Morrice*; verso: c. stamped, *VINCENZO / FABRICANTE / DI OGGETTO* [—] *BELLE ARTI / CAPRI*, u.r. in graphite, *Ch P*, u.c. in blue pencil, *146*

Labels: in black ink, F.G. No. / *28812* / "*The Wayside / Juggler*" / *J.W. Morrice*; MMFA 1965, no. 31

Provenance: Frits Thaulow, Dieppe (sold, Galerie Georges Petit, Paris, 7 May 1907, *Catalogue des Tableaux Provenant de l'atelier Frits Thaulow*, no. 147);[1] Charles Pacquement, Paris, by 1924;[2] F.R. Heaton, Montreal, by 1936;[3] Huntly Drummond, Montreal; Guy Drummond, Montreal, by 1965[4] (sold, Pinney's Auctions, Montreal, March 1988, no. T50); G. Blair Laing Ltd., Toronto, 1988.

30438

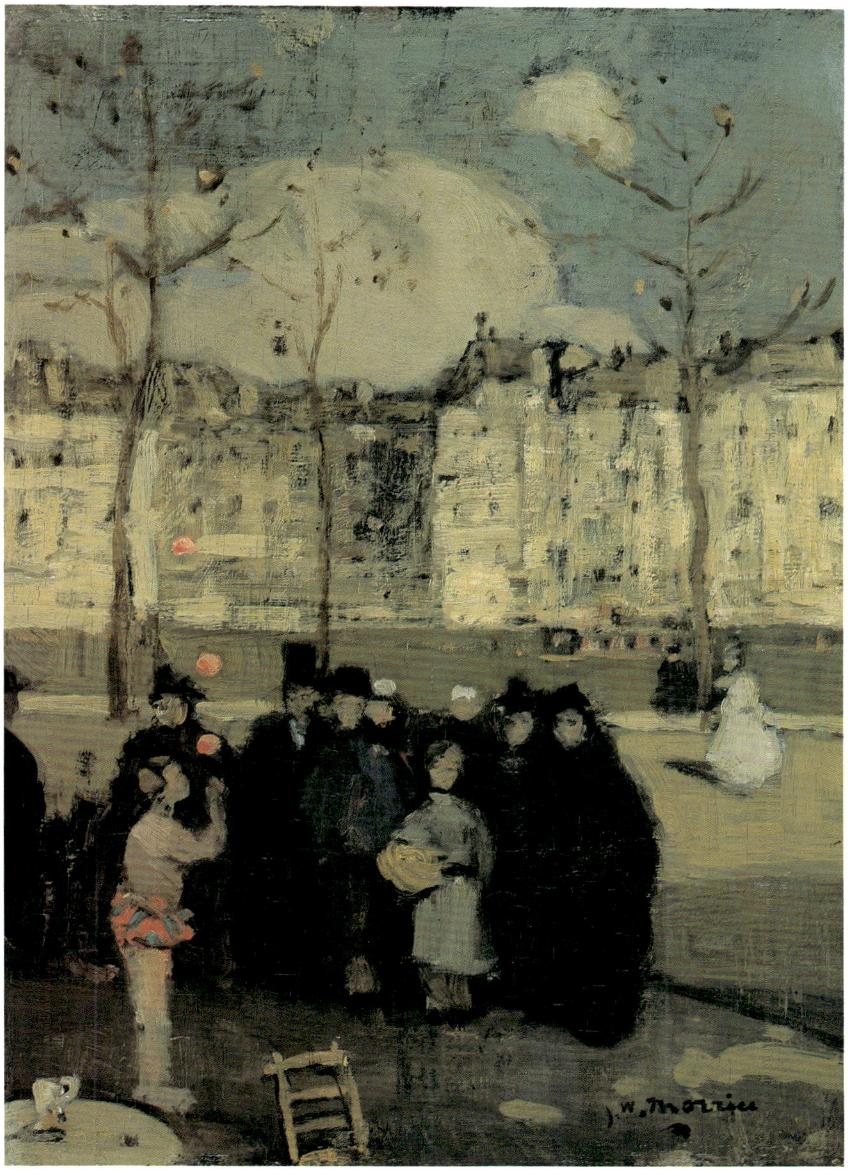

The life of the quays of Paris attracted Morrice over many years, even before he moved to his studio on the Quai des Grands-Augustins. Seated at a café table, Morrice could watch the passing scene, which might sometimes include a wandering *saltimbanque* performing his act on the street. Here a tightly huddled group of passersby, including a messenger boy or girl in the foreground, have stopped to take in the spectacle. In the background, a young woman in a white dress creates a counterpoint to the bright tangerine balls and pantaloons of the juggler. The cropped café table and chair in the lower-left corner invite us to sit and watch. A serene calm pervades the air, and the strong horizontal of the brown river, the barge, and the buildings on the far shore reaffirm this tranquil moment. The balls float in space, stopped momentarily before they resume their slow, repetitive rhythm.

This small work is painted on a wood panel possibly acquired by Morrice in Capri. It was formerly in the collection of the Norwegian painter Frits Thaulow. After Thaulow's death it was sold at auction and subsequently was acquired by the French industrialist and collector Charles Pacquement, who loaned it to the Morrice memorial section at the 1924 Salon d'Automne and to the exhibition at Galeries Simonson in 1926. By 1936 it was in the collection of F.R. Heaton, owner of the famous Montreal gallery W. Scott & Sons, and was loaned by him to the 1937 Morrice retrospective. Huntly Drummond, who had an excellent collection of Morrice paintings, later purchased this work, and it then passed to Guy Drummond, who loaned it to the 1965 Morrice retrospective. It was purchased by Blair Laing in 1988.

1. Sylvia Antoniou, *Maurice Cullen* (Kingston: Agnes Etherington Art Centre, 1982), p. 50, n. 53.
2. Loaned by Charles Pacquement to the Morrice memorial section of the Salon d'Automne, Paris 1924, no. 2508. None of Pacquement's Morrices were included in the sale of his collection at Galerie Georges Petit, Paris, 12 December 1932. They may have been sold privately prior to 1936; Buchanan (1936a, pp. 163–65) catalogues three works in Montreal collections as having come from Pacquement's collection.
3. Buchanan 1936a, p. 163.
4. Johnston 1965, p. 63.

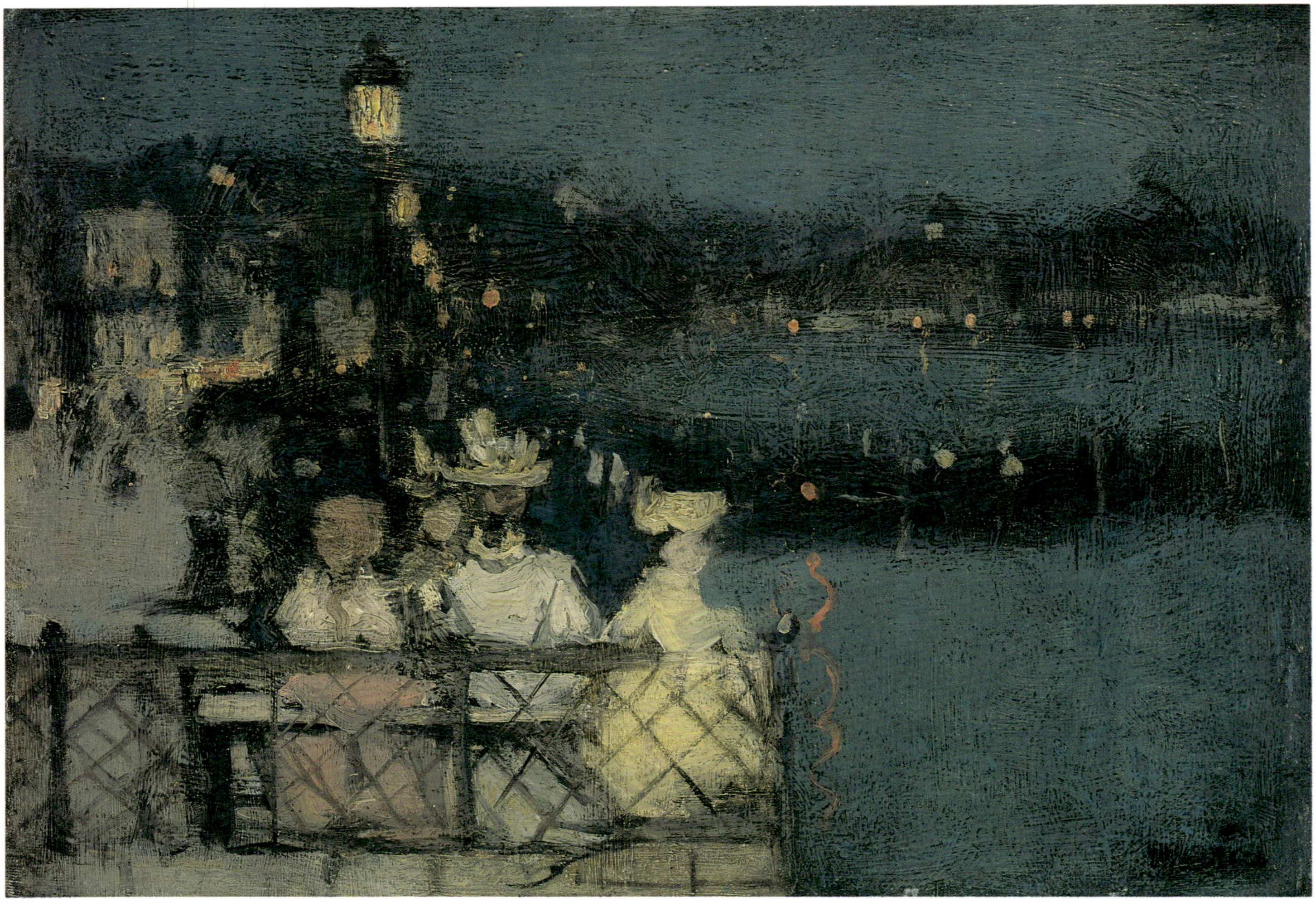

30

Study for "Venice, Festival"

c. 1897–1901

Oil on wood, 17.8 × 25.3 cm

Inscriptions: signed l.r., *Morrice*; verso: r. stencilled in black ink, *357VP*

Labels: Exhibition *A PAINTER'S CHOICE / JAMES WILLIAM MORRICE / VENETIAN SCENE BY NIGHT* / Exhibition arranged by the / ART EXHIBITIONS BUREAU / 6½ Suffolk Street / Pall Mall East, London, S.W.1; typed, WILDENSTEIN & CO., LTD. / 147 NEW BOND STREET / LONDON, W.1 / Exhibition *JAMES WILSON MORRICE* / DATE *July 4 – Aug 2 1968* Cat. No. – / Artist / Title *Venetian Scene, 1903* / Name & Address *Sir Gerald Kelly, K.C.V.O.*; in black ballpoint pen, *T / 191F*; in blue ballpoint pen, *76-16* / "*SEATED FIGURES / SAN MARCO SQ. / VENICE*"

Provenance: Gerald Kelly, London, c. 1905;[1] Lady Kelly, London (sold, Christie, Manson & Woods [Canada] Ltd., Montreal, 19 October 1973, no. 98); G. Blair Laing Ltd., Toronto, by 1976.

30405

Morrice's next documented trip to Venice, after 1897, was in 1901.[2] In February 1902 he exhibited three Venetian canvases with La Libre Esthétique in Brussels: *Venise, le soir* (fig. 31a), *Venise, fête* (fig. 30a), and *Venise, le Grand Canal* (fig. 9, Introduction). A fourth work, *À Venise, la nuit* (fig. 30c), was exhibited at the Société Nationale des Beaux-Arts in Paris in April. The four works, two of which are unlocated but known from photographs, differ markedly in approach, as do also the related studies (fig. 30b and fig. 13, Introduction).

Study for "Venice, Festival" is painted on a large, thick wood panel. The water and sky are a deep, rich blue, and the dresses of the three young women are pink, grey, and cool yellow. *Study for "Venice, Night"* (fig. 30b), formerly owned by Robert Henri,[3] is painted on a small, thin wood panel. Its colours are more contrasted and the brushwork is more angular and expressive. Both panels are very different from the ethereal works identified as having been painted in Venice in 1897 (see, for example, cat. nos. 11, 12, and 13), but recall more closely the Paris café scenes (see cat. nos. 20 and 21). They also differ considerably from the works that are datable to about 1901 (such as cat. nos. 34 and 35). It is certainly possible, then, that these sketches were painted on an undocumented trip to Venice some time between 1897 and 1901.

Study for "Venice, Festival" was acquired from Morrice by Sir Gerald Kelly, who as a young art student lived in Paris from 1901 to 1908. According to his own account he first met Morrice in 1902 or 1903, the latter being the date to which he has attributed this sketch on the back of the panel.[4] The two artists became good friends, and Morrice on occasion would advise the younger painter. In 1935 Kelly gave the National Gallery four sketches that they had worked on together, as well as a sketchbox that Morrice had advised him to buy.[5]

According to Donald Buchanan, Morrice later tried to buy back this sketch.[6] However, it remained with Kelly, who was to become president of the Royal Academy (1949–54), and Kelly loaned it to the 1968 Morrice exhibition during its London showing.[7]

1. Buchanan (1936a, p. 91) gives the date as 1905.
2. Dorais 1978, p. 27; Cloutier 1985, p. 27.
3. Johnston 1965, p. 66. The sketch is inscribed on the verso in brown ink, "Painted by / James Wilson Morrice / owned by / Robert Henri / 58 W 57 / NY City." Henri moved to this address in September 1901; see Henri Diaries, p. 213, entry for 28 September 1901.
4. Buchanan 1936a, p. 50; letter from Kelly to W.R. Johnston, 2 May 1966, Archives, Montreal Museum of Fine Arts, Morrice 1965 exhibition files. See also Derek Hudson, *For the Love of Painting: The Life of Sir Gerald Kelly, K.C.V.O., P.R.A.* (London: Peter Davies, 1975), pp. 12–31.
5. Buchanan 1936a, pp. 148–50.
6. Buchanan 1936a, p. 91.
7. "Morrice's Art in Retrospect," *The Times* (London), 8 July 1968.

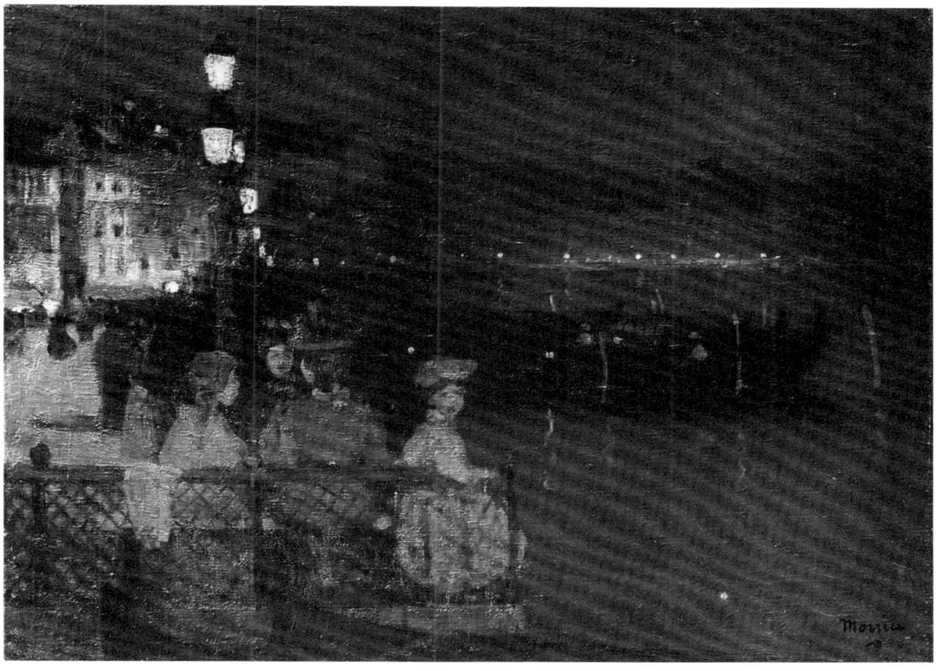

Fig. 30a
Venice, Festival, c. 1901, oil on canvas, 50 × 73 cm (?). Present location unknown. Photograph by E. Crevaux, Paris.

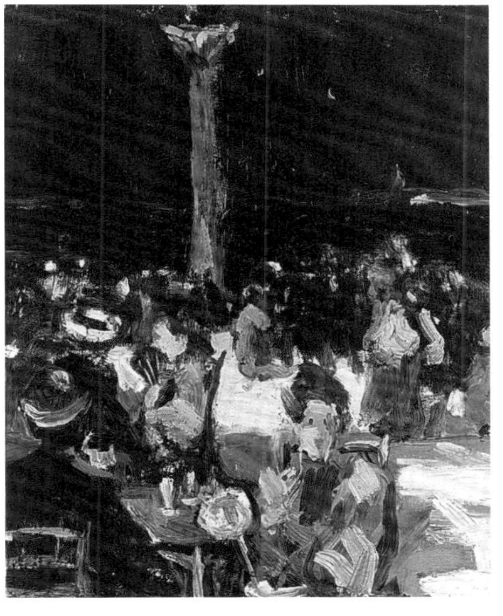

Fig. 30b
Study for "Venice, Night", c. 1897–1901, oil on wood, 15.2 × 12.7 cm. Private collection.

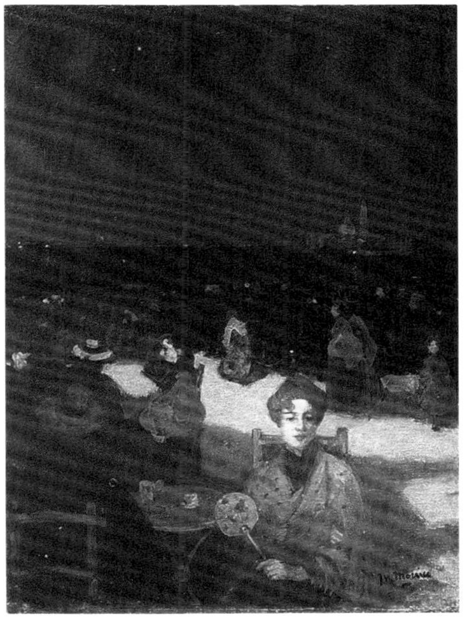

Fig. 30c
Venice, Night, c. 1901, oil on canvas, 81.5 × 60.5 cm. National Gallery of Canada (3140). Photograph by E. Crevaux, Paris.

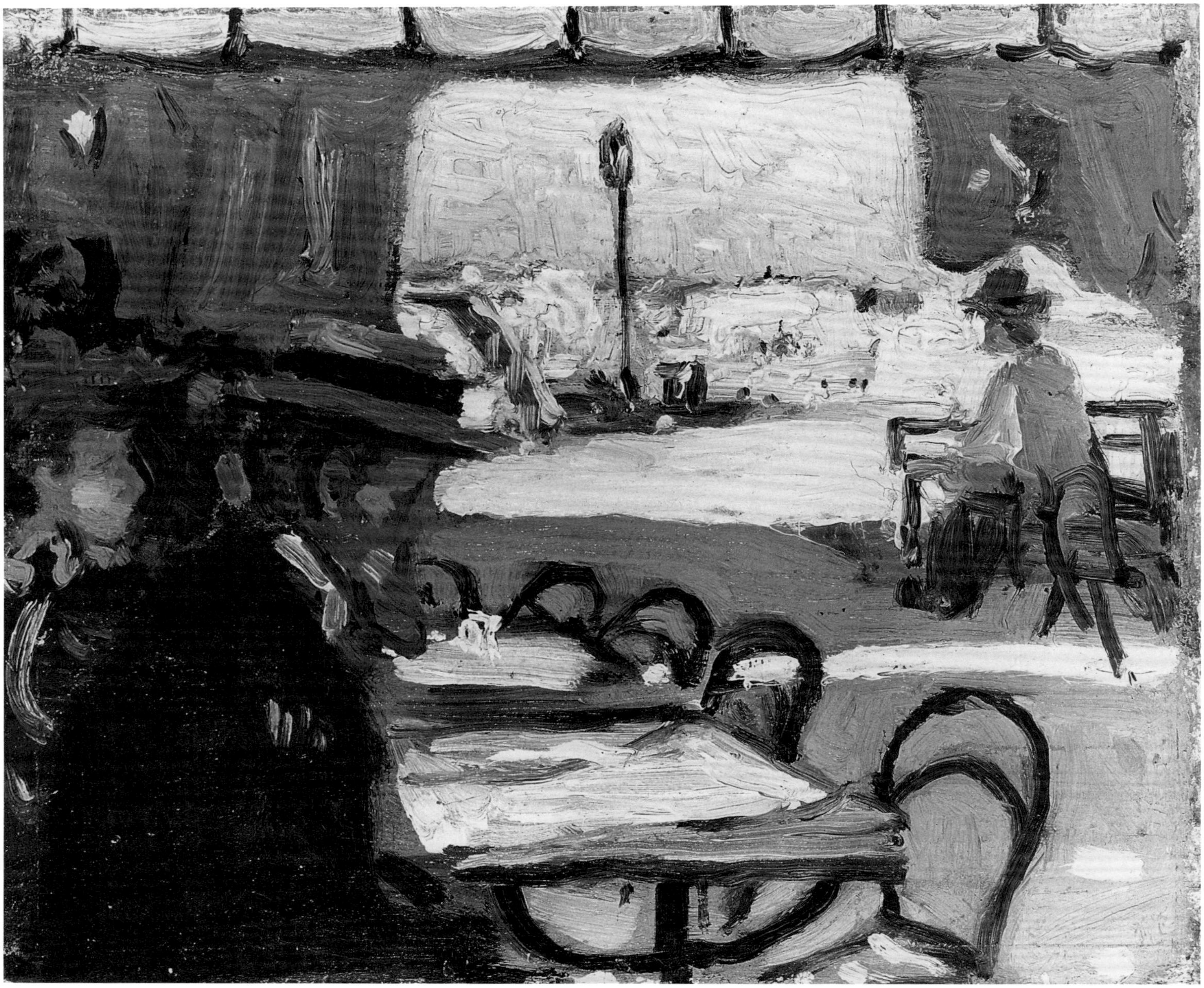

31

Café, Venice

c. 1897–1901

Oil on wood, 12.5 × 15.4 cm

Inscriptions: verso: c.l. in graphite, *6* (crossed out); back of frame: u.l. in graphite, *1965*

Labels: partly torn, HEYDENRYK frame [—] / *Heydenryk / N.Y.*; in blue ballpoint pen, *Blair Laing*; in blue ballpoint pen, *G.B.L. / CAFE IN / VENICE / 5*; in graphite, *12*

Provenance: Private collection, England(?); John Nicholson, London and New York; G. Blair Laing, Toronto, c. 1952–56.[1]

30444

In June 1902 Morrice wrote to the American illustrator and Whistler biographer Joseph Pennell: "I enclose wretched photo of one of my Salon pictures. You may remember I made the sketch one evening with you at the Café Oriental under the influence of an absinthe."[2] The painting, *Venice, Evening* (fig. 31a), depicts a man – possibly Pennell himself[3] – reading a newspaper, with a view of Santa Maria della Salute in the background. *Café, Venice* may be another representation of Pennell, seated in the foreground at a table, with the awning framing the composition at the top and a view of the Riva degli Schiavoni and houses beyond.[4] The specificity of the figure seems to indicate that it is a portrait.

The dating of this sketch is problematic in much the same way as is the dating of *Study for "Venice, Festival"* (cat. no. 30). From a stylistic comparison, we can at least say with confidence that it was painted about the same time as *Cardplayers* (fig. 13, Introduction), which was used as a study for *Venice, the Grand Canal* (fig. 9, Introduction), one of the paintings exhibited by Morrice in Brussels in February 1902.

1. See cat. no. 7, n. 1.
2. Letter from Morrice to Pennell, 1 June [1902], Pennell Papers, container 248. See also Dorais 1978, pp. 27–28, 33, nn. 37–38.
3. See the photograph of Pennell in Elizabeth Robins Pennell, *The Life and Letters of Joseph Pennell* (Boston: Little, Brown & Co., 1929), vol. 1, facing p. 340. A drawing for this reading figure is in the Paris–Venice Sketchbook (fig. 31b). The figure does not appear in the main compositional drawing for *Venice, Evening* (see fig. 12, Introduction).
4. McTavish 1984, p. 40, no. 2c.

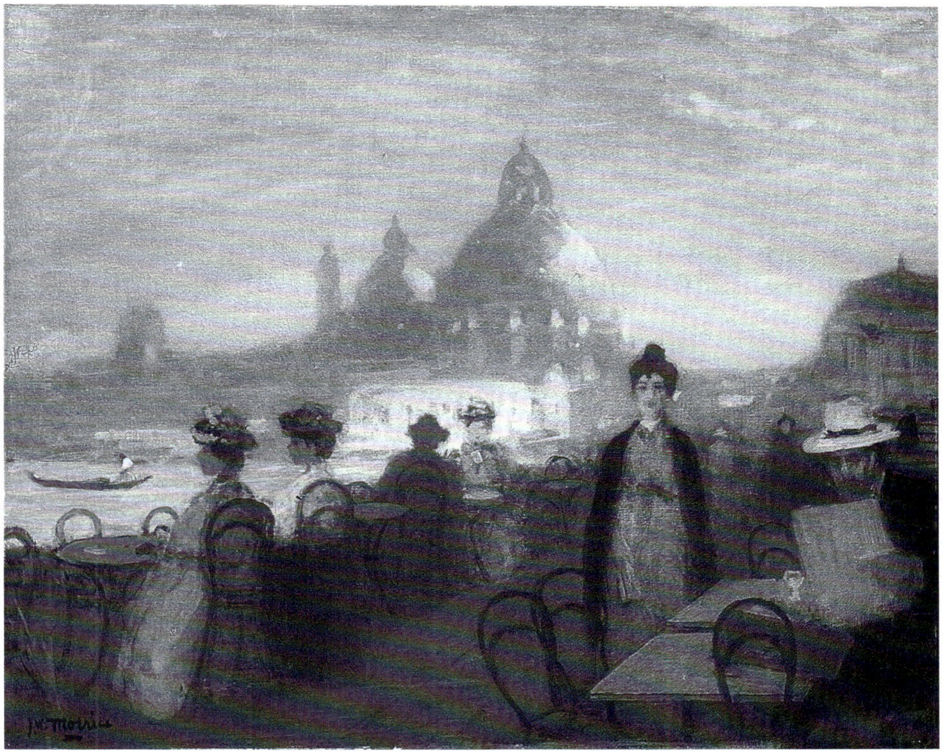

Fig. 31a
Venice, Evening, c. 1901, oil on canvas, dimensions and present location unknown. Photograph by E. Crevaux, Paris.

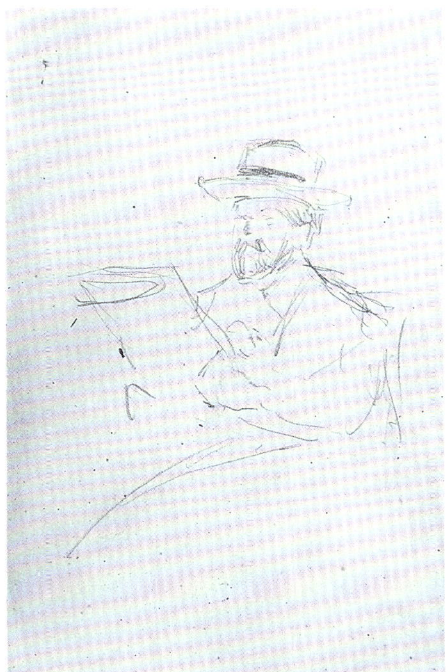

Fig. 31b
Paris–Venice Sketchbook. p. 38r, 1901, graphite on wove paper, 17.2 × 11.4 cm. National Gallery of Canada (7419).

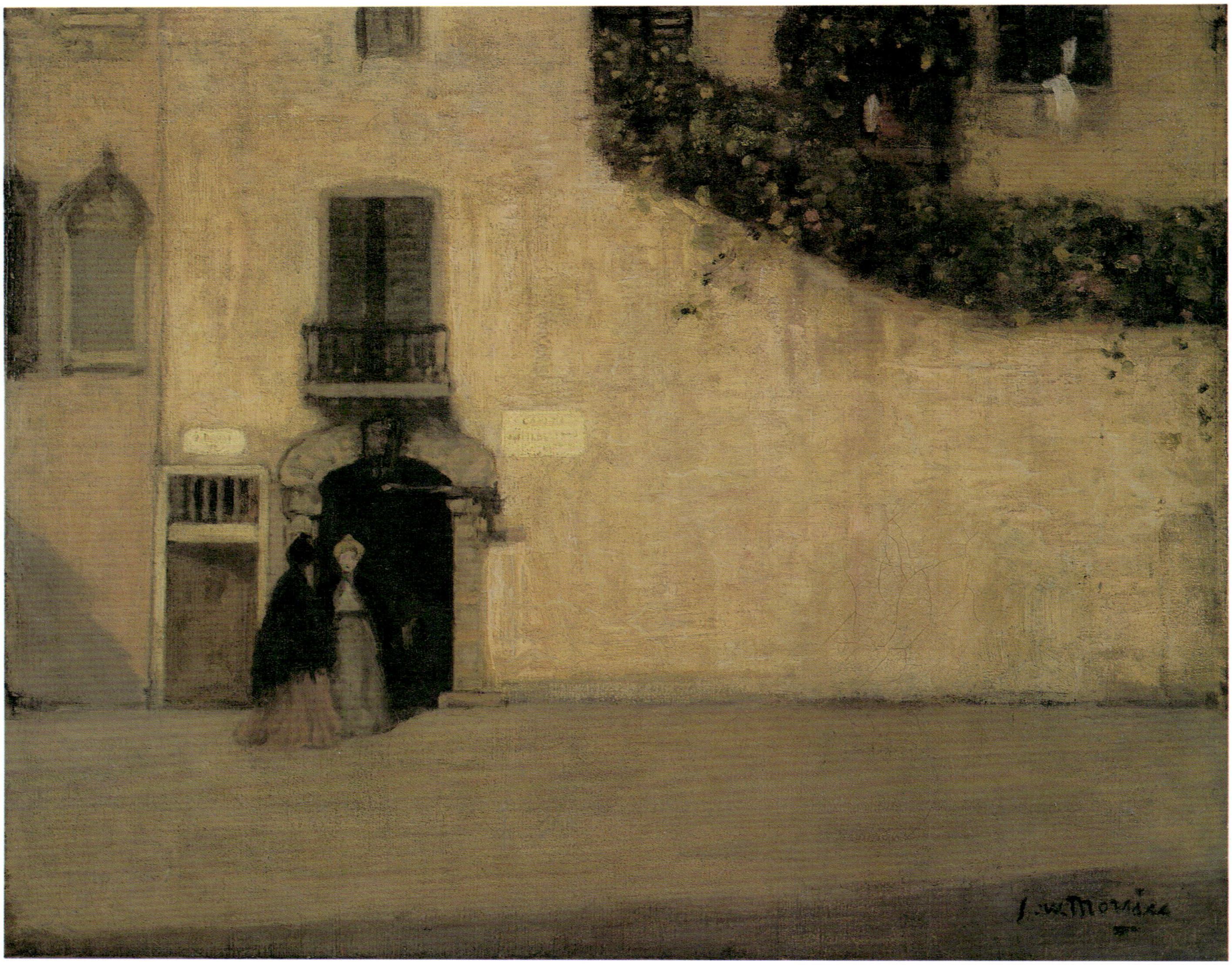

32

Campo San Giovanni Nuovo, Venice

c. 1901–02

Oil on canvas, 50.5 × 61.8 cm

Inscriptions: signed l.r., *J.W. Morrice*; stretcher: on crossbar, l.c. in black ink, *Madame* [—] *Rouché*, c. stamped, *MODÈLE DÉPOSÉ / B*, u.c. in white chalk, *16*; back of frame: c.r. in white chalk, *MORRICE*

Labels: Wildenstein 1968, no. 12; typed, *MORRICE EXHIBITION / TITLE: CAMPO SAN GIOVANNI NUOVA, VENICE / FROM: LAING GALLERY, TORONTO*, in blue ballpoint pen, *12*; typed, NATIONAL GALLERY OF CANADA / Title of Exhibition / *J W MORRICE / RETROSPECTIVE EX*, Catalogue No. *12#* / Box No. *1*; typed, *CAISSE N° 1 / 12 CAMPO SAN GIOVANNI / NUOVA VENICE*; typed, Laing Galleries 194 Bloor Street West Toronto 5 Canada / "*CAMPO SAN GIOVANNI NUOVA, VENICE*" / *c. 1903, Venice / By / JAMES WILSON MORRICE / (1865–1924)*; in blue ink, *G.B.L. / #27 / CAMPO SAN / GIOVANNI*

Provenance: Jacques Rouché, Paris, by 1926;[1] Mme Robert André, Paris, by descent; G. Blair Laing, Toronto, 1962.

30466

Morrice frequently reworked his paintings, and many of his alterations can be documented through early photographs and illustrations or by examining details that now show through the overpaints. This canvas was photographed and reproduced in an article that appeared in *L'art décoratif* in 1905.[2] In the photograph (fig. 32a) we can see a priest in the foreground at the right. Infrared examination of the canvas indicates that this figure too was the product of an alteration: Morrice had originally painted a woman in a long dress, similar to the two women by the door, confronting the viewer in the same manner as the priest (fig. 32b). In the same photograph, a dark form at the right gives evidence of yet another figure that at one time had been included in the composition. In the canvas, as it exists today, the dark-coloured figures show through the light-coloured overpaints. Other alterations by the artist include the reworking of the foreground to diminish the demarcations of the paving stones, the diminution of the foreground shadow and of the door or gate at the right, and the addition of a new signature.

The elimination of foreground figures was the most common type of modification that Morrice made to his paintings (see, for example, cat. nos. 46 and 74), and may be the result of his new perception of space, a change most noticeable in his large North African canvases of the early 1920s. The modifications to this canvas may also have been made around that period – assuming the work had not yet left Morrice's studio, of which we cannot be certain.[3]

This painting was formerly in the collection of Jacques Rouché, one of Morrice's most important early collectors. The author of a book on modern stage design[4] and director of the Paris Opera from 1914, he owned at least eight canvases by Morrice[5] as well as works by Morrice's friend Albert Marquet.[6] Blair Laing purchased the painting from Rouché's daughter, Mme. Robert André, in 1962, in a contest of wills he loved to recount.[7]

1. Loaned by Jacques Rouché to Paris 1926, no. 12.
2. Gustave Soulier, "Les peintres de Venise," *L'art décoratif*, 7e année (January–June 1905), p. 62 (repr.).
3. The 1905 photograph was reproduced in *The Studio* in August 1913 (Ciolkowska 1913b, p. 182), which suggests that the painting was altered after that date.
4. Jacques Rouché, *L'art théâtral moderne*, 1910 (Paris: Librairie Bloud & Gay, 1924).
5. To the 1924 Salon d'Automne he loaned: *La Plage à St. Malo*; *Les Tuileries*; *Les quais*; and *Effet de neige sur les quais*. To the 1926 exhibition at Galeries Simonson he loaned: *La plage à St. Malo*; *Le Cirque de Concarneau*; *Venise, Campo San Giovanni Nuovo*; *Petite place à St. Malo*; *Paris, les Tuileries*; and *Venise, le Grand Canal*. He loaned four works to the 1927 exhibition of Canadian art at the Jeu de Paume in Paris and four works to the 1937 Morrice exhibition in Ottawa. All of these are now in Canadian collections, except for *Petite place à St. Malo*, which I have not been able to identify.
6. Laing 1979, p. 217; Laing 1984, p. 194. See also Buchanan 1936a, p. 137.
7. Laing 1979, pp. 217–18; Laing 1984, pp. 194–98.

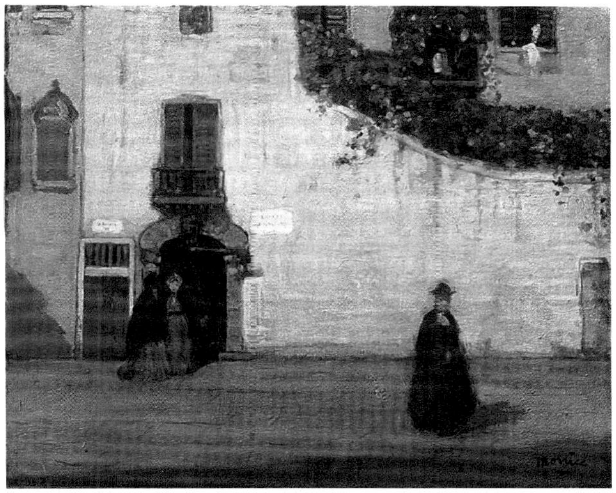

Fig. 32a
Photograph of *Campo San Giovanni Nuovo, Venice*, taken prior to 1905 by E. Crevaux, Paris.

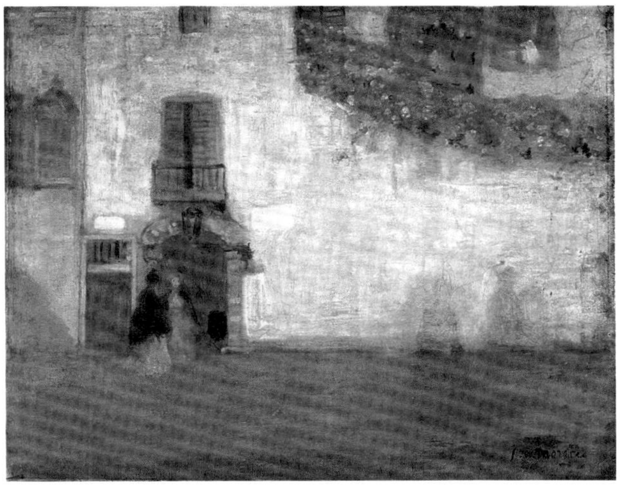

Fig. 32b
Infrared photograph of *Campo San Giovanni Nuovo, Venice*.

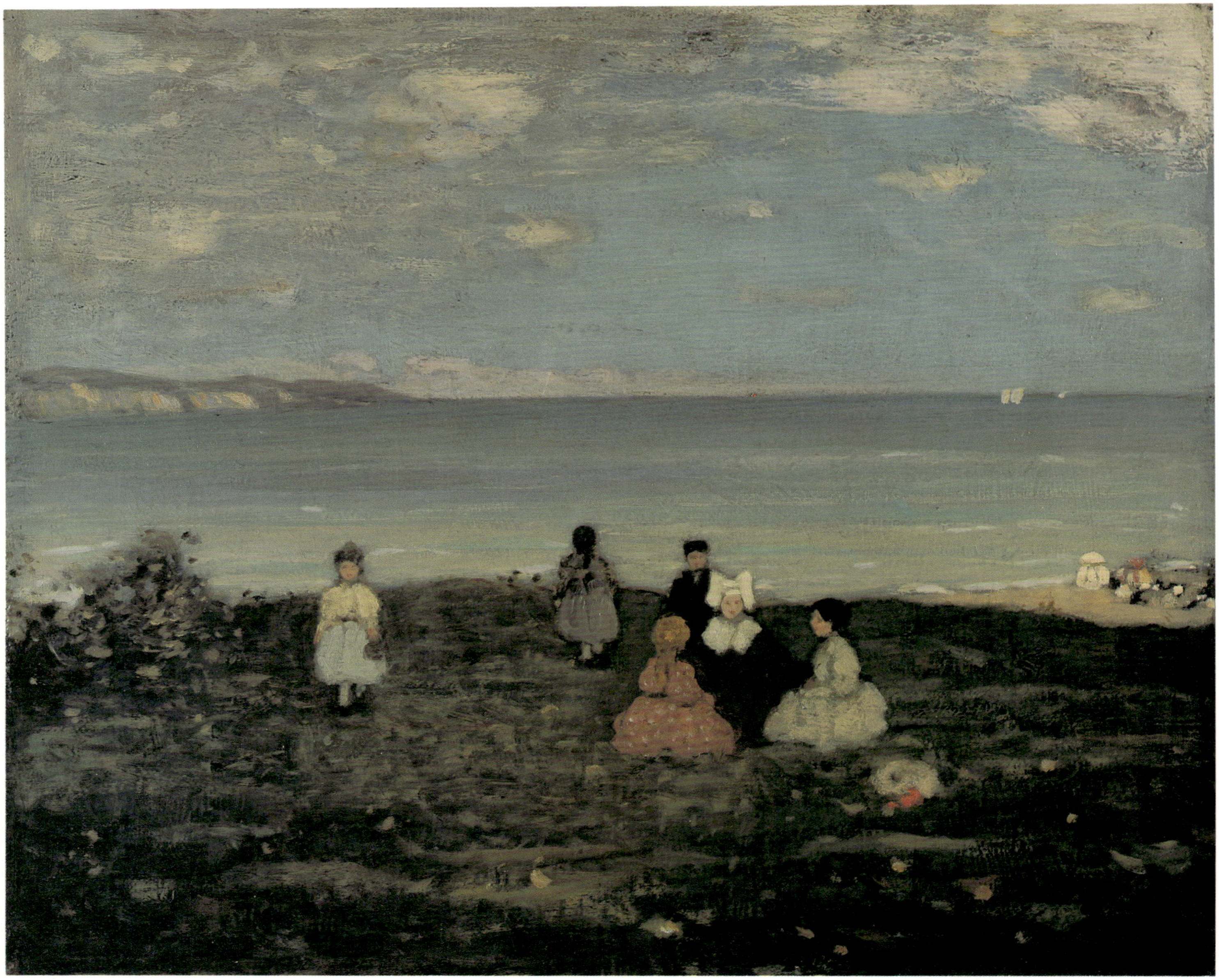

33

On the Cliff

c. 1901–02

Oil on canvas, 49.9 × 61 cm

Inscriptions: signed l.r., *J.W. Morrice*; stretcher: on crossbar, in black crayon, *12 / 8112*, in red crayon, *13*

Labels: in graphite, *76-15*; Art Gallery of Ontario crating label, Norton Gallery exhibition, no. 17; in black ink, *1*; MMFA 1985, no. 40; in blue ballpoint pen, *ON THE / CLIFFS / 76-15*

Provenance: Daniel R. Wilkie, Toronto, 1908;[1] Mrs. W.A.H. Kerr, Toronto, by descent, by 1920[2] (sold, Sotheby Parke Bernet [Canada] Ltd., Toronto, 17 May 1976, lot 77); G. Blair Laing Ltd., Toronto, 1976.

30404

In 1899 Morrice exhibited a painting at the spring Salon of the Société Nationale des Beaux-Arts that was titled simply *Paysage* (fig. 33a). Structured into three horizontal bands linked by the verticals of the young trees, the painting shows a clear indebtedness to the work of Puvis de Chavannes. In *Charenton, Washing Day* (fig. 33b), first exhibited in February 1900,[3] he employs a similar composition, with a young girl in the foreground, a woman hanging up the laundry, and the tree trunks creating a rhythm of verticals linking the horizontals of foreground, water, and foliage. In *On the Cliff* Morrice depicts similar groupings on the grass with an expansive view of the ocean and cliffs beyond. At the right is a bird's-eye view of a beach with bathing tents, a compositional device seen also in *The Beach, St-Malo* (fig. 33c), first exhibited in October 1901.[4] *On the Cliff* is a transitional work, unique in its combination of elements and centrality of focus on the group of figures. The curve of the cliff and beach play against the horizon line. The figures, comfortable in their intimacy and distance, move in parallel existences; one young child gazes out across the water while another examines the viewer. The enamel-like surface is touched with highlights that stand out like brilliant jewels.

That Morrice recognized the importance of this painting is evidenced by its impressive exhibition history – it was shown in Paris, Philadelphia, Pittsburgh, Cincinnati, Chicago, Buffalo, Boston, St. Louis, Venice, and London,[5] before being sold at the first exhibition of the Canadian Art Club in 1908 to its president, Daniel R. Wilkie. At that time Morrice wrote to his friend Edmund Morris: "By the way you got the title of my picture wrong. It is 'On the Cliff, Normandy' and *not* 'Morning off the Coast, St. Augustin.' Where is St. Augustin?" And he added: "I hope my picture will be sold – I don't think $500 is too much for it as it is one of my best things."[6]

1. Letters from Morrice to Edmund Morris, 21 and 22 February and 17 March [1908], Morris Papers. The painting was loaned by D.R. Wilkie to the *Exhibition of Works by Members of the "Société des Peintres et Sculpteurs" (formerly the Société Nouvelle of Paris)*, Fine Arts Academy, Buffalo, N.Y., 16 November–26 December 1911, no. 112, as *On the Beach*.
2. Loaned by Mrs. W.A.H. Kerr to the *Loan Collection of Paintings Contributed by Private Collectors and Public Institutions in the City of Toronto*, Art Gallery of Toronto, 6 January–8 February 1920, as *Figures*, 19 × 23¾ inches. Daniel Wilkie had died in November 1914. See B.E. Howard, "The Amazing Career of Daniel Robert Wilkie," *Canadian Banker* LVIII:2 (Spring 1951), pp. 70–77.
3. Cloutier 1985, p. 133.
4. Ibid., p. 142
5. Ibid., p. 144; *Sesta Esposizione Internazionale d'Arte della Citta di Venezia*, 1905, Sala Internazionale, no. 3c, as *Sulla Spiaggia* (repr.).
6. Letters from Morrice to Morris, 21 and 22 February [1908], Morris Papers. From the second letter it would appear that the painting sold for $400.

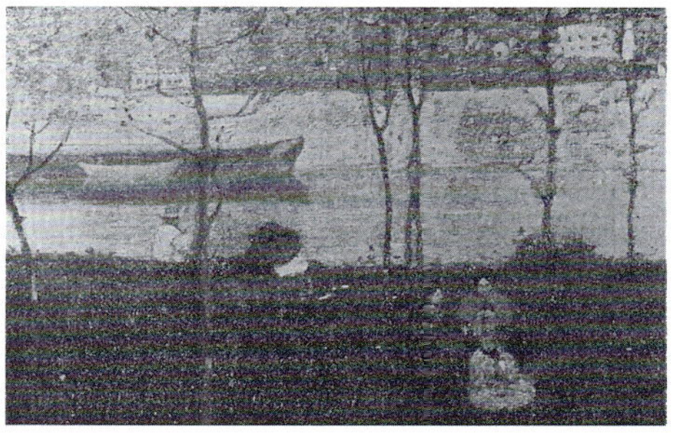

Fig. 33a
"J. Morrice. – Au bord de l'eau (Paysage). Salon de 1899." *La Revue des Deux Frances*, 3ᵉ année (July 1899), p. 497. Dimensions and present location of *Paysage* unknown.

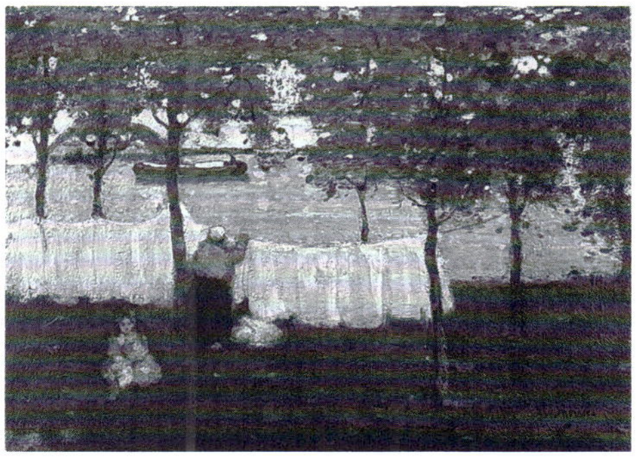

Fig. 33b
Charenton, Washing Day, 1899, oil on canvas, 43.9 × 59.6 cm. Art Gallery of Hamilton. Bequest of F. Eleanore Morrice, 1981 (81.46).

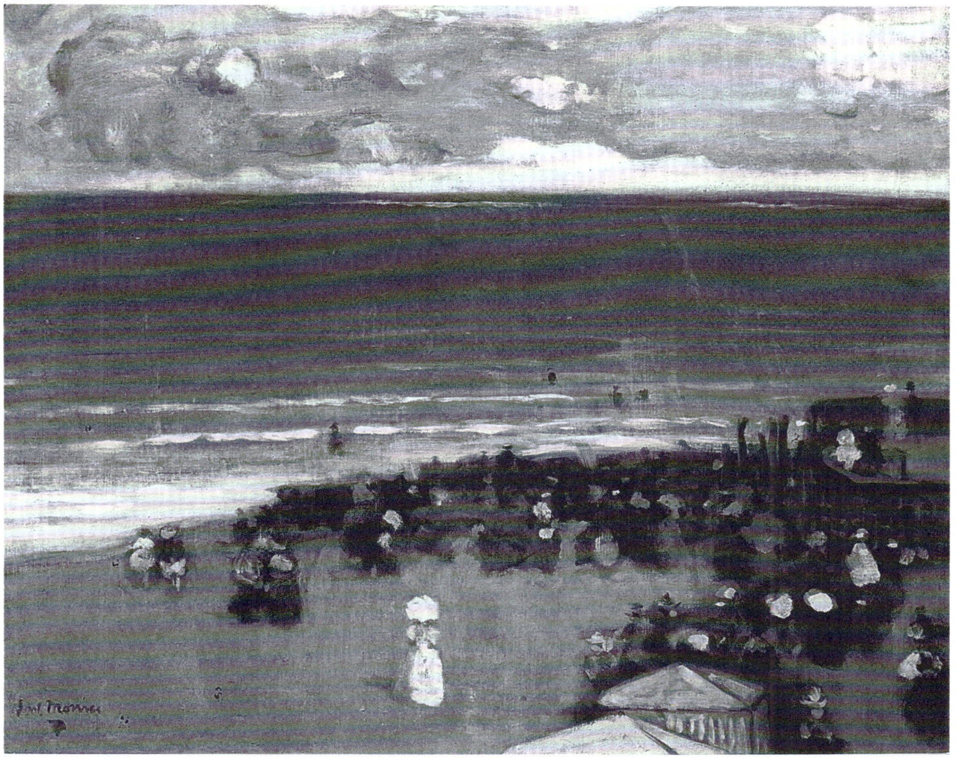

Fig. 33c
The Beach, St-Malo, 1901, oil on canvas, 49.5 × 59.6 cm. Private collection.

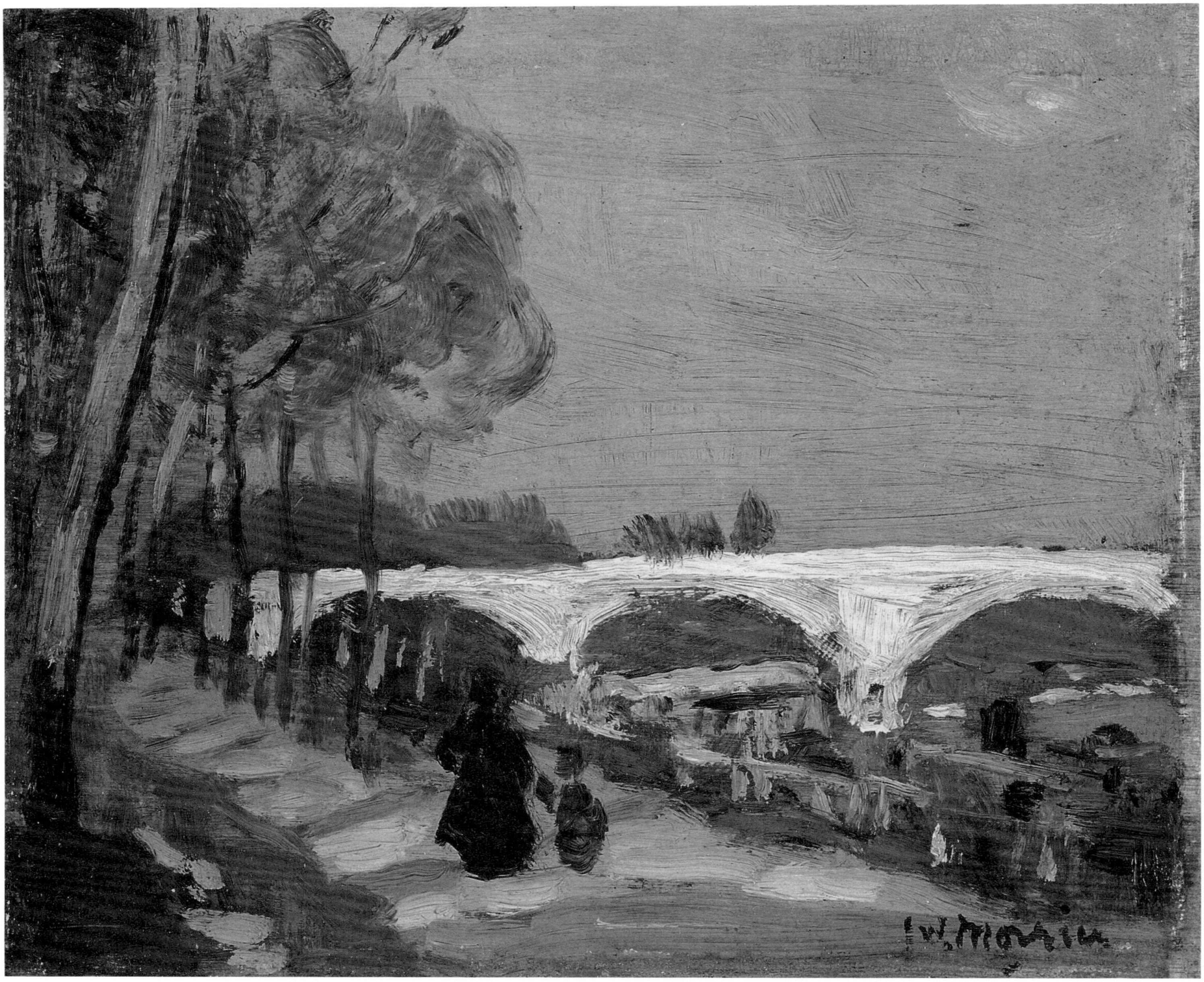

34

At Charenton

1901

Oil on wood, 12.2 × 15.2 cm

Inscriptions: signed l.l., *J.W. Morrice*; verso: u.l. in graphite (artist's hand), *à Charenton*, u.c. in graphite, *424*, c. in graphite, *29*

Labels: typed, Artist *JAMES W. MORRICE, R.C.A.* / Title *A CHARENTON* / Property of *M. JACQUES DUBOURG* / Return Address *PARIS, FRANCE* / Insurance Value $, in graphite, *49* / *Cat 49*; stamped, *DOUANES PARIS EXPOSITIONS*; in blue ballpoint pen, *G.B.L* / *"AT CHARENTON"*

Provenance: Jacques Dubourg, Paris, by 1937;[1] G. Blair Laing, Toronto, 1976.

30462

The bridges of the Seine were Morrice's first love and he would draw and paint them often, whether close to his studio or at nearby Charenton, an eastern suburb on the north bank of the river just south of the Bois de Vincennes. We know that Morrice made a day trip to Charenton in March 1899 together with Robert Henri and his wife Linda,[2] but he would return there numerous times. At least four of his canvases depict this part of the Seine.[3]

A drawing for this particular view is found in the sketchbook of about 1901 in the National Gallery of Canada (fig. 34a). Clearly visible in it are the mother and child walking along the embankment, the funnel of the barge docked at the right, and the white arched bridge traversing the river. In the oil sketch the figures are more definitely delineated, but in a shorthand of strokes. The red of the barge complements the rich green of the grass bordering the walk. The shadows of the trees and figures mark a progression along the path, and the cream yellow of the bridge echoes the darker sandy walk. The trees are lightly brushed in, and the blue of the sky is rubbed. Only a wisp of a cloud is visible in the sky.

1. Loaned by Jacques Dubourg to Ottawa 1937, no. 49.
2. Letter from Henri to his parents, 28 March 1899, Henri Papers.
3. *Charenton, Washing Day* (fig. 33b); *Le Pont de Charenton* (reproduced in Leblond 1981, facing p. 198); *Charenton (le soir)*, exhibited at the 1904 Salon (described in Leblond 1981, p. 205); and *Sunday at Charenton* (see Cloutier 1985, p. 227).

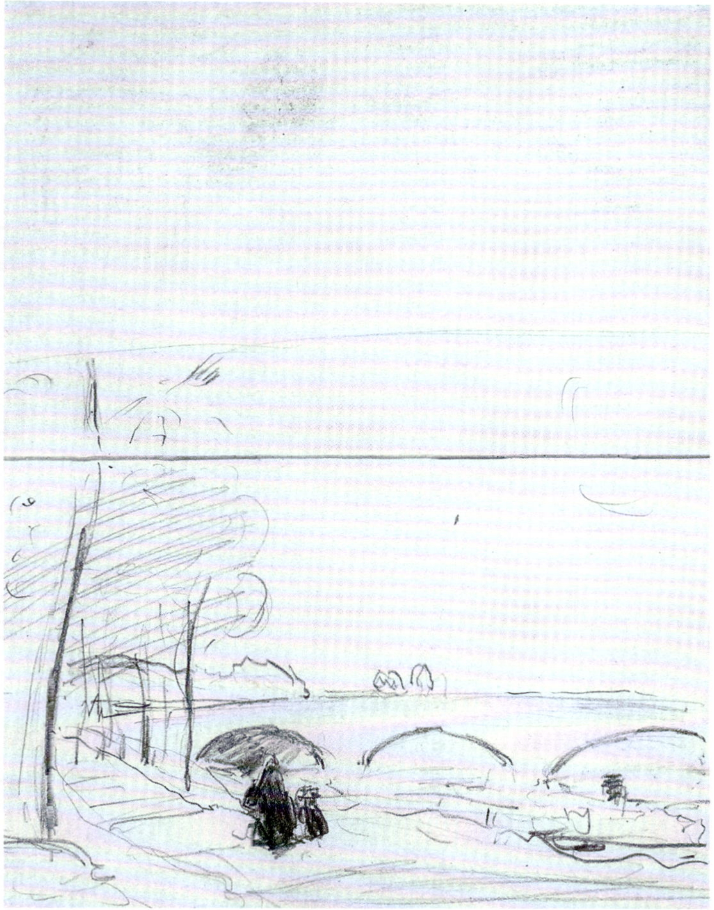

Fig. 34a
Paris–Venice Sketchbook, pp. 7v–8r, c. 1901, graphite on wove paper, 11.4 × 17.2 cm. National Gallery of Canada (7419).

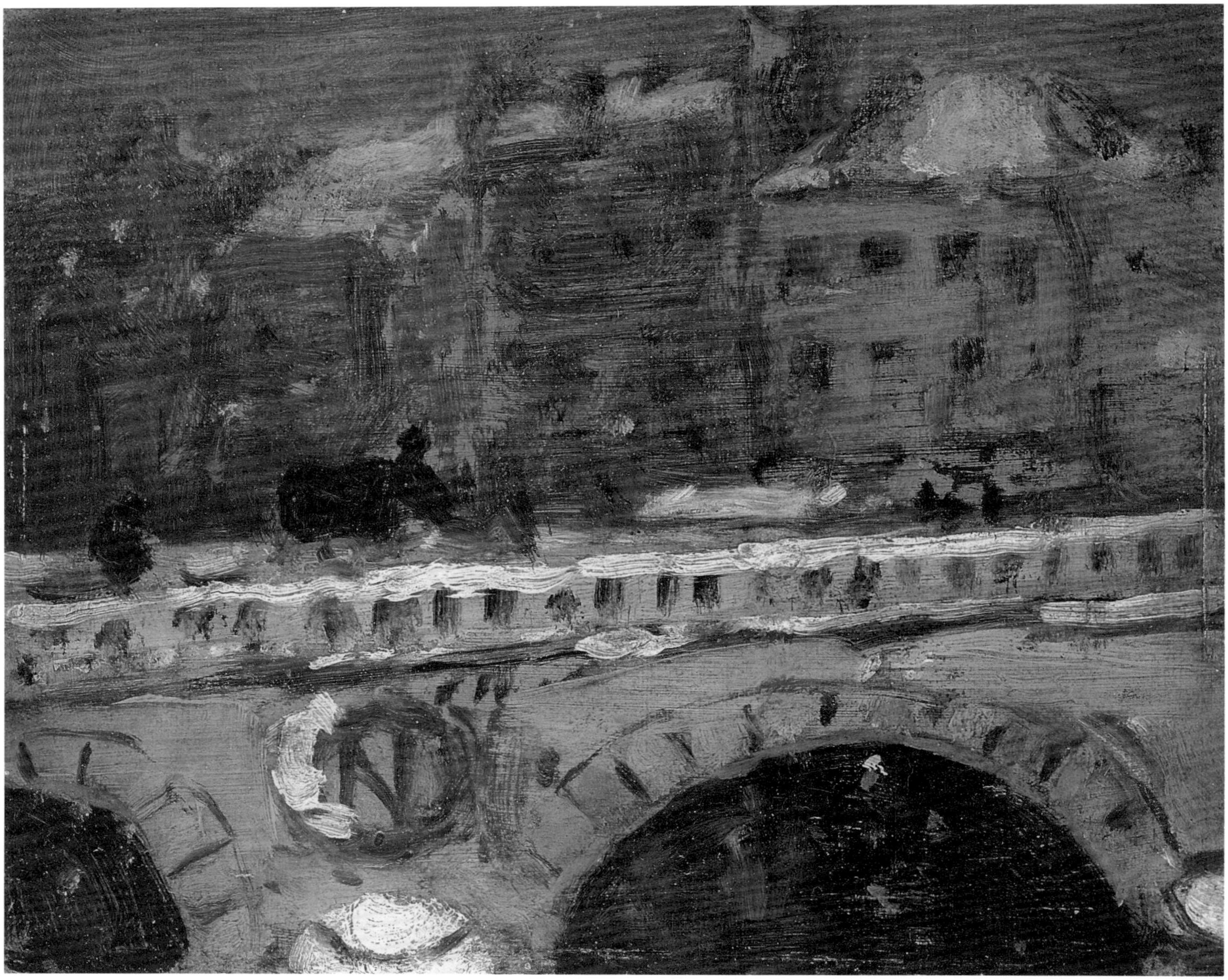

35

Pont St-Michel

c. 1901

Oil on wood-pulp board, 12.6 × 15.4 cm

Inscriptions: verso: u.l. in graphite, *S19*, u.c. in graphite, *PARIS*, c. stamped, *STUDIO / J.W. MORRICE*

Provenance: Estate of the artist. Lawrence T. Porter, St. Andrews East, Quebec; G. Blair Laing, Toronto, 1980.

30475

On 2 October 1899 Morrice moved into a new studio situated at 45 Quai des Grands-Augustins, just near Pont St-Michel, opposite Île de la Cité.[1] He would remain there until about 1916. From his studio window he had a view of Notre-Dame Cathedral and the bustling activity of the quays and the river Seine. Pont St-Michel, depicted here, goes from Boulevard St-Michel, just adjacent to Morrice's studio, to Île St-Louis, and is emblazoned with the Napoleonic monogram.[2] Morrice painted several winter views of the Seine.[3] In one study on a large wood panel showing Pont au Double and the facade of Notre-Dame Cathedral (fig. 35a), the thickly brushed foreground is constructed of intersecting angles, with the trees uniting the lower and upper parts of the composition.

The sketch of Pont St-Michel in the Laing collection is painted on a wood-pulp board in a muted palette of browns, greys, black, and white, with touches of red and yellow (the latter on the wheels of the carriage). The foreground is composed of the lumbering arches of the bridge, depicted at an angle. The sombre colouring of a winter day is relieved by the almost comic personality of the buildings, so sketchily roughed in.

1. Letter from Robert Henri to his family, 2 October 1899, Henri Papers.
2. I am indebted to Lucie Dorais for correcting my previous identification of the bridge as Pont au Change, which is on the other side of Île St-Louis and has wider arches.
3. See, for example, *Early Snow on the Quai des Grands-Augustins* (reproduced in colour in Laing 1984, p. 61). From installation views of Paris 1927, this work can be identified as *Effet de neige sur les Quais*, from the collection of Jacques Rouché. See also *On the Quays, Paris* (reproduced in Ciolkowska 1913b, p. 181; present whereabouts unknown).

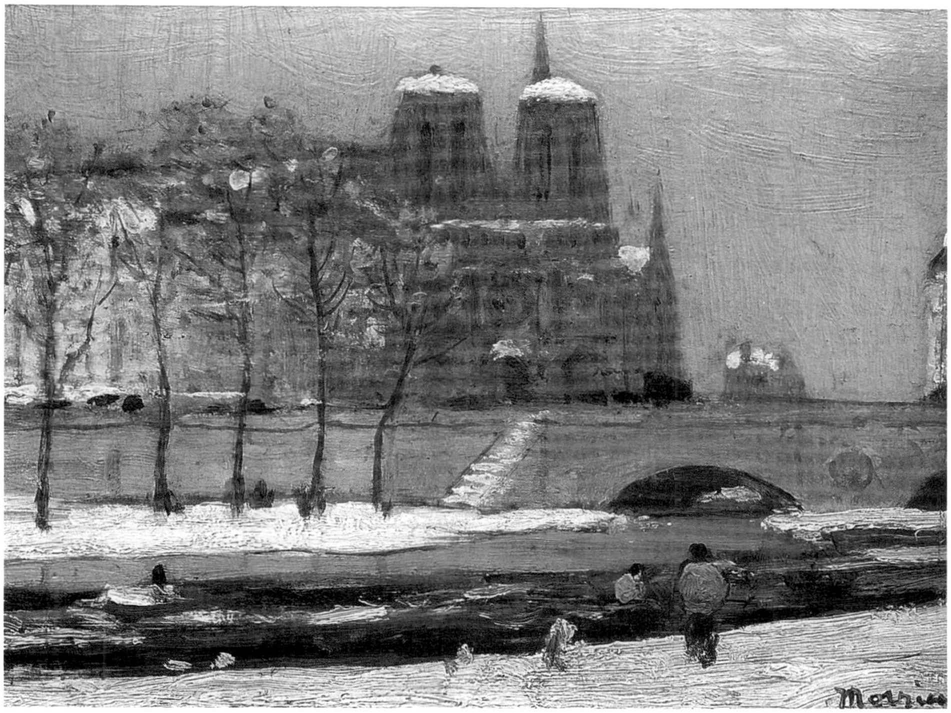

Fig. 35a
Notre-Dame, c. 1898, oil on wood, 19 × 25.4 cm. McMichael Canadian Art Collection, Kleinburg. Gift of R.S. McLaughlin, Oshawa (1968.7.18).

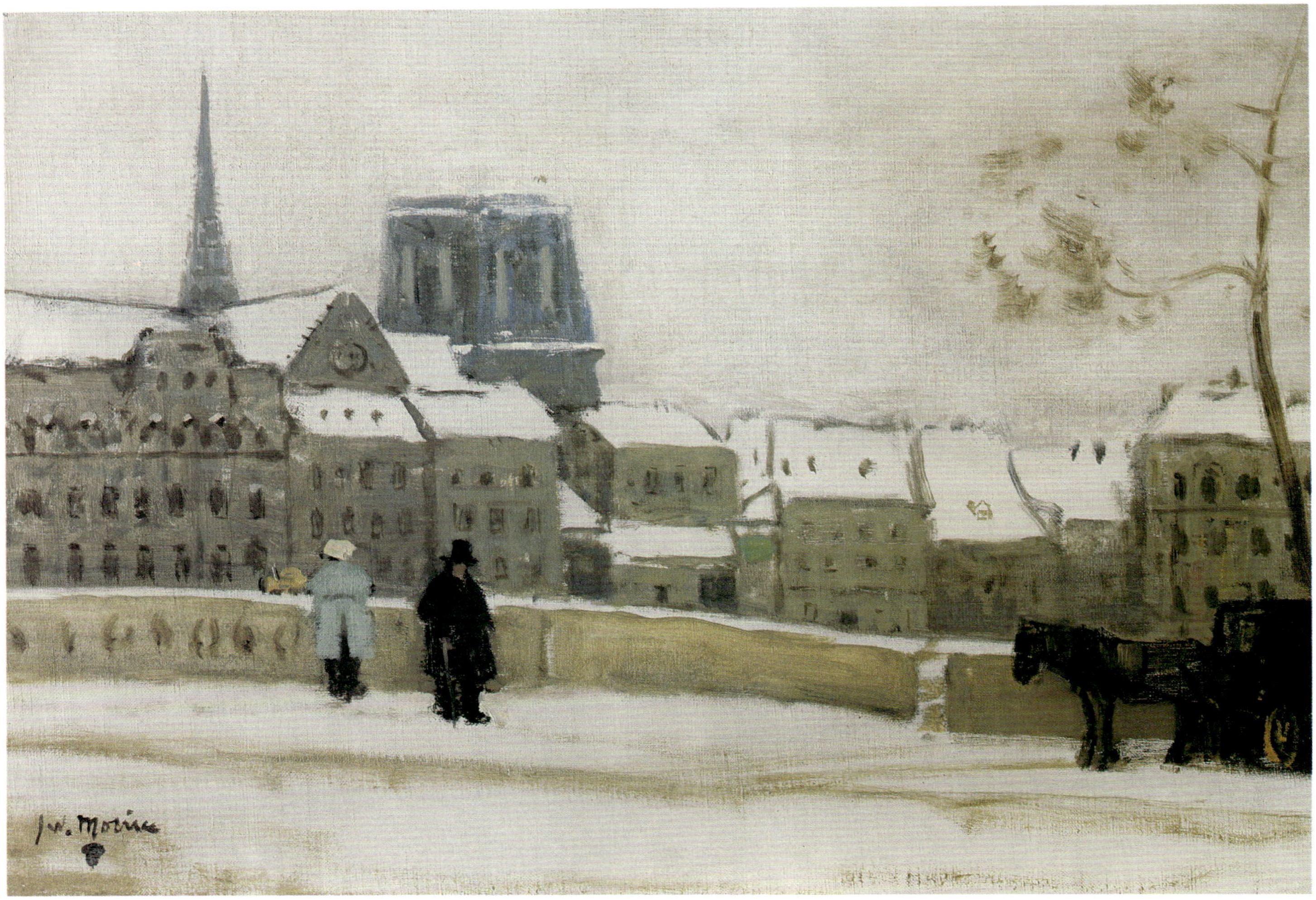

36

Notre-Dame, Paris

c. 1901–02

Oil on canvas, 38.3 × 55.2 cm

Inscriptions: signed l.l., *J.W. Morrice*; stretcher: u.l. in graphite, *1*, l.c. in graphite, [—]*N*[—]; on crossbar, c. stamped, *H. CHALBO boulevard de Montparnasse / 74 / Paris 15*

Labels: Art Gallery of Ontario crating label, Norton Gallery exhibition, no. 18; MMFA 1965, no. 33; in blue ballpoint pen, *79-25 / NOTRE DAME / DE PARIS*

Provenance: Dr. Francis Shepherd, Montreal, by 1925;[1] Dorothy Shepherd, Montreal, by descent, 1929.[2] Stevens Art Gallery, Montreal, 1945.[3] Lucille Gagnon, Montreal, by 1965;[4] by descent to a niece of Lucille Gagnon; G. Blair Laing Ltd., Toronto, 1979.[5]

30416

A similarly comic personality characterizes the brown buildings in this view of Pont Louis-Philippe and the snow-covered towers of Notre-Dame.[6] In the foreground, a baker in a blue coat leans over the parapet while a top-hatted man in a black coat walks toward the waiting carriage.

In this painting Morrice has combined studies that he originally did in two separate drawings (figs. 36a and 36b). The paint is applied thinly, creating a dry surface; in some areas it has been rubbed into the canvas. These techniques mark a major departure from his previous canvases, in which he had built up the paint in thick enamel-like surfaces. Here the colour is restrained, composed predominantly of browns, greys, and whites, save for the blue smock of the baker (echoed in the blue of the right tower) and a green roof between the two men and the horse.

This work was listed in one of Morrice's sketchbooks as "Notre Dame, l'hiver."[7] It was exhibited at the Third Annual Exhibition of the Canadian Art Club in Toronto in January 1910 as *Notre Dame, Paris*. It was later acquired by Dr. Francis Shepherd, a trustee of the National Gallery of Canada and president of the Art Association of Montreal.

1. Loaned by Dr. Francis Shepherd to Montreal 1925, no. 101.
2. Included in the *Memorial Exhibition: Paintings and Bronzes from the Collection of the late Francis J. Shepherd*, Art Association of Montreal, 1929, no. 47.
3. Advertisement in *The Gazette* (Montreal), 31 March 1945 (clipping in artist's file, Library, Montreal Museum of Fine Arts).
4. Loaned by Lucille Gagnon, widow of the painter Clarence Gagnon, to the exhibition *James Wilson Morrice 1865–1924* (Johnston 1965), no. 33.
5. Laing 1984, p. 62.
6. For a photograph of the same view, see Dorais 1978, p. 25.
7. Paris–Venice Sketchbook (National Gallery of Canada, 7419), p. 62r. This sketchbook dates from about 1901.

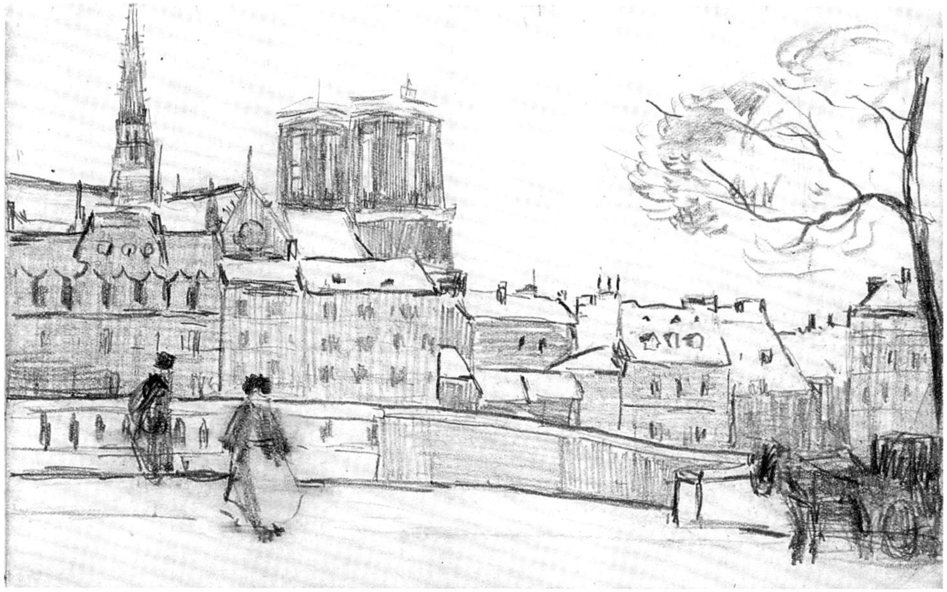

Fig. 36a
Paris–Venice Sketchbook, p. 12r, c. 1901, graphite on wove paper, 11.4 × 17.2 cm.
National Gallery of Canada (7419).

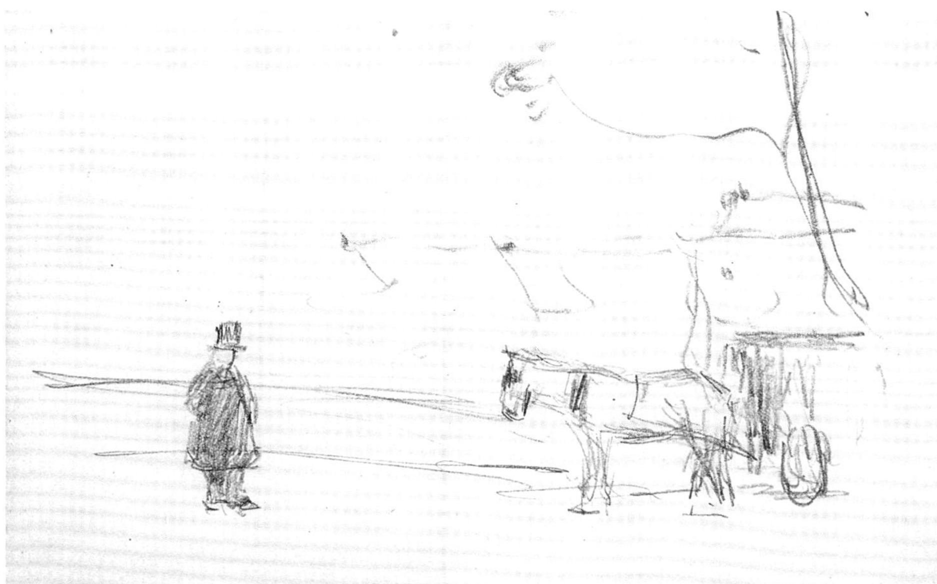

Fig. 36b
Paris–Venice Sketchbook, p. 11r, c. 1901, graphite on wove paper, 11.4 × 17.2 cm.
National Gallery of Canada (7419).

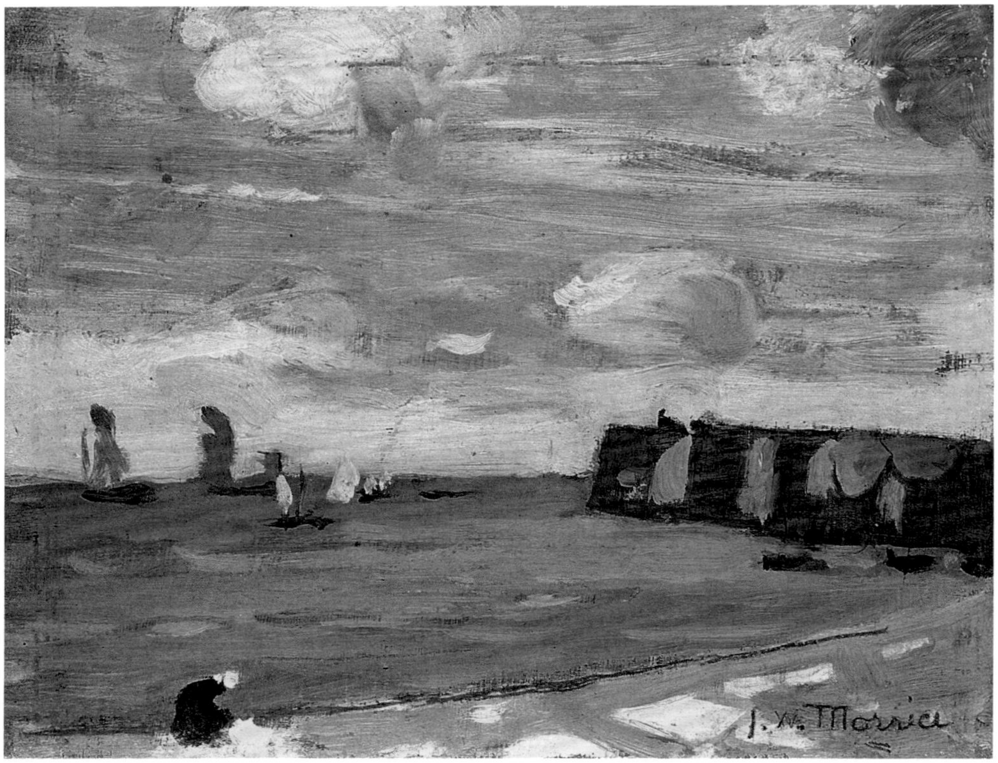

37

Harbour Entrance

c. 1902–04

Oil on wood, 12.2 × 15.2 cm

Inscriptions: signed l.r., *J.W. Morrice*

Labels: in blue ballpoint pen, *G.B.L / A BRITTANY / PORT*

Provenance: Percyval Tudor-Hart, Sillery, Quebec; Mrs. Percyval Tudor-Hart, Sillery, Quebec (sold, Jacoby's House of Antiques Co. Ltd., Montreal, 2 May 1974, lot 75). G. Blair Laing, Toronto, 1974.

30471

Morrice's many travels are difficult to trace. On the spur of the moment, without even telling Léa, he might leave his Paris studio to sketch in Brittany or Normandy or any other spot his fancy took him. His sketchbooks contain notes of train schedules for various destinations. In one sketchbook we find views of Dieppe, Paramé, Mers, Venice, Quebec City, and Montreal. It is in this same book that we find a number of studies related to this oil sketch – drawings of sails and clouds, of women laying out their wash on the beach, and of sails drying on a pier (see figs. 37a and 37b).

In the oil sketch, the clouds skitter across the sky, the sails mark the horizon, and the pier and curving beach establish the foreground where the stooped woman lays out her sheets. The shoreline is defined by the bare wood, which also provides the dominant tone of the pier, drawn in black with white and blue sails.

This sketch was formerly in the collection of Mrs. Percyval Tudor-Hart, widow of the Quebec painter whose work was praised with that of Morrice at the 1899 Paris Salon.[1]

1. R. Booyer, "Un Salonnier aux Salons de 1899," *L'artiste: Journal de la littérature et des beaux-arts*, n.s., vol. 2 (April–June 1899), pp. 117, 141–45. See also Alasdair Alpin MacGregor, *Percyval Tudor-Hart, 1873–1954: Portrait of an Artist* (London: P.R. Macmillan Ltd., 1961), p. 235.

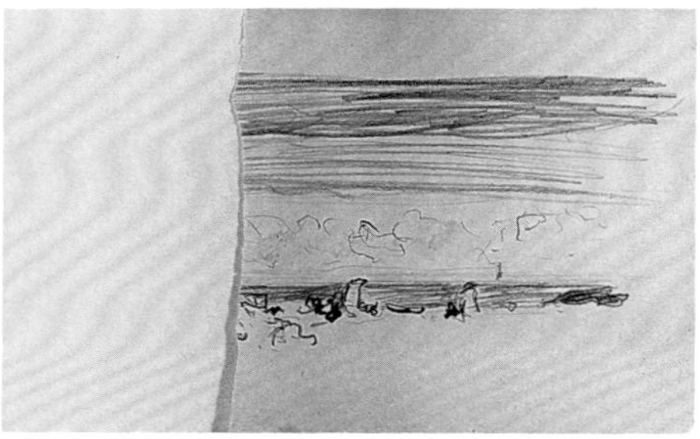

Fig. 37a
Sketchbook 16, p. 44r, c. 1902–06, graphite on wove paper, sheet 10.6 × 16.7 cm (torn). Montreal Museum of Fine Arts. Gift of David R. Morrice, 1973 (Dr.1973.39).

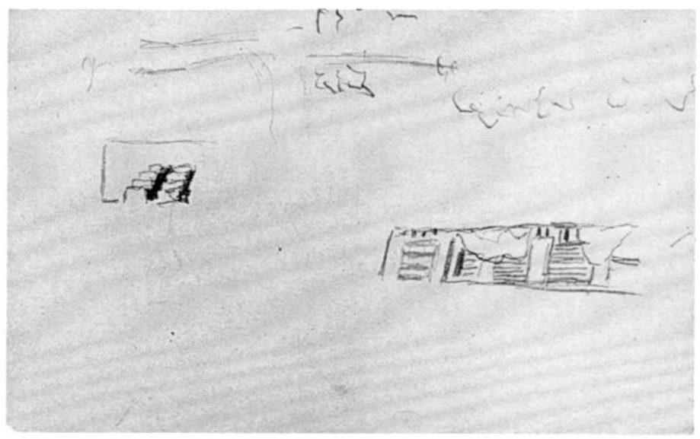

Fig. 37b
Sketchbook 16, p. 40r, c. 1902–06, graphite on wove paper, 10.6 × 16.7 cm. Montreal Museum of Fine Arts. Gift of David R. Morrice, 1973 (Dr.1973.39).

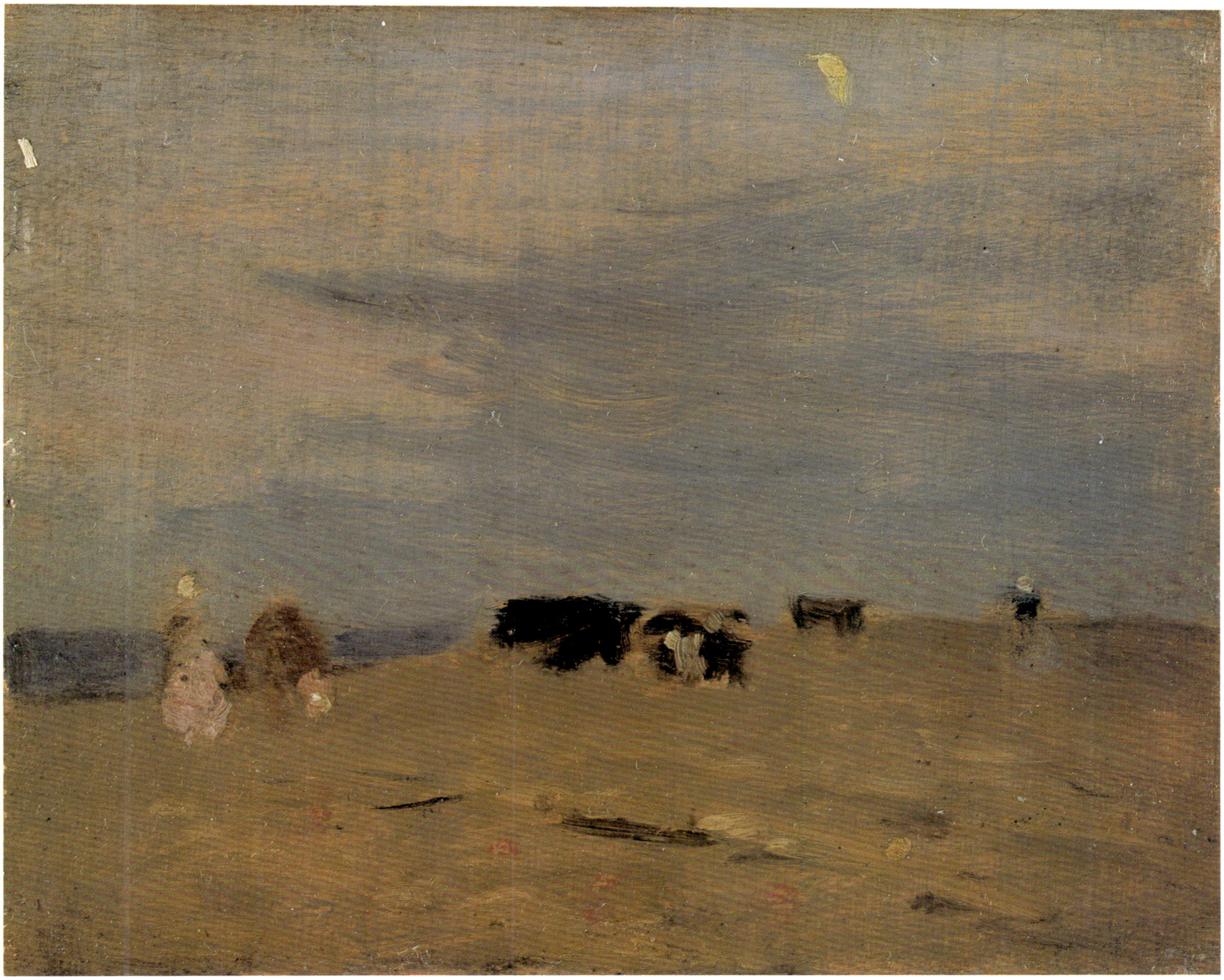

38

Pastorale, Brittany

c. 1902–04

Oil on wood, 12.2 × 15 cm

Inscriptions: verso: c.l. in graphite, *85.00*, c. stamped, *STUDIO / J.W. MORRICE*, in stamp in graphite, *322*, l.c. stamped, *ESTATE / F.R. HEATON*, b. in black ink (Joseph Shima's hand), *Pastorale – Brittany*

Labels: partly torn, CONTINENTAL GALLERIES / OF FINE ART / [—]mond St. MONTREAL. Tel. PLa[—]

Provenance: Estate of the artist; F.R. Heaton, Montreal; Continental Galleries of Fine Art, Montreal; Lawrence T. Porter, St. Andrews East, Quebec; G. Blair Laing, Toronto, c. 1980.

3048C

A young child herds cows in a field overlooking a body of water, her pink dress contrasting with the subtle browns of the hill dotted with touches of red. The sky is composed of pink, mauve, and blue rubbed gently onto the wood, and the clouds sweep by revealing a crescent moon above.

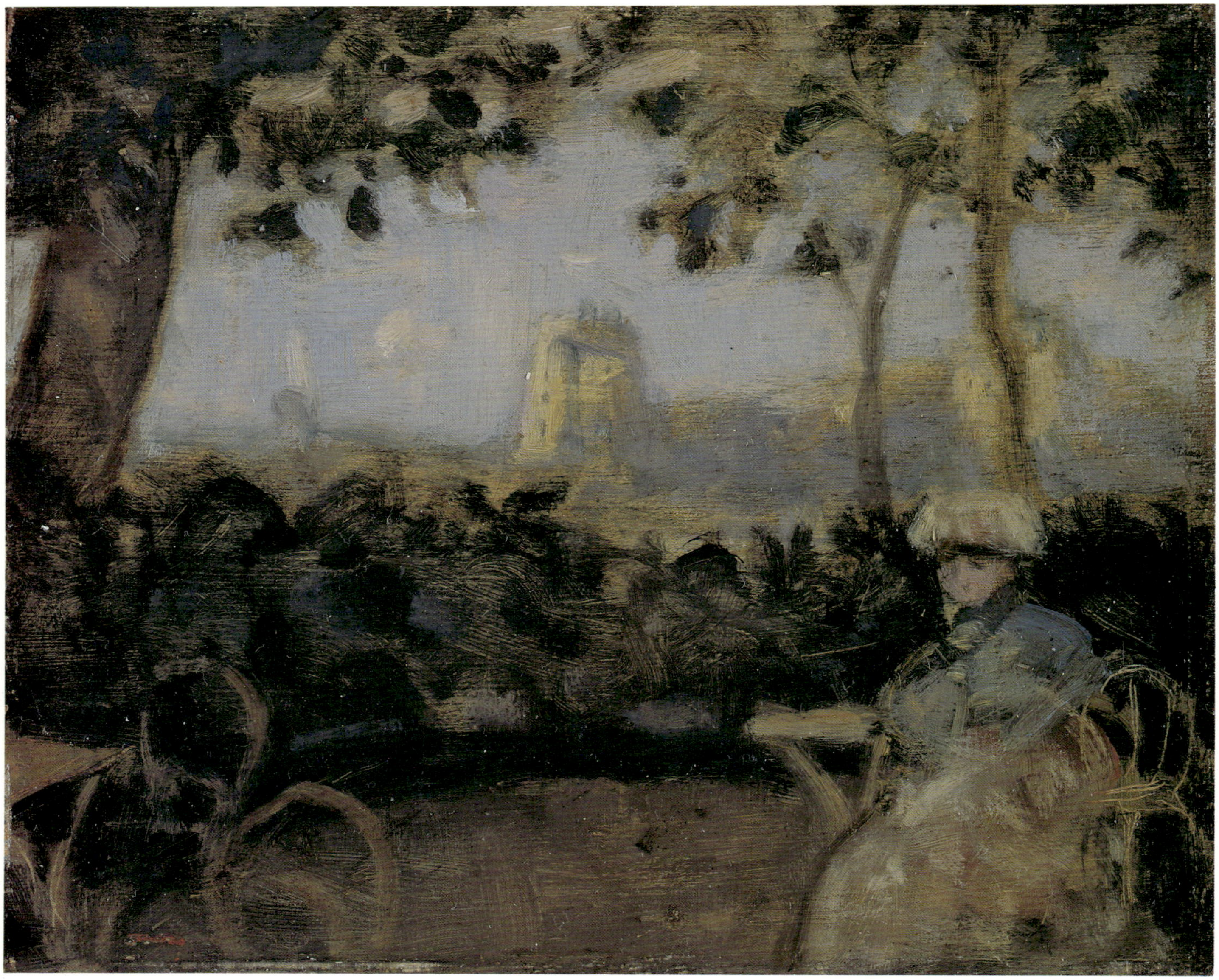

39

Le Bosquet

c. 1903–04

Oil on wood, 12.4 × 15.1 cm

Inscriptions: verso: t. in graphite (artist's hand), *Morrice / 45 Quai des G*[ds] *Augustins / Chez M Guichardaz / 29 rue du Dragon*, l.l. in graphite (artist's hand), *le Bosquet*, l.l. in graphite, *38*, l.r. in graphite, *218* / [—], c. stamped, *STUDIO / J.W. MORRICE*, u.r. in graphite, *#7204*, in graphite, *6 × 4⅞*

Labels: in blue ink, *CAFE PARIS / 86-10*

Provenance: Estate of the artist. Walter Klinkhoff Gallery, Montreal; private collection, Town of Mount Royal, Quebec (sold, Fraser Bros., Montreal, 23 October 1986, lot 77); G. Blair Laing Ltd., Toronto, 1986.

30434

This delicate little sketch depicts a woman seated at an outdoor café that is surrounded by shrubbery. Leafy trees create a canopy over her and frame a view of distant apartment buildings and a pinky-mauve sky. The woman's dress is brushed with a transparent white over the red skirt and blue blouse, and at the extreme right Morrice has scratched in a phantom round-backed chair. The tree trunks are outlined in a darker brown and the foliage is dabbed in lightly over a thinly rubbed green.

"Le Bosquet" ("The Grove"), the title inscribed by the artist on the back of the panel, may possibly be the name of the outdoor café. A drawing of this same café (fig. 39a) can be found in the sketchbook in which Morrice drew a study for his 1904 Salon canvas *En pleine mer*,[1] confirming a date of about 1903–04. In the oil sketch Morrice further develops the transparency of the foliage already suggested in *At Charenton* (cat. no. 34) and *Notre-Dame, Paris* (cat. no. 36), producing a diaphanous study of filtered light. This same interest in refined and delicate colour effects is seen in his 1901 canvas *Le Pont Royal* (fig. 39b),[2] as well as in his 1904 Salon canvas *Le Quai des Grands-Augustins*,[3] purchased by the French government that year.

It is not certain in which city Morrice painted this sylvan café. At the back of the sketchbook in which he did the first drawing he has noted train schedules from Paris to London, Hamburg, St-Malo, Boulogne, and Rennes. Might this lovely spot be in one of those cities?

César Guichardaz, whose name and address on the Rue du Dragon in Paris are inscribed on the back of the panel, was Morrice's supplier of paints, brushes, and canvas for many years.[4]

1. See Cloutier 1985, p. 145.
2. *Le Pont Royal* was shown at the third exhibition of the International Society of Sculptors, Painters and Gravers in London, 7 October–10 December 1901, no. 115 (repr.). This painting was formerly in the collection of Jacques Rouché (Buchanan 1936a, p. 162, as *Sur les Quais*).
3. See Cloutier 1985, pp. 164–65.
4. Guichardaz's name and address first appear in Sketchbook 1 (Montreal Museum of Fine Arts, Dr.1973.24, back endpaper, verso), which is datable to about 1901–03. See letter from Morrice to Edmund Morris, 30 December [1910], Morris Papers.

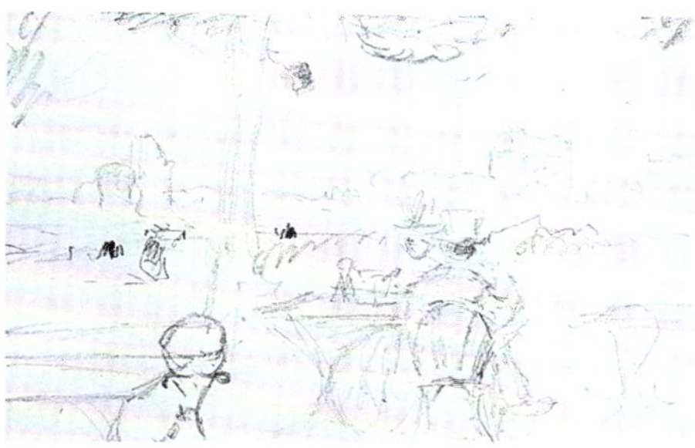

Fig. 39a
Sketchbook 5, p. 22r, c. 1903–04, graphite on wove paper, 10.5 × 16.7 cm. Montreal Museum of Fine Arts. Gift of David R. Morrice, 1973 (Dr.1973.28).

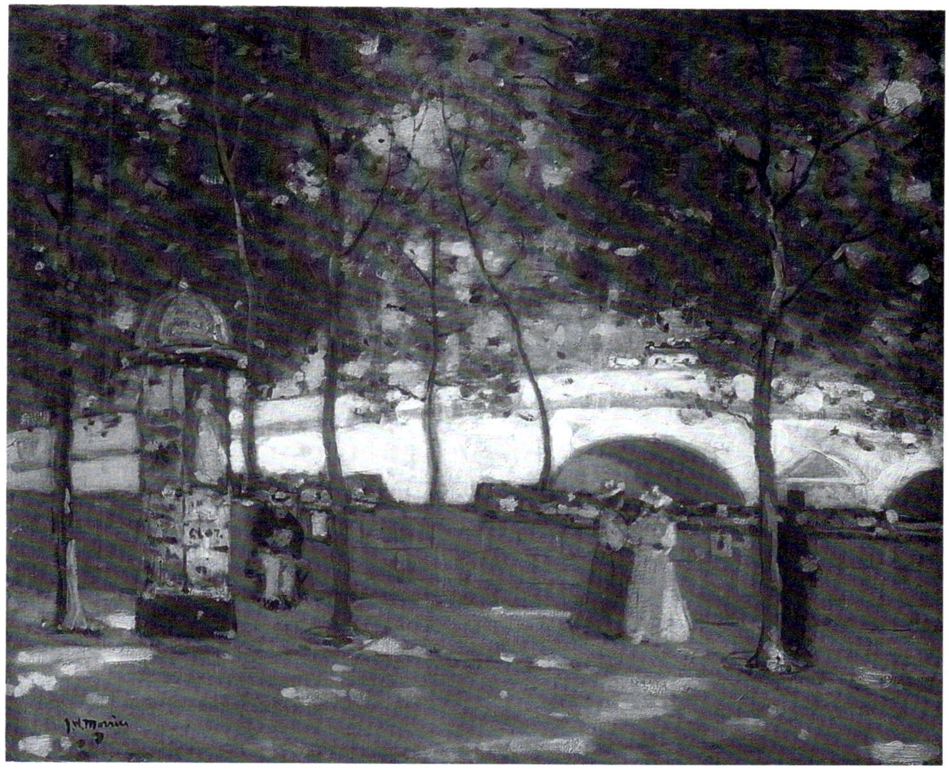

Fig. 39b
Pont Royal, 1901, oil on canvas, 58.4 × 71.1 cm. Private collection. Photograph by E. Creveux, Paris.

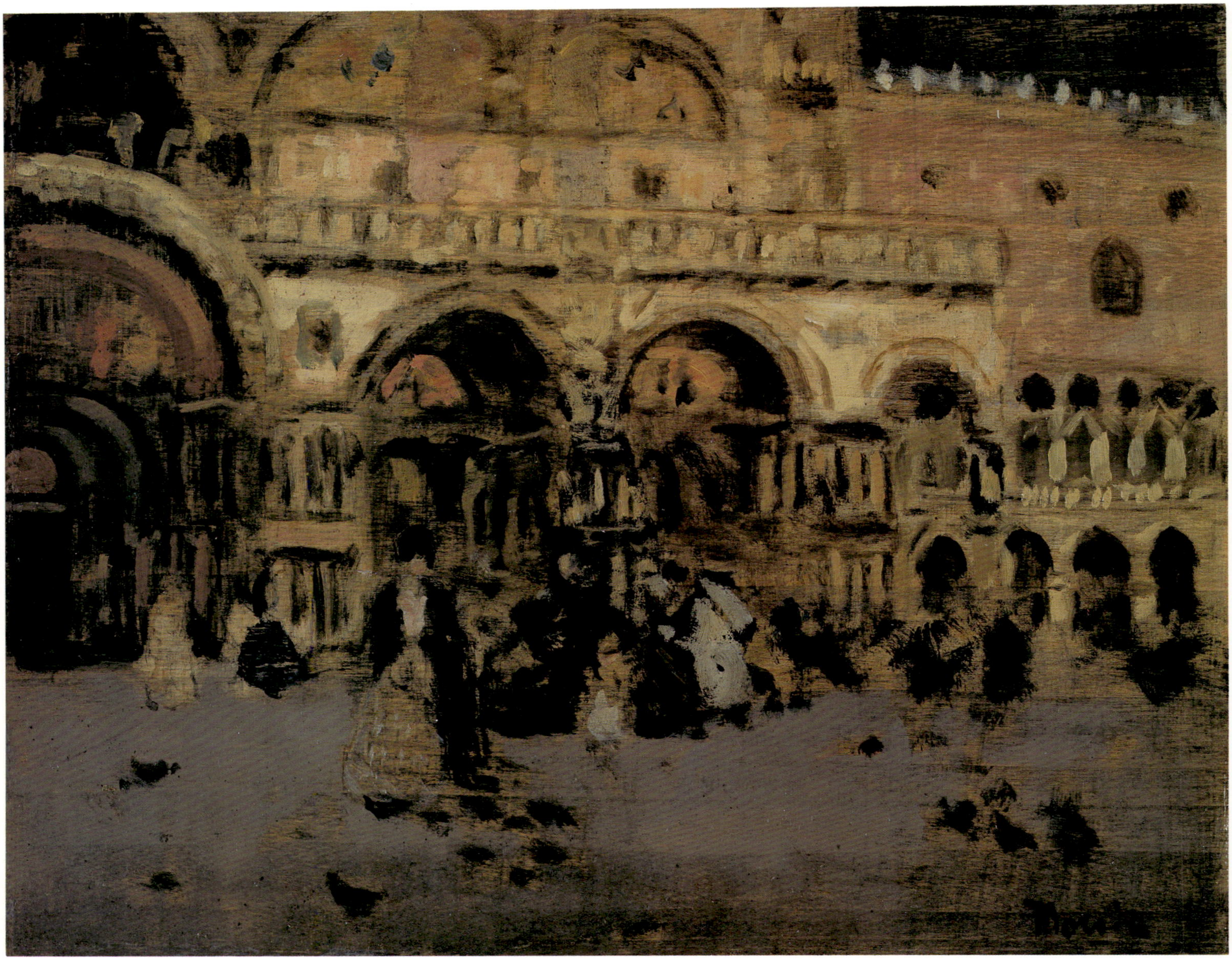

40

San Marco Square, Venice

c. 1902–04

Oil and graphite on wood, 25.6 × 33.1 cm

Inscriptions: signed l.r., *Morrice*

Labels: in blue ballpoint pen, *San Marco / Sq. / 81-38*

Provenance: (Sold, Sotheby Parke Bernet [Canada] Inc., Toronto, 10 November 1981, lot 20); G. Blair Laing Ltd., Toronto, 1981.

30424

Of Morrice's studies of the facade of San Marco in Venice, this large panel is certainly one of the richest and most subtle. The paint is rubbed onto the wood, creating glowing bands of rich blue-grey in the foreground, pink and cream in the building, and deep blue in the sky at the upper right. The grouping of the figures, including as usual a single isolated woman facing the viewer, forms a V in front of the facade, while touches of colour representing birds break up the remainder of the foreground. As David McTavish has noted, Morrice overpainted the flagpole that is situated in front of San Marco, retaining only the base, around which he groups several figures.[1]

The facade of San Marco was a subject Morrice treated on many occasions.[2] In one sketch (fig. 40a), on a panel just about the same size as this one, he has included the mosaics above the central portal, his bright daubs of colour creating a mosaic effect in themselves.[3] In his 1901 Venice sketchbook he listed the many churches in which he could see the paintings of Tintoretto.[4] Undoubtedly it was the art and architecture of Venice itself that did so much to enrich the colour and subtlety of Morrice's palette.

1. McTavish 1984, p. 41, no. 27.
2. Other oil sketches of the facade of San Marco are in the Montreal Museum of Fine Arts (1981.69), the Samuel E. Weir Collection and Library of Art, Queenston, Ontario (982.59), and the Winnipeg Art Gallery (G-79-2).
3. The work had been purchased by Blair Laing from Georges Manoury in Paris (Laing 1984, p. 214). Manoury had arranged for the collection and shipping of the French paintings for the 1937 Morrice exhibition. He wrote at the time: "I knew [Morrice] very well and love his works" (letter from Manoury to H.O. McCurry, 18 August 1937, Archives, National Gallery of Canada, file 5.5–Morrice 1937).
4. Paris–Venice Sketchbook (National Gallery of Canada, 7419), p. 60v. See also Dorais 1978, p. 28.

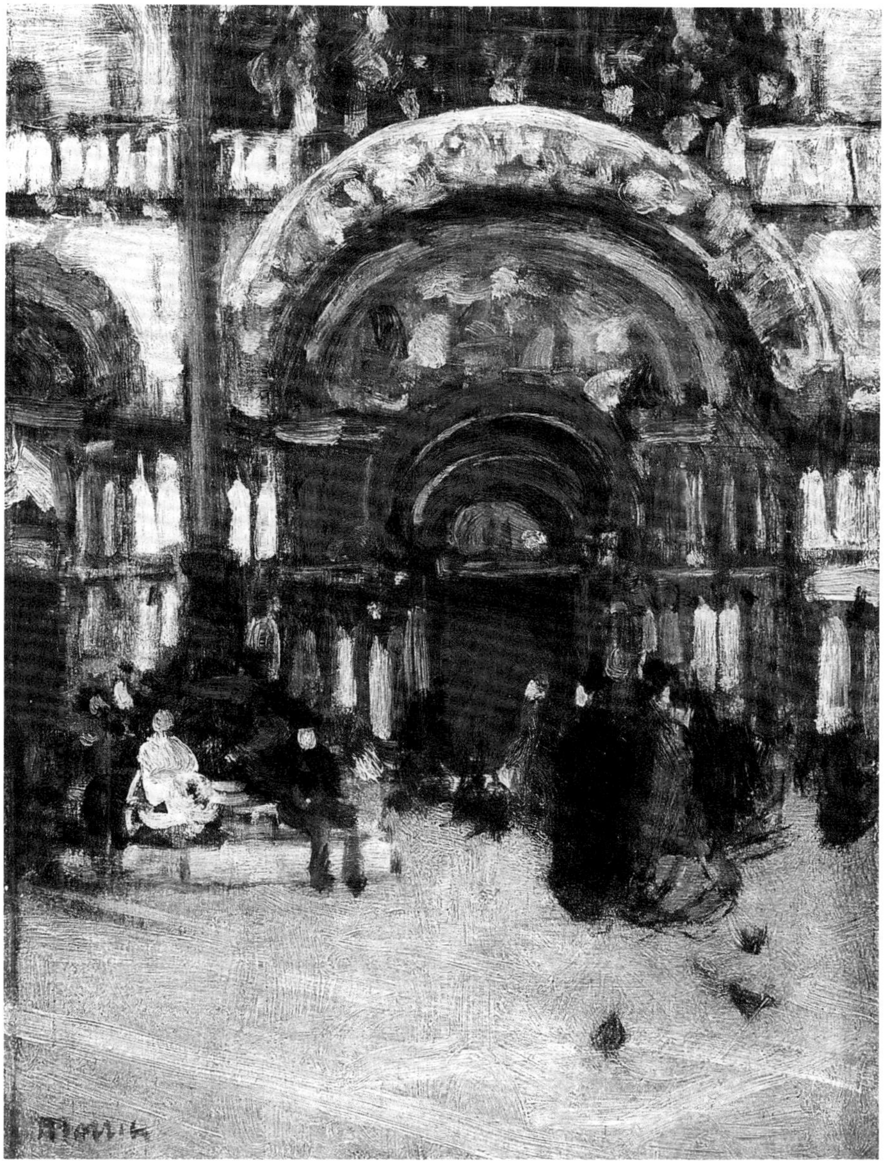

Fig. 40a
Le Porche de l'église San Marco, c. 1902–04, oil on wood, 33.6 × 24.7 cm. Art Gallery of Hamilton. H.L. Rinn Bequest, 1956 (56.86.L).

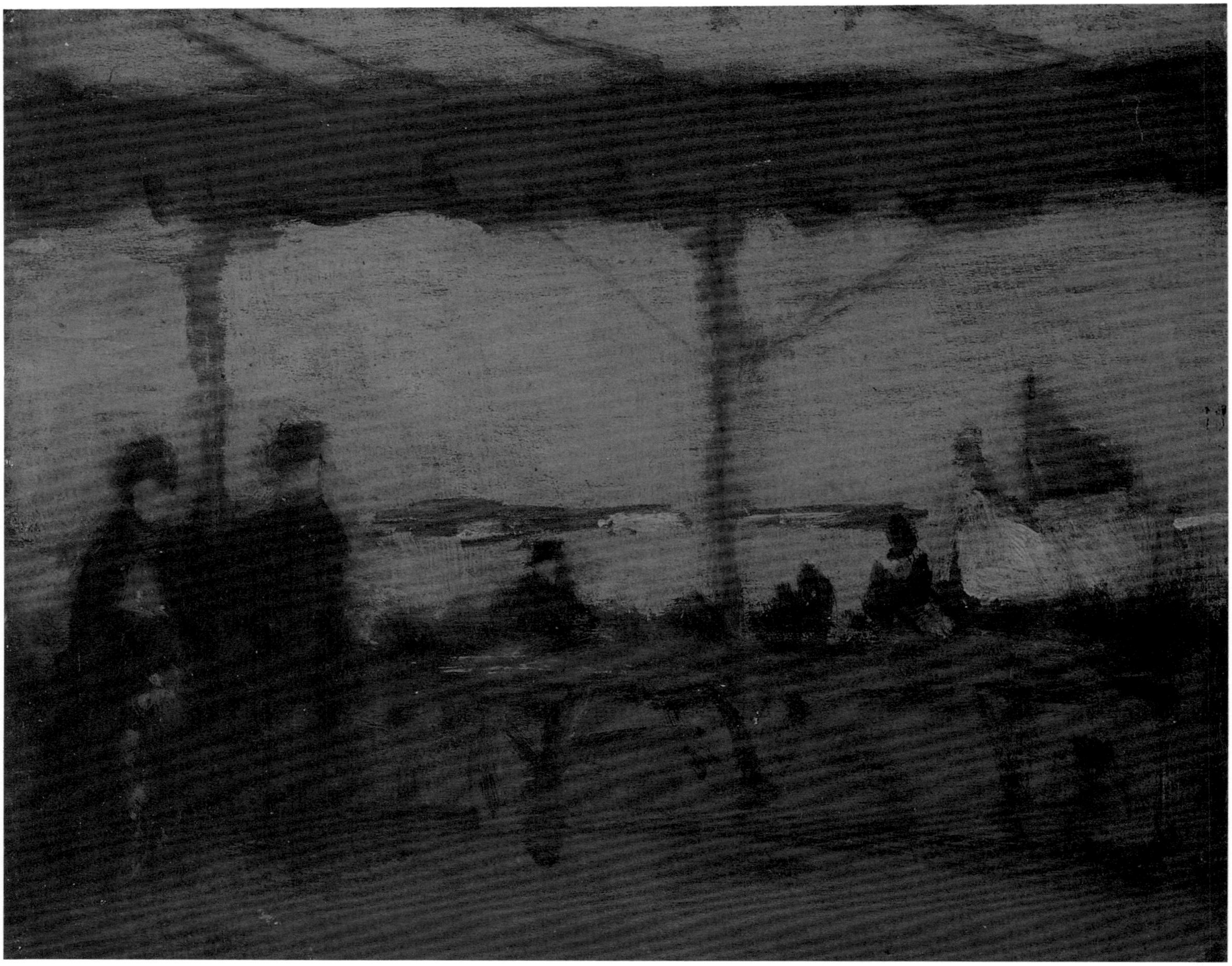

41

Study for "Venice, Looking out over the Lagoon"

c. 1902–04

Oil and graphite on wood, 12.3 × 15.3 cm

Inscriptions: verso: c. stamped, *STUDIO / J.W. MORRICE*

Labels: in blue ballpoint pen, *VENICE LOOKING / OUT OVER THE / LAGOON*

Provenance: Private collection, Montreal; G. Blair Laing, Toronto, 1969.

30458

In this oil study for the canvas in the Montreal Museum of Fine Arts (fig. 41a), Morrice has arranged the composition in horizontal bands divided into three vertical units. The drawing of the tables and figures is loose and summary, the dominant colours rubbed onto the wood. The main verticals and horizontals were painted first, after which he brushed in the sky and then in graphite added diagonal supports for the canopy.

One of the women at the left looks out at the viewer while the other gazes at the yellow and red sails. The soft pale-blue of the water and the muted pink-mauve glow of the sky are separated by a few yellow strokes and bare wood. All the final elements are merely hinted at, but the dominant colour relationships and the mood are already defined.

In the canvas the overall tonality is lighter, and the sky is pink, daubed with yellow and turquoise to create a glowing surface. The awning, reddish brown in the sketch, is now green and pink. At the right Morrice has added a seated figure reading a newspaper and a charming still life in green, red, and brown.

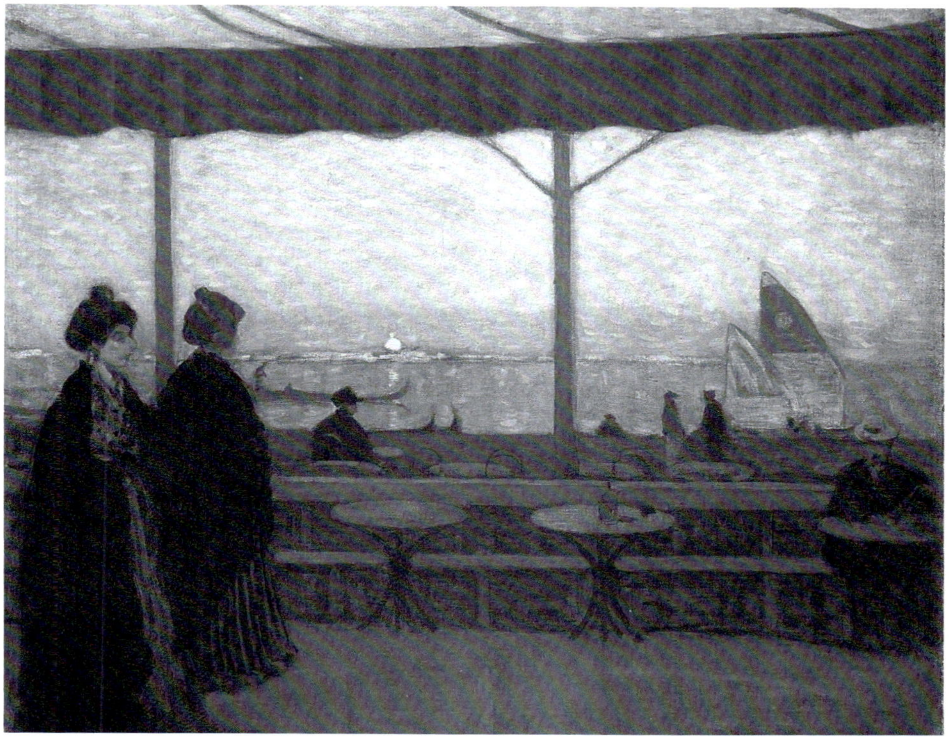

Fig. 41a
Venice, Looking out over the Lagoon, c. 1904, oil on canvas, 60.6 × 73.9 cm. Montreal Museum of Fine Arts. Gift of the artist's estate, 1925 (925.334).

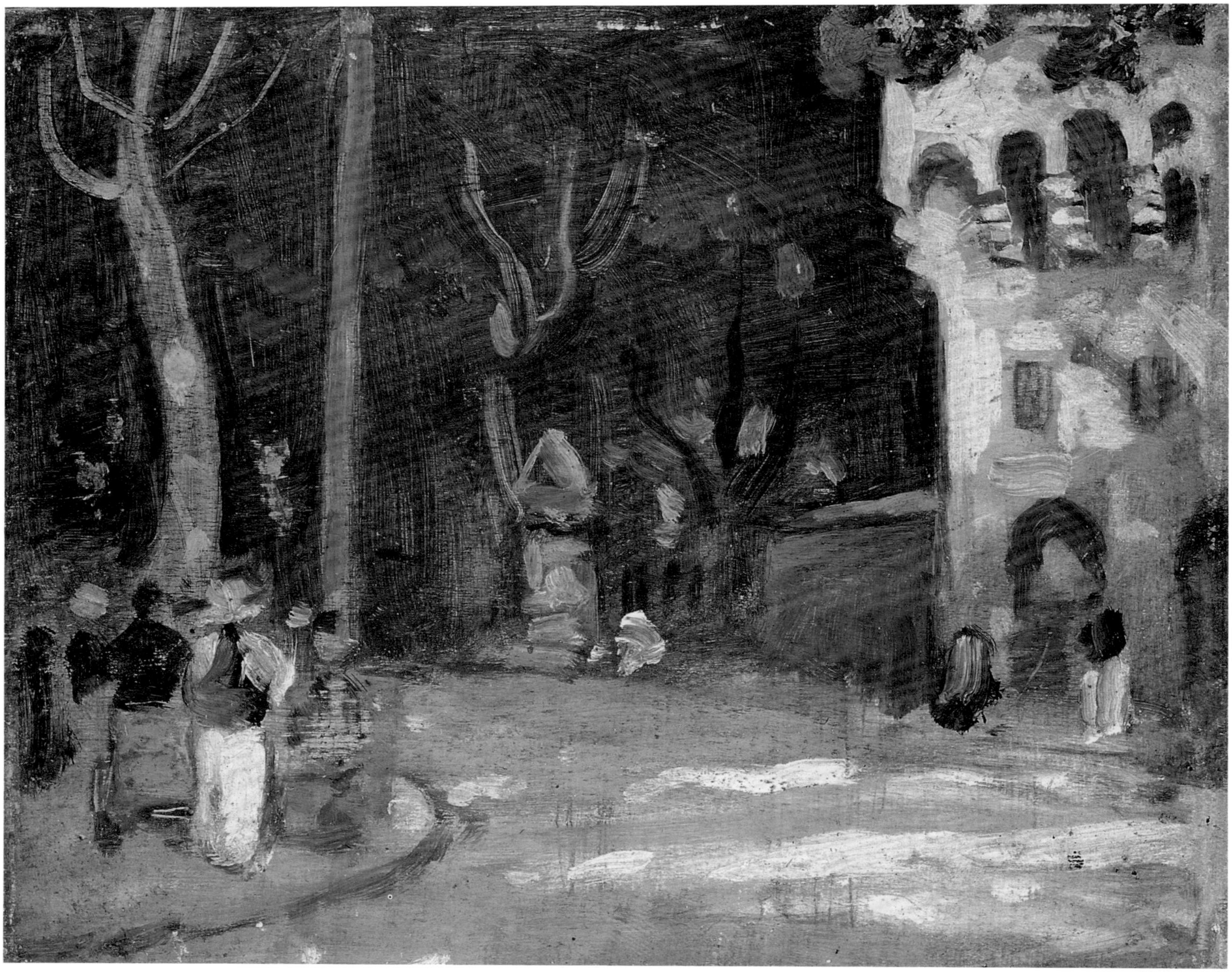

42

Street in Marseilles

1904

Oil and graphite on wood, 12.5 × 15.3 cm

Inscriptions: verso: c. stamped, *STUDIO / J.W. MORRICE*

Labels: typed, Laing Galleries 194 Bloor Street West Toronto 5 Canada / *"PARIS STREET" C. 1905 / By / J.W. MORRICE*; in blue ballpoint pen, *PARIS / STREET / 86-9*

Provenance: Estate of the artist. Mrs. Percyval Tudor-Hart, Sillery, Quebec (sold, Jacoby's House of Antiques Co. Ltd., Montreal, 2 May 1974, lot 76). G. Blair Laing Ltd., Toronto; private collection, Town of Mount Royal, Quebec (sold, Fraser Bros., Montreal, 23 October 1986, lot 34); G. Blair Laing Ltd., Toronto, 1986.

30433

In 1904 Morrice travelled to Avignon, Martigues, Marseilles, and Venice.[1] Among the visual records of the trip is a drawing (fig. 42a) of the unidentified building in this oil sketch – almost certainly a scene in Marseilles.

The foliage here is painted in the same rich greens evident in *Study for "Bullring, Marseilles"* (cat. no. 43). The open mauve-grey foreground is crossed with bands of light, while the pole and curving tree echo the form of the building's facade. The figures, standing still, look away from the viewer.

1. Letter from Morrice (in Avignon) to Joseph Pennell, 9 July 1904, Pennell Papers; letter from Morrice (in Venice) to J.W. Beatty, Carnegie Institute, Pittsburgh, 14 August [1904], Carnegie Institute Papers, Archives of American Art, Washington, D.C., microfilm 8, letter 50851.

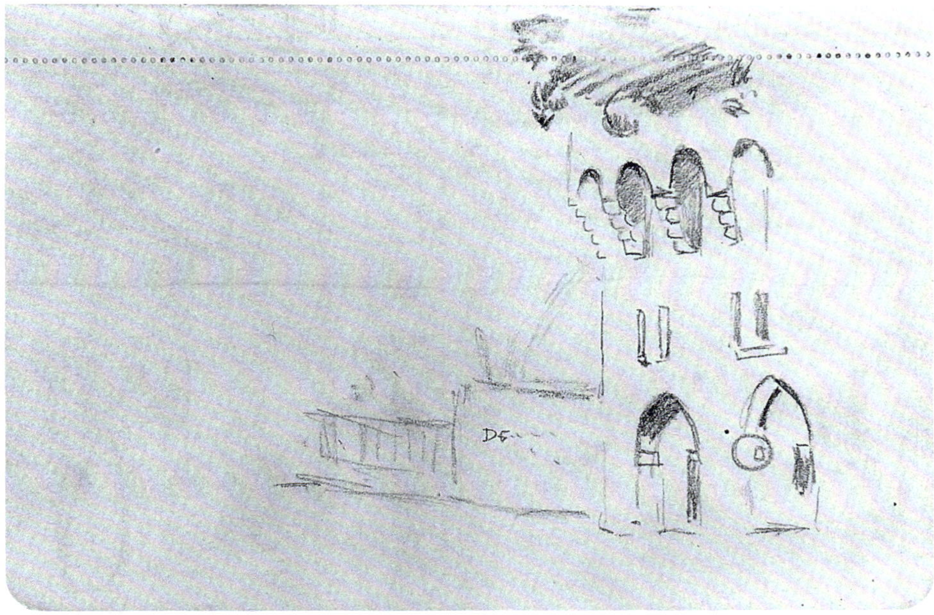

Fig. 42a
Sketchbook 18, p. 8r, 1904, graphite on wove paper, 11.5 × 17.3 cm. Montreal Museum of Fine Arts. Gift of David R. Morrice, 1973 (Dr.1973.41).

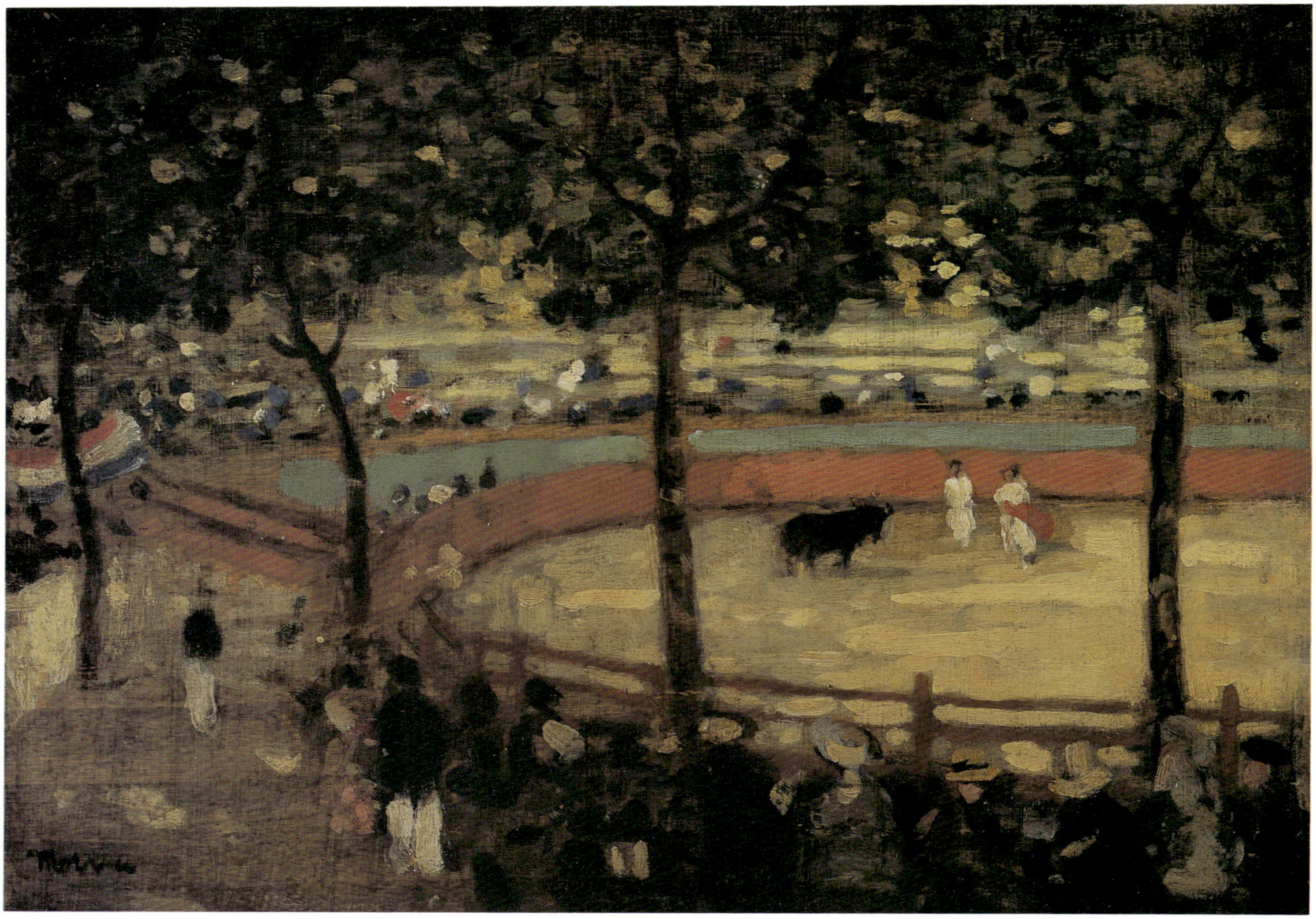

43

Study for "Bullring, Marseilles"

1904

Oil on wood, 23.5 × 32.9 cm

Inscriptions: signed l.r., *Morrice*

Labels: Laing Galleries 194 Bloor Street West Toronto 5 Canada; OKanada, no. 37

Provenance: Charles Pacquement, Paris; Jacques Dubourg, Paris; G. Blair Laing, Toronto, 1973.

30463

In the same sketchbook that Morrice used to delineate the architecture of the building in Marseilles (fig. 42a) there is a graphite sketch (fig. 43a) for this oil sketch, which is, in turn, a study for the well-known canvas *Bullring, Marseilles* (fig. 43b), first exhibited in 1905. In the drawing Morrice has identified all the basic elements: the bullring, the foreground spectators, and the bullfighter and bull. The tree trunks and foliage provide a structure, just as the awning does in *Venice, Looking out over the Lagoon* (see cat. no. 41). In the oil sketch he has eliminated the boy sitting on the wall at the left (replacing him with a standing figure) and has generally defined the lights and darks and the play of light on the sand and tree trunks. The dominant unifying elements are the red and green of the far wall of the bullring, the sandy yellow repeated in the ring and on the wall at the centre left, and the green of the foliage. The French tricolor at the centre left provides a colourful accent. Donald Buchanan's description of Morrice's procedure for the preparation of the canvas is equally applicable to the sketch: "His method now was to brush in small patches of pure colour, then he would take a cloth and rub the colours together until the surface became radiant as a ruby. Finally, here and there, a touch of colour would be added to produce heightened brightness in the details."[1] In the foliage Morrice has rubbed green onto the wood and then added short touches of light and dark green and yellow.

In the canvas Morrice has enlarged the width and depth of the ring. The figures in the foreground, particularly the silhouetted woman at the lower right, are more defined and painted in a greater variety of coloured accents. The tree trunks, outlined and in places reinforced at the edges with scratching, play a more dominant role. As a result of the greater emphasis on the figures and the tree trunks, the focus of attention shifts away from the confrontation in the ring. The paler and more unified colouring reinforces this more distanced and decorative effect.

1. Buchanan 1936a, p. 97.

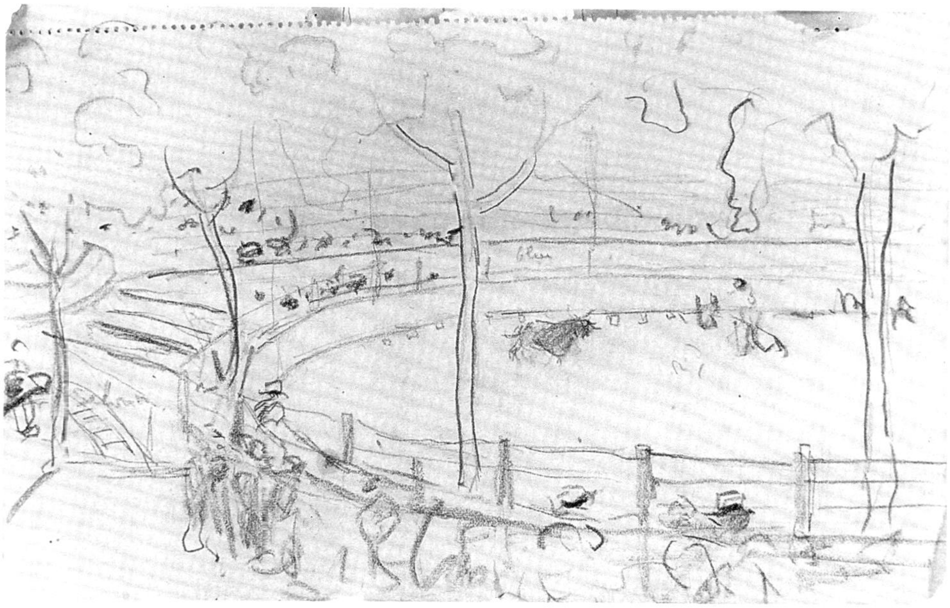

Fig. 43a
Sketchbook 18, p. 15r, 1904, graphite on wove paper, 11.5 × 17.3 cm. Montreal Museum of Fine Arts. Gift of David R. Morrice, 1973 (Dr.1973.41).

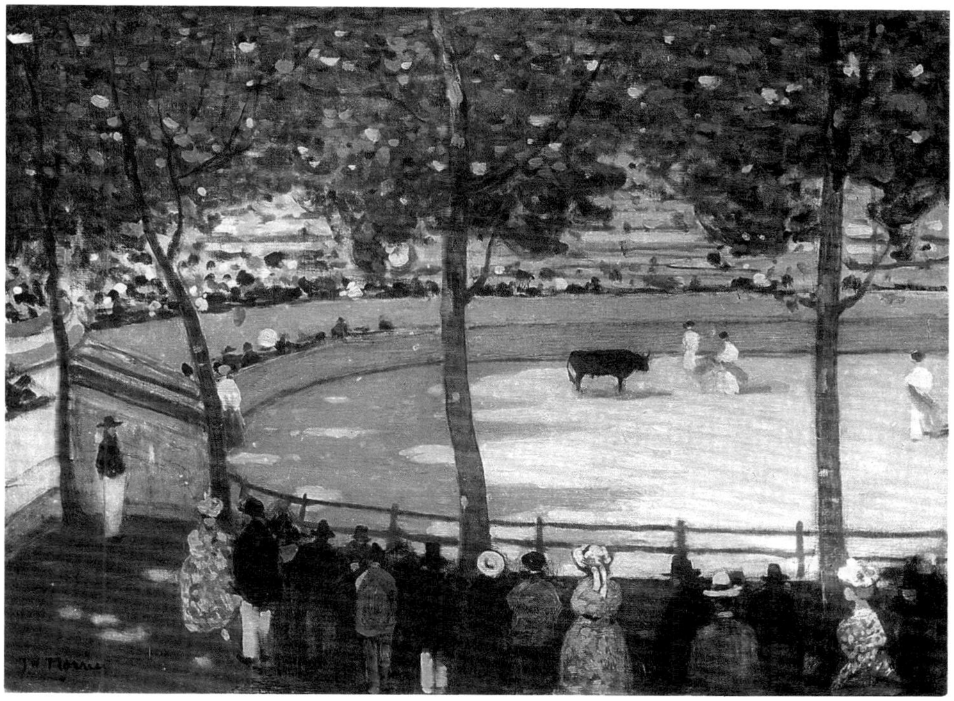

Fig. 43b
Bullring, Marseilles, 1904–05, oil on canvas, 58.4 × 79.3 cm. Private collection. Photograph by E. Crevaux, Paris.

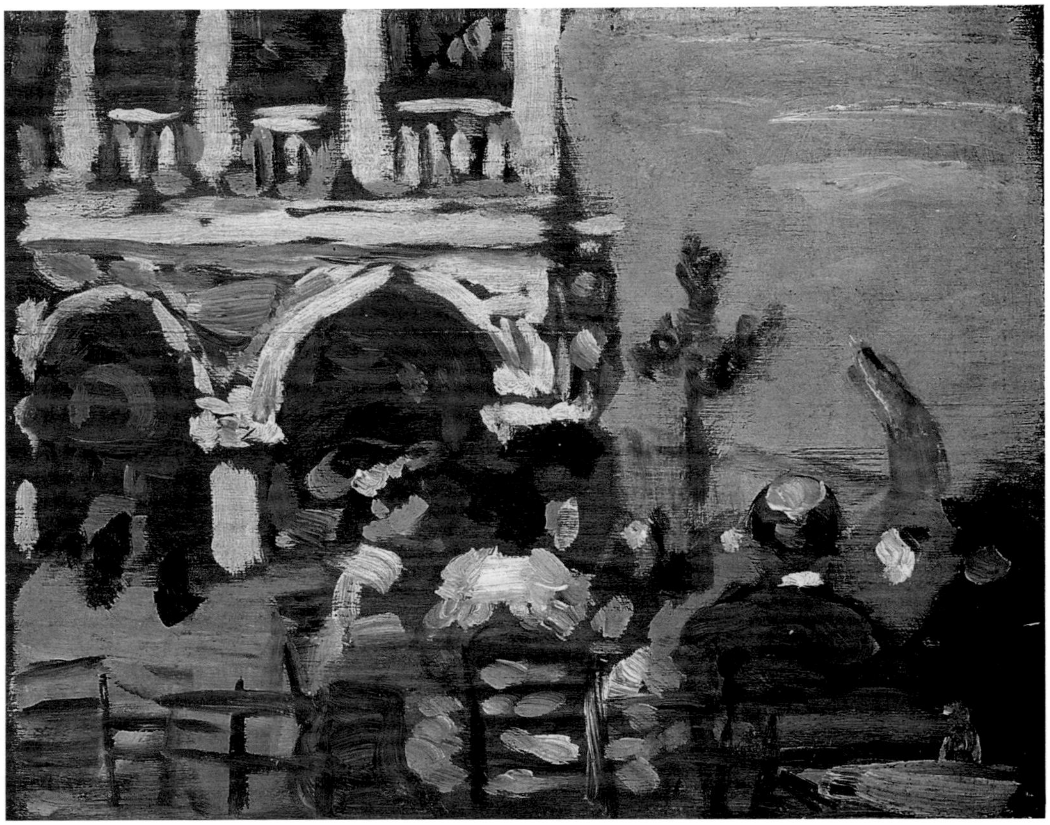

44

Seated Figures, San Marco Square, Venice

1904

Oil on wood, 12.3 × 15.3 cm

Inscriptions: verso: t. in graphite, *Mr Arthur Browning*, u.l. in graphite, *2*, c. stamped, *STUDIO / J.W. MORRICE*

Labels: in blue ballpoint pen, *76-103 / VENICE*; in blue ballpoint pen, *76-103*

Provenance: Estate of the artist. Arthur Browning, Montreal. Walter Klinkhoff Gallery, Montreal. (Sold, Sotheby Parke Bernet [Canada] Ltd., Toronto, 17 May 1976, lot 126); G. Blair Laing Ltd., Toronto, 1976.

30407

After leaving Marseilles Morrice continued on to Venice, and his sketchbook includes several drawings of figures seated in cafés, one of them (fig. 44a) very close to this oil sketch. Morrice must have been seated in the same café from which he sketched his *Doge's Palace* (cat. no. 11), but his approach here differs considerably. Concentrating on the figures and the architecture, he constructs the main forms with a few broad strokes of colour, merely suggesting the less important elements such as the chairs at the lower left or the sailboat passing by in the lagoon.

According to the inscription on the back, this sketch was formerly in the collection of Arthur Browning, one of the members of the exhibition committee of the Art Association of Montreal that organized the 1925 memorial exhibition and an active benefactor of that association until the time of his death in 1957.[1]

1. Annual reports of the Art Association of Montreal / Montreal Museum of Fine Arts, 1925 to 1958.

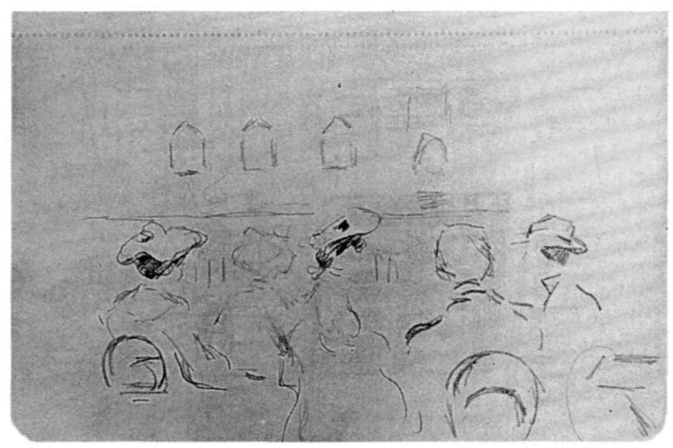

Fig. 44a
Sketchbook 18, p. 76r, 1904, graphite on wove paper, 11.5 × 17.3 cm. Montreal Museum of Fine Arts. Gift of David R. Morrice, 1973 (Dr.1973.41).

45

Church in Brittany

c. 1905–06

Oil on canvas, 51.2 × 62 cm

Inscriptions: signed l.l., *J.W. Morrice*; stretcher: on crossbar, u.c. in black crayon, *Box / 3 / 770* (crossed out) / *766*, c. stamped, *MODÈLE DÉPOSÉ / B*

Provenance: Watson Art Galleries, Montreal; R.S. McLaughlin, Oshawa, 1926;[1] by descent to a member of the McLaughlin family (sold, Sotheby's, Toronto, 8 November 1988, lot 207); G. Blair Laing Ltd., Toronto, 1988.

30439

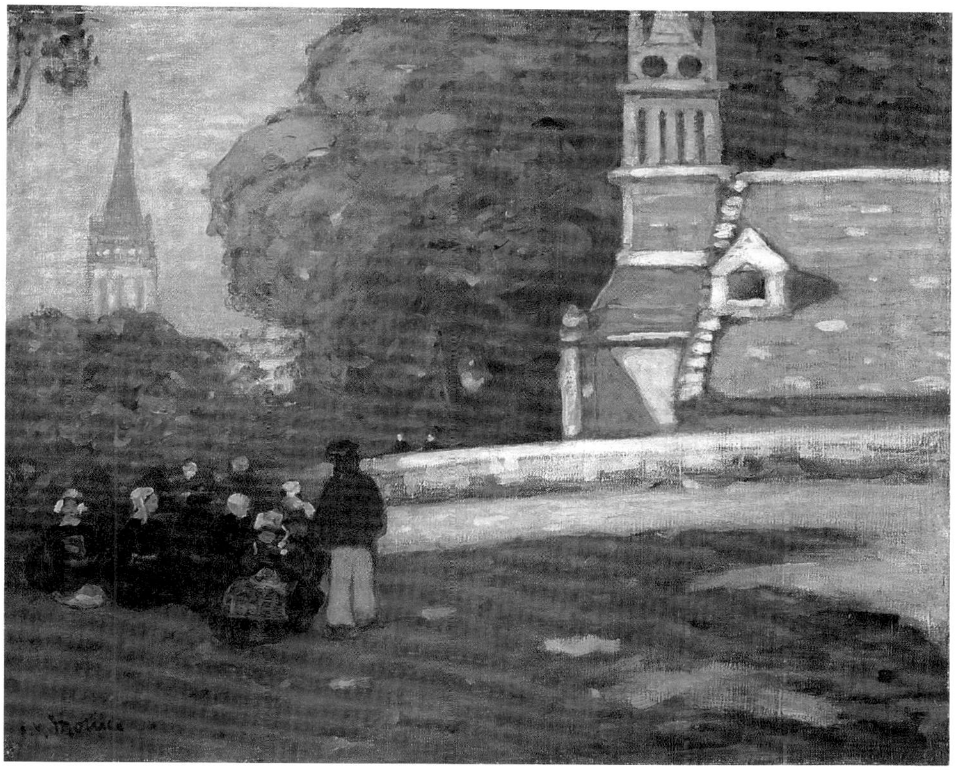

This painting most likely depicts a group of Bretons congregating before or after a procession at a pardon. Its composition recalls above all Dagnan-Bouveret's well-known 1887 Salon canvas *Breton Women at a Pardon*.[2] In that canvas the grouping of women seated on the grass and two men standing, all in local costume, fills the entire foreground. In the background is a church with a pointed spire and additional groupings of figures. In Morrice's canvas the figures are not individualized and are secondary to the landscape setting with its dappled colour and light.

Morrice exhibited two canvases of Breton pardons. At the International Society in London in January 1908 he submitted a canvas titled *A Pardon, Brittany*, which may be the same as that shown with the Canadian Art Club in Toronto and in Montreal in January and March 1910. A second painting, titled *Pardon, Bretagne*, was shown with the Société de Peintres et de Sculpteurs in March 1910.[3] It is possible that this canvas is one of those two works.[4]

There are no known studies for this very structured composition in which the curve of the wall and field play against the horizontals and verticals of the architecture. The decorative massing of the trees, the patterned shadows, and the branch cleverly introduced into the upper-left corner are a gentle foil to the solidity of the architecture and to the massed group of black-robed Bretons. The sky, trees, and shadows are composed of a thin uniform tone brushed with lighter and darker tones, each accent distinct. This treatment recalls Morrice's Venetian and Marseilles canvases of 1904 and 1905 (see figs. 41a and 43b), though the colours are richer and more striking in their contrasts. The churches of yellow stone with lavender and blue roofs remain to be identified.

1. Watson Papers, stock no. 766, sold to R.S. McLaughlin, 3 November 1926, as *In Brittany*.
2. Pascal Adolphe Dagnan-Bouveret (1852–1929), *Breton Women at a Pardon*, 1887, Calouste Gulbenkian Foundation, Lisbon. See Gabriel P. Weisberg, "Vestiges of the Past: The Brittany 'Pardons' of Late Nineteenth-Century French Painters," *Arts Magazine* LV:3 (November 1980), p. 137 (repr.).
3. Galerie Georges Petit, Paris, 1910, *Exposition de Peintres et de Sculpteurs*, no. 104. The month is confirmed by a letter from Morrice to Edmund Morris, 20 March 1910, Morris Papers.
4. Buchanan (1936a, p. 166) catalogues a work titled *Breton Pardon* in the collection of Mrs. Thaxter Shaw, Montreal, which differs from *Church in Brittany* and which he says was that exhibited at the International Society in 1908.

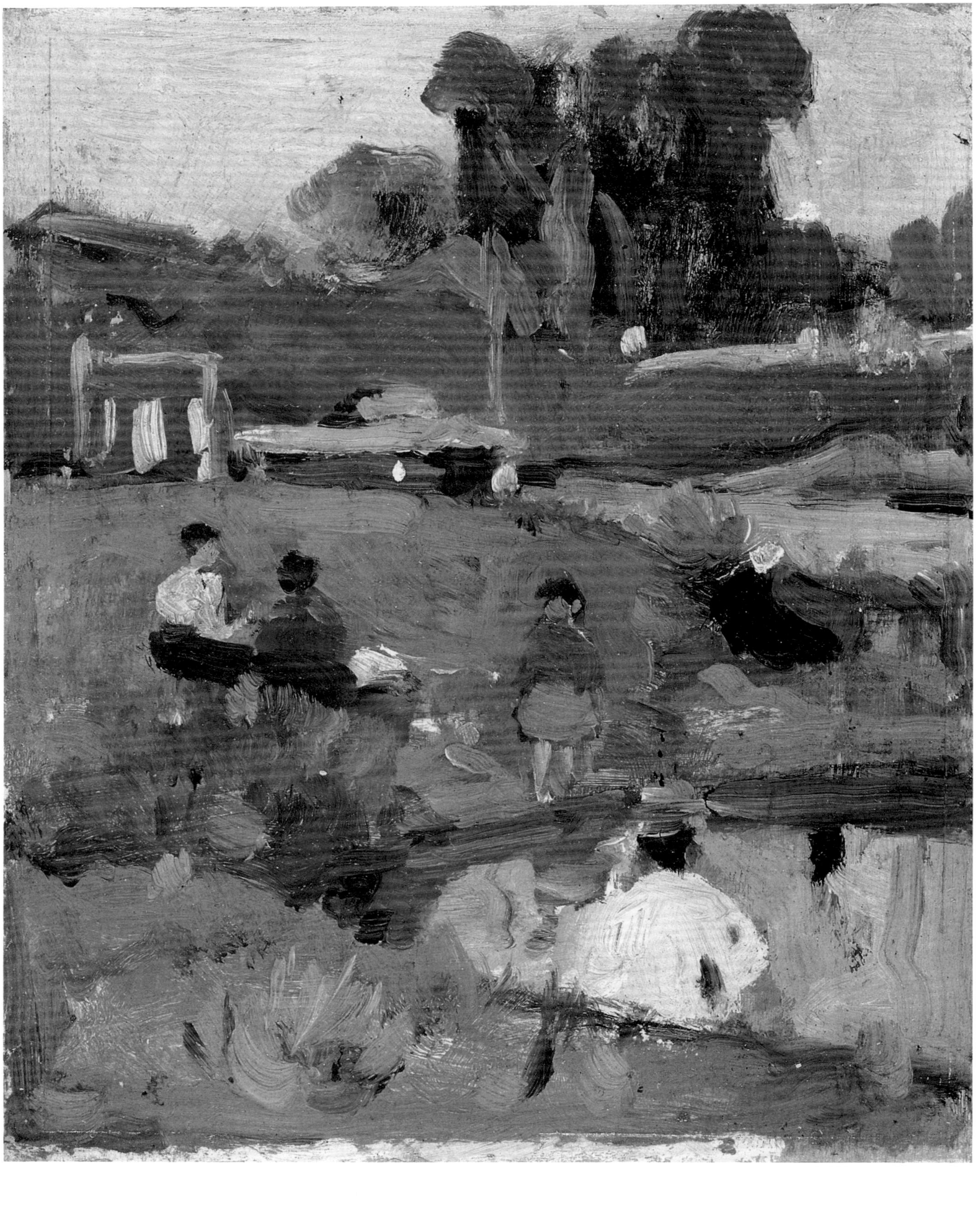

46

Study for "At a Country Fair"

c. 1905–07

Oil on wood, 15.5 × 12.8 cm

Inscriptions: back of frame: u.l. in graphite, *NIC*[HOLS]*ON / N° 2*

Labels: partly torn newspaper clipping, in graphite, *T*[ruth]; in graphite, *19*; typed, *G. Blair Laing, / Toronto, Ontario. / "Paris Park"*, in graphite, *8 / #36*; MMFA 1965, no. 43; in blue ballpoint pen, *G.B.L. / IN A PARIS / PARK / 3*

Provenance: Private collection, England(?); John Nicholson, London and New York; G. Blair Laing, Toronto, c. 1952–56.[1]

30442

This work was acquired by Blair Laing from John Nicholson and was probably, at one time, in the same collection as *Fishing Boats* (cat. no. 7). Pasted on the back of the panel is a clipping from the 23 November 1905 edition of the London newspaper *Truth* containing a review of the 1905 Salon d'Automne. The reviewer writes: "A young Canadian painter, Mr. Morrice is among the exhibitors. I like his work extremely. Look at his small picture – the size of your hand – of a nurse in a Paris park with these little dotties – blue, red, and white – playing in front of her." Of the works listed in the exhibition, only *Les Tuileries, Étude* might correspond to the picture described in the review. Yet this hilly park with its natural pond is definitely not the formal gardens of the Tuileries adjacent to the Louvre;[2] Donald Buchanan has suggested that it may be Clamart, near the Bois de Meudon, southwest of Paris.[3] As with *Fishing Boats*, we may surmise that the review is not of this particular work but testifies to a previous owner's admiration for comparable works by Morrice.

In this sketch a man in a white jacket and straw-coloured hat sits by the side of the pond with his back to us. A young child in a blue shirt and pink skirt stands on the opposite side. Sitting on the grass to her right is a figure all in black, and to her left are two women in black skirts, one wearing a white blouse and the other a red blouse. Behind them is a sketchily defined structure with a red flag flying from the right side.

In a closely related sketch (fig. 46a), the figures are more dominant and houses are defined at the upper right. The trees on the hillside are more massive and extend to the top of the panel, accentuating the verticality of the composition, and the rhythm of the receding diagonals is more clearly articulated.

In the canvas (fig. 46b), which more closely approximates the second sketch, the man in the foreground has been removed (probably after first having been included, as a faint "shadow" remains). The composition is based on curving diagonals that lead the eye back and forth across the canvas, but it is also vertically anchored by the rising trees and by the young girl standing just off centre.[4] The rich colours applied with a fluid brush in the sketches are translated in the canvas into lovely glowing hues, especially in the yellow sky touched with pink and blue.

1. See cat. no. 7, n. 1.
2. My thanks to Lucie Dorais for correcting my initial error in the cataloguing of this work.
3. Donald Buchanan catalogue of paintings by J.W. Morrice, Archives, National Gallery of Canada. According to Buchanan, the canvas now known as *At a Country Fair* is most probably the work titled *Clamart* that was exhibited at the Goupil Gallery in London in 1922.
4. A similar grouping of trees can be seen in *Horse Race, St-Malo* (reproduced in Cloutier 1985, p. 176).

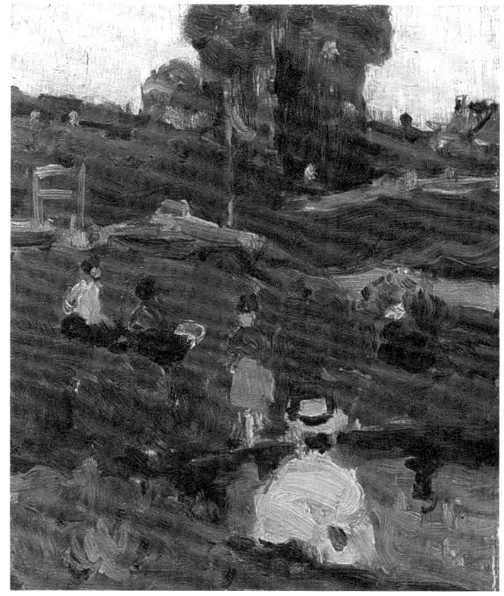

Fig. 46a
Study for "At a Country Fair", c. 1905, oil on wood, 15.2 × 12.7 cm. Art Gallery of Ontario, Toronto. Gift of Mrs. Alan G. Law, 1929 (1331).

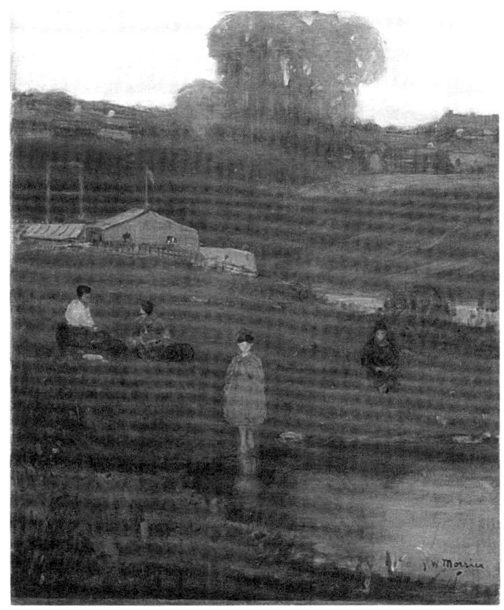

Fig. 46b
At a Country Fair, c. 1905–07, oil on canvas, 80.7 × 65.7 cm. Beaverbrook Art Gallery, Fredericton. Gift of Mrs. Howard W. Pillow, 1958 (59.148). Photograph by E. Crevaux, Paris.

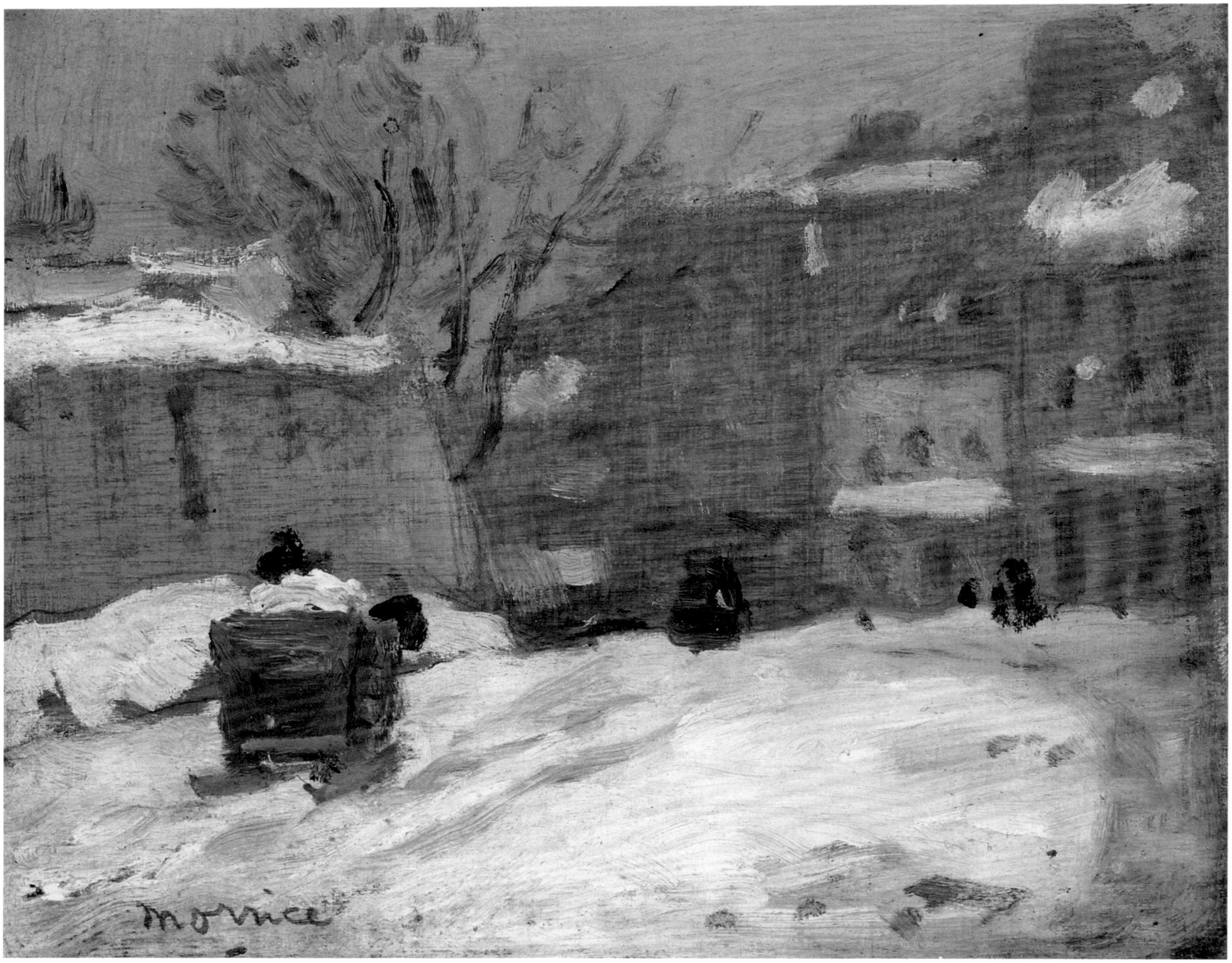

47

Street in Quebec

1906

Oil and graphite on wood, 12.2 × 15.2 cm

Inscriptions: signed l.l., *Morrice*; back of frame: u.r. in black crayon, *Box 5*, stamped, *DOUANES EXPOSITIONS PARIS*

Labels: in blue ink, N°. *78*; DORURE ENCADREMENTS / HAVARD FRÈRES / 123, BOUL. MONTPARNASSE / TÉLÉPH. DANTON 65-68

Provenance: Jacques Dubourg, Paris, by 1937;[1] Mme Jacques Dubourg, Paris, 1981; private collection, Quebec City, 1983; G. Blair Laing, Toronto, 1983.[2]

30483

Morrice returned to Canada in December 1905 to spend Christmas with his family, and he sketched in Quebec City and in Montreal.[3] The results of this trip were exhibited in Paris the following spring at the Salon of the Société Nationale des Beaux-Arts, under the titles *Effet de neige (Montréal)*, *Effet de neige (Québec)*, *Effet de neige (boutique)*, and *Effet de neige (traîneau)*, causing him to be caricatured as "Our Lady of the Snows."[4] This sketch relates very closely to (and may perhaps be a study for) the canvas reproduced in the 1906 Salon catalogue as *Effet de neige* (fig. 47a) – most likely *Effet de neige (Québec)*. In the canvas the composition is closed off by a row of old houses rather than by the taller buildings depicted here.[5]

The paint in this sketch is applied very thinly to delineate the forms of the buildings, but the snow is more thickly painted. The warm tones of the natural wood are a major element of the composition.

1. Loaned by Jacques Dubourg to Ottawa 1937, no. 50, as *Rue à Montréal, neige*.
2. Laing 1984, pp. 206, 208.
3. Minute books of the Pen and Pencil Club, Montreal, 3 and 17 February 1906, Archives, McCord Museum of Canadian History, Montreal. See also Bruce St. John, ed., *John Sloan's New York Scene* (New York: Harper & Row, 1965), pp. 15–16, entries for 22, 23, and 24 February 1906.
4. Letter from Morrice to Robert Henri, 23 June [1906], Henri Papers.
5. Two related drawings, in Sketchbook 15 (Montreal Museum of Fine Arts, Dr. 1973.38, pp. 30r and 36r), probably dating from early 1908, are studies for *Mountain Hill, Quebec* (fig. 47b); see Cloutier 1985, pp. 188–89.

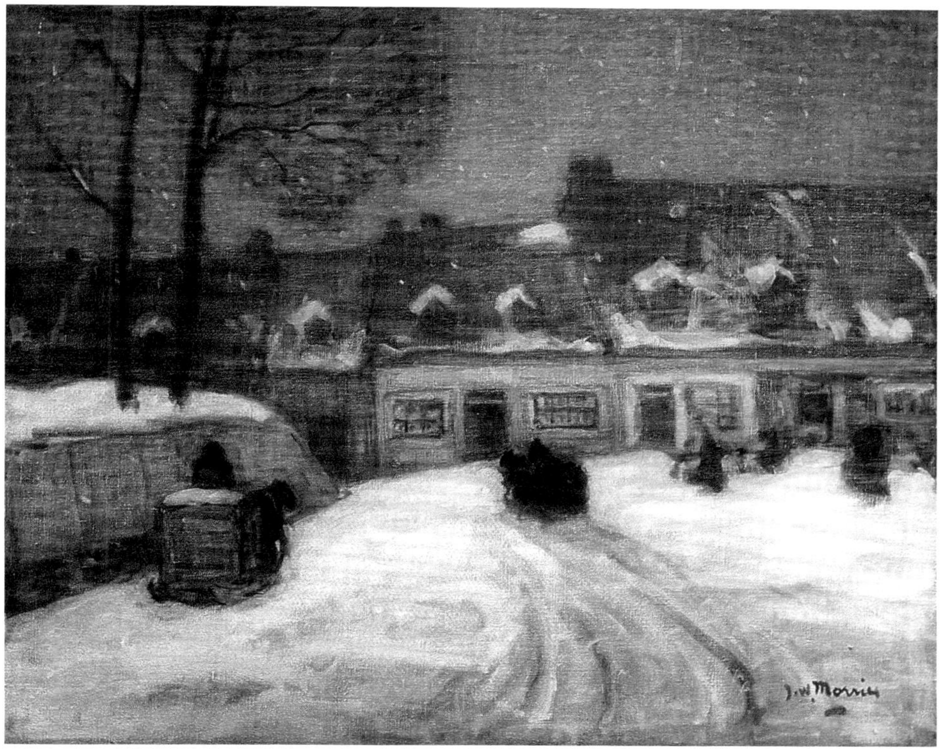

Fig. 47a
Snow Effect (Quebec), 1906, oil on canvas, dimensions and present location unknown. Photograph by E. Crevaux, Paris.

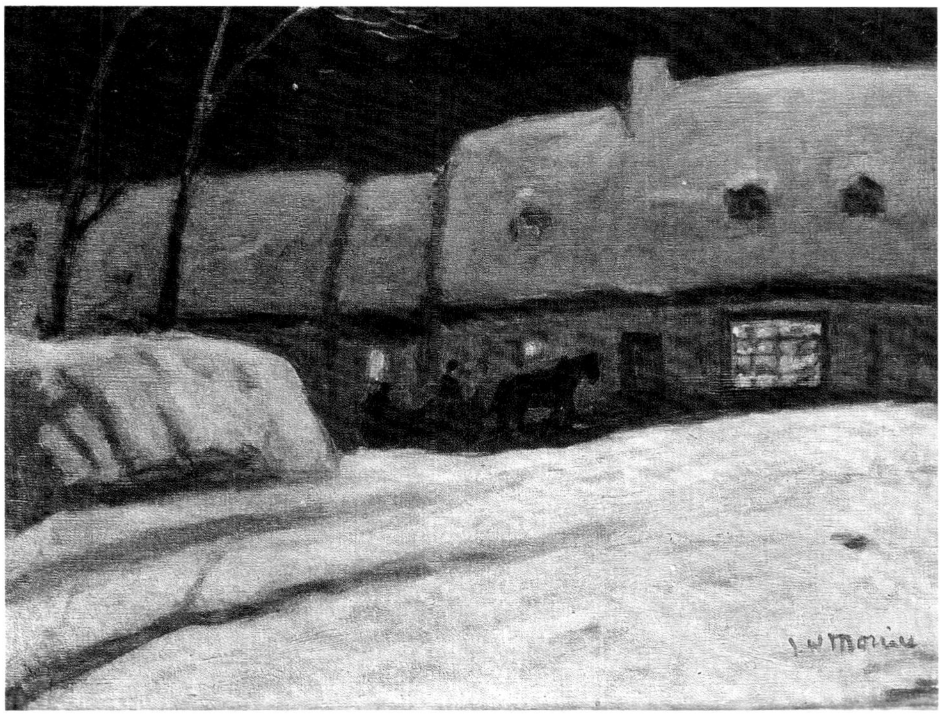

Fig. 47b
Mountain Hill, Quebec, c. 1909–10, oil on canvas, 50.8 × 61 cm. Private collection.

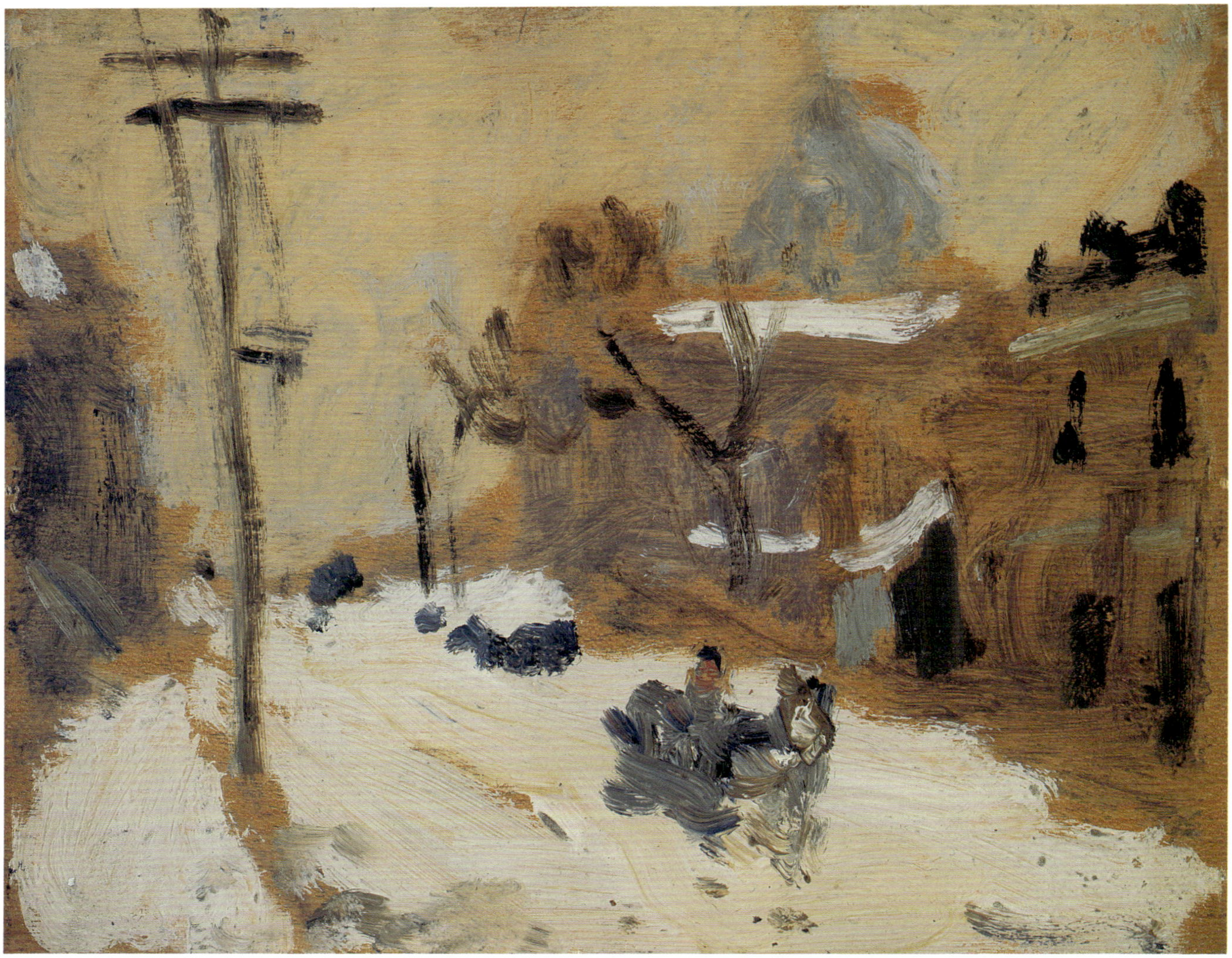

48

Cathedral and Street, Montreal, Winter

1906

Oil on wood, 12.7 × 15.2 cm

Inscriptions: verso: c. stamped, *STUDIO / J.W. MORRICE*, r. in graphite, *W.J.M. 26 / 6 / 52 / 16 / 10 / 26 / 78* (numerical calculation), l.l. in white chalk, *C25*

Labels: in blue ballpoint pen, *77-32 / CATHEDRAL / LOWER MONTREAL*

Provenance: Estate of the artist. Gellett family, Montreal. G. Blair Laing Ltd., Toronto, 1977.

30410

With its lightly brushed bare wood delineating the main architectural elements, and its rubbed sky and thicker white for the snow, this sketch closely approximates *Street in Quebec* (cat. no. 47) and may safely be dated to the same Canadian trip. In his memoirs, the Montreal art dealer William Watson notes that during that visit Morrice stayed at the Windsor Hotel on Dominion Square, where he painted a view of Peel Street looking down the hill.[1] The present work may perhaps have been sketched on Cathedral Street (one block east), looking up the hill toward the dome of St. James Cathedral (now called Mary Queen of the World Cathedral), visible at the upper right of the sketch. Morrice has included the telephone poles, which surely would have been eliminated in any larger canvas.

Watson also tells of meeting Morrice in Montreal that winter, and of Morrice's complaints about the difficulty of painting out-of-doors in the cold – how the paint stiffened, and how his hands grew numb and inflexible "so that one could hardly feel what was being painted."[2] What an appropriate phrase for this sketch so hastily and freely realized, the facts just barely defined but the felt emotion and unity of perception so deftly expressed.

1. Watson 1974, pp. 15–17.
2. Ibid, p. 16.

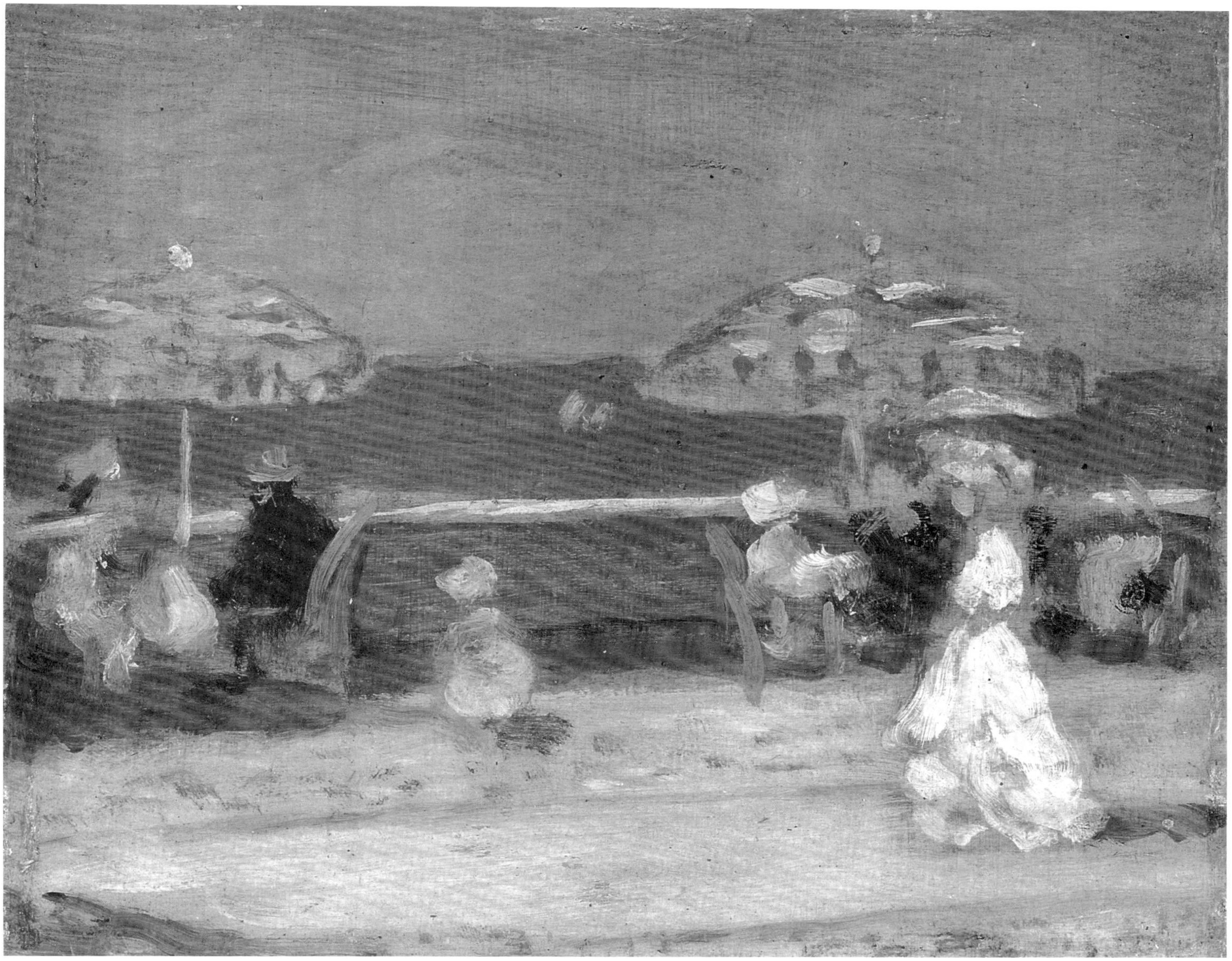

49

Study for "Dieppe"

c. 1906

Oil on wood, 12.3 × 15.3 cm

Inscriptions: verso: u.r. in graphite, *MRS JM*, c. stamped, *STUDIO / J.W. MORRICE*

Labels: in blue ballpoint pen, *85-7 / PROMENADE / DIEPPE*

Provenance: Estate of the artist. Mrs. R.E. MacDougall, Montreal; by descent to a member of the MacDougall family (sold, Sotheby's, Toronto, 28 May 1985, lot 684); G. Blair Laing Ltd., Toronto, 1985.

30428

Morrice visited Dieppe on numerous occasions from as early as 1892. Easily accessible by train from Paris, Dieppe was frequented by a stimulating international crowd that included such artists as Aubrey Beardsley, Jacques-Émile Blanche, Charles Conder, Frits Thaulow, and Walter Sickert. There is very little documentation concerning the dates of Morrice's visits to Dieppe, nor is it known with whom he associated there, but his stays are clearly evidenced by his drawings and paintings.

We do know that Morrice worked near Dieppe in June 1906.[1] In a sketchbook that he used from about 1902 to 1906 there is a drawing of women seated under a striped umbrella (fig. 49a) that may relate to *Study for "Dieppe"* and to the canvas *Dieppe* (cat. no. 50). In the oil sketch Morrice has very roughly rendered the various elements. Details such as the green chairs are merely suggested with a few lines, but the overall effect is captured for further development in the canvas. A woman in a white summer dress walks from the right, while a young child toddles toward the group at the left. The decorative red and white umbrellas frame the rich blue-green sea flecked with two white sails. Above is a light-blue and pink summer sky.

1. Letter from Morrice to Robert Henri, 23 June [1906], Henri Papers.

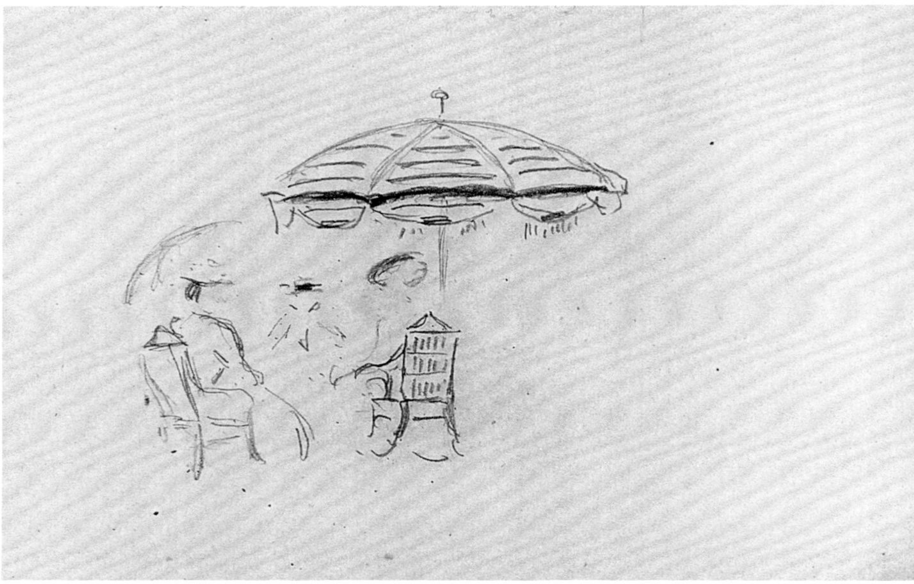

Fig. 49a
Sketchbook 16, p. 19r, c. 1906, graphite on wove paper, 10.6 × 16.7 cm. Montreal Museum of Fine Arts. Gift of David R. Morrice, 1973 (Dr.1973.39).

50

Dieppe

c. 1906

Oil on canvas, 50.3 × 61.2 cm

Inscriptions: signed l.l., *J.W. Morrice*; stretcher: on crossbar, in black ink, *4*, in blue crayon, *39*, in red crayon, *Box #9*

Labels: verso: partly torn, in black ink, Title *Dieppe* / Artist *J W Morrice* / Address *99 Notre Dame W. Montreal* / Agent *W* [Scott &] *Sons* / Agent's address *99* [Notre Dame] *St. West* / *Montreal*; partly torn, in black ink, [—] Title of / Picture *Dieppe* / *45 Quai des Grands Augustins, Paris, France* / Price; partly covered by other label, in black ink, [CAN]ADIAN / *James W* [Morrice] / *"Dieppe"*; partly torn, typed, *DIEPPE* / [F]*ISHER, ESQ.* / *147 SPADINA AVENUE* / *TORONTO*; 12 Paris / B / DÉPOSÉ / F; in graphite, *GBL #6* / *MORRICE* / *"DIEPPE"*; in graphite, *11*; brass plaque, CANADIAN ARTISTS / PATRIOTIC FUND / EXHIBITION – 1915

Provenance: A.B. Fisher, Toronto, 1915; G. Blair Laing, Toronto, c. 1956–60.[1]

30445

In this canvas based on the preceding sketch (cat. no. 49) Morrice has strengthened the foreground shadow, creating an intimate environment for the casual conversations of the summer holidayers. In enlarging the composition he has broken up the extended space between the umbrellas by adding towels hanging over the wall. He has expanded the group at the right to include three adults and a young girl, and the child at the centre now faces the viewer. The sailboats are diminutive elements on the deep-blue water below a paler-blue sky crossed by wispy clouds. The bright orange of the umbrellas is echoed in the parasol held by the young woman walking across the foreground.

This work incorporates elements seen in a number of other paintings by Morrice. The child we have seen in a watercolour of about 1900 (fig. 23b) and the young woman walking in the foreground was in Marseilles in 1904 watching a bullfight (fig. 43b). The foreground shadow used as a framing device appears in *Red Houses, Venice*,[2] and the unified colour and simplified composition recall the 1906 Salon canvas *Effet de neige (Montréal)*.[3]

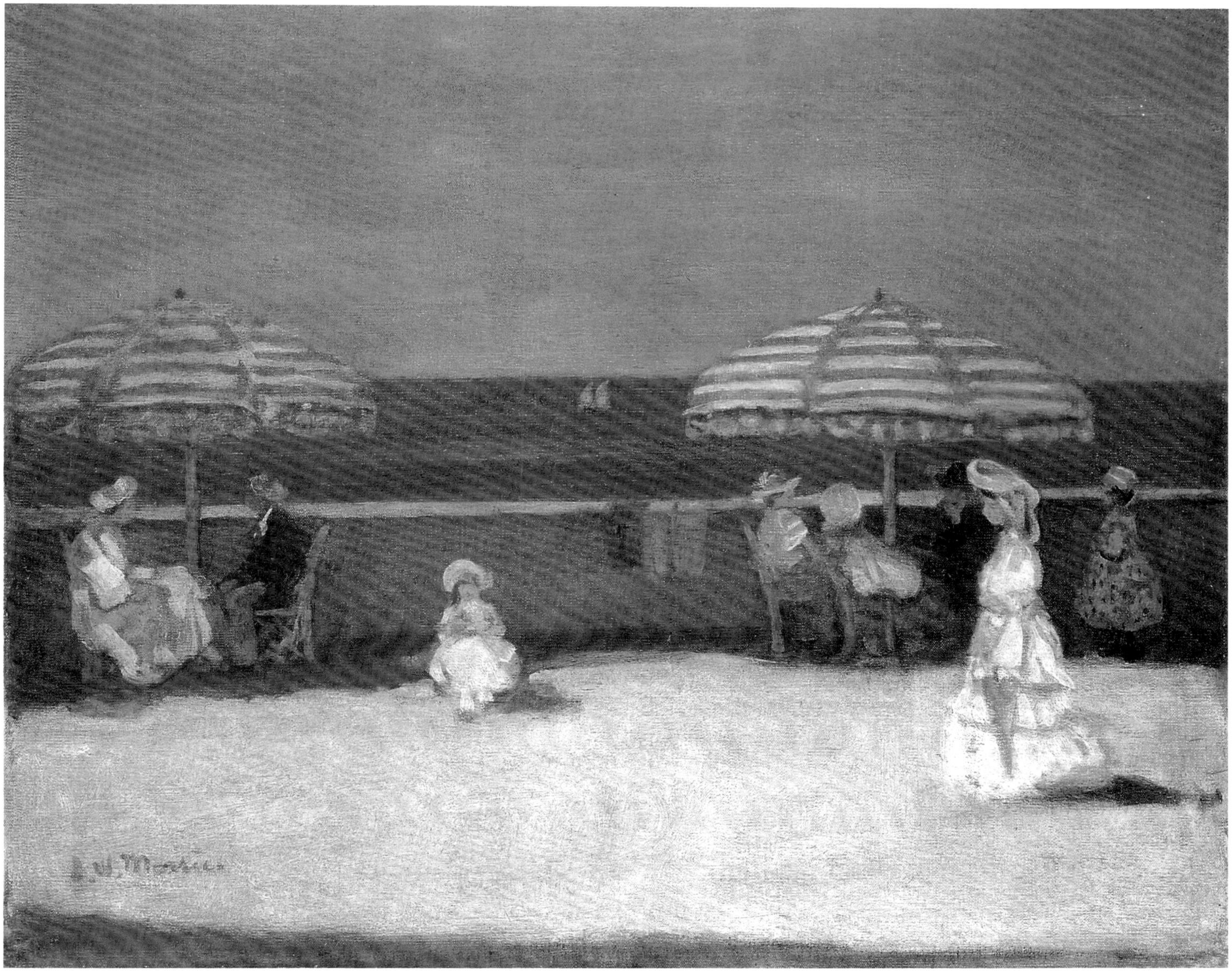

This canvas was donated by Morrice, most likely at the request of the president of the Royal Canadian Academy, William Brymner, to the exhibition of paintings and sculptures given by Canadian artists in aid of the Patriotic Fund, organized by the Academy in 1914. It was bought by Newton MacTavish for A.B. Fisher,[4] an executive of the T. Eaton Company and member of the Toronto Arts and Letters Club. Mr. Fisher loaned the painting to a number of exhibitions over the years. It was acquired by Blair Laing from Mr. Fisher shortly before the latter's death.

1. In Laing 1979, p. 226, Blair Laing gives the date of acquisition as 1960. In Laing 1984, p. 202, he gives the date as 1958. In his cataloguing notes (now in the archives of the National Gallery of Canada) he gives the date as 1956.
2. Montreal Museum of Fine Arts (925.335), reproduced in Dorais 1985b, p. 53, and dated by Dorais 1906 or 1907
3. Reproduced in Dorais 1985b, p. 49, as *Canadian Square in Winter*.
4. An annotated copy of the *Catalogue of Pictures and Sculptures Given by Canadian Artists in Aid of the Patriotic Fund* in the library of the National Gallery of Canada gives MacTavish as the purchaser of *Dieppe* (no. 35), but it was Fisher who loaned it to the 1925 Morrice memorial exhibition in Montreal. See Laing 1984, p. 176.

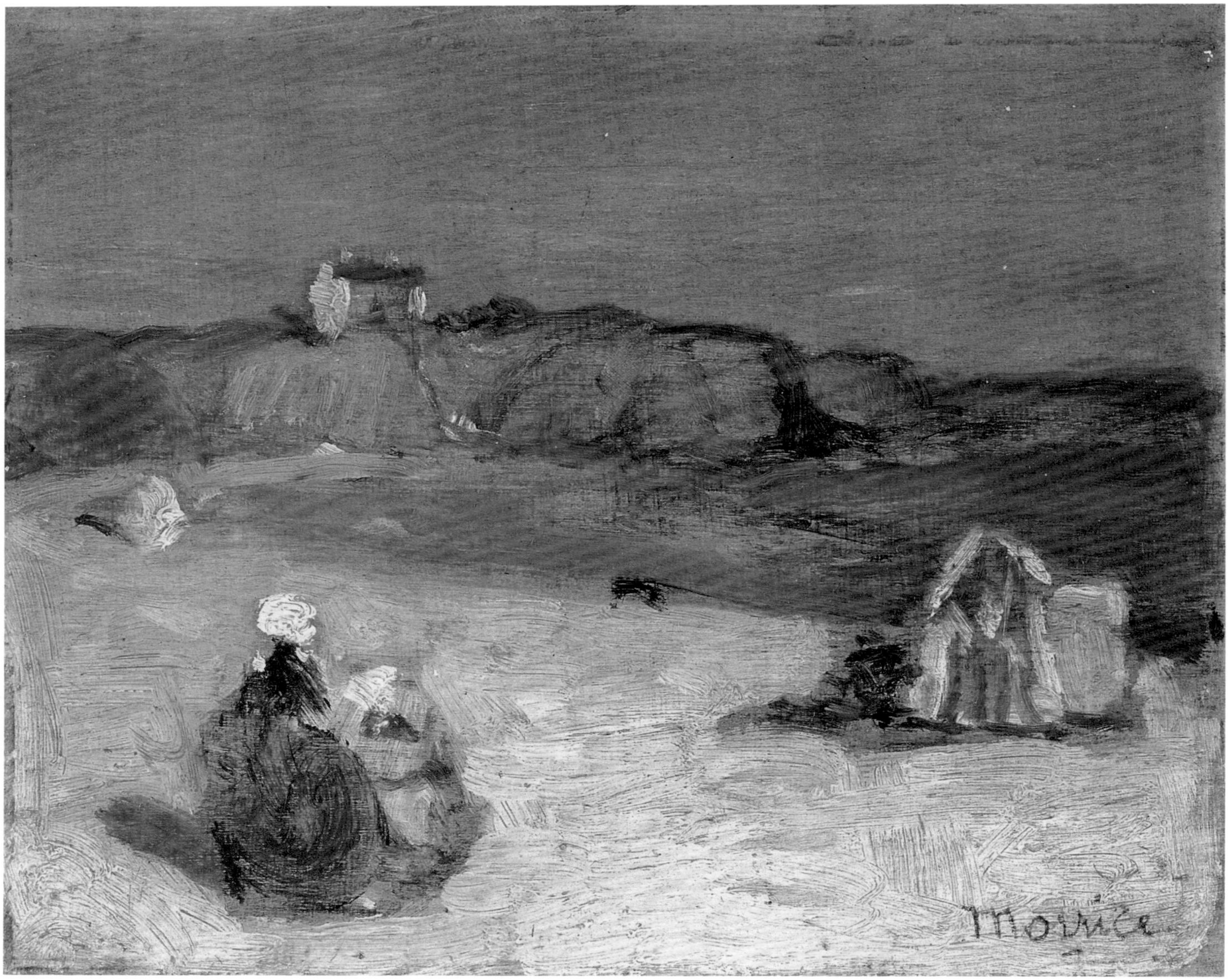

51

Le Pouldu, Brittany

1906

Oil on wood, 12.2 × 15.2 cm

Inscriptions: signed l.r., *Morrice*; verso: u.c. in graphite, *Bretagne*, c.l. in graphite, *5⅞ / 4¾*

Labels: typed, *G. Blair Laing, / Toronto, Ontario. / "Le Pouldu"*; MMFA 1965, no. 75; in blue ballpoint pen, *75*

Provenance: Clarence Gagnon, Paris; Lucille Gagnon, Paris and Montreal; G. Blair Laing, Toronto, 1960.

30453

After leaving Dieppe, Morrice spent the summer of 1906 in Brittany, painting at Le Pouldu in the company of several fellow artists – including the Englishman Gabriel Thompson, the American Robert Henry Logan, and the Pole Mela Muter – and on occasion visiting the American painter Charles Fromuth at Concarneau.[1] Some of the sketches he painted that summer were much admired by the English writer Arnold Bennett, at that time resident in Paris, who saw them in the fall and purchased one for himself.[2]

Le Pouldu had been a popular painting site for some time and was best known for the work produced there by Paul Gauguin in 1889 and 1890. It was perhaps Morrice's admiration for that artist that attracted him there. Gauguin had painted the village itself and the surrounding landscape, but what Morrice liked most about Le Pouldu was its "fine coast & small beach."[3]

There are several oil sketches of the beach at Le Pouldu[4] characterized by the sweeping curve of the foreground and the cliff and house beyond. In the present work the sand is yellow and pink, the cliffs thinly brushed, and the sky rubbed with red rising into the blue above. A touch of pale green glows at the edge of the water. In a related canvas (fig. 51a) that shows the same curve of the beach, the water and the cliffs play a more dominant role and the house on the cliff has been omitted. In the foreground are a group of women and children and a lone rider on a white horse.

This sketch was formerly in the collection of Clarence Gagnon, who had arrived in Paris in 1904 with specific instructions from his teacher William Brymner to get in touch with Morrice.[5] Gagnon's admiration for Morrice is especially evident in his works painted in Venice, St-Malo, and Dinard.[6]

1. Fromuth Journals, vol. 1, pp. 235, 249, entries for 21 July and 19 September 1906.
2. Bennett 1971, pp. 157–58, entry for 21 October 1906. The sketch purchased by Bennett was sold at Sotheby's, London, on 31 July 1931, lot 76. It was purchased by O.J. Stevenson of Guelph, who had written an essay on Morrice (published in Stevenson 1927). See the letter from Stevenson to McCurry, 29 March 1937, Archives, National Gallery of Canada, file 5.5–Morrice 1937.
3. Letter from Morrice to Robert Henri, 22 December [1906], Henri Papers.
4. See *On the Sands, Le Pouldu*, from the collection of R.B. Angus, Montreal, sold at Christie, Manson & Woods (Canada) Ltd., Montreal, 2 May 1973, lot 80, and *A Beach Scene*, sold at Sotheby's, Toronto, 17 May 1989, lot 216. A sketch was with Stevens Gallery, Montreal, and was described in *The Gazette* ("Panels by Morrice at Stevens Gallery") on 20 September 1941: "The third work is gayer in vein and hints at the France of happier days – cliffs bathed in a mellow light, figures near the sea, with a dark breakwater and a colourful bathing shelter supplying the strong contrasts. A foreground of lovely tone adds much to this work, which is big in feeling. This little work called 'The Beach, Le Pouldu' was evidently painted on the sketching excursion that produced the larger canvas – which introduces figures and a white horse – now hanging in the Mount Royal Club."
5. Letter from Brymner to Gagnon, 28 April 1904, Clarence Gagnon Papers, Archives, McCord Museum of Canadian History, Montreal.
6. McTavish 1984, pp. 26–27; René Boissay, *Clarence Gagnon* (La Prairie: Marcel Broquet, 1988), pp. 75–81.

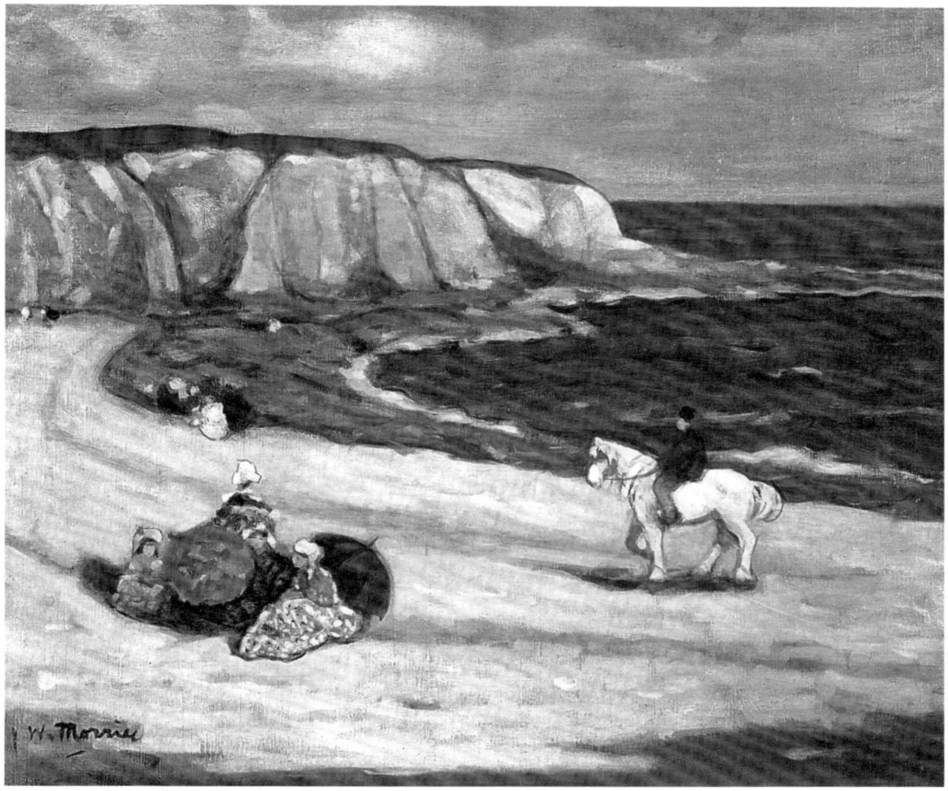

Fig. 51a
The Beach, Le Pouldu, c. 1906–08, oil on canvas, 50.2 × 75.6 cm. Mount Royal Club, Montreal. Gift of James Reid Wilson, 1914.

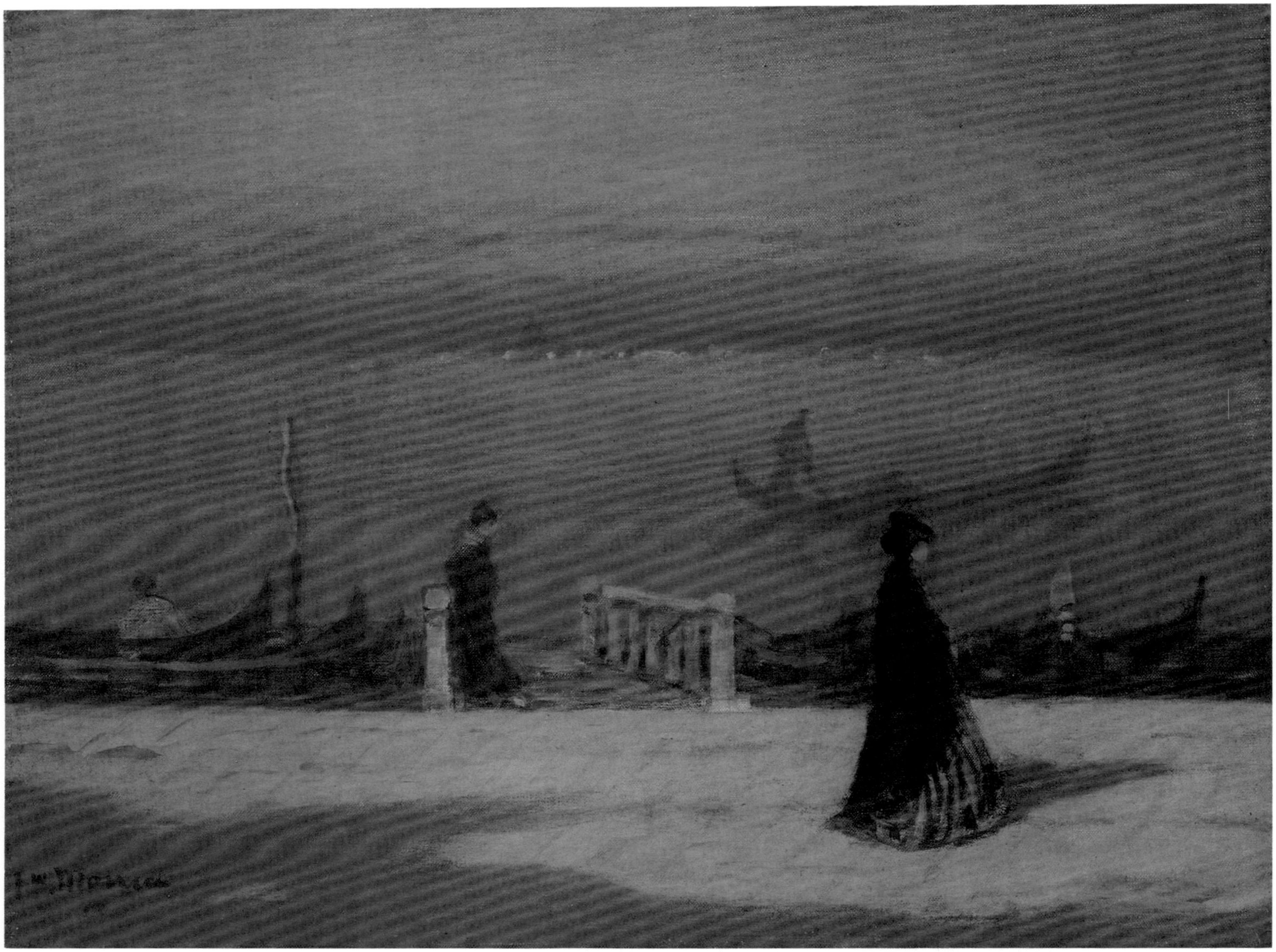

52

Nocturne, Venice

c. 1906

Oil on canvas, 45.2 × 55.2 cm

Inscriptions: signed l.l., *J.W. Morrice*; verso: u.c. in graphite, *55 × 42*

Labels: in blue ink, *85-8 / NOCTURNE, / VENICE*

Provenance: (Sold, Christie, Manson & Woods International Inc., New York, 15 March 1985, lot 178); G. Blair Laing Ltd., Toronto, 1985.

30429

Venice inspired some of Morrice's most lyrical paintings. From the simplicity of *Prow of a Gondola* (cat. no. 12) to *Nocturne, Venice*, Morrice was attracted by the remarkable light of that Mediterranean city. He returned to Venice on a number of occasions and continued to exhibit his Venetian canvases at major Parisian exhibitions up to the First World War.

In the sketch for this work (fig. 52a) Morrice defined the foreground in a curve of cream paint, leaving the bare wood to represent the shadows. The rhythm of the woman's gait echoes the curves of the pole behind her. In the middle distance a gondola is being poled across the water, which is painted in blue and banded by a collar of lights. The sky above rises from brown to purple to a darker blue. The underdrawing, especially evident in the foreground, seems to bear no relation to the painted design.

In the canvas the contrast between the lights and darks is diminished. The luminous foreground has become the main focus, and the distant lights and churches are barely distinguishable. By eliminating most of the securing poles Morrice has extended the breadth of the water. Now it is just the graceful passage of the woman in her black shawl that defines the movement of the picture.

While the sketch (fig. 52a) would appear to relate to *Study for "Venice, Looking out over the Lagoon"* (cat. no. 41), the richly evocative colour and simplified composition of the canvas relate more closely to *Dieppe* (cat. no. 50).

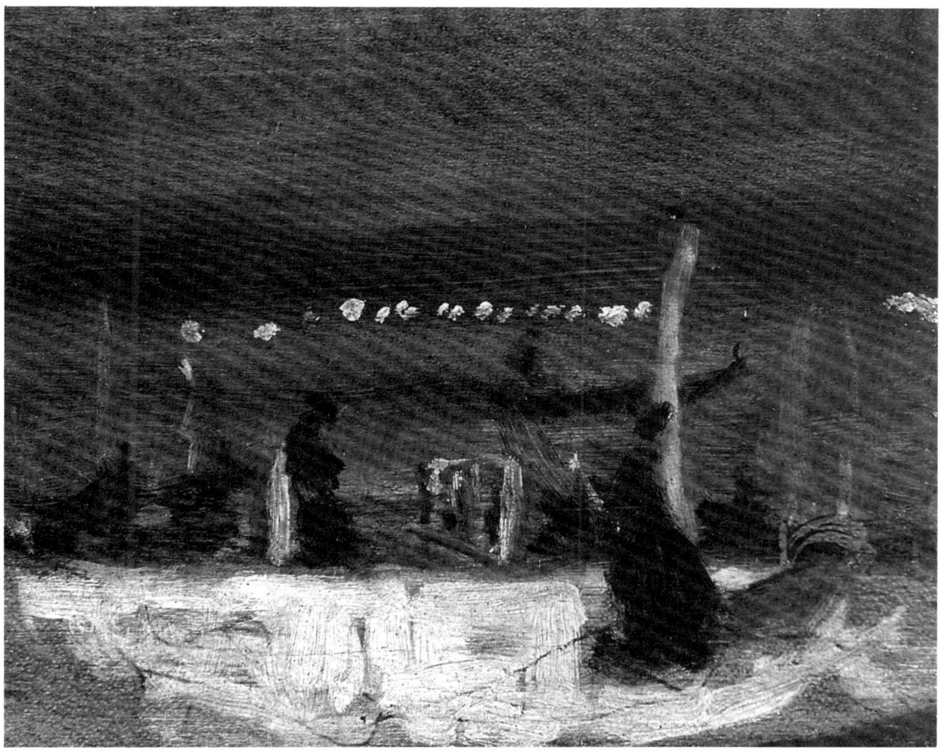

Fig. 52a
Evening in Venice, c. 1904, oil and graphite on wood, 12.4 × 15.4 cm. Edmonton Art Gallery. Purchased 1979 with funds donated by the Women's Society (79.18).

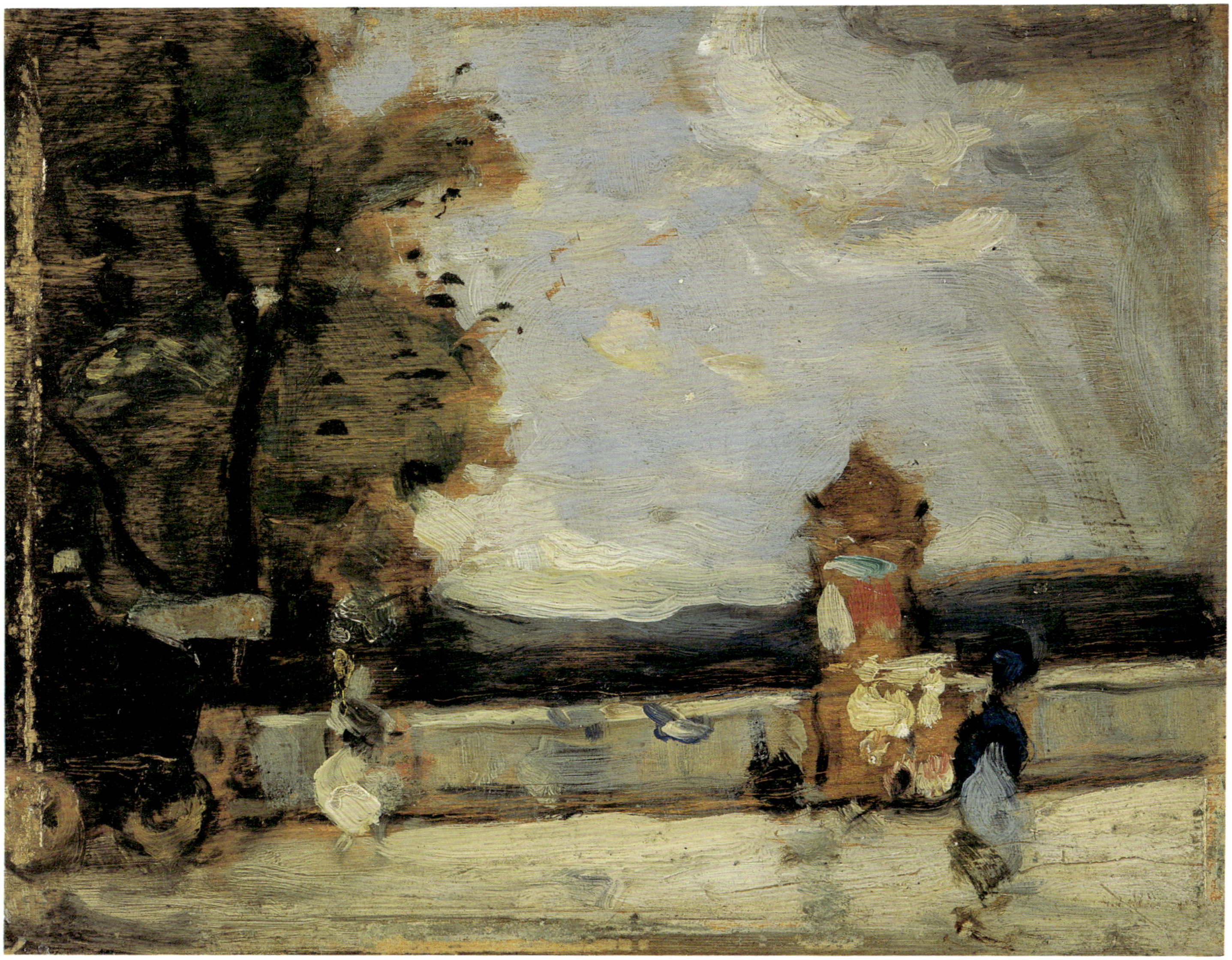

53

Kiosk and Carriage

c. 1906–08

Oil on wood, 12.3 × 15.4 cm

Inscriptions: verso: l. in graphite, *Miss Mary Mack*, c. stamped, *STUDIO / J.W. MORRICE*, c.r. in graphite, *9*, u.c. in graphite, *200*

Labels: in blue ink, *98*; in blue ballpoint pen, *KIOSK / PARIS / 86-86* (last "6" crossed out)

Provenance: Estate of the artist; W. Scott & Sons, Montreal; Mary Mack, Cornwall, Ontario (sold, Sotheby & Co. [Canada] Ltd., Toronto, 31 October 1972, lot 40). G. Blair Laing Ltd., Toronto. Kastel Gallery Inc., Montreal. Private collection, Town of Mount Royal, Quebec (sold, Fraser Bros., Montreal, 23 October 1986, lot 19); G. Blair Laing Ltd., Toronto, 1986.

30432

Poster-covered kiosks serve as colourful accents in many of Morrice's sketches of urban scenes (see, for example, cat. no. 24 and fig. 39b). In a sketchbook that Morrice used between 1902 and 1906 there is a drawing of two such columns in an unidentified locale (fig. 53a). In another oil sketch, *Kiosk and Square, Paris* (fig. 53b), from about the same period as the present work, the column dominates an outdoor café scene.

The foliage in both these sketches is treated in a similar manner, with touches of dark green over a thin, rubbed ground coat of the same colour. This is in contrast to the more broadly painted foliage seen in the oil sketches of 1909 (see, for example, cat. no. 57). The kiosks in both sketches are painted in red, yellow, and blue with the bare wood showing through. Whereas in *Kiosk and Square, Paris* the forms are large and rounded, in *Kiosk and Carriage* the brushwork is more angular and nervous, accentuating the animation of the passing view. A carriage rushes to the left, leaves blow from the trees, and women hurry by as the rain approaches from the right. In the centre the kiosk crowns an expansive landscape view. Morrice's favourite themes are treated with immediacy and charm and with a sense of delight in keen observation.

Mary Mack, a Cornwall, Ontario, artist and alderman, was most likely the previous owner of this sketch.[1] Her name is written on the back of the panel in the same hand as the inscriptions on the backs of *North African Town* and *Plane Tree and Tent, North Africa* (cat. nos. 69 and 71), suggesting that all three works had a common source.

1. In a letter to the National Gallery of Canada, 25 June 1972, Miss Mack states that she owns a "small Morrice" (Archives, National Gallery of Canada).

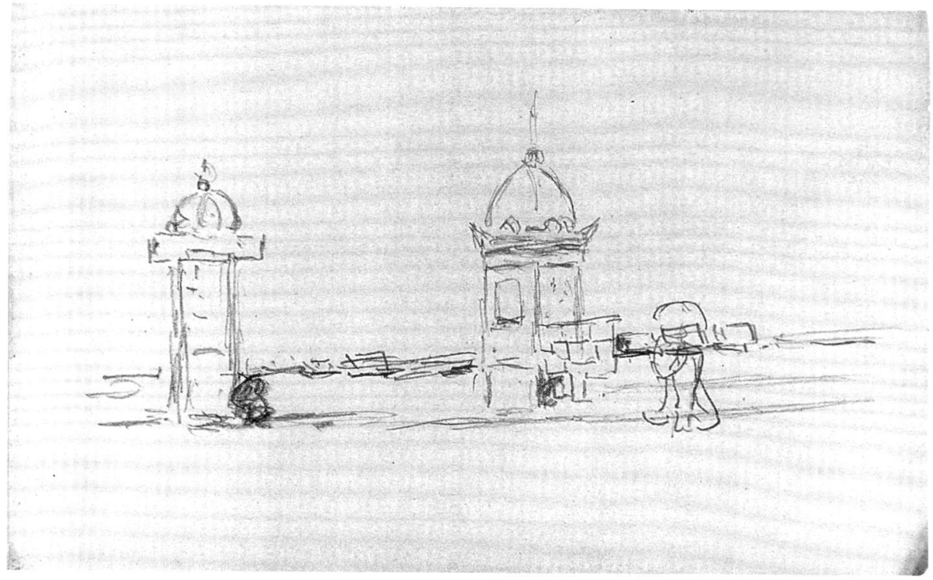

Fig. 53a
Sketchbook 16, p. 64v, c. 1906, graphite on wove paper, 16.7 × 10.6 cm. Montreal Museum of Fine Arts. Gift of David R. Morrice, 1973 (Dr.1973.39).

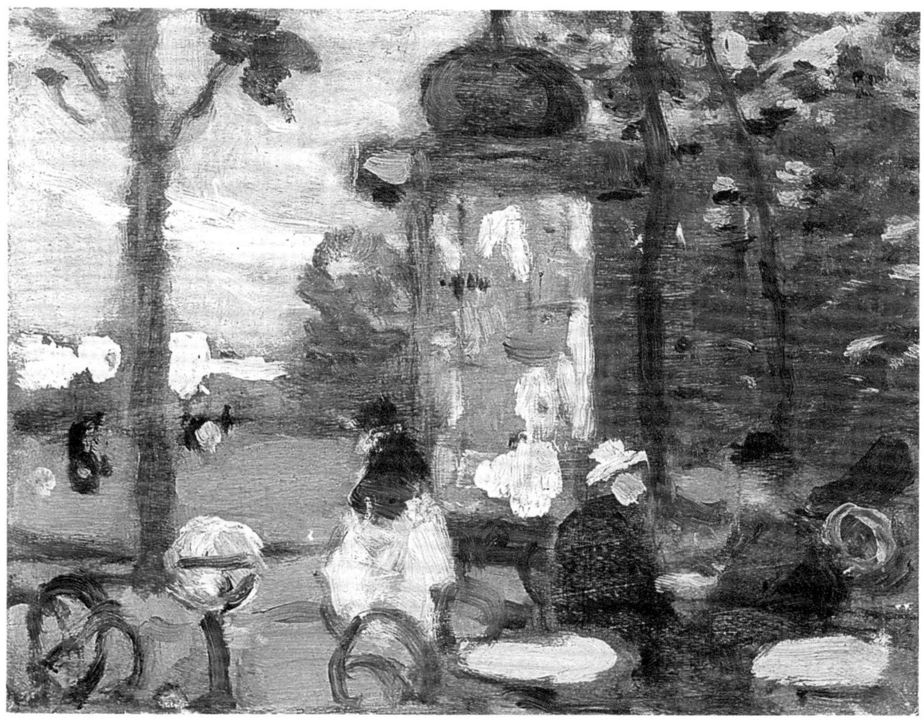

Fig. 53b
Kiosk and Square, Paris, c. 1906–08, oil on wood, 12.2 × 15.4 cm. National Gallery of Canada (3190).

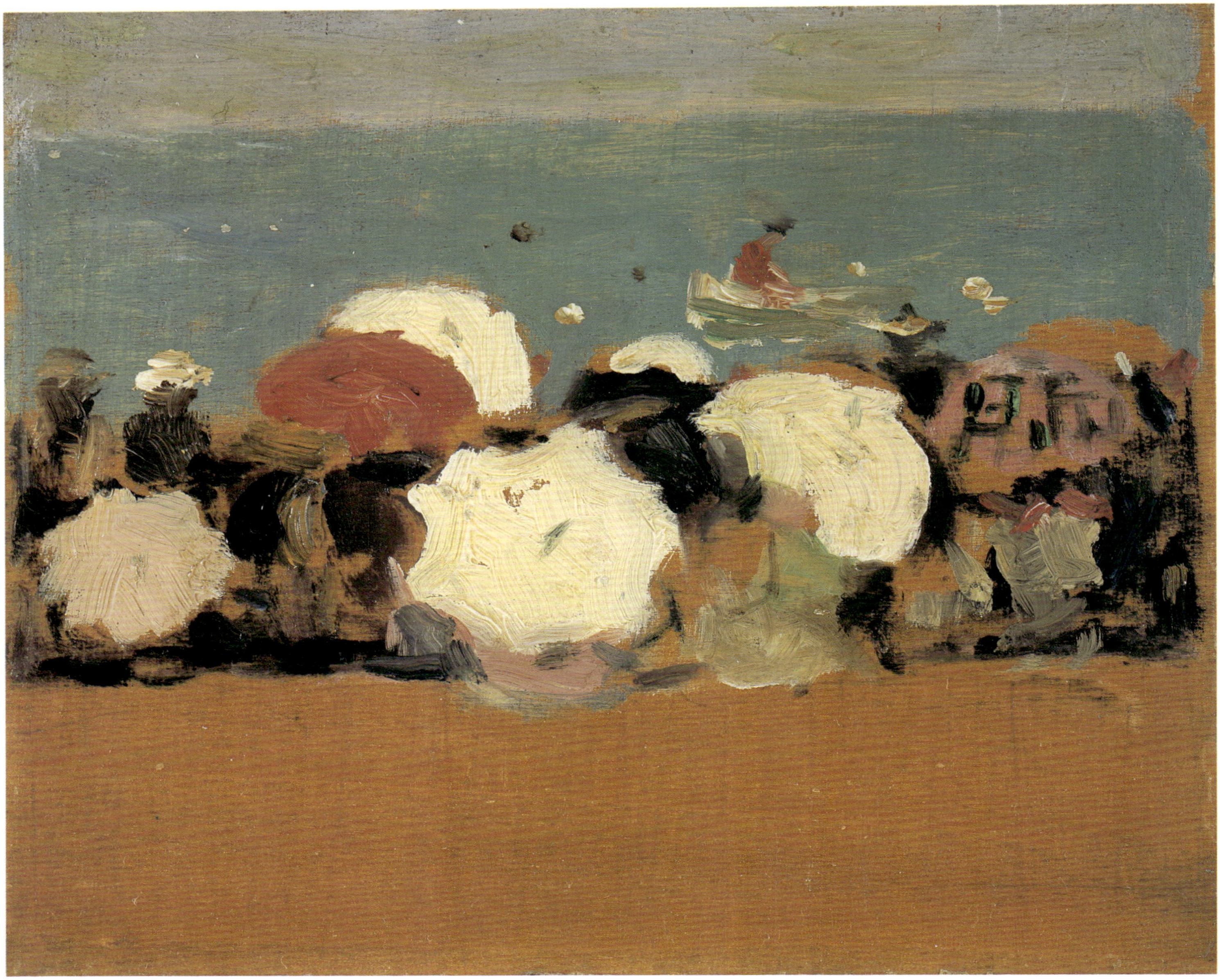

54

Beach and Parasols

c. 1905–06

Oil on wood, 12.6 × 15.4 cm

Inscriptions: verso: u.r. in graphite, *#40*, u.c. in graphite, *Top*, c.r. in graphite, *2*

Labels: partly torn, typed, "[Be]*ach Scen*[e with P]*arasols*; MMFA 1965, no. 76; in blue ballpoint pen, *GBL #15 / Beach & / Parasols*

Provenance: Private collection, England(?). John Nicholson, London and New York; G. Blair Laing, Toronto, c. 1952–56.[1]

30454

In many of his sketches Morrice uses the bare wood of the panel as a tonal element. Among the works in the Laing collection, we see early examples of this in *Flour Mill at Old Dordrecht* (cat. no. 6) and *The Beach, St-Malo* (cat. no. 26), and it is especially evident in his 1906 Quebec studies (see cat. nos. 47 and 48). In *Beach and Parasols* almost the entire lower third of the composition is left unpainted – it is merely touched with a breath of colour. Immediately above, the row of umbrellas is broadly brushed, with colour massed at the centre and thinning out at the sides. A lone figure in a red shirt rows across the blue water, and a light-blue sky caps this summer scene. The treatment of the water and sky is similar to that in *Study for "Dieppe"* (cat. no. 49), and the use of the subtly tinted wood is seen also in a sketch in the Montreal Museum of Fine Arts (fig. 54a), although in the latter the colours are more muted and less festive.

1. See cat. no. 7, n. 1.

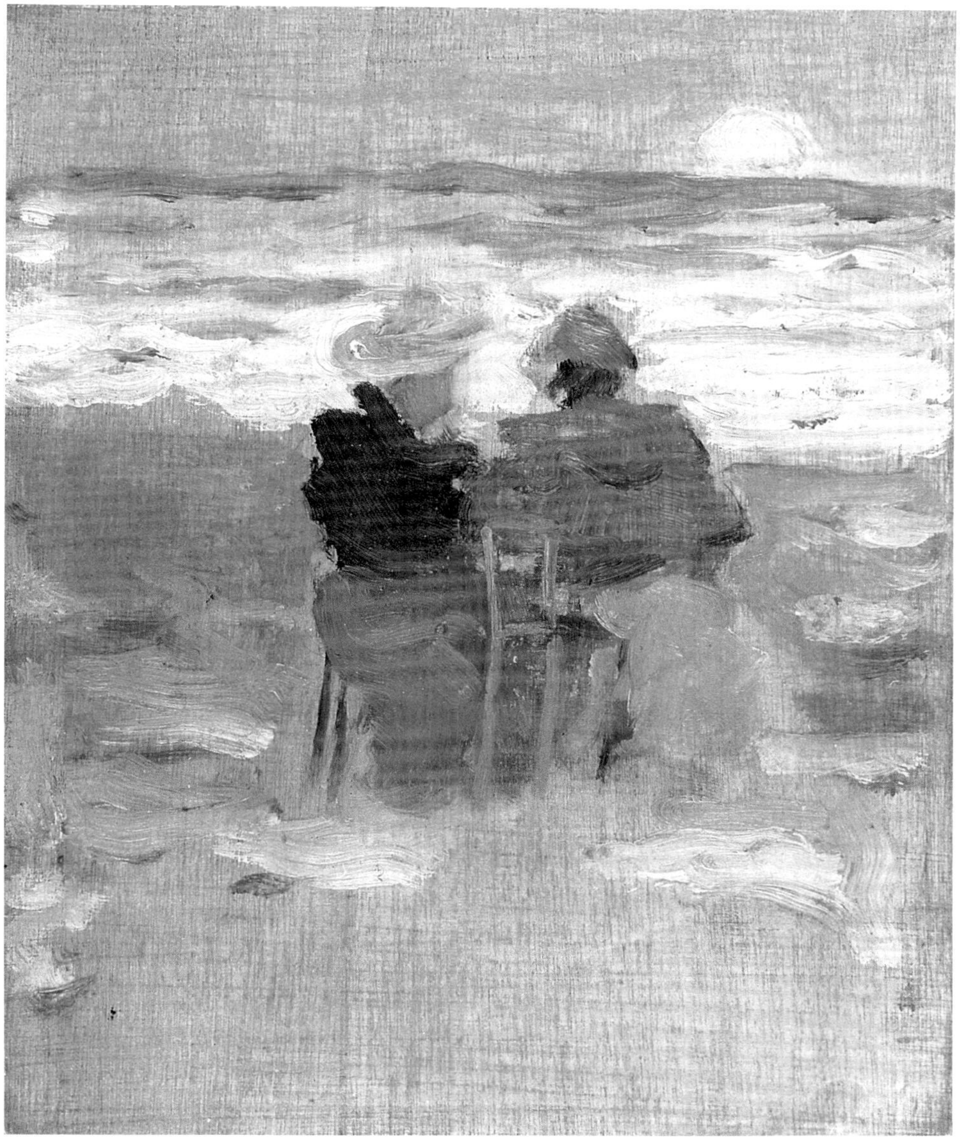

Fig. 54a
Figures in an Evening Coast View, c. 1905–08, oil on wood, 15.5 × 10.7 cm. Montreal Museum of Fine Arts. Bequest of F. Eleanore Morrice, 1981 (1981.73).

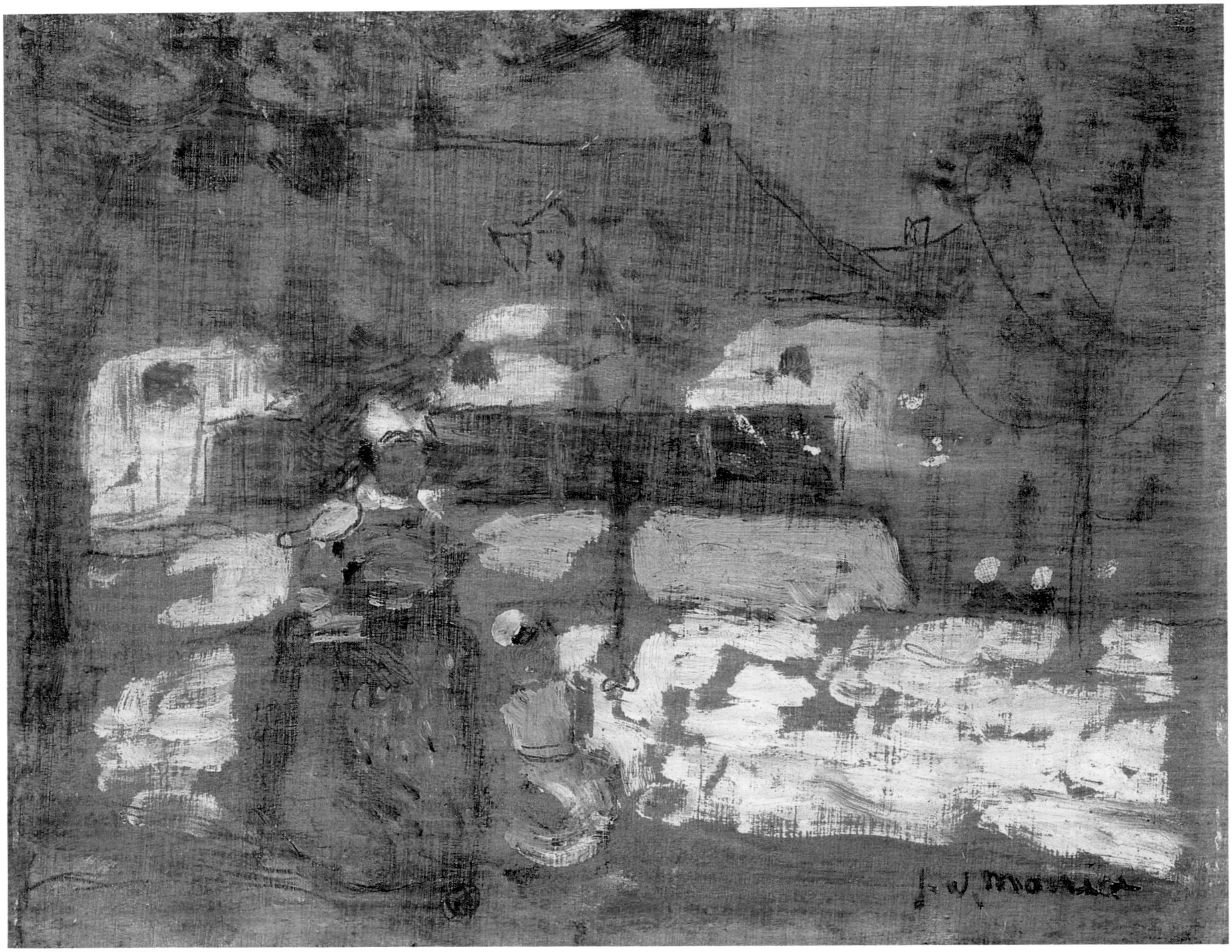

55

Street, Brittany

c. 1909–10

Oil and graphite on wood, 12.2 × 15.5 cm

Inscriptions: signed l.r., *J.W. Morrice*; verso: c. stamped, *STUDIO / J.W. MORRICE*, in stamp in graphite, *319*, b. in blue ballpoint pen, *6 × 4¾ / 198-909-2 AW*, u.r. in graphite, *76499*; back of frame: c.l. in graphite, *838 120 / 14° × 12 / 838 120 / 14° × 12*, b. partly covered by label, in red chalk, *1211* × [—]

Labels: in blue ballpoint pen, *82-10 /* "*STREET / BRITTANY*"

Provenance: Estate of the artist. (Sold, Phillips Ward-Price, Toronto, 27 July 1982, lot 107); G. Blair Laing Ltd., Toronto, 1982.

30425

In *Street, Brittany* the colour of the wood becomes the dominant unifying tone, giving the sense almost of a tinted drawing. Morrice has defined in graphite the general form of the tree at the right and the large house, then freely brushed in the trees and foreground, as well as the figures, and finally reinforced certain details with graphite again. The roof, sky, and foreground are rubbed with a thin application of paint, while the centre of the composition is more solidly brushed. The apron of the Breton woman is dotted with green, adding a light and decorative note to this charming sketch.

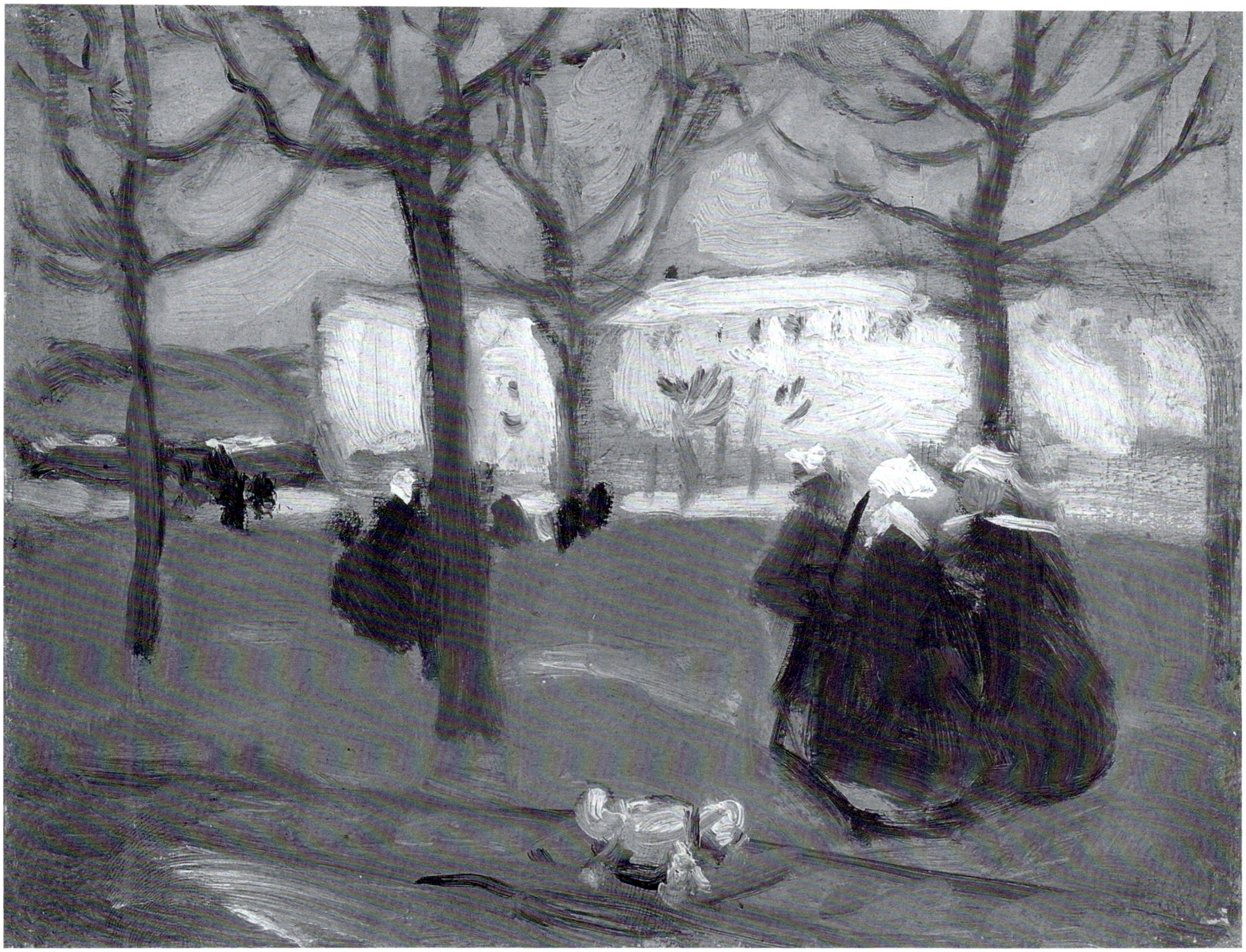

56

A Brittany Town

c. 1909–10

Oil and graphite on wood, 13.2 × 16.9 cm

Inscriptions: verso: u.l. in black ink, *981YT*, u.r. in graphite, *288*, t. in black ink, *Painted by my brother J.W. Morrice / Annie Morrice Law*, c. stamped, *STUDIO / J.W. MORRICE*, l.r. in graphite, *small co*[—], in graphite, *N.E.*, l.l. in graphite, *V.G*

Provenance: Estate of the artist; Annie Morrice Law, Montreal. Private collection, England (?) (sold, Christie, Manson & Woods Ltd., London, 14 October 1977, lot 73); G. Blair Laing, Toronto, 1977.

30447

Figures walking or standing in treed public squares constituted a favourite subject for Morrice, seen in works as early as the 1899 canvas *La Communiante* (fig. 57b). The composition of this sketch is very similar to that of *Street, Brittany* (cat. no. 55), the women walking amidst the leafless trees that define the rhythm across the panel. At the back of the flat brown square is a large cream-yellow building, with the blue water and a green-capped cliff visible in the distance at the left. A touch of brilliant red at the base of the farthest tree pulls us into the composition. In the foreground is a white dog – the same dog seen in Morrice's paintings of the Quai des Grands-Augustins and at the racecourse at St-Malo.[1]

1. See Cloutier 1985, pp. 164, 176.

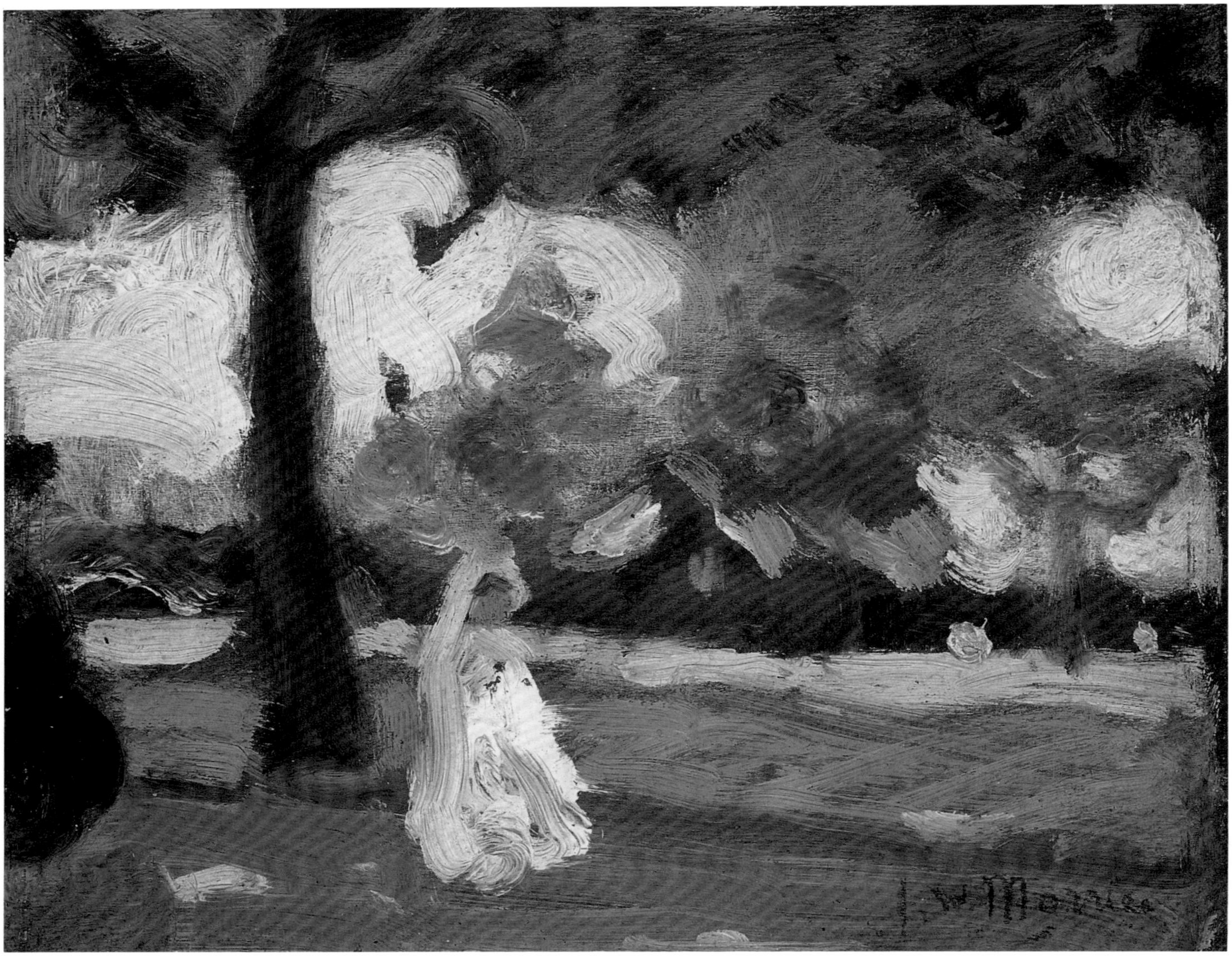

57

Study for "The Communicant"

1909

Oil on wood, 12.3 × 15.4 cm

Inscriptions: signed l.r., *J.W. Morrice*; verso: u.l. in graphite (artist's hand), *La Communiante*

Labels: in black ink, *Edwin Holgate / La Communicant*; u.c. in blue pencil, *GGS 1914 / 154*; in brown ink, *78/9*; in blue ballpoint pen, *77-3 / La Communicant*

Provenance: Edwin Holgate, Montreal, by 1925;[1] G. Blair Laing Ltd., Toronto, 1977.

30409

This study of a young girl going to her first communion is boldly laid down with rapid, direct strokes. The figures, clouds, and foreground tree are solidly brushed, while the receding sky and background foliage and trees are most delicately suggested. The triangular foreground plane is solidly anchored by the vertical tree, which extends its boughs across the top of the composition – a structural device that appears frequently in Morrice's sketches of 1909 and 1910. The dominant colours are brown, white, and grey.

This work is a study for the well-known canvas *La Communiante* (fig. 57a), first exhibited in March 1910.[2] In the canvas the dappled foreground is more integrated in colour. The blue of the sky becomes the dominant tone, and light and shadow play across the trunk of the tree and the child's dress. The pink house in the background recedes into the foliage, and another figure has been added, walking near the house. The rolling rhythm of the sketch is retained in the canvas but the contrasting tones have been transmuted into subtle harmonies of colour. The bare wood in the sketch becomes canvas merely covered with a ground near the foliated trees, enhancing their transparency.

In 1899 Morrice had treated the subject of a young communicant standing proudly in a public square with her black-robed guardian (fig. 57b). Here she stands alone, fragile and beautiful, a hooked bare branch above her head.

This sketch was formerly in the collection of the Montreal painter Edwin Holgate, who most likely acquired it from Morrice when he was studying in Paris in the early 1920s. Holgate's name appears in two of Morrice's sketchbooks – first as "Edwin Welgate" in a book dating from about 1914 and then as "E.H. Holgate" in a book from about 1921–22.[3] The inscription "GGS 1914 / 154" refers to the inclusion of this sketch in the autumn Salon of the Goupil Gallery in London in 1914.[4]

1. Loaned by Edwin Holgate to Montreal 1925, no. 53.
2. Galerie Georges Petit, Paris, 1910, *Exposition de Peintres et de Sculpteurs*, no. 99.
3. In Sketchbook 10 (Montreal Museum of Fine Arts, Dr.1973.33), p. 74r is inscribed, "Edwin Welgate / 10 Rue Asseline XIV / (Montreal)." In Sketchbook 21 (Montreal Museum of Fine Arts, Dr.1973.44), p. 68v is inscribed, "E.H. Holgate / 10 Rue Assaline / XIV."
4. See Cloutier 1985, p. 48.

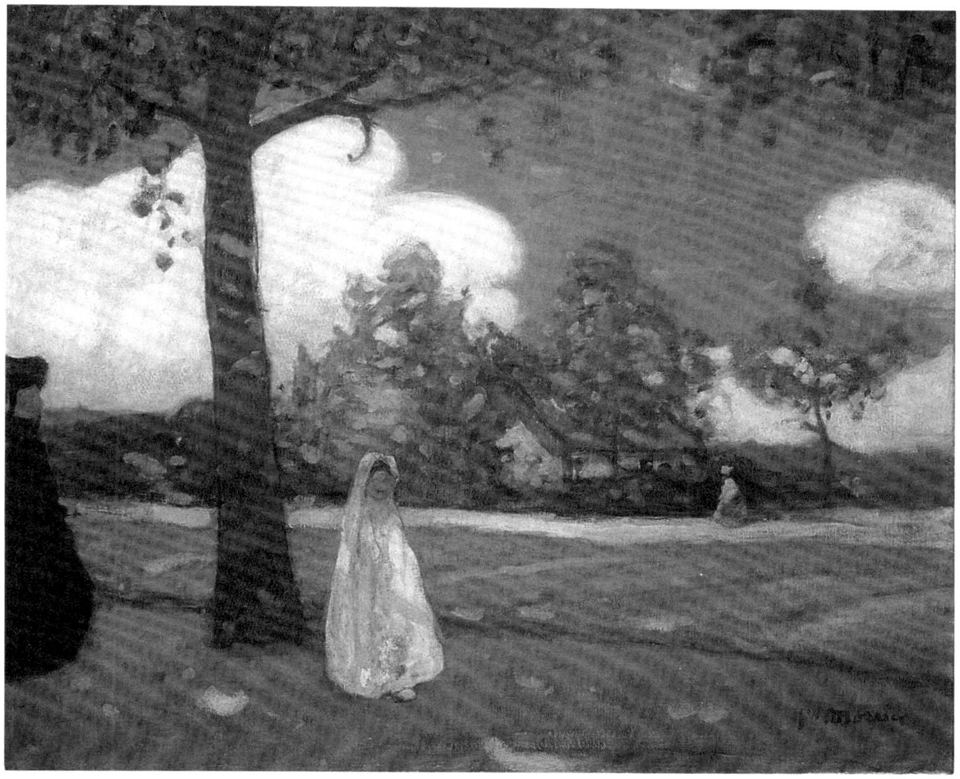

Fig. 57a
The Communicant, c. 1910, oil on canvas, 60.2 × 73.4 cm. National Gallery of Canada (6760).

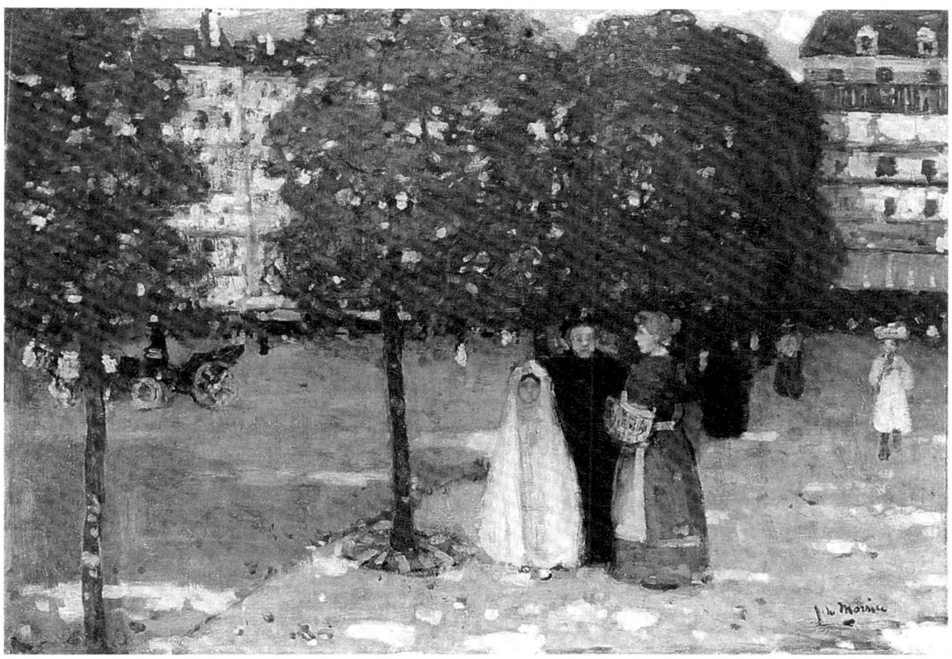

Fig. 57b
The Communicant, 1899, oil on canvas, 83 × 118 cm. Musée du Québec, Quebec City (A-78.98-P).

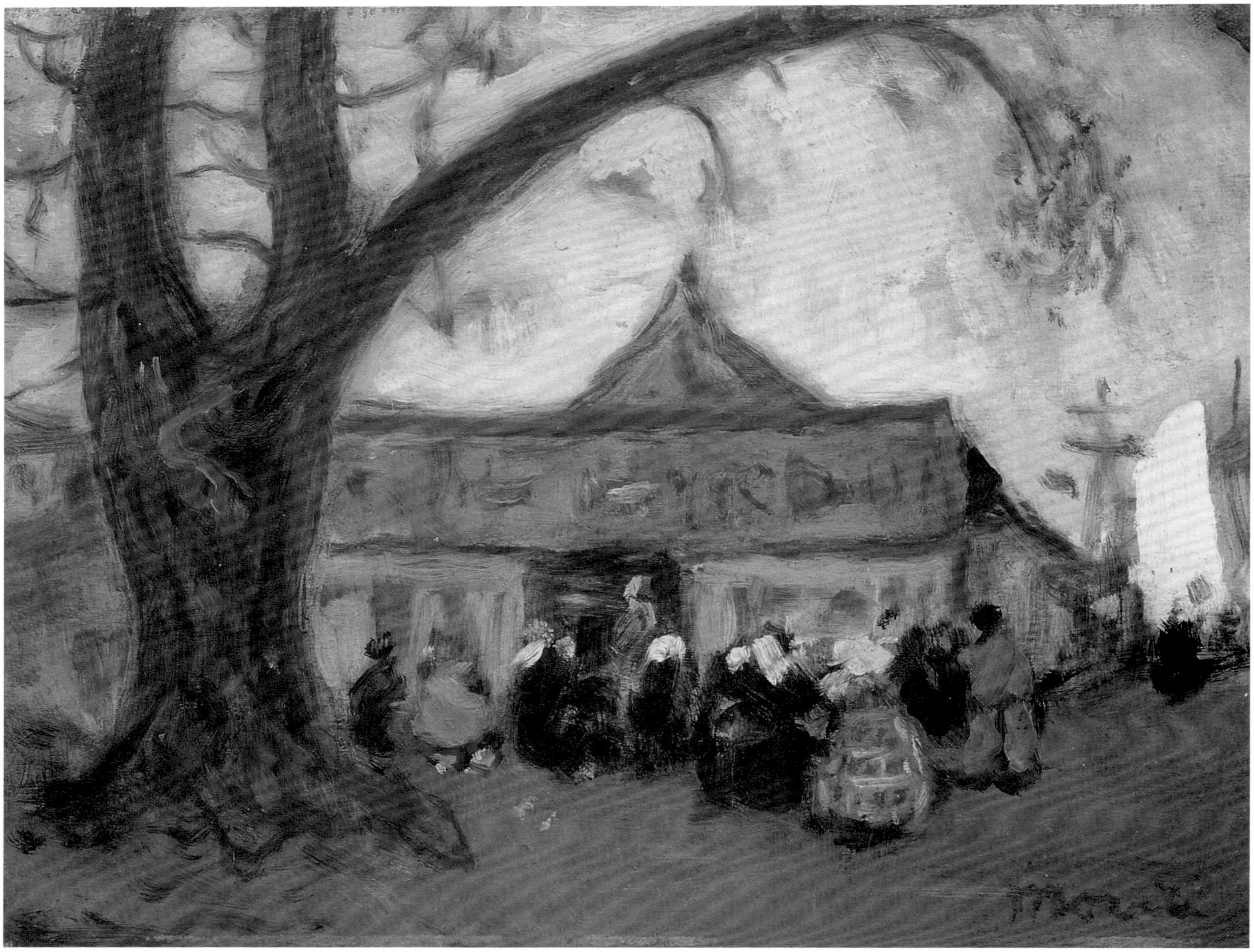

58

Circus, Concarneau

c. 1909–10

Oil on wood, 13.2 × 17 cm

Inscriptions: signed l.r., *Morrice*; u.r. in black ink, *2*

Labels: in graphite and blue ballpoint pen, *22*; in blue ballpoint pen, *76-2* / *THE CIRCUS* / *CONCARNEAU*

Provenance: (Sold, Christie, Manson & Woods [Canada] Ltd., Montreal, 24 October 1974, lot 164); G. Blair Laing Ltd., Toronto, 1974.

30403

Morrice spent most of the winter of 1909–10 painting in a studio in Concarneau. It was a most productive stay, resulting in some of his best-known canvases, including *Circus, Concarneau* (fig. 58c), formerly in the collection of Jacques Rouché.[1] The oil sketch was preceded by two drawings, one of them being a study of the tree with two saplings (fig. 58a). In the second drawing (fig. 58b) the saplings frame the tent of the *Cirque d'hiver*, with the Bretons converging on the entrance. The large tree is especially dominant in the oil sketch, the bough extending over the figures and tent, with the space opening at the right to a view of the sails of the ships in harbour. A few strokes of white paint have all but obliterated a late customer at the right but are an effective balance to the somewhat ghoulish tree. The dominant browns in the ground and in the tree and the yellow of the sky frame the tent with its horizontal blue-green and red sign.

In the canvas (for which there may have been another oil sketch) the saplings have reemerged and only a curving branch in the upper-left corner serves to remind us of the tree. The figures cluster together to watch a clown, while the sails of the ships create elegant patterns in the background on this sunny, rather than overcast, day.

1. See cat. no. 32, n. 5.

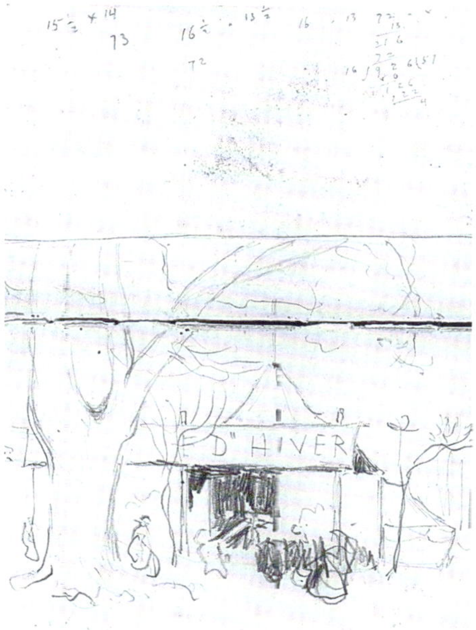

Fig. 58b
Sketchbook 15, pp. 23v–24r, c. 1909–10, graphite on wove paper, 22.4 × 16.6 cm (overall). Montreal Museum of Fine Arts. Gift of David R. Morrice, 1973 (Dr.1973.38).

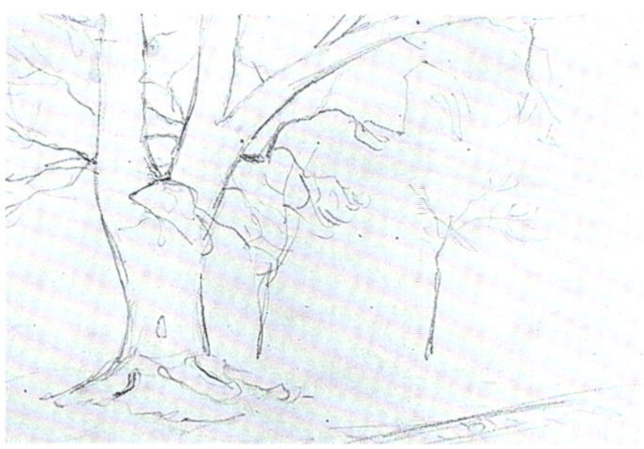

Fig. 58a
Sketchbook 15, p. 20r, c. 1909–10, graphite on wove paper, 11.2 × 16.6 cm. Montreal Museum of Fine Arts. Gift of David R. Morrice, 1973 (Dr.1973.38).

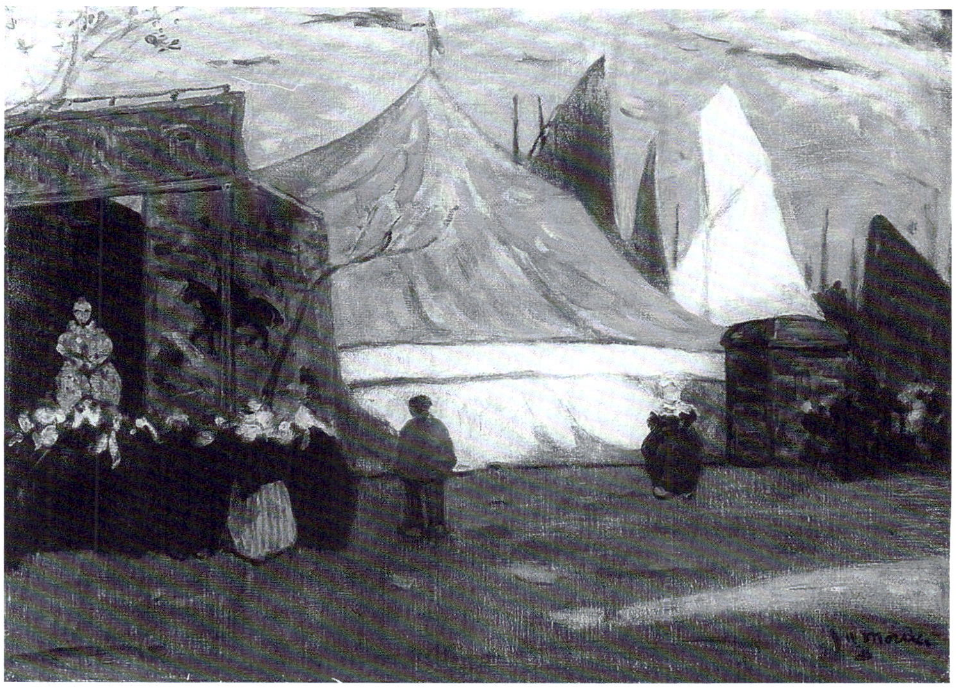

Fig. 58c
Circus, Concarneau, 1910, oil on canvas, 60.6 × 81.3 cm. Beaverbrook Canadian Foundation, Beaverbrook Art Gallery, Fredericton (59.348).

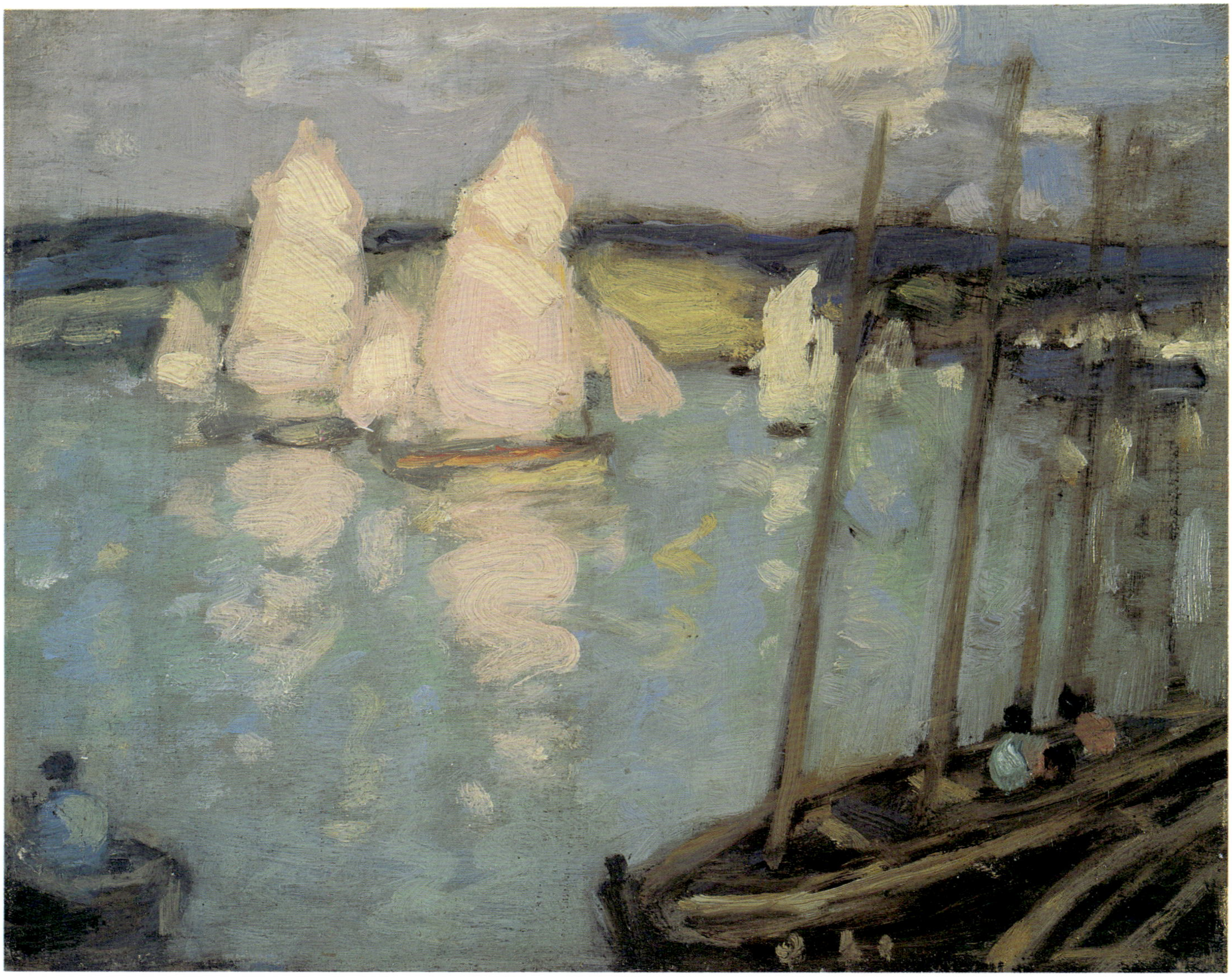

59

Study for "Boats, Concarneau"

1910

Oil on wood, 12.5 × 15.4 cm

Inscriptions: verso: u.l. in graphite (artist's hand), *J.W. Morrice*

Labels: partly torn, W. [SCOTT & SO]NS, / [—] WEST, / MONTREAL, in brown ink, *Sailing Boats*, in brown ink, *Fishing Boats* (crossed out); in blue ballpoint pen, *76-41* / *FISHING* / *BOATS CONCARN* / *EAU*

Provenance: W. Scott & Sons, Montreal. John A. MacAulay, Winnipeg; G. Blair Laing, Toronto, 1974.

30484

Fluidly brushed and glowing with colour, this sketch provides a vivid contrast to the much more restrained *Circus, Concarneau* (cat. no. 58). The foreground boats frame the reflections of the glowing pink sails in the mauve and blue water, and mauve clouds rise above the yellow, green, and blue hills beyond. The figure in the boat at the left is observable also in the gondola at the left in *Nocturne, Venice* (cat. no. 52). An additional drawing to clarify the details of the fishing boat (fig. 59a) may have followed the oil sketch.

The canvas derived from these studies was exhibited in Paris in March 1910 as *Concarneau, bateaux* (fig. 59b).[1] Here three – rather than two – boats frame the right corner, and the figure on the left now faces the viewer. The pink and yellow sails on the red and yellow boat are reflected in the turquoise water and set against the lime-green foreground hill. The far hills are a deep, rich emerald green. Mauve and white clouds rise above the landscape. A photographic reproduction of the canvas in an American periodical in 1913 was aptly titled "The Emerald Shore."[2]

1. Galerie Georges Petit, Paris, 1910, *Exposition de Peintres et de Sculpteurs*, no. 101
2. Borgmeyer 1913, p. 352.

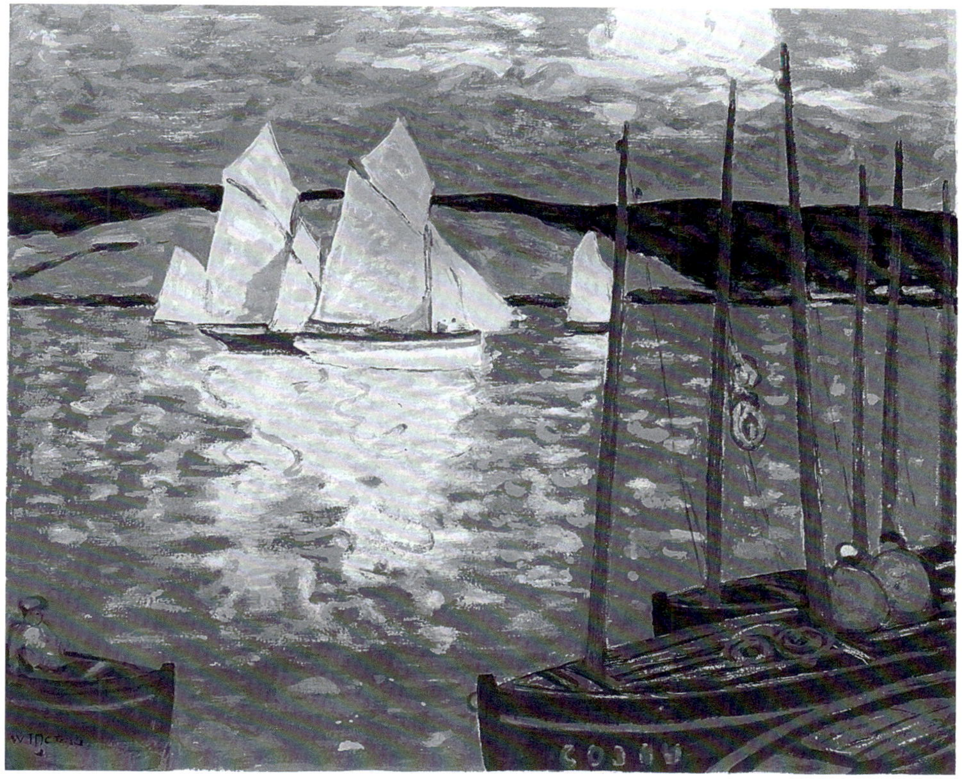

Fig. 59b
Boats, Concarneau, 1910, oil on canvas, 60 × 72 cm. Private collection.

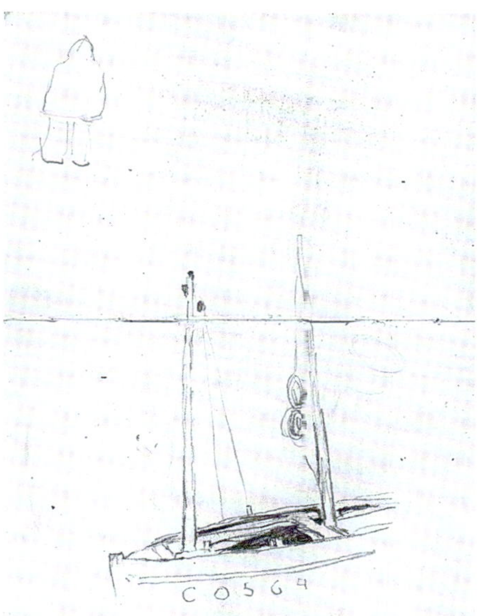

Fig. 59a
Sketchbook 15, pp. 7v and 8r, 1910, graphite on wove paper, 22.4 × 16.6 cm (overall). Montreal Museum of Fine Arts. Gift of David R. Morrice, 1973 (Dr.1973.38).

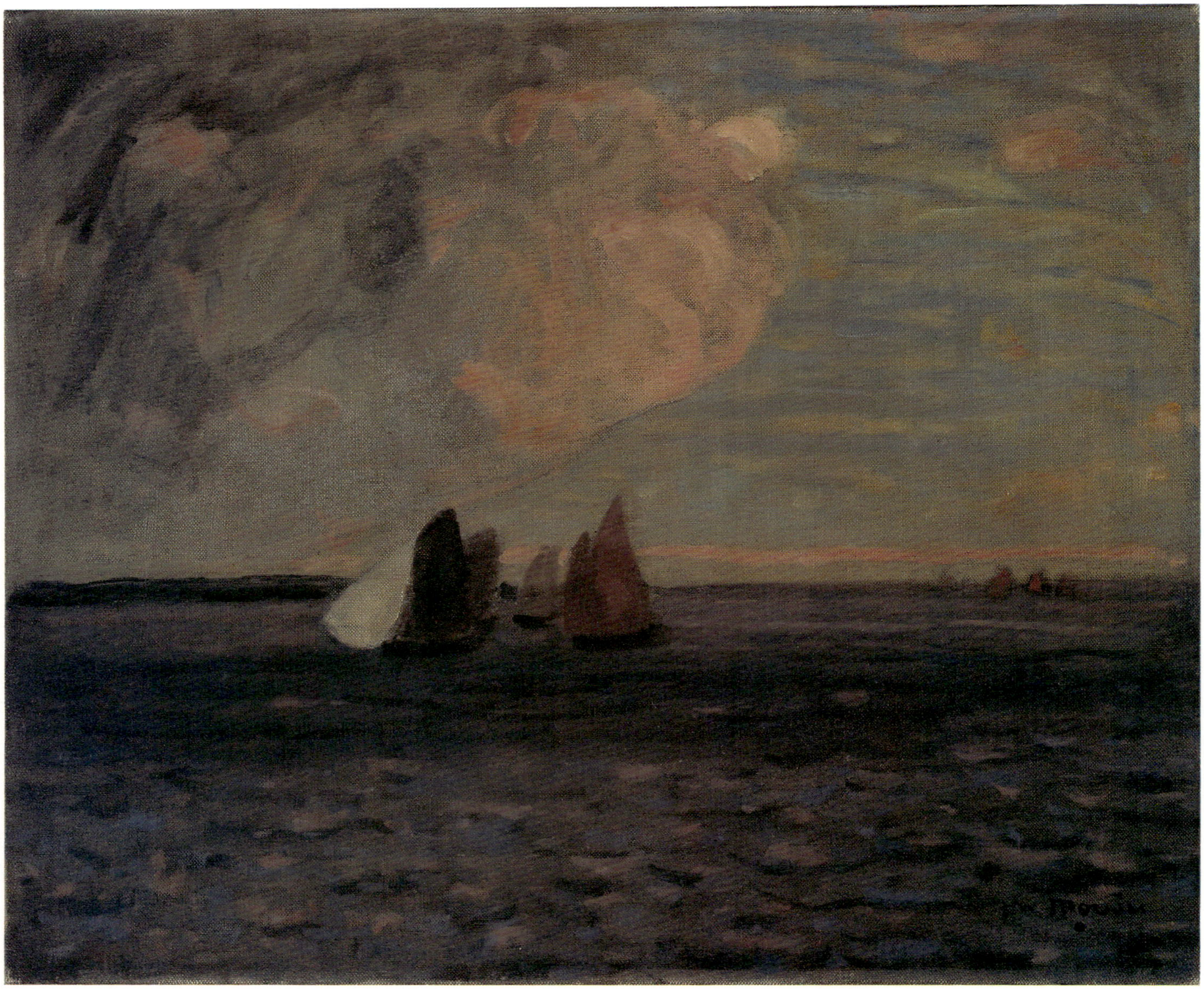

60

Fishing Boats, Nantes

c. 1909–10

Oil on canvas, 54.5 × 65.2 cm

Inscriptions: signed l.r., *J.W. Morrice*; verso: c.l. stamped, *TOILE DETREMPE* / [—] *DE* / *BLANCHET* / [—] *PARIS*, l.l. stamped, *DOUANES* [—] *PARIS*, l.r. stamped, [—]; stretcher: u.l. in graphite, *1905–06*, u.r. in graphite, ****, r. in blue pencil, *PM36.150*, l.r. stamped, [—]; on crossbar, u.c. in orange pencil, *Nantes*, c. stamped, *DOUANES EXPO* [—] / *PARIS*

Labels: in blue ballpoint pen, *Barques de Pêcheurs – Nantes / (ex Henri Matisse through Pierre Matisse)*; in black ink, *Mr Morrice*; in blue pencil, *A Mr. Guichardaz 29 rue du / Dragon*; in black ink, THE ART GALLERY OF TORONTO, GRANGE PARK, *1st SHPT* / No. *10 PICT* / Date *16/11/53* / From *MONT MUS* / *Box IV #10 of 10*; CONTINENTAL GALLERIES / OF FINE ART / 1450 Drummond St. – MONTREAL – Tel. PLateau 1072; in blue ballpoint pen, *75-22* / *FISHING* / *BOATS* / *NANTES*; in black ballpoint pen, *75-42*

Provenance: César Guichardaz, Paris; Pierre Matisse Gallery, New York, by 1937;[1] Continental Galleries of Fine Art, Montreal, 1942;[2] Lawrence M. Hart, Montreal, by 1950;[3] Continental Galleries of Fine Art, Montreal; John A. MacAulay, Winnipeg, 1955;[4] G. Blair Laing Ltd., Toronto, 1974(?).

30402

It was John Lyman who best described the transformation that typically takes place from the sketch to the canvas in Morrice's painting: "His subject is transferred from physical light into a spiritual light. Not a self-emanating radiance like Renoir or Redon, but an immaterial suffusion. . . . from the sketch to the picture the material elements are signally reduced while at the same time the essential elements grow to fullness. . . . he made his sketches principally to record the material elements of his composition, while the subject proper is distilled & concentrated by memory . . ."[5]

Lyman's observations are especially true in the case of this particular work. In the sketch (fig. 60a) the more angular brushwork defines the "material elements" and their general interrelationships, but the movement is less defined. The dramatic sky effects are merely hinted at with touches of black brushed on the bare wood at the left and on the right edge of the pink cloud.[6] In the canvas Morrice paints a vision of glowing and contrasting colour, rolling rhythm, and subtle tensions. The pink in the sky is reflected in the water, highlighting the foreground waves, while a dark cloud at the upper left casts a shadow in the middle distance in front of the white, brown, and red sails of the boats. Red sails identify the boats at the right on the horizon, which is bounded by a bright, horizontal pink cloud. The freedom of the brushwork in the clouds contrasts with the orderly rhythm of the waves in the foreground.

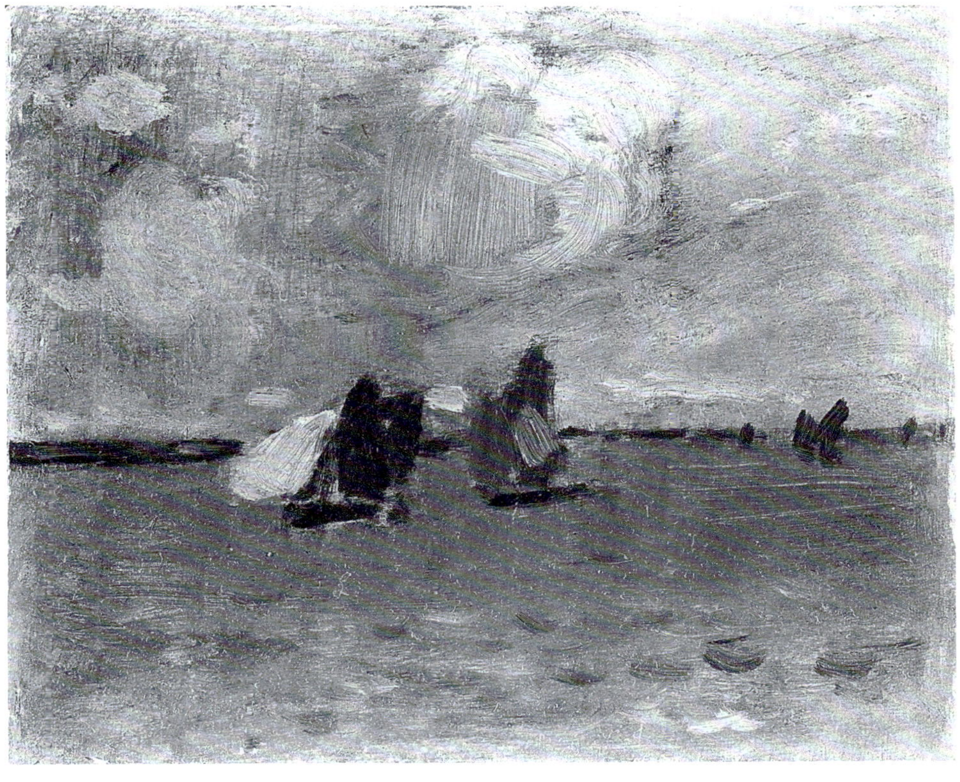

Fig. 60a
Fishing Boats, c. 1909, oil on wood, 12.7 × 15.2 cm. Private collection.

1. Correspondence in curatorial file for Morrice's *Landscape, Trinidad* (2417), Art Gallery of Ontario, Toronto. Matisse was offering both works for sale in 1937.
2. Letter from Pierre Matisse to Mrs. Joseph Shima, Continental Galleries, 26 September 1949 (letter with Continental Galleries, Montreal, 1977).
3. Loaned by Lawrence M. Hart to the Canadian National Exhibition, Toronto, September 1950, no. 156.
4. Correspondence in curatorial file for Morrice's *At the Front* (6357), National Gallery of Canada.
5. Lyman 1980, p. 40.
6. The sketch is reproduced in colour in Laing 1984, p. 207.

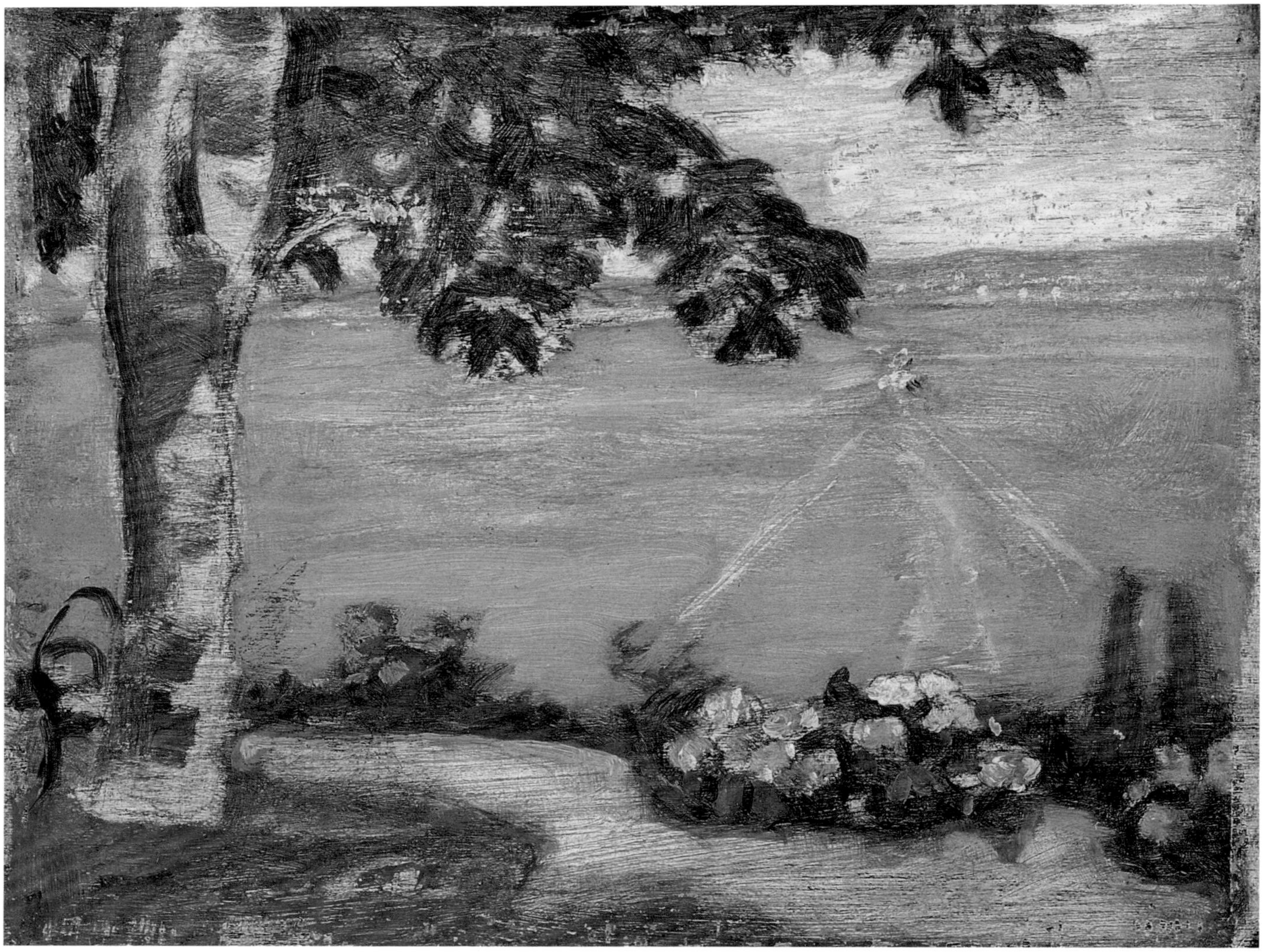

61

Landscape

c. 1910

Oil and graphite on wood, 13.2 × 17 cm

Inscriptions: verso: c. stamped, *STUDIO / J.W. MORRICE*, c.l. in graphite, *170*

Labels: in blue ink, *GBL / LAKE IN / SOUTH FRANCE*

Provenance: Estate of the artist. A member of the Porteous family, Montreal; G. Blair Laing, Toronto, c. 1980.

30472

Whether this sketch represents a lake in the south of France, as Blair Lang believed,[1] or Île d'Orléans near Quebec City (as I have surmised) is uncertain. This could indeed be a view from Île d'Orléans, where the Porteous family, friends of the artist,[2] had their summer home. Morrice visited Canada in the summer of 1910 to celebrate his parents' fiftieth wedding anniversary.[3]

In this sketch Morrice first drew in the tree and foliage, outlining the colour areas in the foreground in graphite. Over the thin rubbed blue of the water he scratched in the wake of the boat, then painted in the more solid blue of the foreground water. The treatment of the foliage as broad, angular masses is characteristic of other sketches he did around this same period.[4]

1. Laing 1984, pp. 142–43.
2. Letter from Morrice to Edmund Morris, 24 January [1912], Morris Papers.
3. Sketchbook 15 (Montreal Museum of Fine Arts, Dr.1973.38), back endpaper, recto; "Canadian Academy Exhibition Open Soon," *Montreal Star*, 3 November 1910; letter from Morrice to Newton MacTavish, 3 November 1910, MacTavish Papers.
4. For example, *Roadside Scene* (oil and graphite on wood, 12.2 × 15.3 cm), McMichael Canadian Art Collection, Kleinburg (1968.7.27), inscribed recto, lower right, "June 2nd/11."

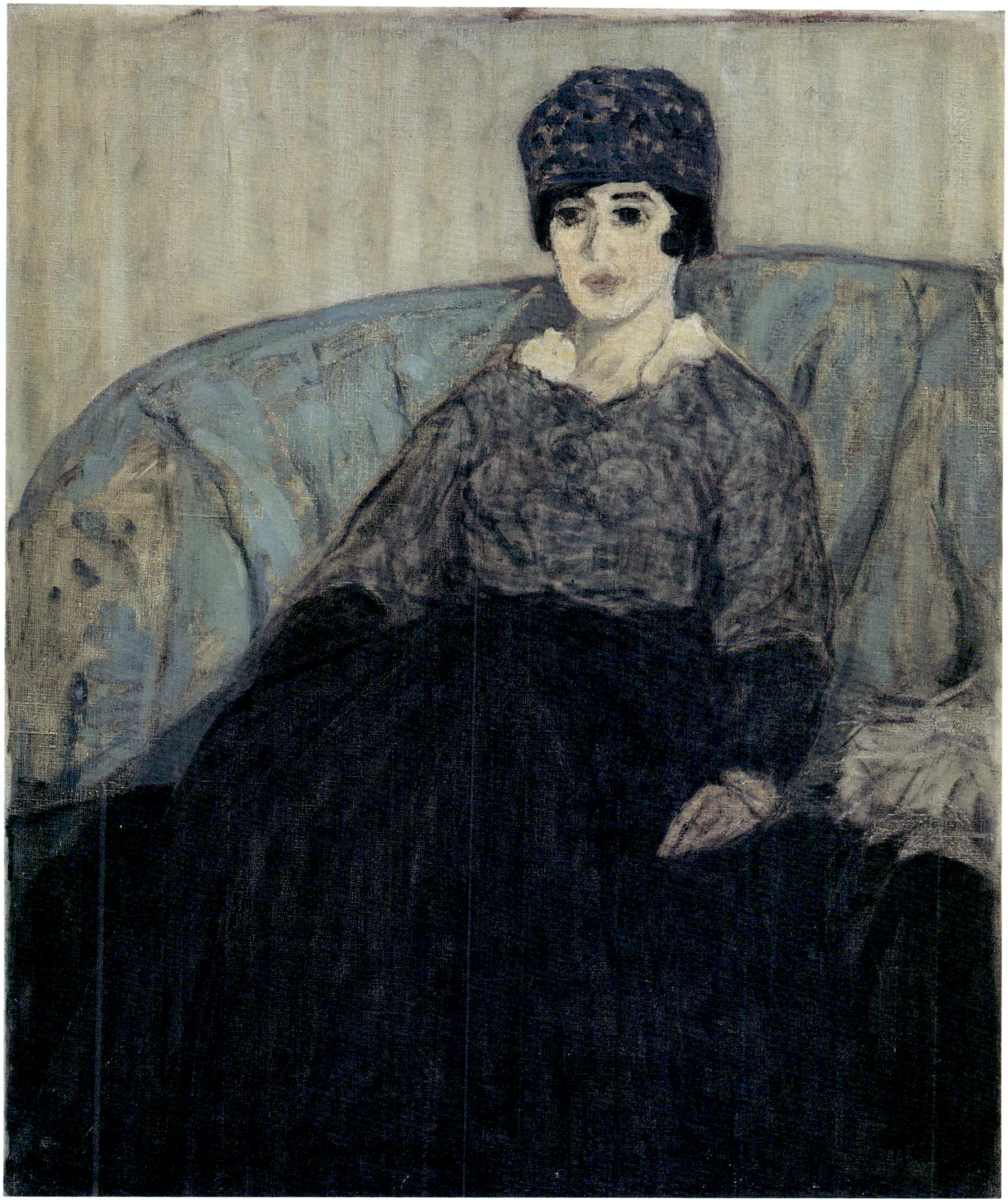

62
Blanche Baume

62

Blanche Baume

c. 1911–12

Oil on canvas, 61.2 × 50.5 cm

Inscriptions: signed l.r., *Morrice*; stretcher: u.l. in graphite, [—]*80.00* (partly crossed out), u.c. in graphite, *Blanche by J.W. Morrice*, in graphite, *2796 $35.00*, u.r. in graphite, *$5000.00*, l.c. stamped, *12 Paris* [—] *F / 61 × 30*; on crossbar, l.c. in graphite, *GRR***, c. in graphite, *0/2796*; back of frame: l.c. in graphite, *BLAIR LAING*, l.r. in graphite, *SCHA*[—]

Labels: in blue ballpoint pen, *Note Mlle Blanch Baume / posed for several of / Morrice's portraits. This / version was selected by / the National Gallery for a / full size reproduction No NG 41-54. / William R Watson*

Provenance: Estate of the artist;[1] Galeries Simonson, Paris;[2] W. Scott & Sons, Montreal, by 1932;[3] W.R. Watson, Montreal (sold, Sotheby & Co. [Canada] Ltd., Toronto, 23 October 1973, lot 70). G. Blair Laing, Toronto, 1974.

30479

Around 1911 Morrice went back to figure painting for the first time in many years, and in April 1911 exhibited a canvas titled *La toilette* (most likely the female nude now in the Art Gallery of Ontario in Toronto; see fig. 63a) at the International Society in London. It was considered "indecent" by the art critics, and Morrice commented, "they must have dirty minds."[4]

There are at least eight paintings of women, including nudes, that have several internal cross-references (similar backgrounds or textiles, or identical models) which permit us to date them to the same period, that is from about 1911 to 1914.[5] Two studies are of Morrice's longtime model Blanche Baume in variant colour schemes: this version is painted in blue, while the one in the Montreal Museum of Fine Arts (fig. 62a) is in red.[6] Both figures are seated on a similar high-back sofa and are shown wearing a long-skirted dress and turban. Behind them both, the striped wallpaper is represented in vertical bands.

In the blue version, the dark skirt and lower sleeves occupy almost the entire bottom half of the composition and the blouse is painted in loose, transparent-blue lines over brown, calling to mind the fluid drawing of the dark cloud in *Fishing Boats, Nantes* (cat. no. 60). The sofa's curves are defined with dark lines and it is toned with turquoise blue and mottled areas of brown. A feather or fur muff, its busy brushwork echoing that of the blouse, is at the sitter's left. The background is painted in cream-yellow bands, with the lighter bands in a pale robin's-egg blue.

In the Montreal painting the outlines are more pronounced, resulting in a more abstract silhouette, further enhanced by the wooden moulding at the top of the sofa back. The patterned cushions reinforce the decorative effect. Both works are notable for their emphatic brushwork and linear rhythms, as well as for their effective colour harmonies.

This was not the first time that Morrice had painted two variant canvases of similar compositions. There are two versions of *The Beach, St-Malo*,[7] both probably dating to 1903; the larger version came from the collection of Jacques Rouché and may have been painted on commission. There are also variant compositions of the *Quai des Grands-Augustins*;[8] the larger one was purchased by the French government in 1904, and it is possible that the smaller canvas was painted to capitalize on this success. As well, there is a second version of the painting in the Musée de Picardie (fig. 5, Introduction).[9]

Buchanan has identified six portraits of Blanche Baume, ranging in date from the mid-1890s to about 1914.[10] According to his account, Baume was a rather well-known model who had posed for one of the nude figures representing the rivers of Asia on Denys Puech's monument to François Garnier erected in 1898 on the Avenue de l'Observatoire.[11]

An inscription on a label on the back of this work refers to a silkscreen reproduction of the painting made by Peter Markgraf in 1967. Markgraf's are among the finest reproductions ever made of Canadian paintings.

1. According to Buchanan (1936a, p. 182), this painting was exhibited at the French Gallery, London, in April 1925, and all the paintings in that show were from the artist's estate.
2. Paris 1926, no. 44, as *Femme en bleu*.
3. Montreal 1932, no. 22, as *Blanche*.
4. Letter from Morrice to Edmund Morris, 2 April [1911], Morris Papers.
5. See also cat. no. 63 and Cloutier 1985, nos. 71, 72, 83, and 84. There is an unfinished nude in the Musée d'art contemporain de Montréal (A77.2.P.1), and a nude formerly in the Mendel Collection, reproduced in *The Mendel Collection: Opening Exhibition* (Saskatoon: Mendel Art Gallery and Civic Conservatory, 1964), p. 6.
6. Reproduced in colour in Cloutier 1985, p. 194.
7. Montreal Museum of Fine Arts (947.980), oil on canvas, 54.6 × 73.7 cm; private collection, Toronto (formerly in the collection of Jacques Rouché, Paris), oil on canvas, 81.3 × 114.3 cm. See Cloutier 1985, pp. 158–59.
8. Musée d'Orsay, Paris (RF 1980-146), oil on canvas, 65 × 80 cm; National Gallery of Canada (73), oil on canvas, 48.9 × 59.7 cm. The latter was first exhibited at the Carnegie Institute, Pittsburgh, November 1905, no. 184 (confirmed by installation photographs). It was purchased by the National Gallery of Canada in 1909; when Sir Edmund Walker, the chairman of the National Gallery's board of trustees, saw the larger canvas at the Luxembourg Museum in Paris, he referred to the National Gallery version as a study, which it clearly is not (Sir Edmund Walker Journal 1899–1919, Thomas Fisher Rare Book Library, University of Toronto,

microfilm 565, entry for 24 June 1909). See Cloutier 1985, pp. 32, 164–65.

9. The second version was, by 1902, in the collection of George Hearn, a noted patron of the Metropolitan Museum of Art in New York (Charles FitzGerald, "Exhibit at the Union League and Lotos Clubs," *The Sun* [New York], 13 December 1902). It was sold with the Hearn collection at the American Art Asoociation, 25 February 1918, lot 160, repr. See also Buchanan 1936a, p. 160, entry for *St. Malo*.
10. Buchanan 1936a, pp. 179–82. These are *Young Woman in a Black Coat* (Montreal Museum of Fine Arts, 937.659), *Woman in a Wicker Chair* (Beaverbrook Art Gallery, Fredericton, 59.149), *Woman in a Grey Hat* and *Olympia* (National Gallery of Canada, 4880 and 6771), as well as *Blanche* and *Blanche Baume*, reproduced here. In addition, a study of a head sold at Christie, Manson & Woods (Canada) Ltd., Montreal, 30 April 1970, lot 21, bears the title *Blanche*.
11. Buchanan 1936a, p. 99, n. 1. See also June Hargrove, *The Statues of Paris* (New York / Paris: Vendome Press, 1989), p. 248.

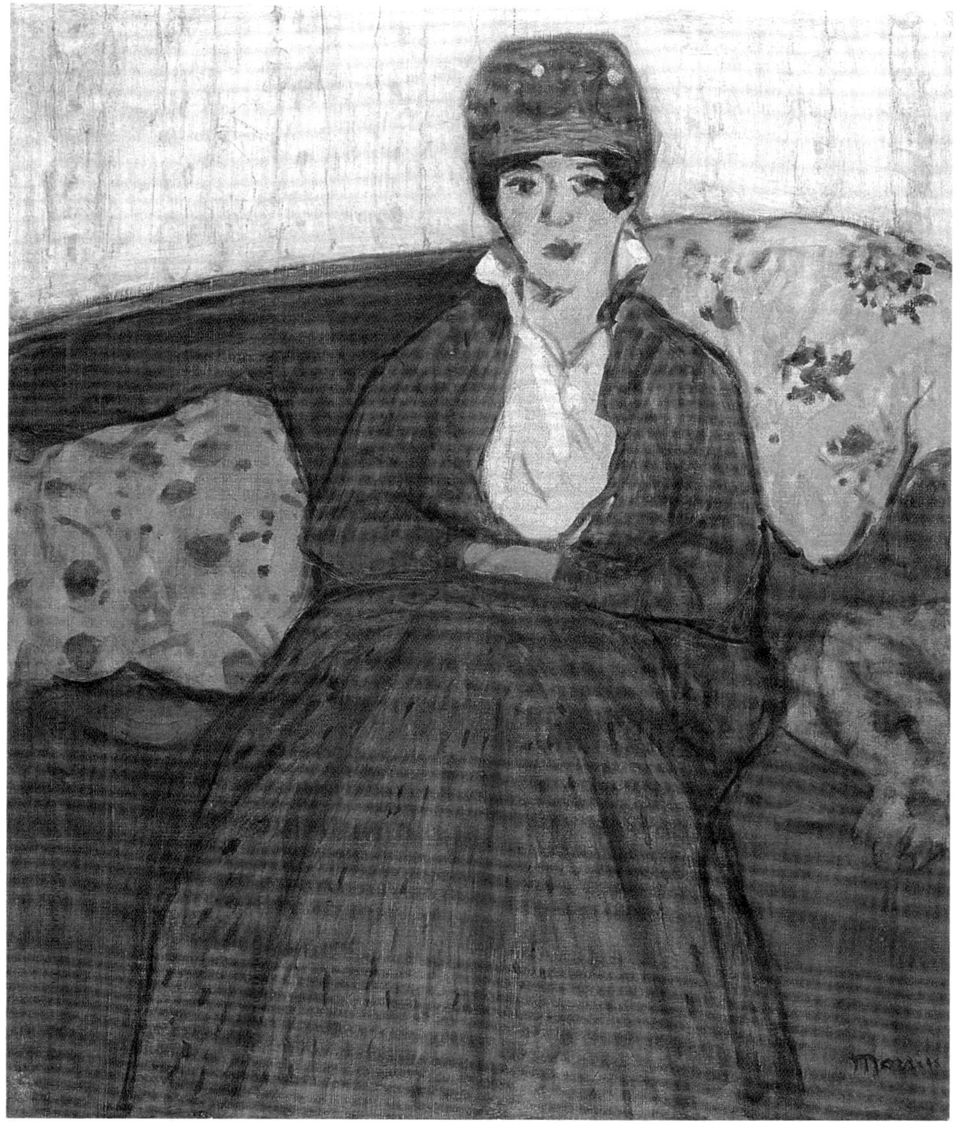

Fig. 62a
Blanche, c. 1911–12, oil on canvas, 62.2 × 50.8 cm. Montreal Museum of Fine Arts. Gift of Dr. G.R. McCall, 1978 (1978.32).

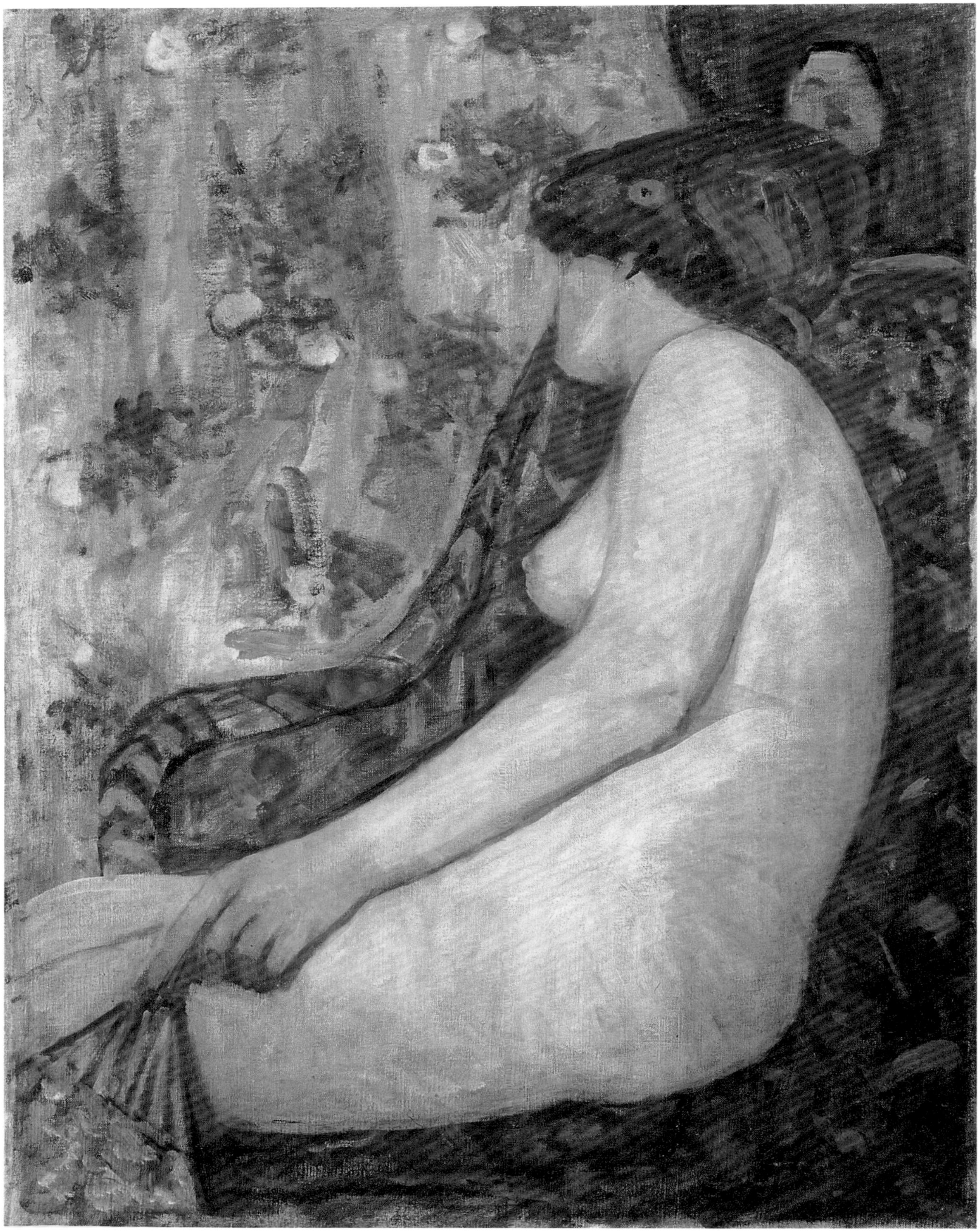

63

Woman with a Fan

c. 1912–14

Oil on canvas, 65 × 50.5 cm

Inscriptions: signed l.r., *Morrice*; verso: l.r. stamped twice, *DOUANES EXPOSITIONS PARIS*; stretcher: l.r. stamped, *DOUANES EXPOSITIONS PARIS*, u.c. stamped, *15 P / 65 × 50*, u.r. scratched, *32*; on crossbar, in graphite, *Cadoret*, in red crayon, *Box 5-12*

Labels: in black ink, *198*; typed, Artist *JAMES W. MORRICE, R.C.A.* / TITLE *FEMME À L'ÉVENTAIL* / Property of *MME. LEA CADORET* / Return Address *PARIS, FRANCE*, in graphite, twice, *32*; in black ink, ROBINOT Frères & Cie. / EMBALLEURS / 86, Boulevard Garibaldi, 86 – Paris (15e) / *Légation du Canada*; partly torn, [Laing Galleries 194 Bloor] Street West Toronto 5 Canada; in black ink, *4*; in black ink, *LAR*

Provenance: Estate of the artist; Léa Cadoret, Juan-les-Pins and Paris;[1] Jacques Dubourg, Paris; G. Blair Laing, Toronto, 1965.

30460

The same material depicted on the cushion in *Blanche* (fig. 62a) is used as a backdrop in the richly coloured *Woman with a Fan*, a three-quarter-length study of a red-haired, seated female nude.[2] The red of the chair and the yellow, red, and green of the background establish the dominant tones, set off by the pink and pale-green fan and the brown wall behind the Japanese mask at the upper right. The loose brushwork in the chair and background contrasts with the silhouette and the more finished flesh tones of the figure. Turned away from the viewer, the model expresses a mood of tranquillity and repose. But what are we to make of the mask? Is it merely a touch of decorative exoticism, a humorous intrusion, or are we to read some other meaning in the painting?

Morrice originally painted this work on a larger canvas; he subsequently reduced its size and mounted it on a new stretcher (the original painted canvas is now folded over the stretcher). He then reworked the surface and composition to conform to the new dimensions. As the painted canvas originally extended further on the right and at the top, the change altered the position of the model in relation to the picture frame, which now confines her more closely.

This is almost certainly the same model depicted in *Nu de dos devant la cheminée* (fig. 63a) and *Nude with a Feather* (fig. 63b). In the former, which is the earliest of the three, Morrice has limited himself to muted browns and flesh tones, posing the model leaning against a mantlepiece, with framed sketches all around her. In the other two works the colour is much more vibrant, and the patterned textiles are exploited for both their decorative and sensual qualities. In *Woman with a Fan* the curve of the chair and drapery echo the pose of the model, while in *Nude with a Feather* the vertical panels are a foil to the curves of the model and her draped cloak. Several authors have noted Morrice's debt to the French painter Pierre Bonnard in these paintings,[3] Bonnard having been an artist Morrice greatly admired.[4]

After Morrice's death, his later nudes became the property of Léa Cadoret. His family in Montreal may have found them objectionable, and it was only after their inclusion in Donald Buchanan's biography in 1936 and the Morrice retrospective in 1937 that they started to enter Canadian collections.

1. Buchanan 1936a, p. 181.
2. The material also appears in *Flowers* (oil on canvas, 46 × 38 cm) in the National Gallery of Canada (15536).
3. O'Brian 1982b, pp. 27–31; Cloutier 1985, p. 193; Dorais 1985a, pp. 68–69; Dorais 1985b, p. 19.
4. Bennett 1971, p. 174, entry for 18 January 1907; letter from Morrice to Edmund Morris, 20 June 1911, Morris Papers.

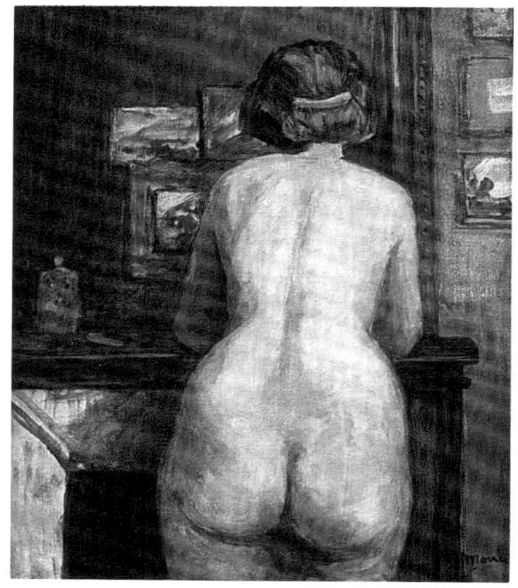

Fig. 63a
Nu de dos devant la cheminée, c. 1911, oil on canvas, photograph by E. Crevaux, Paris, showing original dimensions, 57.2 × 47 cm. Painting presently in the collection of the Art Gallery of Ontario, Toronto. Gift of Mr. and Mrs. Jules Loeb, Toronto, 1987 (87/340).

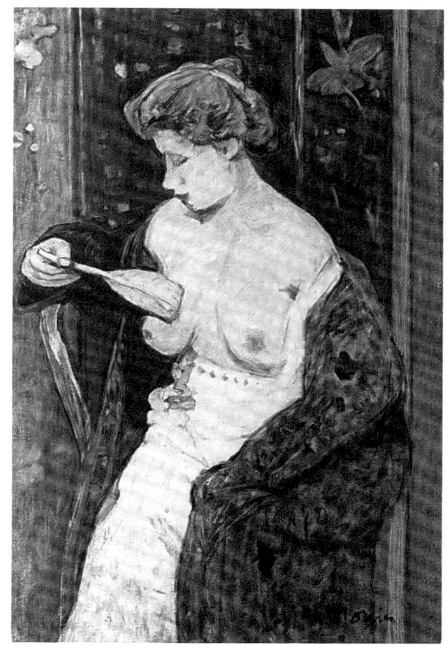

Fig. 63b
Nude with a Feather, c. 1912–14, oil on canvas, 81 × 54 cm. Montreal Museum of Fine Arts. Bequest of F. Eleanore Morrice, 1981 (1981.65).

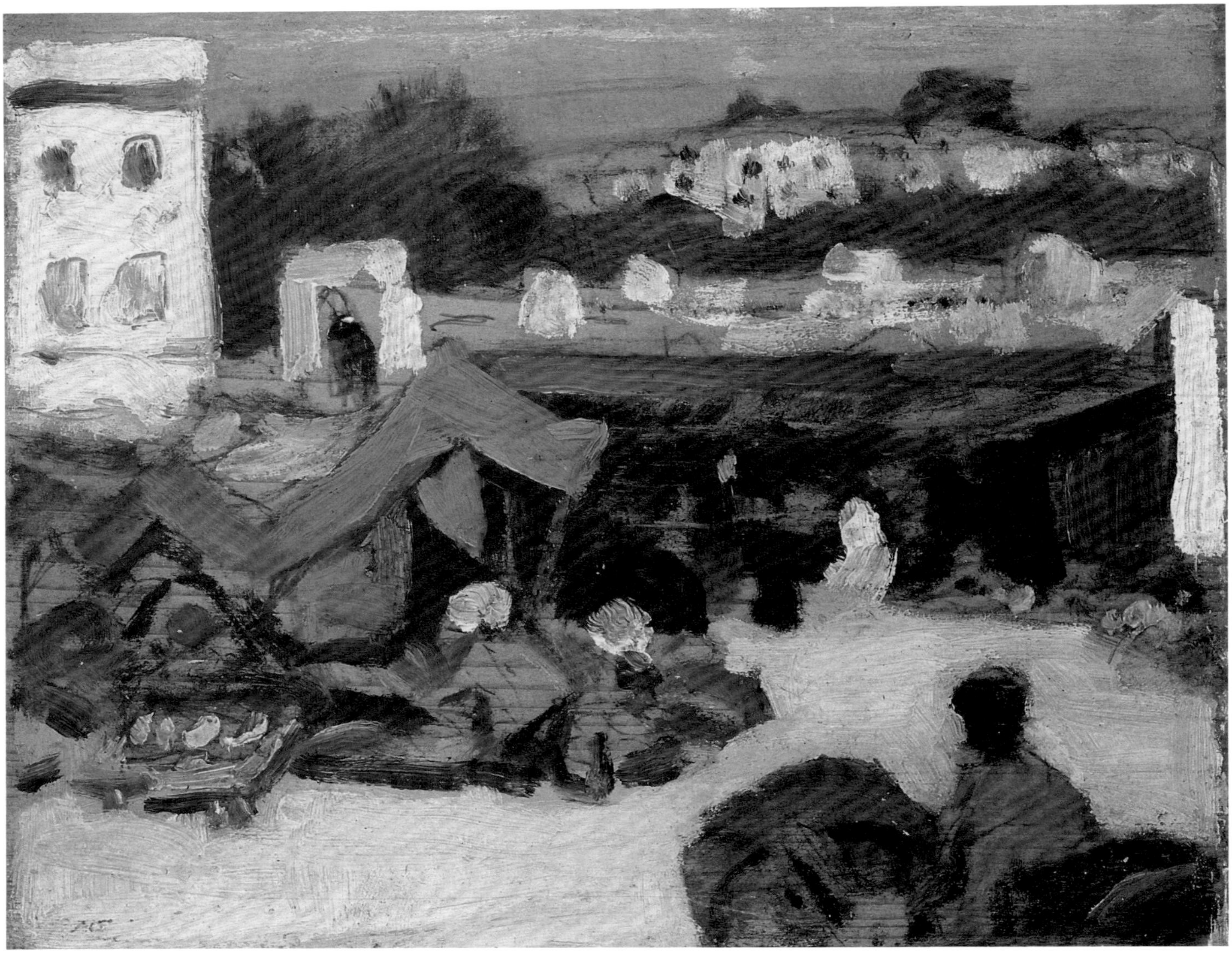

64

Arab Market, Tangiers

1912

Oil and graphite on wood, 12.2 × 15.4 cm

Inscriptions: verso: c. stamped, *STUDIO / J.W. MORRICE*, b. in graphite, *Arab Market Tangier*

Labels: in blue ballpoint pen, *78-26 / "MOROCCO / MARKET"*

Provenance: Estate of the artist. Vilma Lafontaine, Montreal; Laing Galleries, Toronto, 1960; Dr. G.H. Henderson, Halifax; G. Blair Laing Ltd., Toronto, 1978.

30412

In early February 1912 Morrice departed for Gibraltar and Tangiers. It was in the Moroccan port city that he encountered Henri Matisse, whom he had known in Paris through the Salon d'Automne, and possibly as early as the 1890s.[1] In October Morrice exhibited four Tangiers paintings at the Salon d'Automne: *Tanger*; *Tanger, la plage*; *Tanger, paysage*; and *Tanger, boutique*. Then in December he returned to Tangiers, where he stayed until early March before going on to Gibraltar and Spain.[2] In April 1913 he exhibited one additional painting, *Tanger, le soir*, at the International Society in London. Later in the year, at the Salon d'Automne, he exhibited a canvas of the Rock of Gibraltar together with five new Tangiers paintings: *Tanger, les environs*; *Tanger, fenêtre*; *Tanger, jardin*; *Tanger, ville*; and *Tanger, danseuse*. In March 1914 he returned once more to North Africa, this time to visit Tunis.[3]

The inscription on the back of this sketch, identifying the subject as an Arab market in Tangiers, is very likely correct, and the sketch probably is from Morrice's first visit to North Africa. On the first page of his North African sketchbook we find a faint, rubbed drawing of this same market (fig. 64a). The angularity of the foreground tents and the schematic treatment of the houses on the hillside relate to the sketch for the canvas exhibited in 1912 as *Tanger, paysage*.[4]

In his earlier oil sketches Morrice sometimes used graphite for the preliminary drawing or to add or reinforce details (see, for example, cat. nos. 40 and 41). Around 1910 he began using graphite in conjunction with oil paint in a more expressive manner (see cat. no. 55), but still essentially for definition or reinforcement.[5] In this sketch, however, Morrice has drawn in the composition in graphite and then added colour to fill in the main forms, allowing the graphite to animate the spaces visible between the paint strokes. This is especially apparent in the hills and in the forms below the tents, where the combination of graphite and paint becomes even more complex and dynamic.

Morrice painted a second view of this market (fig. 64b), in which he depicts a stairway in the foreground leading to some seated figures who are watching the milling throng. Other figures are also seen on the balcony at the right. In both works, touches of bright pink enliven the arch on the far side of the market.

1. Letter from Morrice to Edmund Morris, "Thursday," Morris Papers. See also Laura Coyle, "Chronology," in Cowart et al. 1990, p. 258.
2. Letters from Morrice to Edmund Morris, 1 November [1912] and 1 January 1913, Morris Papers; Danièle Giraudy, "Correspondance Henri Matisse–Charles Camoin," *Revue de l'art* XII (1971), pp. 14–16; Coyle, op. cit.
3. Letter from A.Y. Collins to Maurice Cullen, 12 March 1914, Archives, Art Gallery of Hamilton.
4. The sketch and canvas are reproduced in Dorais 1985b, pp. 64–65. The canvas is in the National Gallery of Canada (6108).
5. See also the portrait of William Brymner in the Montreal Museum of Fine Arts (943.809), reproduced in Johnston 1965, p. 54. The portrait dates from Morrice's visit to Canada in the summer of 1910 (Dorais 1985a, pp. 63, 71, n. 12).

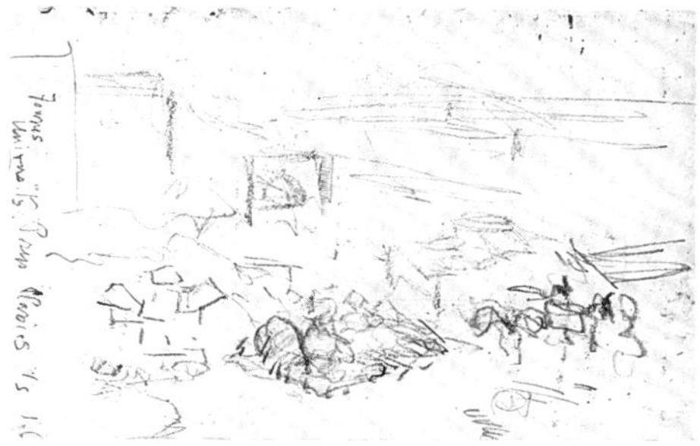

Fig. 64a
Sketchbook 6, p. 1r, 1912, graphite on wove paper, 10.7 × 16.7 cm. Montreal Museum of Fine Arts. Gift of David R. Morrice, 1973 (Dr.1973.29).

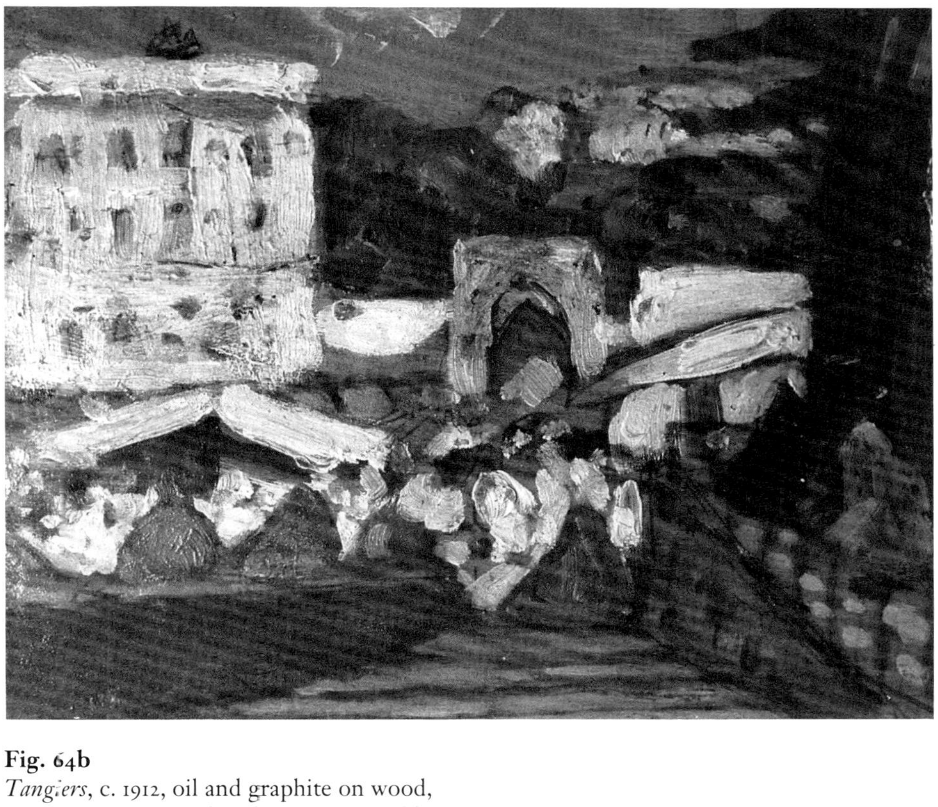

Fig. 64b
Tangiers, c. 1912, oil and graphite on wood, 13 × 16.7 cm. City of Lethbridge, Donald Buchanan Collection.

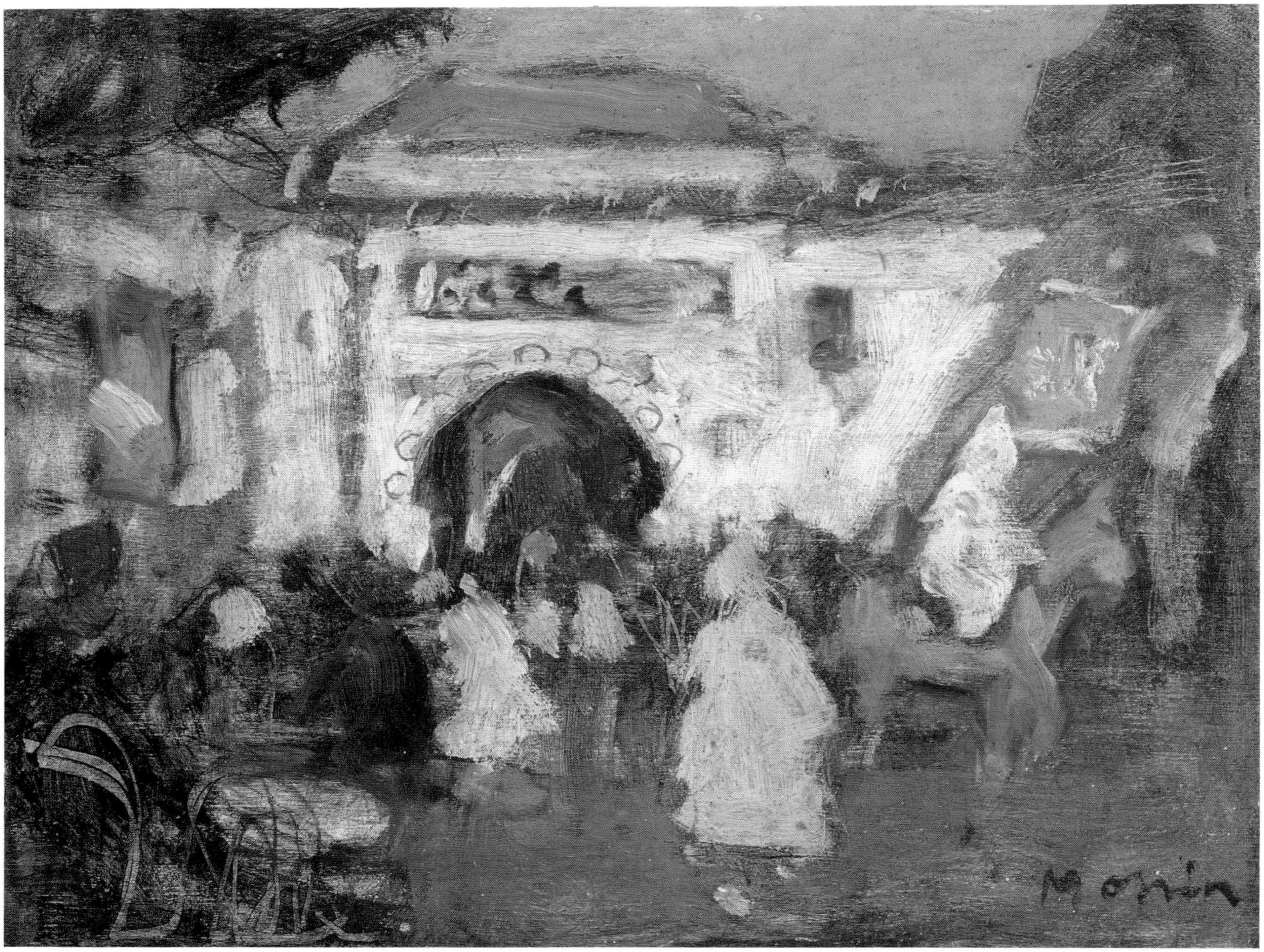

65

A City Gate, North Africa

c. 1912

Oil and graphite on wood, 13.1 × 17 cm

Inscriptions: signed l.r., *Morrice*; verso: in graphite, *J.W. Morrice*

Labels: in blue ballpoint pen, GBL / "MARRAKESCH"

Provenance: Private collection, London; G. Blair Laing, Toronto, 1972.

30474

Blair Laing originally identified this sketch as representing a procession in Algiers.[1] He subsequently placed the scene in Marrakesh, relying somewhat hesitantly on the claim made by the biographer of the American painter Robert Henry Logan that Morrice had travelled with Logan to Marrakesh in 1910.[2] However, it is difficult to believe that Morrice would have ventured into what was still a rather dangerous zone for European travellers; it was only in 1912 that the Treaty of Fez was signed, formally establishing most of Morocco as a French protectorate.

The gate painted here was depicted by Morrice in another oil sketch, *A North African Market Scene* (fig. 65b), and may be the same as one he drew in his North African sketchbook (fig. 65a). As in *Arab Market, Tangiers* (cat. no. 64), he has freely drawn in the forms in graphite and then brushed the paint over them, in some instances following the initial composition and in others ignoring the underdrawing. He has then come back with graphite and with the end of his brush, or some other implement, in order to add detail (the chairs at the lower left, the decoration on the arch) or to affirm a line. In *North African Market Scene* the graphite underdrawing is more evident (especially in the figures at the lower left), and more of the wood shows through. Accent colours of red, yellow, and green animate the predominantly white and brown street scene.

1. Laing 1979, p. 205.
2. Laing 1984, pp. 86–87; Tally 1980, p. 23.

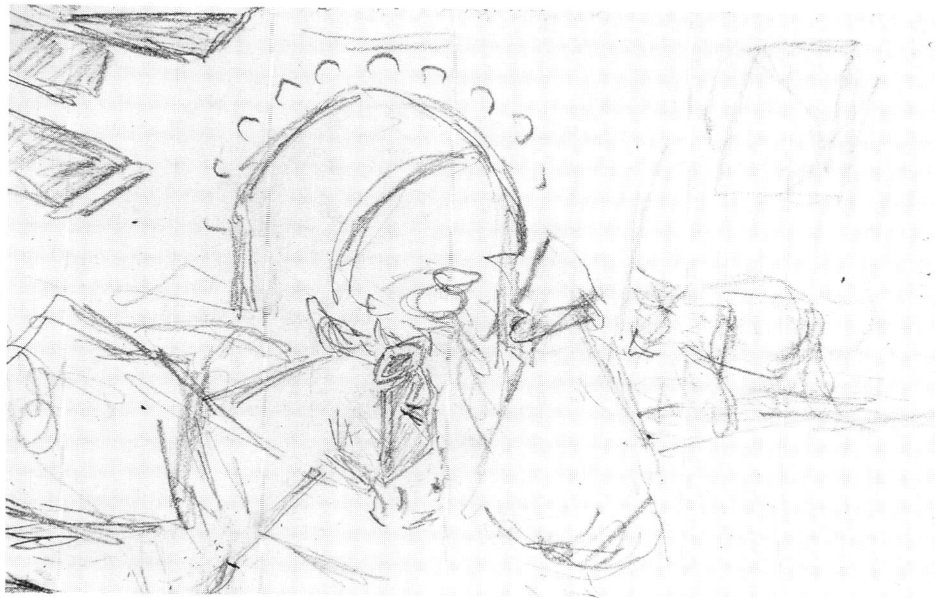

Fig. 65a
Sketchbook 6, p. 4r, c. 1912, graphite on wove paper, 10.7 × 16.7 cm. Montreal Museum of Fine Arts. Gift of David R. Morrice, 1973 (Dr.1973.29).

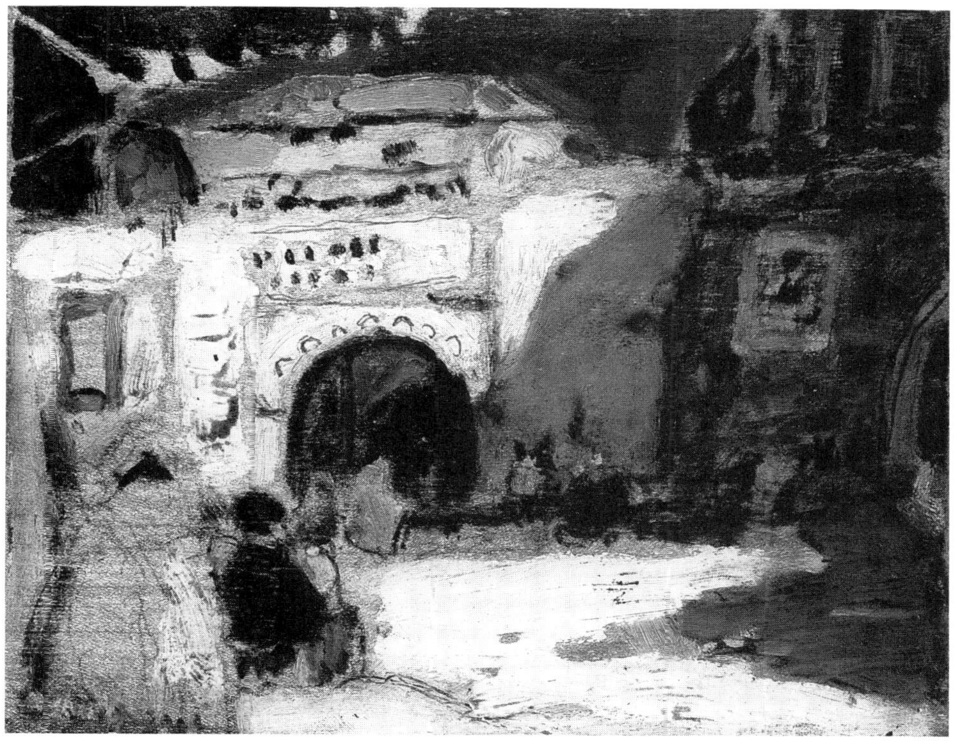

Fig. 65b
A North African Market Scene, c. 1912, oil and graphite on wood, 12.2 × 15.5 cm. McMichael Canadian Art Collection, Kleinburg. Bequest of David R. Morrice, 1979 (1979.3.1).

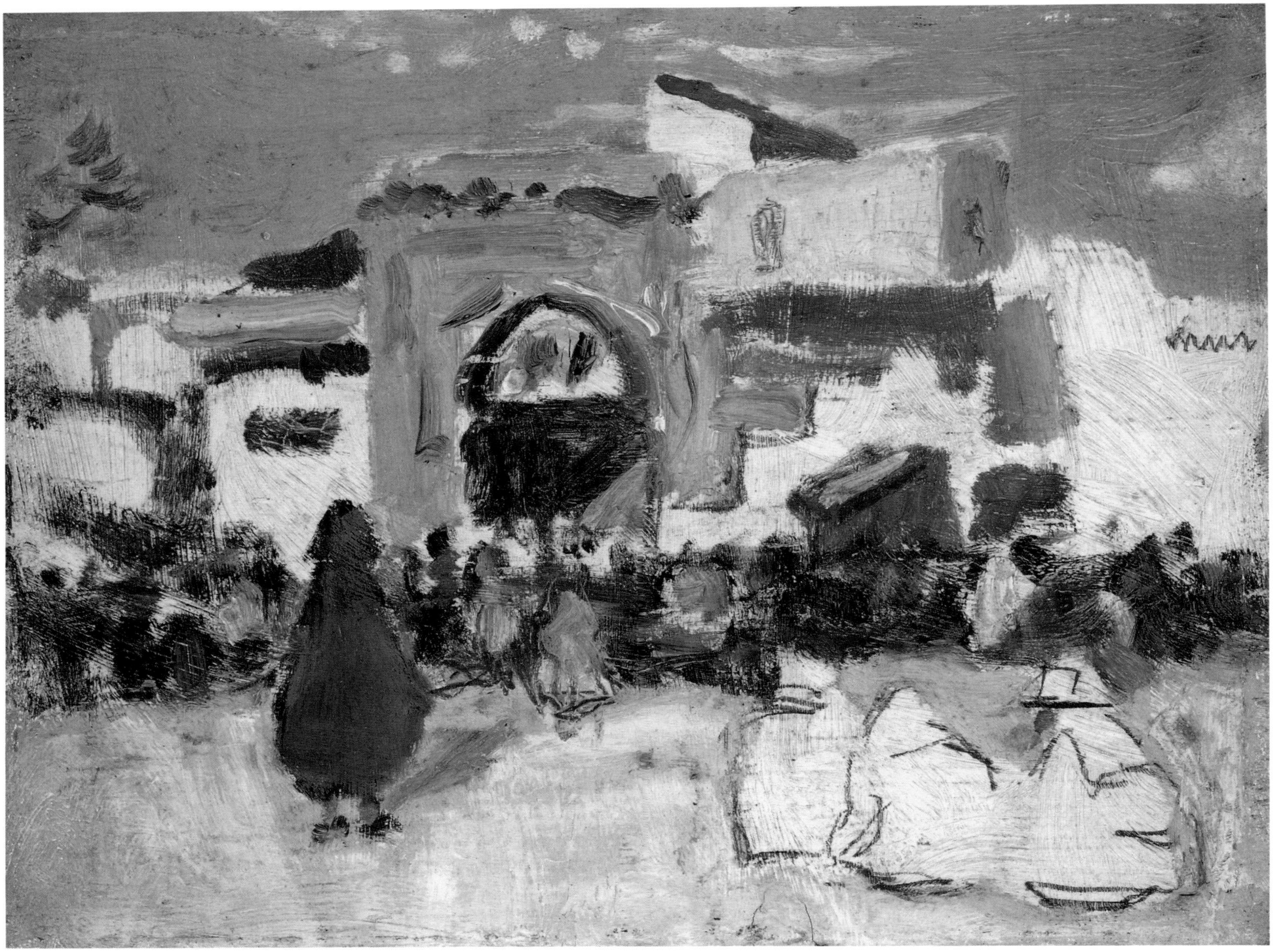

66

North African Market

c. 1912

Oil and graphite on wood, 13 × 17.1 cm

Inscriptions: back of frame: l… in black ballpoint pen, *From Mrs. James Law / Montreal, P.Q.*

Labels: MMFA 1965, no. 97; Wildenstein 1968, no. 31; typed, NATIONAL GALLERY OF CANADA / Title of Exhibition / *J W MORRICE / RETROSPECTIVE EX* / Catalogue No. *31#* / Box No. *10*, in graphite, *Nov Dec / 1965*; typed, *MORRICE EXHIBITION / TITLE: EASTERN MARKET (PANEL) / FROM: LAING GALLERY, TORONTO*, in black ballpoint pen, *#31*, in graphite, *FROM Mrs. James Law / Montreal*; in blue ink, *GBL / "EASTERN / MARKET"*, in graphite, / *#13*

Provenance: Mrs. James Law, Montreal. G. Blair Laing, Toronto, 1965.

30452

In this sketch of a North African market scene in front of a massive pink gate, Morrice has painted the surrounding wall and buildings in a mosaic of coloured shapes. Graphite affirms details in the architecture and is used to draw in the three foreground figures over the white paint that defines their general forms. Morrice often incorporated in his paintings a figure addressing the viewer; here instead he has placed the woman in black, depicted from the rear.

In the preliminary drawing for this oil sketch (fig. 66a) Morrice clarified the details of the architecture and the grouping of the market throng. The present whereabouts of the drawing, which had been removed from Morrice's North African sketchbook in 1953, are unknown.[1]

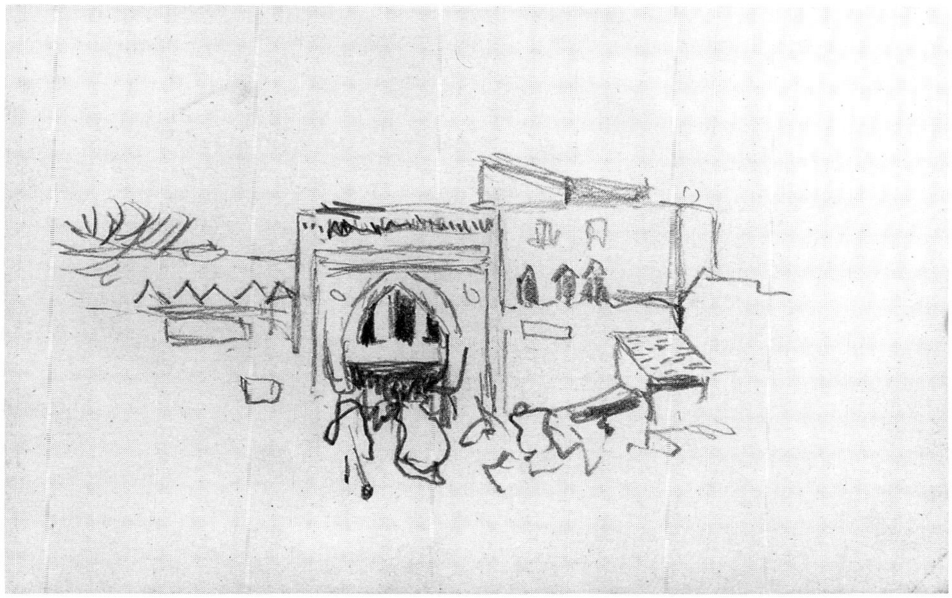

Fig. 66a
A City Gate in North Africa, c. 1912, graphite on wove paper, probably 10.7 × 16.7 cm. Originally in Sketchbook 6; present location unknown.

1. In 1953 certain selected pages from Morrice's sketchbooks, then with David Morrice, were removed for photography and reproduction in *Canadian Art* and for exhibition at the National Gallery of Canada. Markers in the sketchbooks identified where the pages came from, but the pages were never put back in place after they were returned to David Morrice. Unlike some of the other removed pages, this drawing was not bequeathed to the Montreal Museum of Fine Arts. See Archives, National Gallery of Canada, file 2.6–Morrice; Buchanan 1953; Moisan 1983, nos. 82, 83, and 84.

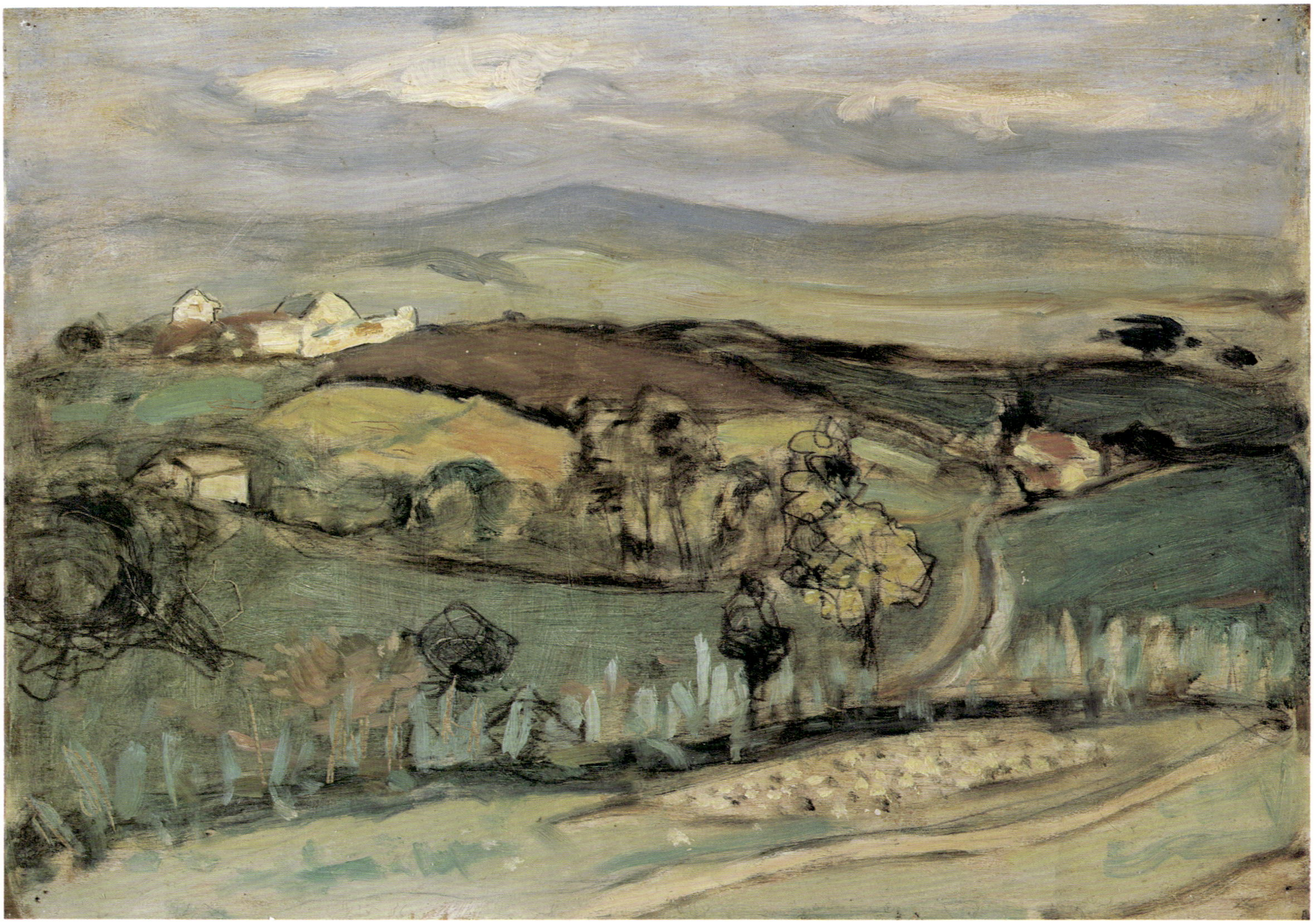

67

Study for "Environs of Tangiers"

1913

Oil and graphite on wood, 23.7 × 33 cm

Inscriptions: verso: u.c. in black ink (Joseph Shima's hand?), *Landscape in Provence / by James W. Morrice, R.C.A.*, u.l. in green pencil, *M193*; back of frame: u.c. in graphite, *In Provence*

Labels: typed, THE / NATIONAL GALLERY OF CANADA OTTAWA / *Paintings in Ottawa Collections* / OHMS *April 9, 1959. / Name Eugene M. Henry / Address 128 Lisgar Road, Rockcliffe / Title Landscape in Provence / J.W. Morrice RCA / Value $900.00*; in blue ink, *81-4 / L'SCAPE / PROVENCE*

Provenance: Continental Galleries of Fine Art, Montreal. Eugene Henry, Ottawa; by descent to a member of the Henry family; G. Blair Laing Ltd., Toronto, 1981.

30421

If any generalizations can be made about the differences between the sketches realized during the Tangiers trips of 1912 and 1913, it is that the later works are characterized by a greater fluency of line, more liquid paint, smoother surfaces, and more open space. This sketch is a study for a canvas (fig. 67a) that Donald Buchanan identified as being the *Tanger, les environs* that was exhibited at the Salon d'Automne in November 1913.[1] It is painted on a large panel, of approximately the same size as the sketch for the painting *Gibraltar*, which was also exhibited that fall.[2]

There is a lyrical freedom of handling in this sketch, the composition of which is defined by curving intersecting rhythms that extend into the mountains and sky. The dappled white and black in the foreground is gently confined by the drawing in black and surmounted by light-green dabs of paint. The fields on the crest of the hill in front of the red-roofed, white buildings are painted in rich brown, grey, and pink. The paint is applied thinly in some areas and thickly in others, with lines defining the major areas. Graphite accents form open lyrical spaces.

In the canvas the far hills are more thinly painted in black, and the sky rises from a pale yellow to light blue. At the centre, the fields echo the yellow of the sky and the trees become a more emphatic anchor for the surging landscape.

1. Buchanan 1936a, pp. 175–76.
2. The sketch *Gibraltar* (fig. 67b) is in the Montreal Museum of Fine Arts; the canvas (66 × 81.2 cm) is in the Art Gallery of Ontario, Toronto (89/112).

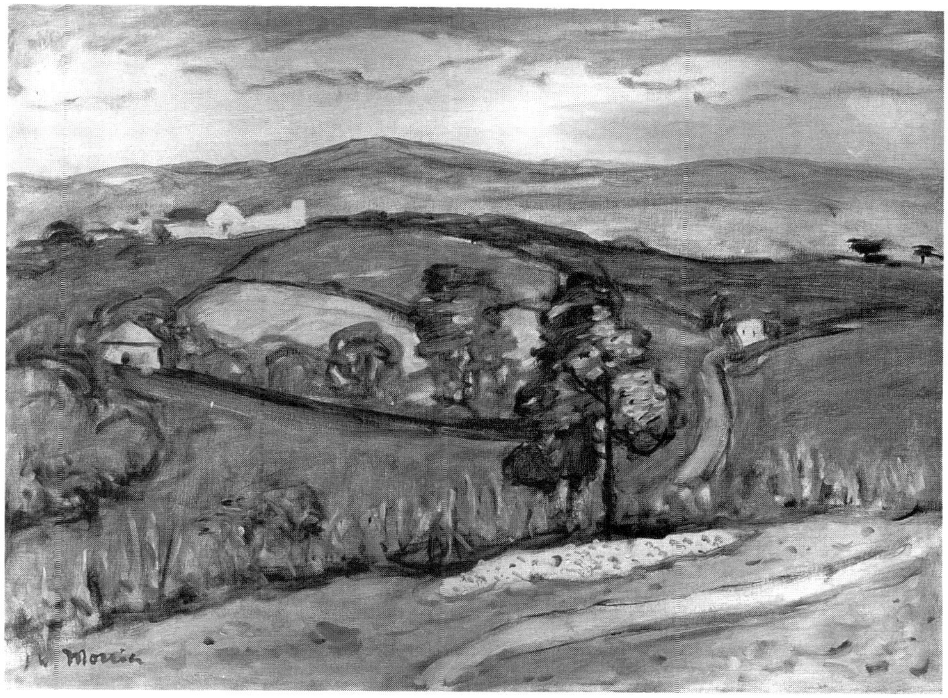

Fig. 67a
Environs of Tangiers, 1913, oil on canvas, 50.8 × 72.4 cm. Private collection.

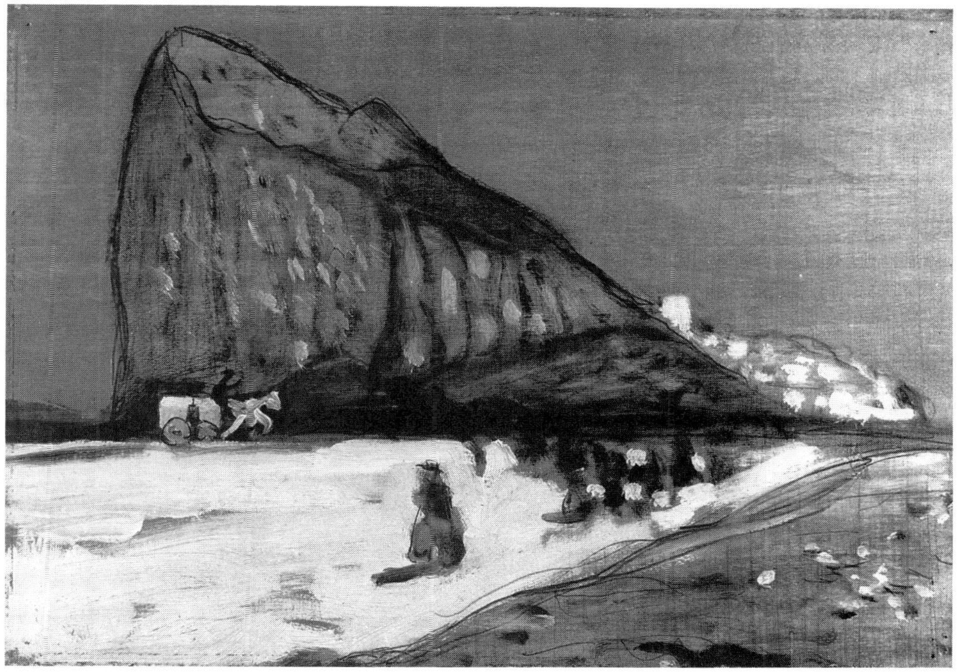

Fig. 67b
Gibraltar, 1913, oil and graphite on wood, 23.6 × 32.8 cm. Montreal Museum of Fine Arts. Bequest of David R. Morrice, 1981 (1981.13).

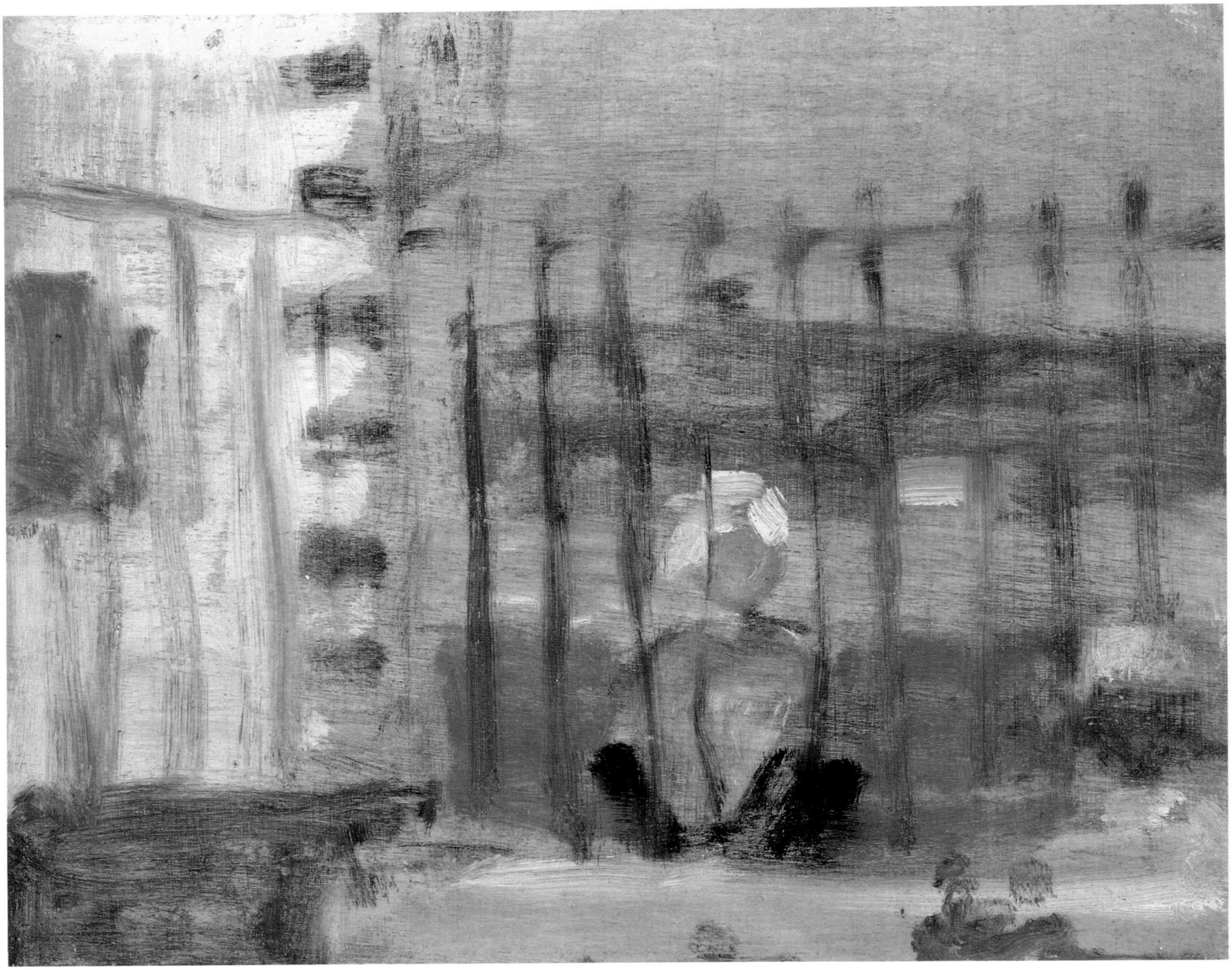

68

Through a Garden Fence

c. 1912–13

Oil on wood, 12.1 × 15 cm

Inscriptions: verso: t. in blue ink, *Through a Garden Fence Tunis*, c. stamped, STUDIO / J.W. MORRICE

Labels: in blue ballpoint pen, GBL / GARDEN / FENCE

Provenance: Estate of the artist. Continental Galleries of Fine Art, Montreal, c. 1942; Lawrence T. Porter, St. Andrews East, Quebec; G. Blair Laing, Toronto, 1980.

30477

Thinly rubbed and sketchily drawn, this amusing little study has been identified in an unknown hand as having been painted in Tunis, which would date it to 1914. Yet this work bears little relationship to the known Tunis sketches, or to any of the other known North African works, except for the portrait of Henri Matisse (fig. 68a), identified as having been painted in Tangiers.[1] There, as in this sketch, the grill has been painted in simple vertical green lines over alternating bands of colour, with the paint thinly rubbed at the top. At the left in both works is a single window, and a balcony is sketchily drawn above the fence.

Writing of the time spent with Morrice in Tangiers, Matisse recalled: "... Apart from the time that we were at work, we were always together. I would go with him to some café, where I would have as many glasses of mineral water as he would of whisky."[2] At what café in Tangiers, one wonders, did Morrice drink his whisky and Matisse his mineral water under the bold gaze of this delightful child?

1. First published in Johnston 1965, pp. 56, 79. Dorais (1985a, p. 53) questions the identification as Matisse. In the recent catalogue *Matisse in Morocco* (Cowart et al. 1990, p. 258) the portrait is presumed to be of Matisse.
2. Letter from Matisse to Armand Dayot, quoted in Paris 1926, p. 7.

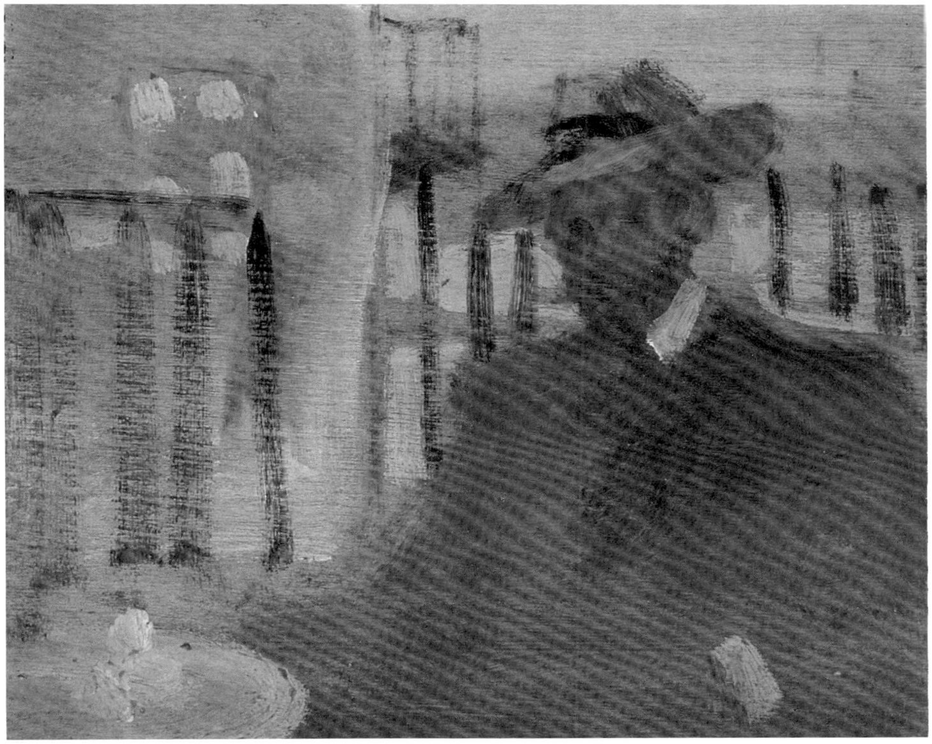

Fig. 68a
Portrait of Henri Matisse, c. 1912–13, oil on wood, 12.1 × 15.2 cm. Private collection.

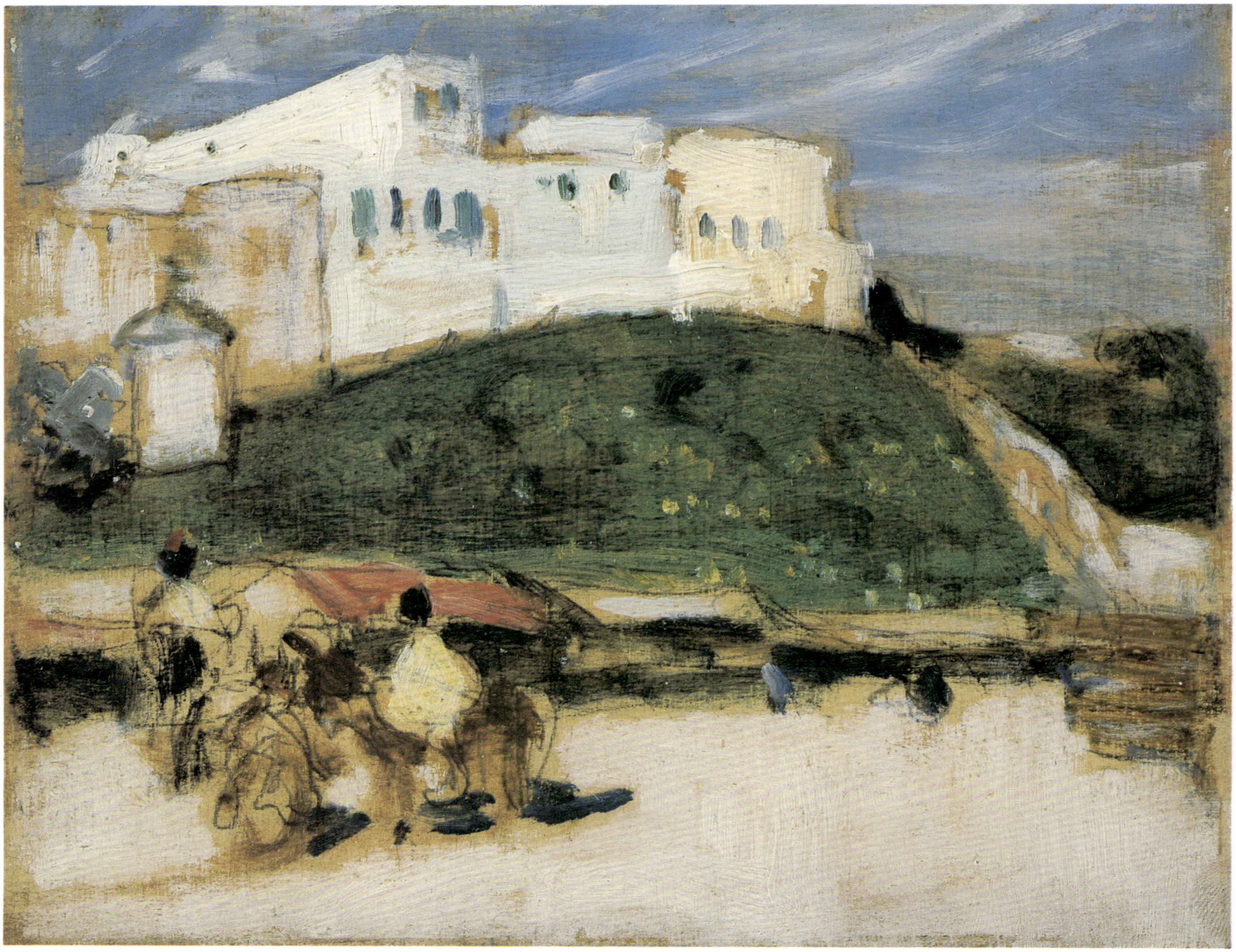

69

North African Town

c. 1912–14

Oil and graphite on wood, 13.3 × 17 cm

Inscriptions: verso: u.c. in graphite, *2438ARG14 / 6⅜ × 5*, r. in graphite, *Miss Murray*, c. stamped, *STUDIO / J.W. MORRICE*, l.l. in graphite, *207*

Labels: in blue ballpoint pen, *86-2 / "NORTH AFRICAN / TOWN"*

Provenance: Estate of the artist. Miss Murray (?). (Sold, Joyner Fine Art Inc., Toronto, 27 May 1986, lot 110); G. Blair Laing Ltd., Toronto, 1986.

30431

Wisps of clouds blow over pastel-coloured buildings at the crest of a grass-covered hill by the market. The graphite underdrawing is loosely and summarily put down. Then the paint is brushed, rubbed, and dabbed, leaving the uncovered graphite to suggest and animate forms. With great sureness and lyricism, Morrice sings the praises of the sun-filled landscape.

The name "Miss Murray" inscribed on the back of this panel (most probably the identity of a previous owner) is in the same hand as on catalogue numbers 53 and 71.

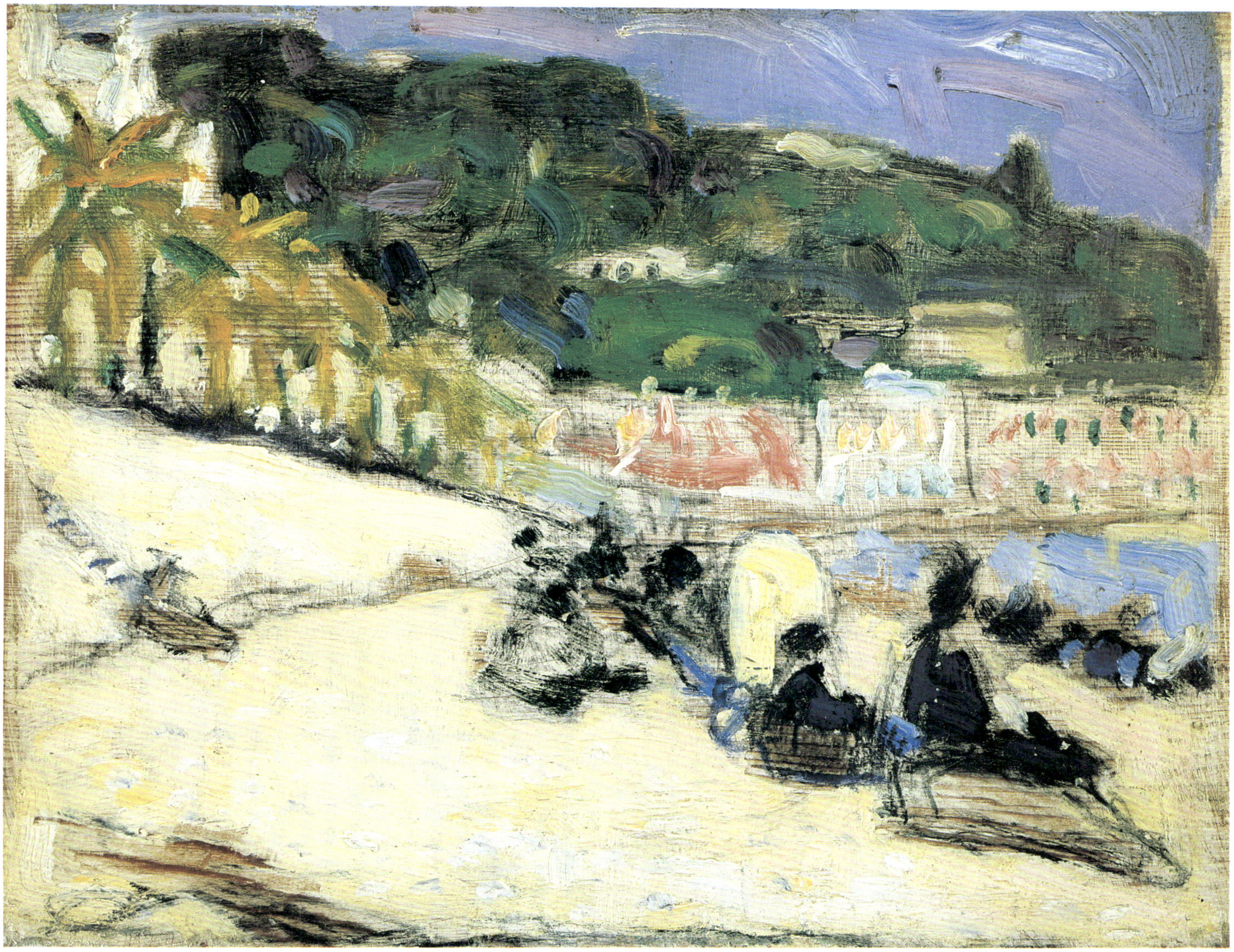

70

Beach, Côte d'Azur

c. 1912–14

Oil and graphite on wood, 12.3 × 15.5 cm

Inscriptions: verso: c. stamped, *Studio / J.W. Morrice*, c.r. in black ballpoint pen, *71504*, l. in graphite, *as #62 / Plain metal / 8072*

Labels: in blue ballpoint pen, A BEACH / COTE / D'AZUR / 86-11

Provenance: Estate of the artist. Kastel Gallery Inc., Montreal. Private collection, Town of Mount Royal, Quebec (sold, Fraser Bros., Montreal, 23 October 1986, lot 90); G. Blair Laing Ltd., Toronto, 1986.

30435

Under a fluidly painted blue and lavender sky brushed with white, the rich green foliage of the hill crowns the buildings and bathers on the beach, drawn in graphite and thinly painted. The open foreground allows us to catch our breath after the orgy of lush colour above.

John Lyman wrote in his journal in 1927: "I have been inclined to think that the greatest change in [Morrice's] style was in the latter years, but as one looks closely at canvases of different periods (after the earliest) the perception of change vanishes almost completely . . . in the impression of unvarying personality."[1] From the beaches of St-Malo (see cat. nos. 26 and 27) to the Côte d'Azur there is a significant change in brushwork, drawing, and colour, and yet Morrice still evokes the same atmosphere of luxury, calm, and sensual delight. The title of Matisse's famous canvas *Luxe, calme et volupté* evokes well Morrice's world of tranquillity bathed in coloured light.

1. Lyman 1980, p. 41.

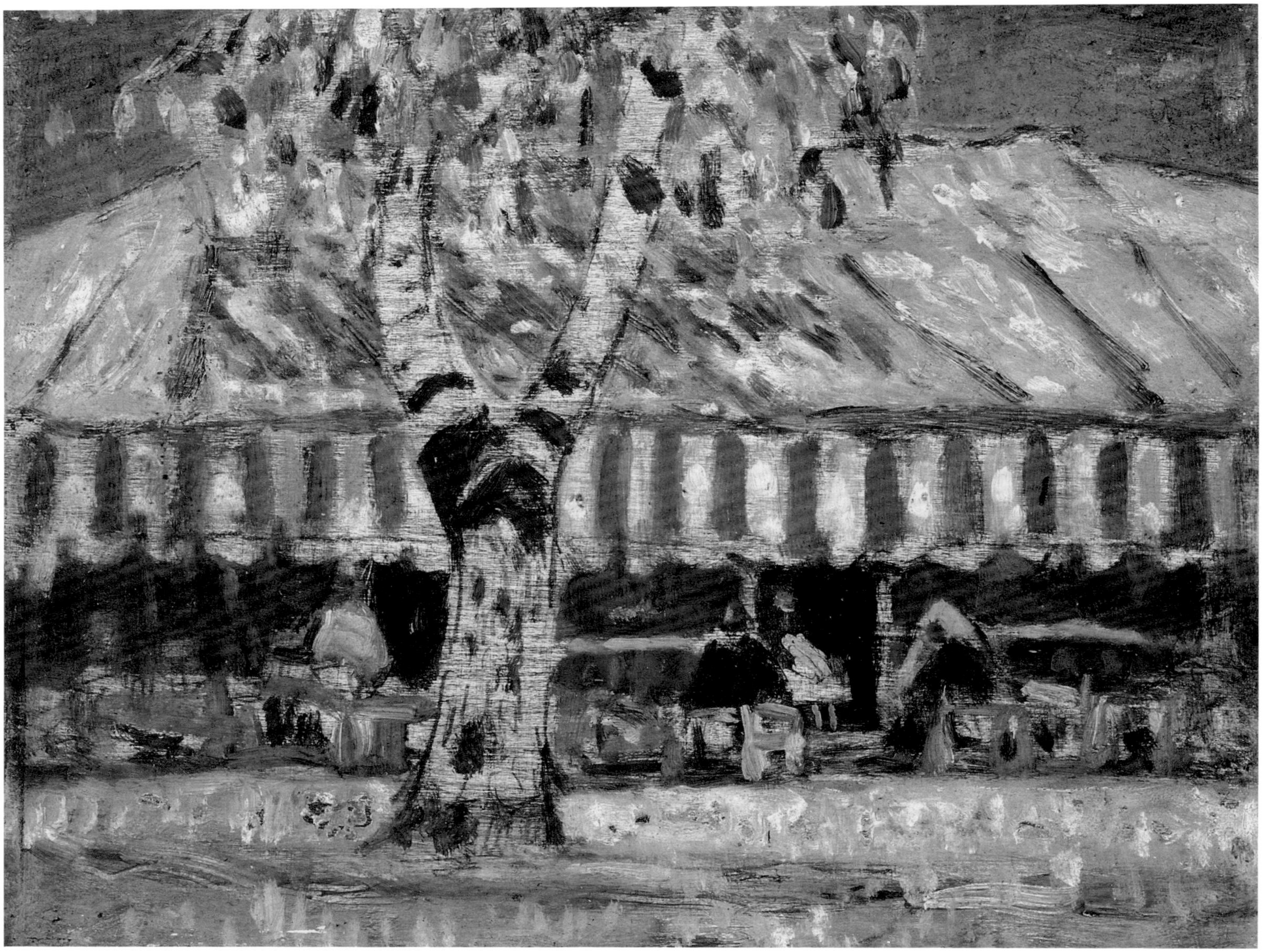

71

Plane Tree and Tent, North Africa

1914

Oil and graphite on wood, 13.2 × 17 cm

Inscriptions: verso: u.c. in graphite, *Miss S. Robertson*, c. in black ink, *JAMES WILSON MORRICE*, c. stamped, *STUDIO / J.W. MORRICE*

Labels: in blue ballpoint pen, *84-10* / "*PLANE TREE / & TENT MOROCCO*"

Provenance: Estate of the artist. Miss S. Robertson (?). (Sold, Sotheby Parke Bernet [Canada] Inc., Toronto, 14 May 1984, lot 75); G. Blair Laing Ltd., Toronto, 1984.

30426

In front of a café stands a dappled tree. Customers are seated outside, while the waiter rests in the doorway. A solid blue sky frames the tree, and light and shadow play across the tent, its awning painted in alternating dark green and mint green. In the preparatory drawing (fig. 71a),[1] the café tables are grouped in clusters, whereas in the oil sketch they become a unified horizontal band parallel to the awning. The few sparse tufts of grass in the foreground are painted in short vertical strokes, as in *Study for "Environs of Tangiers"* (cat. no. 67). However, the emphatic simplicity of this sketch and the solid blue sky recall more *Study for "Afternoon, Tunis"* (fig. 71b), which Morrice painted in 1914, on his last visit to North Africa before the outbreak of war.

1. The drawing was identified correctly in Moisan 1983, p. 85, as having been removed from Sketchbook 10, the sketchbook that contains Morrice's London and West Indian drawings. For this reason it was erroneously titled *Terrace Café, West Indies*. The drawing most certainly dates from his trip to Tunis in 1914 preceding his stay in London after the outbreak of war.

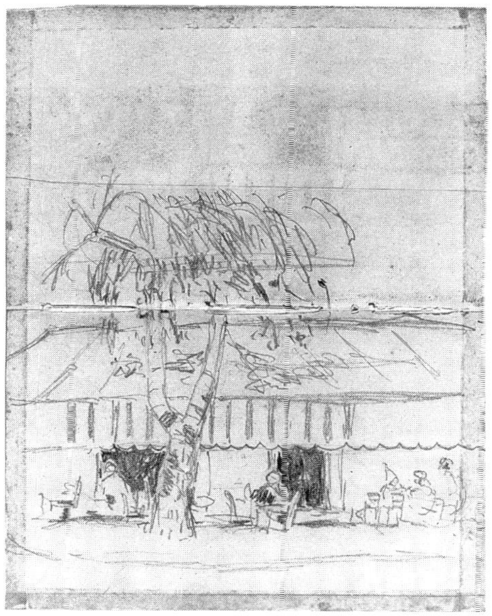

Fig. 71a
Sketchbook 10, pp. 5v–6r, 1914, graphite on wove paper, 21.2 × 16.5 cm (overall). Montreal Museum of Fine Arts. Gift of F. Eleanore and David R. Morrice, 1973 (Dr.1973.19).

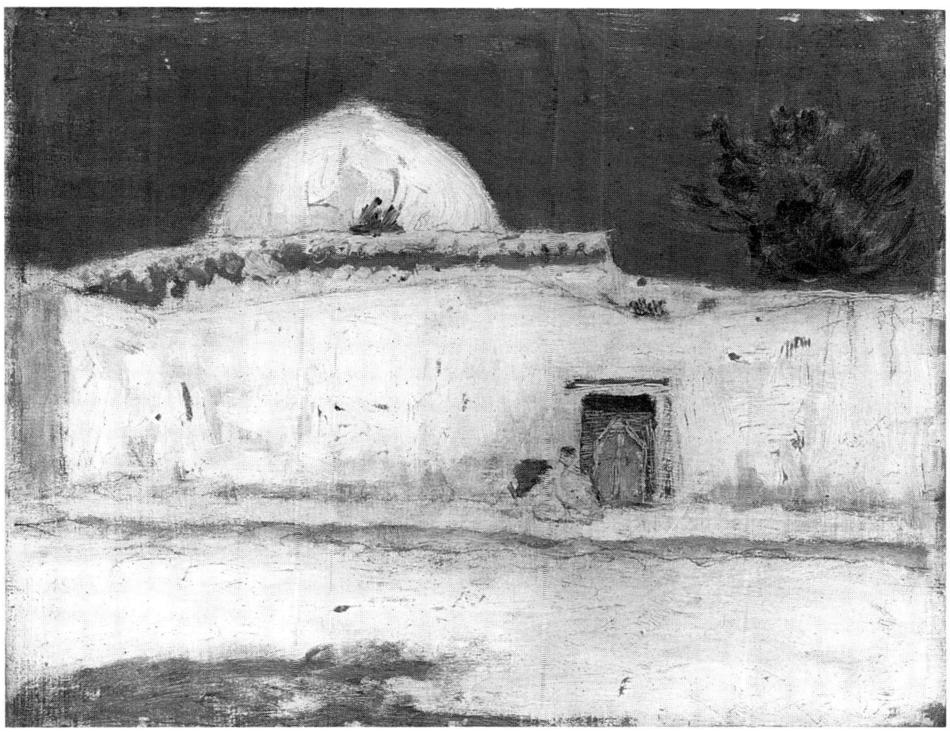

Fig. 71b
Study for "Afternoon, Tunis," 1914, oil and graphite on wood, 13.3 × 16.6 cm. Montreal Museum of Fine Arts. Gift of Mrs. Alan G. Law, Montreal, 1925 (925.340-B).

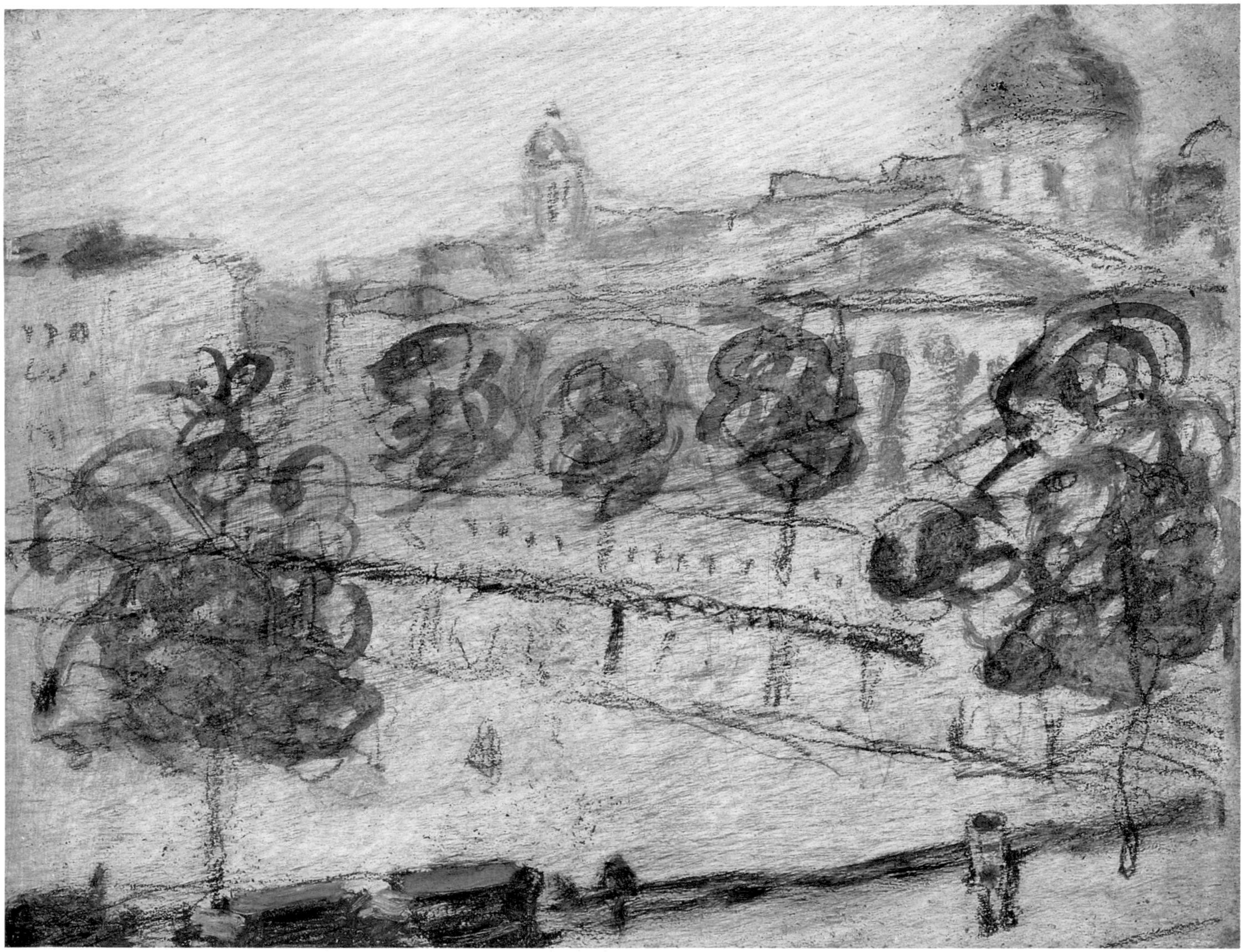

72

Trafalgar Square, London

1914

Oil and graphite on wood, 13.3 × 17 cm

Inscriptions: verso: c. stamped, *STUDIO / J.W. MORRICE*, l.l. in graphite, *X-510-13*

Labels: in blue ballpoint pen, *81-2 / VIEW OF / LONDON*

Provenance: Estate of the artist. J. Robertson; G. Blair Laing Ltd., Toronto, 1981.

30420

On 3 August 1914 Germany declared war on France and invaded Belgium, and on the following day Great Britain declared war on Germany. Cafés in Paris were forced to close early as the country prepared for combat. Not wanting to be confined to his bachelor quarters during long evenings, Morrice left Paris on 11 August[1] and shortly afterward showed up in London in the company of numerous other expatriates fleeing the oncoming conflagration.[2] Pursuing his usual work patterns, he sketched around Trafalgar Square and near the Houses of Parliament. At the latter site his sketching aroused the suspicions of a policeman, who proceeded to arrest him on suspicion of being a spy. Following a brief investigation Morrice was released.[3]

In the drawing that preceded this work (fig. 72a), Trafalgar Square, with its leafy trees lined up in front of the National Gallery, looks almost like the Quai des Grands-Augustins. In the lower-left corner of the oil sketch Morrice has included several blue-roofed cars – among the very few automobiles he ever painted (see also fig. 72b). In the lower-right corner a man in a red sandwich-board adds a touch of humour to this otherwise depopulated square. Over a thin pink ground the blue roofs of the buildings echo the roofs of the cars, and the summer foliage is drawn in transparent swirls of green almost as thin as watercolour.

1. Sketchbook 10 (Montreal Museum of Fine Arts, Dr.1973.33), p. 1 verso, is inscribed, "left Paris / August 11."
2. Elizabeth Robins Pennell, *The Life and Letters of Joseph Pennell* (Boston: Little, Brown & Co., 1929), vol. 2, p. 145; Bell 1956, p. 168.
3. Buchanan 1936a, pp. 123–25.

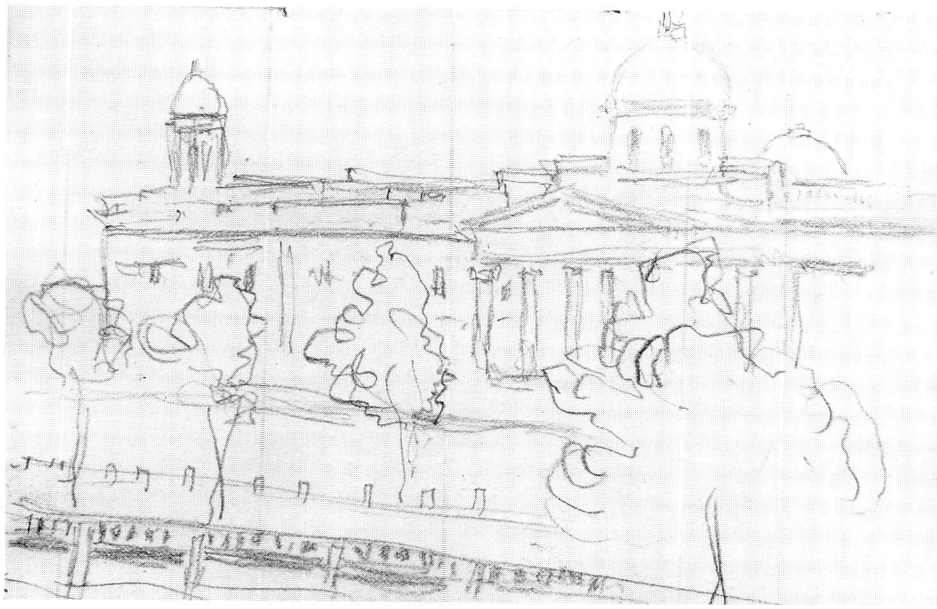

Fig. 72a
Sketchbook 10, p. 30r, 1914, graphite on wove paper, 10.7 × 16.5 cm. Montreal Museum of Fine Arts. Gift of David R. Morrice, 1973 (Dr.1973.33).

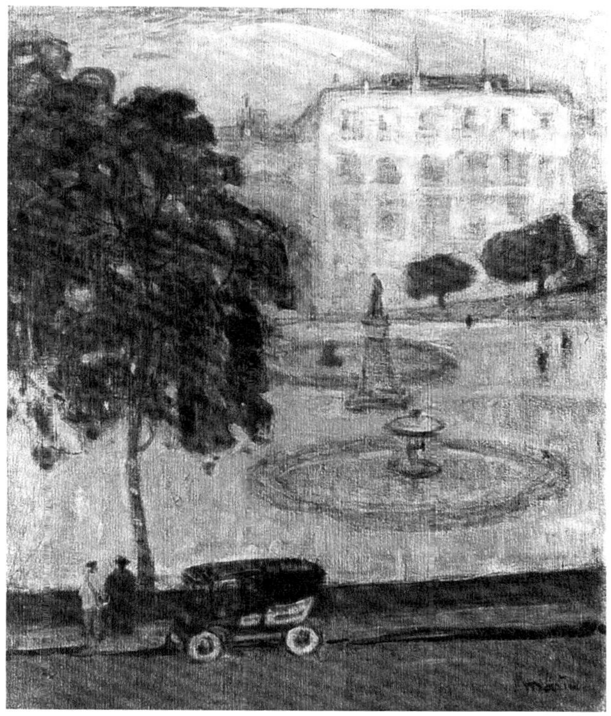

Fig. 72b
Trafalgar Square, London, 1914–15, oil on canvas, 62.2 × 50.8 cm. Private collection

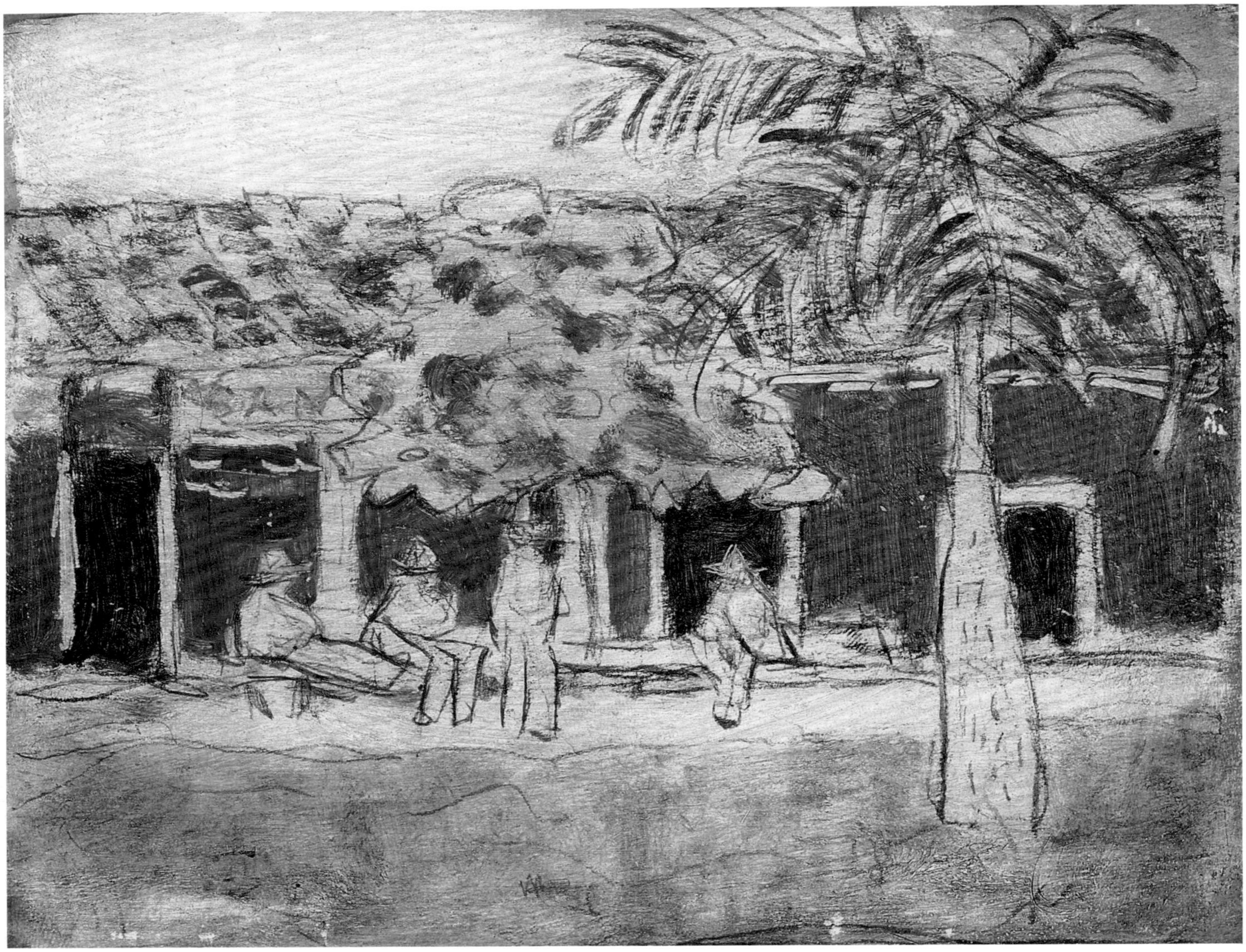

73

Study for "Houses, Cuba"

1915

Oil and graphite on wood, 13.2 × 17 cm

Inscriptions: verso: l.r. in graphite, *Cuba*

Provenance: Charles Pacquement, Paris; Jacques Dubourg, Paris; G. Blair Laing, Toronto, 1972.

30482

By November 1914 Morrice had returned to Paris, and he wrote to Joseph Pennell: "Paris is about the same as usual except at night when everything is closed at 9:30. I am going over to Canada for Xmas."[1] It was not to be a joyful visit, as both his parents died before Christmas.[2] At the instigation of the Van Hornes (Sir William had been responsible for the construction of a railway in Cuba after the Spanish-American War and owned an imposing residence at Camagüey),[3] Morrice decided to avoid the uncertainties of Europe and North Africa and visit Cuba, travelling from Montreal via New York, Washington, and New Orleans.[4] He spent most of his time in Santiago de Cuba and Havana, and made a short trip to Jamaica, spending less than two months in all and returning to France in mid-April.[5] From Paris he soon wrote to Newton MacTavish: "I got some good sketches & I am now working on them."[6]

This sketch shows certain compositional similarities to *Plane Tree and Tent, North Africa* (cat. no. 71), although it is more loosely treated. The trees, figures, and general outlines are drawn in graphite. The colour is largely limited to reds and greens, with touches of browns and blue, and the paint is thinly rubbed in the foreground and sky. Traces of the letters "SAN," strongly reinforced in the preliminary drawing (fig. 73a), are still visible.

In the canvas (fig. 73b) Morrice maintains his focus on the central horizontal. The sky is painted white with touches of blue, and the foreground is a thin green dabbed with darker and lighter accents. The house at the right is a more intense blue-green, the roof tiles are pink and yellow dotted with red, and the foliage of the central tree, surmounting a sinuously curved trunk, plays a more prominent role. One of the men has been eliminated, and instead a new figure appears in front of the palm tree – a child dressed all in white holding a brilliant red kerchief.

1. Letter from Morrice to Pennell, 19 November [1914], Pennell Papers.
2. His mother, Annie Stephenson Morrice, died 26 November 1914; his father, David Morrice, died 19 December 1914 (Morrice family Bible, with David R. Morrice, Montreal, 1977).
3. Walter Vaughan, *The Life and Work of Sir William Van Horne* (New York: The Century Co., 1920), pp. 276–339.
4. Buchanan 1936a, p. 130; letter from Morrice (in Washington) to MacTavish, "Friday," postmarked 24 February 1915, MacTavish Papers; Sketchbook 10 (Montreal Museum of Fine Arts, Dr.1973.33), p. 62v (address of St. Charles Hotel, New Orleans).
5. Sketchbook 10, p. 37r, is inscribed, "Havana to St. Nazaire / April 18 / Transatlantique."
6. Letter from Morrice to MacTavish, 26 May [1915], MacTavish Papers.

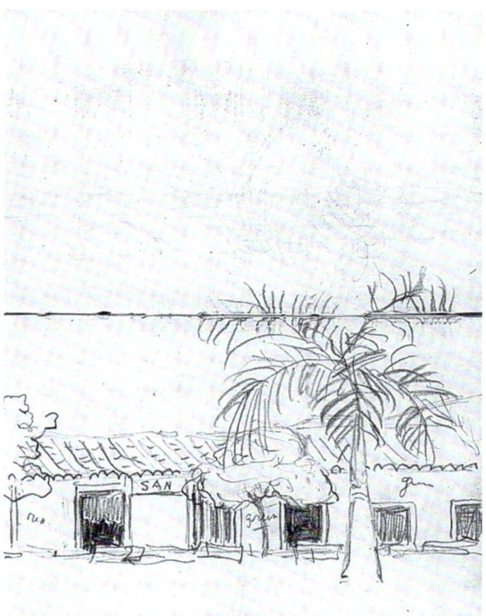

Fig. 73a
Sketchbook 10, pp. 14v–15r, 1915, graphite on wove paper, 21.2 × 16.5 cm (overall). Montreal Museum of Fine Arts. Gift of David R. Morrice, 1973 (Dr.1973.33).

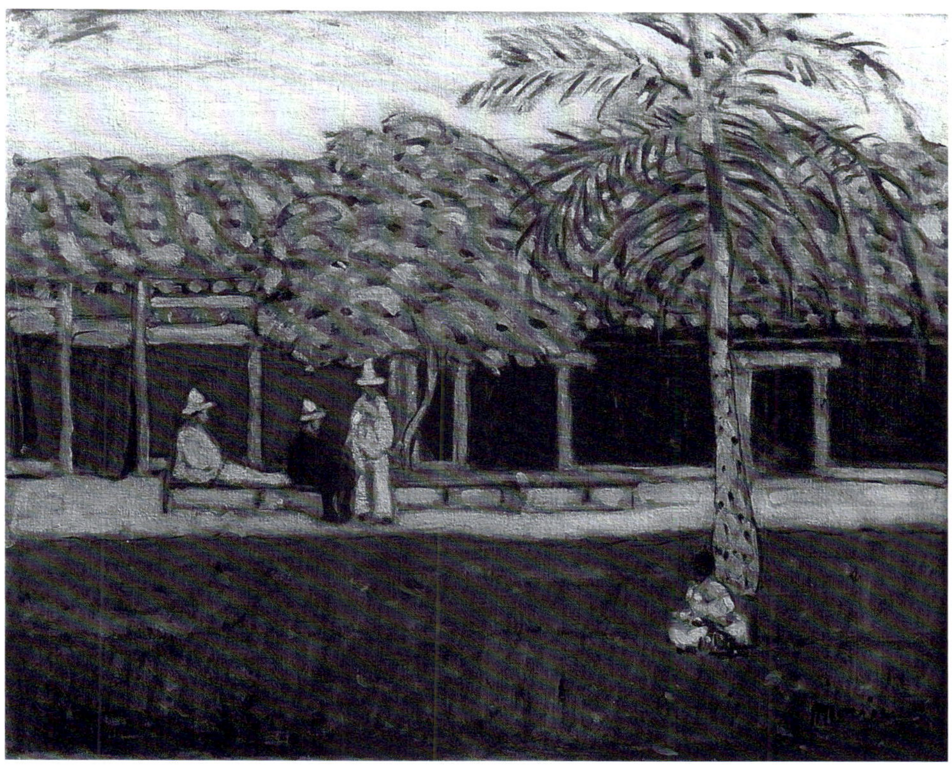

Fig. 73b
Houses, Cuba, c. 1915, oil on canvas, 50.8 × 60.9 cm. Montreal Museum of Fine Arts. Purchase, William G. Cheney Fund, 1939 (939.670).

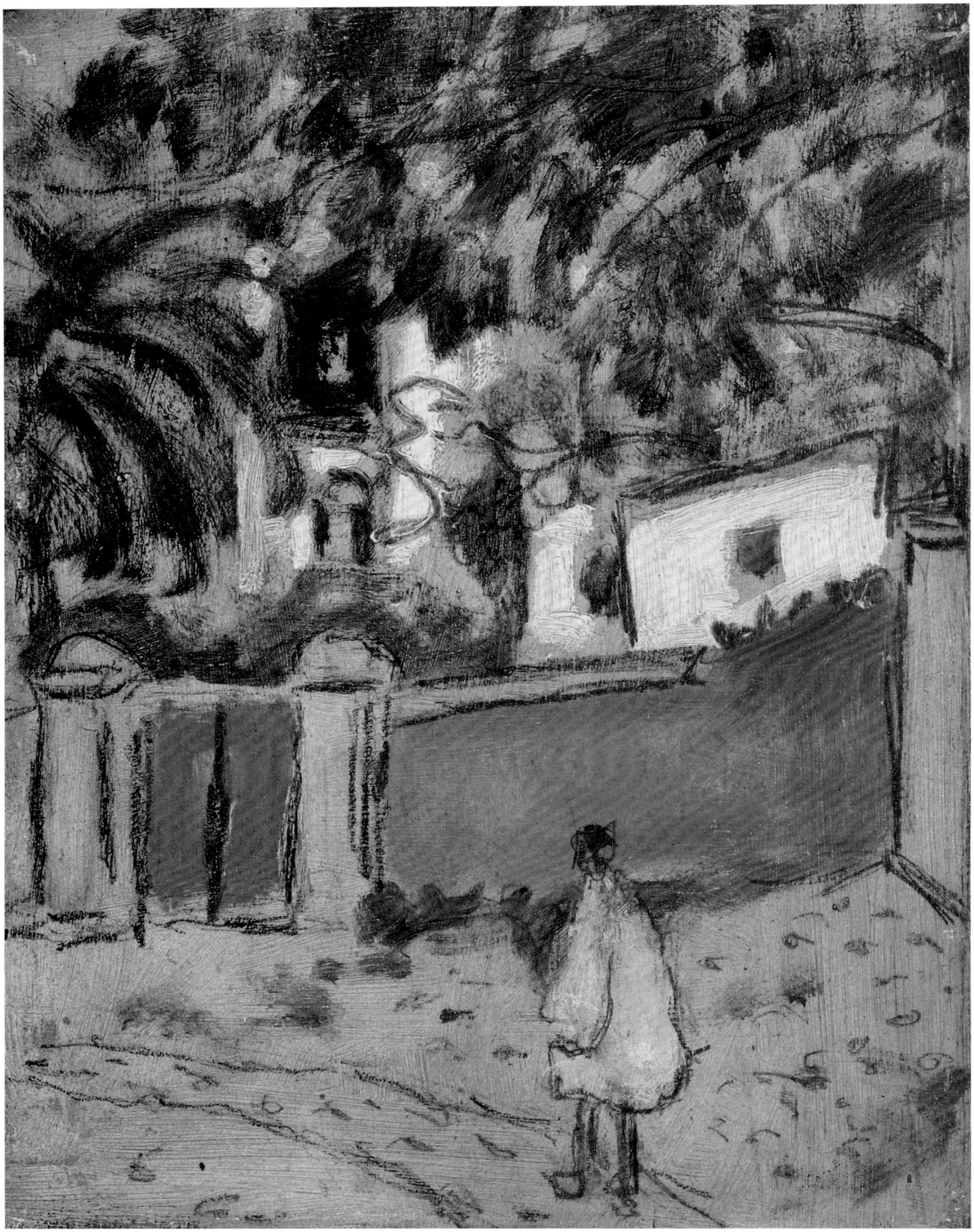

74

A Monastery Gate, Cuba

c. 1915

Oil and graphite on wood, 17 × 13.3 cm

Inscriptions: verso: u.c. partly covered by label, in graphite, *Monastery* / [—], u.c. in brown ink, *15*, c. stamped, *STUDIO / J.W. MORRICE*, in stamp in graphite, *310*

Labels: in blue ballpoint pen, *G.B.L.* / "*AMARBOUT / MOROCCO*"; in graphite, *13*

Provenance: Estate of the artist. Vilma Lafontaine, Montreal; G. Blair Laing, Toronto, 1960.

30455

This oil sketch relates to a watercolour of the same subject (fig. 74a) in which Morrice has scraped out and overpainted the foreground figure. The watercolour was included in the 1934 exhibition at Mellors Fine Arts Limited, at which time it was titled *Monastery Gate, Cuba*. More recently the edifice depicted in these works has been identified as a marabout, or Moslem saint's tomb, in North Africa.[1] The sketch does show close stylistic similarities to *Study for "Houses, Cuba"* (cat. no. 73), and is painted in the identical reds and greens, but the figures are quite dissimilar, and here the walking man appears to be dressed in a jellaba. Yet just as puzzling is the figure in North African garb seen in the lower-right corner of Morrice's *Circus at Santiago, Cuba* (fig. 74b). In the absence of any conclusive evidence one way or the other, the Cuban identification has been retained here.

Based on its stylistic similarities to other works of the period, including *Study for "Houses, Cuba,"* the oil sketch is datable to about 1915. The watercolour, on the other hand, resembles other watercolours that Morrice did in North Africa in the 1920s. That it came after the oil sketch is further confirmed by the elimination of the foreground figure.

Another watercolour version of this oil sketch, apparently painted on a sheet of paper of sketchbook size, was in the collection of the artist T.R. MacDonald, formerly director of the Art Gallery of Hamilton.[2]

1. Conversation with Lucie Dorais, 1984; Laing 1984, p. 98.
2. Letter from T.R. MacDonald to the author, 29 May 1977 (Archives, National Gallery of Canada). MacDonald purchased the watercolour from Sydney Carter of Montreal about 1948–49. On the back it had the F.R. Heaton estate stamp. MacDonald sold it to Walter Klinkhoff Gallery, Montreal, prior to 1977. This may be the same sketchbook-sized watercolour referred to as *Tangiers* in Szylinger 1985, p. 83. In a conversation with the author, 15 October 1991, Szylinger confirmed that there is in a private collection a watercolour of this composition on paper (15.2 × 10.2 cm) that bears the title *Tangiers*. According to Szylinger, there also exists a larger canvas of the subject, similarly titled *Tangiers*.

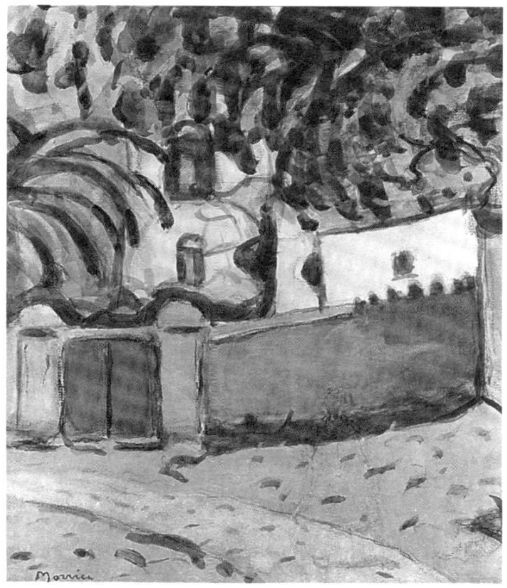

Fig. 74a
Monastery Gate, Cuba, c. 1915–21, watercolour over graphite on illustration board, 31.8 × 26.5 cm. National Gallery of Canada (4303).

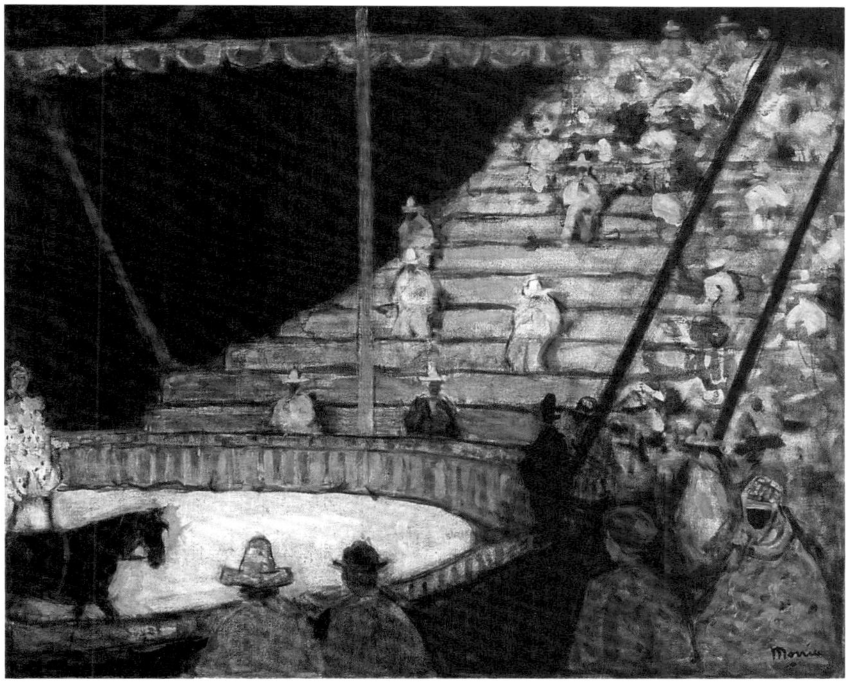

Fig. 74b
Circus at Santiago, Cuba, c. 1915, oil on canvas, 60.3 × 73 cm. Montreal Museum of Fine Arts. Bequest of William J. Morrice, 1943 (943.789).

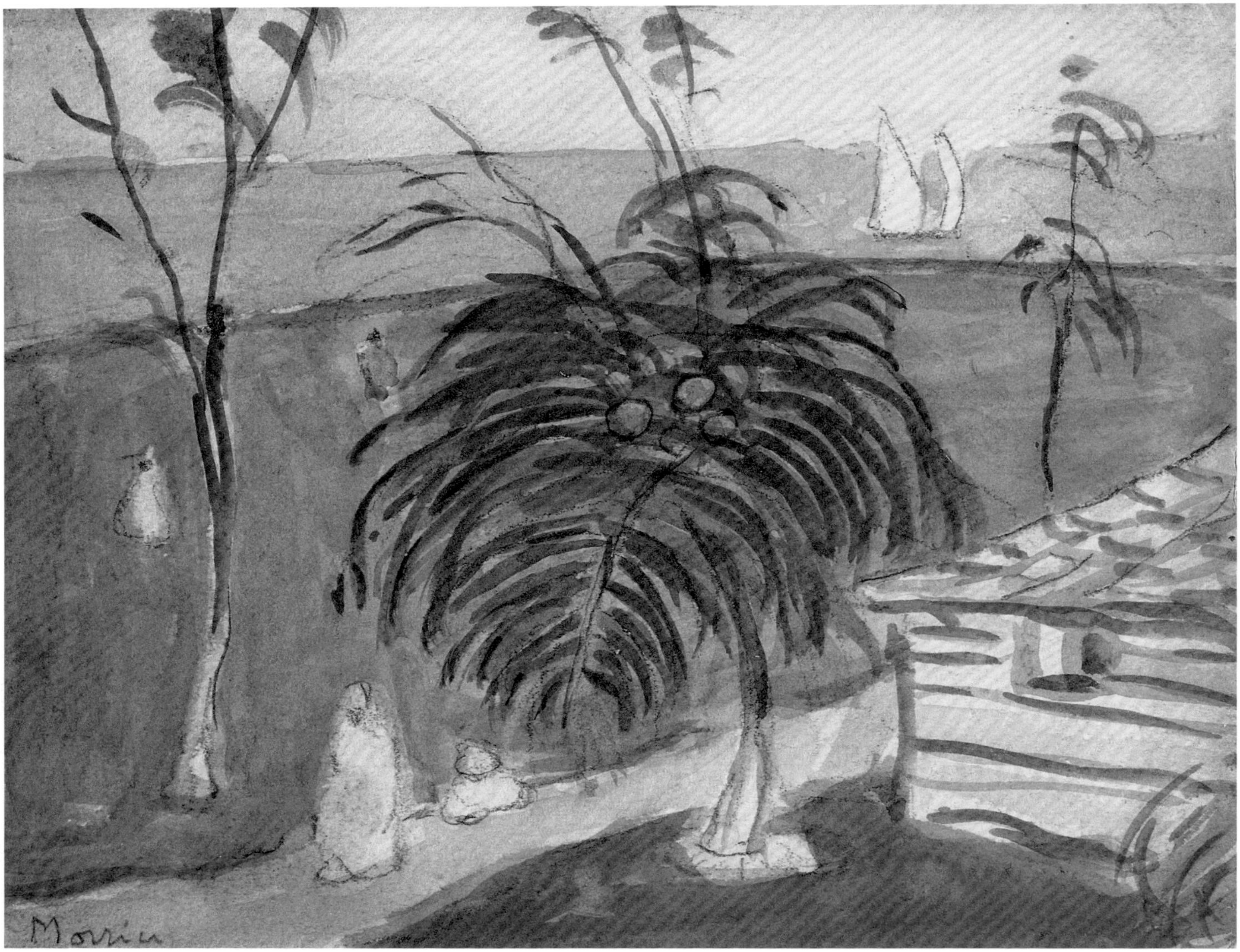

75

Jamaica

1915

Watercolour and graphite on wove paper, formerly laid down on wood-pulp board, 13.6 × 17 cm

Inscriptions: signed l.l., *Morrice*; verso (on original backing board): u.l. in graphite (artist's hand), *Jamaica*, u.r. in graphite, *1643 / Mr. Ogilvie / 392 Mountain St.*

Provenance: John Ogilvy, Montreal; Miss F.D. Ogilvy, Montreal (?). A. Hamilton Gault, Montreal and Taunton, Sussex, England; Mrs. A. Hamilton Gault, Taunton, Sussex; by descent to a niece of Mrs. A. Hamilton Gault; G. Blair Laing, Toronto, c. 1972.[1]

30467

Not included in exhibition

In May 1915, back in Paris, Morrice wrote to Newton MacTavish: "I was only a short time in Cuba & Jamaica. Jamaica I liked enormously but I went down too late & it was impossibly hot."[2] There are hardly any works that can be positively identified as having been painted in Jamaica, but this watercolour on prepared watercolour board is inscribed on the back in Morrice's own hand.

A preliminary drawing (fig. 75a) shows the outlines of the composition. In the watercolour, realized in pale greens, pink, and blue, Morrice has added several figures and also a sailboat on the horizon. A very generalized study, it was probably painted on the spot, unlike his more finished watercolours from after the war. Yet it held his interest, for he later painted a loose, sketchy canvas from it (fig. 75b) whose brushwork suggests a date close to that of *Autumn, Quai des Grands-Augustins* (fig. 77c).

The "Ogilvie" whose name and address appear on the back of this watercolour is most likely the Montreal art dealer John Ogilvy. In 1924, the year after his death, we find Miss F.D. Ogilvy (previously listed in the city directories with John Ogilvy at 223 Stanley Street) at 392 Mountain Street.[3] Might she perhaps be the Miss Florence Ogilvy who loaned *Winter, Ste-Anne-de-Beaupré* to the 1925 memorial exhibition at the Art Association of Montreal?

1. Laing 1984, pp. 210, 212, 214.
2. Letter from Morrice to MacTavish, 26 May [1915], MacTavish Papers.
3. Letter from Morrice (in Montreal) to MacTavish, "Thursday," postmarked 5 February 1915, MacTavish Papers. In the letter and in the inscription on this work Morrice misspells Ogilvy's name "Ogilvie," as on p. 37r of Sketchbook 10 (Montreal Museum of Fine Arts, Dr.1973.33), where he writes "John Ogilvie 223 Stanley Street." On John Ogilvy, see Watson 1974.

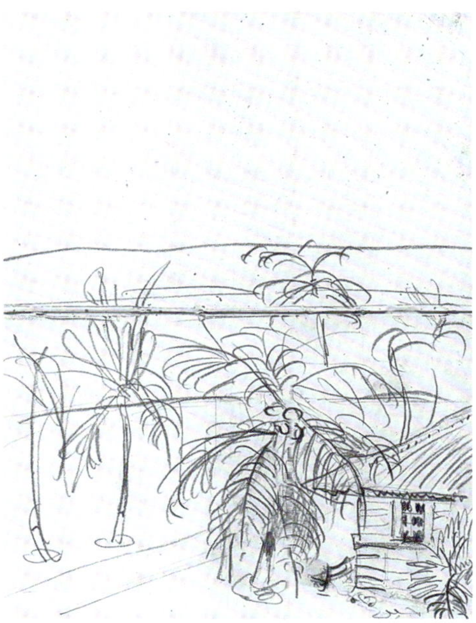

Fig. 75a
Sketchbook 10, pp. 40v–41r, 1915, graphite on wove paper, 21.2 × 16.5 cm (overall). Montreal Museum of Fine Arts. Gift of David R. Morrice, 1973 (Dr.1973.33).

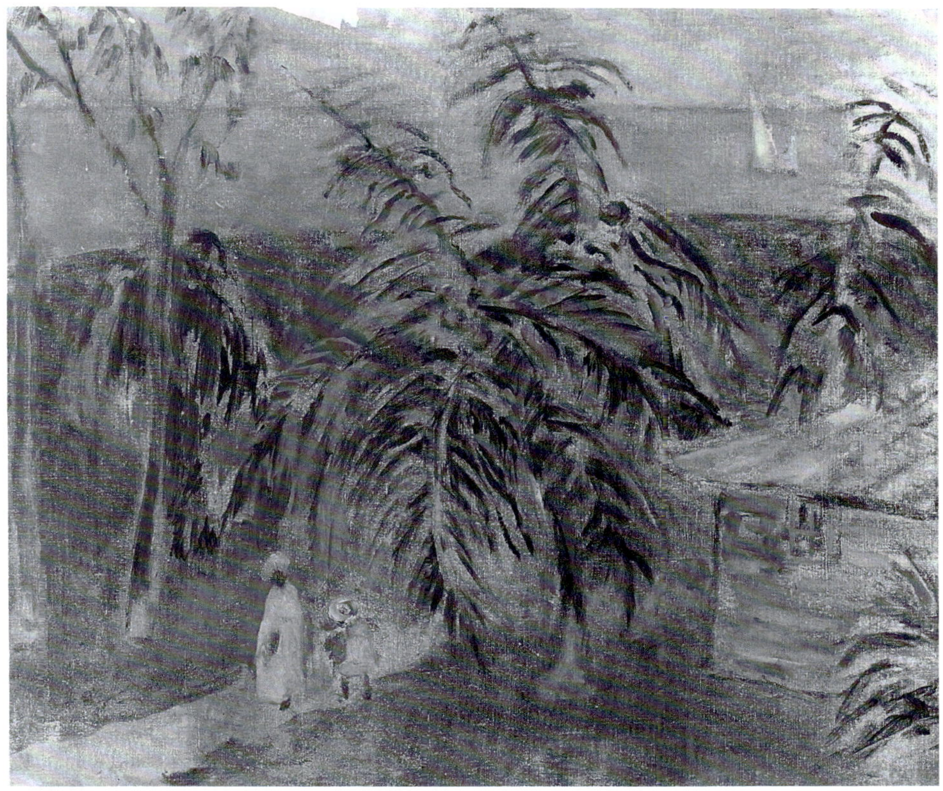

Fig. 75b
Jamaica, c. 1915–16, oil on canvas, 53.3 × 63.5 cm. Present location unknown. Formerly with Continental Galleries of Fine Art, Montreal.

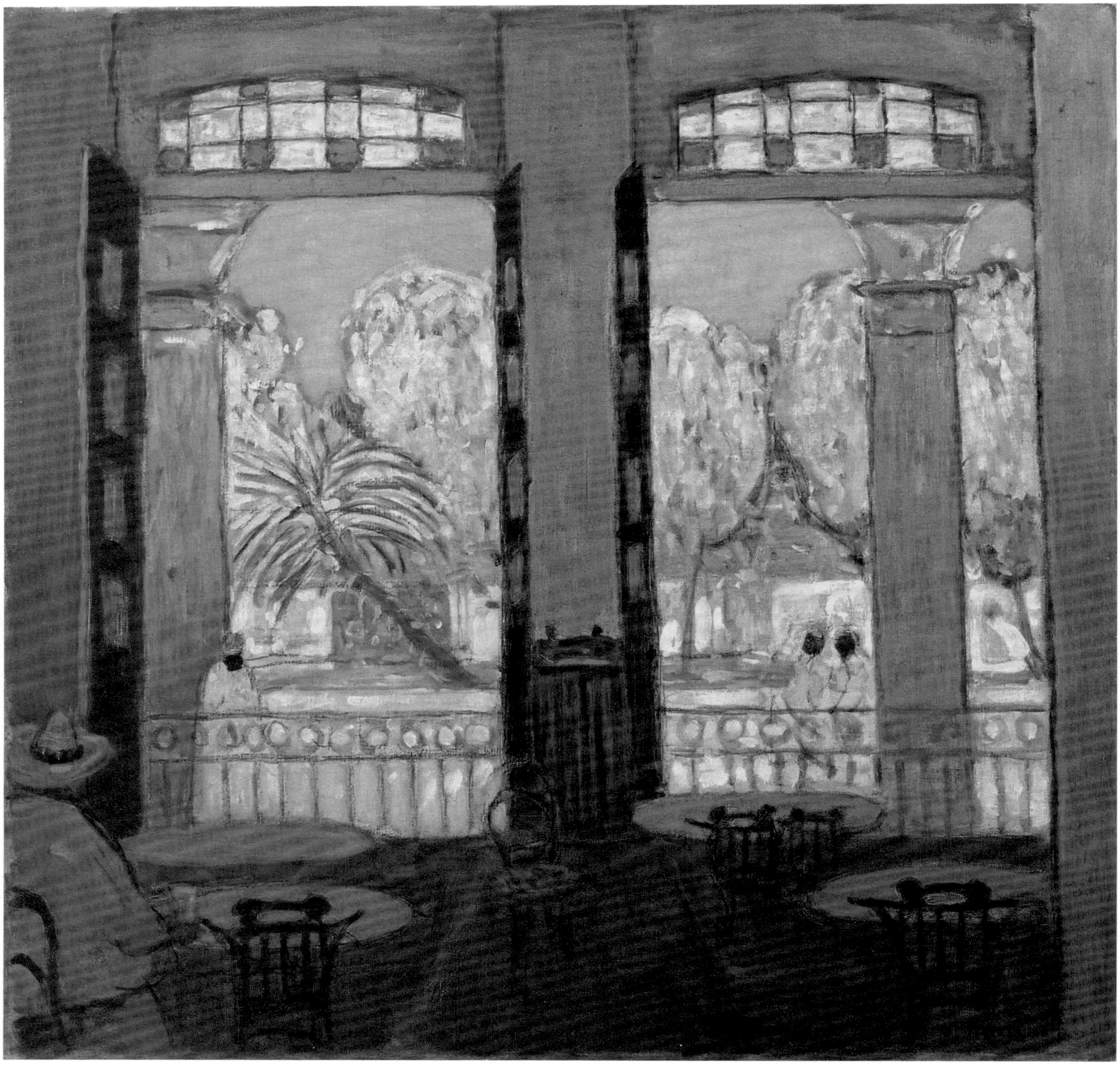

76

Café el Pasaje, Havana

c. 1915–19

Oil on canvas, 65.8 × 67.5 cm

Inscriptions: signed l.r., *Morrice*; stretcher: u.l. in graphite, *Café Il Pasajo / Havana*, c. in black crayon, *Box #5*, in graphite, *0/2802*, in graphite, *18*

Labels: in black ink, THE ART GALLERY OF TORONTO, GRANGE PARK / No. *1 Pict.* / Date 25/5/54 / From *Box 5*; Laing Galleries, Toronto; OKanada, no. 44; in blue ballpoint pen, *75-21* / "*CAFE EL / PASAJE / HAVANA / CUBA*"; in graphite, *75-21*

Provenance: Estate of the artist; Galeries Simonson, Paris, by 1927;[1] W. Scott & Sons, Montreal, by 1932;[2] The Dominion Gallery of Fine Art, Montreal, by 1946;[3] John A. MacAulay, Winnipeg, by 1953;[4] Phyllis MacAulay, Winnipeg, by 1965;[5] G. Blair Laing Ltd., Toronto, 1975.

30401

Whether in Paris, or Venice, or Tangiers, cafés always offered Morrice an ideal vantage point from which to observe and sketch the passing scene. It was in Havana that he conceived this most important of his café views. As in *Venice, Looking out over the Lagoon* (fig. 41a), he depicts the interior of the café, looking out through two windows onto the tree-lined street and the houses beyond.

The composition is defined by three flat verticals, one in the foreground and two in the middle ground.[6] The diagonal of a slanting palm tree cuts across the left window opening. The background is dominated by the delicate-hued yellow trees, with their touches of green and orange, and by the flat blue sky. The horizontals are defined by the railing, the walking figures, the orange-roofed houses, and the coloured-glass lunettes. A lone drinker is seated at the lower-left corner, while the remainder of the foreground is taken up by empty tables. Only the tops of the tables are fully visible, their legs merely suggested by a loose matrix of thin black lines and scratching, used also to reinforce the outlines of the shutters, chairs, and railing. Canvas (covered with a ground layer) and underdrawing can be seen between the lines that depict the branches of the palm tree. The sky is solidly painted, while other areas are more thinly and sketchily treated.

There are no known sketches for this canvas but Donald Buchanan has identified a photograph (fig. 76a) as the study for this view. The photograph was found by David R. Morrice, the artist's nephew, in one of the sketchbooks that he acquired from Léa Cadoret in 1952. Buchanan has suggested that the photograph may have been taken by R.B. Van Horne, with whom (according to Buchanan) Morrice travelled to Cuba.[7]

The photograph is very close to the canvas, except that in the painting Morrice has depicted the well-lit interior, and the street is viewed from a higher, more distant vantage point. As a result the space is more open and more clearly articulated. Other differences include the striking flat vertical at the right, the design of the grillwork, chairs, and glass, the fenestration of the louvres, the arrangement of the trees, and the absence of signage in the painting. The solitary drinker wears a sombrero, and the figures on the street appear to be North African rather than Cuban as in the photograph. Lucie Dorais has identified one other canvas that Morrice painted from a photograph,[8] so it is not impossible that he would have done the same for this café scene.

In a related work (fig. 76b), based on a sketchbook watercolour,[9] Morrice has structured the composition in a similar manner but with only two verticals. The colour is paler, the foliage and sky more transparent, and the design of the grillwork somewhat obtrusive.

It is difficult to determine when Morrice

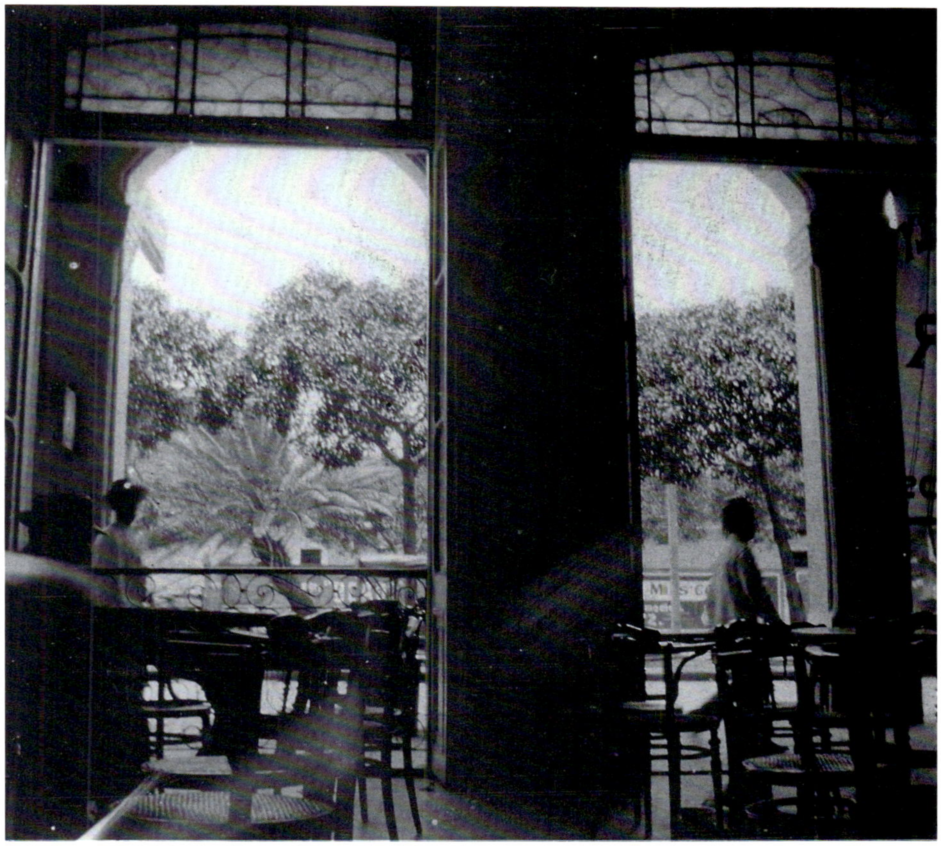

Fig. 76a
Photograph of a café in Havana, taken possibly by R.B. Van Horne in 1915. Montreal Museum of Fine Arts. Gift of David R. Morrice, 1973.

actually painted *Café el Pasaje, Havana*. Exhibition records provide us with hardly any clues, as the annual Salons in Paris were suspended during the war (resuming only in 1919). The two paintings that we are able to date with certainty to 1914–15 are *Afternoon, Tunis* in the Montreal Museum of Fine Arts (purchased in 1915) and *House in Santiago* in the Tate Gallery (acquired by the Contemporary Art Society, London, in 1916).[10] *Café el Pasaje, Havana* may be the work titled *À la Havane, Cuba* exhibited at the Salon d'Automne in 1919, but its first documented showing was at the French Gallery in London in 1925.[11]

Although its synthesis of design and colour make this painting distinctive, some elements in it can also be found in other works. The dappled yellow foliage of the trees recalls *Plane Tree and Tent, North Africa* (cat. no 71) as well as the hanging plant in the costumed portrait *Olympia* in the National Gallery of Canada (6671). The flat treatment of the sky is more typical of Morrice's wartime and post-war canvases, such as *Canadian Troops at the Front*, *Quebec Farmhouse*, and *Landscape, Trinidad*.[12]

A rather cryptic note in Morrice's Cuban sketchbook reads: "Hotel Pasaje, Panama."[13] Possibly a branch operation?

1. Loaned by M. Simonson to Paris 1927, no. 176, as *Café de Papa-jo à la Havane*.
2. Montreal 1932, no. 4, as *Cap Il Pasajo, Havane*.
3. "Paintings by Morrice at Dominion Gallery," *The Gazette* (Montreal), 5 January 1946.
4. Buchanan 1953, p. 108.
5. Johnston 1965, p. 74.
6. Morrice had made use of a similar framing device in two very early paintings, *Plant in a Window* (Beaverbrook Art Gallery, Fredericton, 64.33), from about 1892–93, in which a transparent curtain is depicted on the left edge, and *Terrace in Capri* (Montreal Museum of Fine Arts, 1981.12), possibly painted about 1894 and then reworked at a later date.
7. Buchanan 1953, p. 108. See also Buchanan 1936a, p. 130, where it is stated that their trip took place before the war. There is no documentation to support this claim.
8. Dorais 1985b, pp. 21–22. The painting is *Landscape, Trinidad* in the National Gallery of Canada (15535).
9. See Cloutier 1985, p. 225.
10. Ibid., pp. 219, 226.
11. Buchanan 1936a, p. 176.
12. See Cloutier 1985, pp. 214, 228, 232–33, 235.
13. Sketchbook 10 (Montreal Museum of Fine Arts, Dr.1973.33), p. 37r.

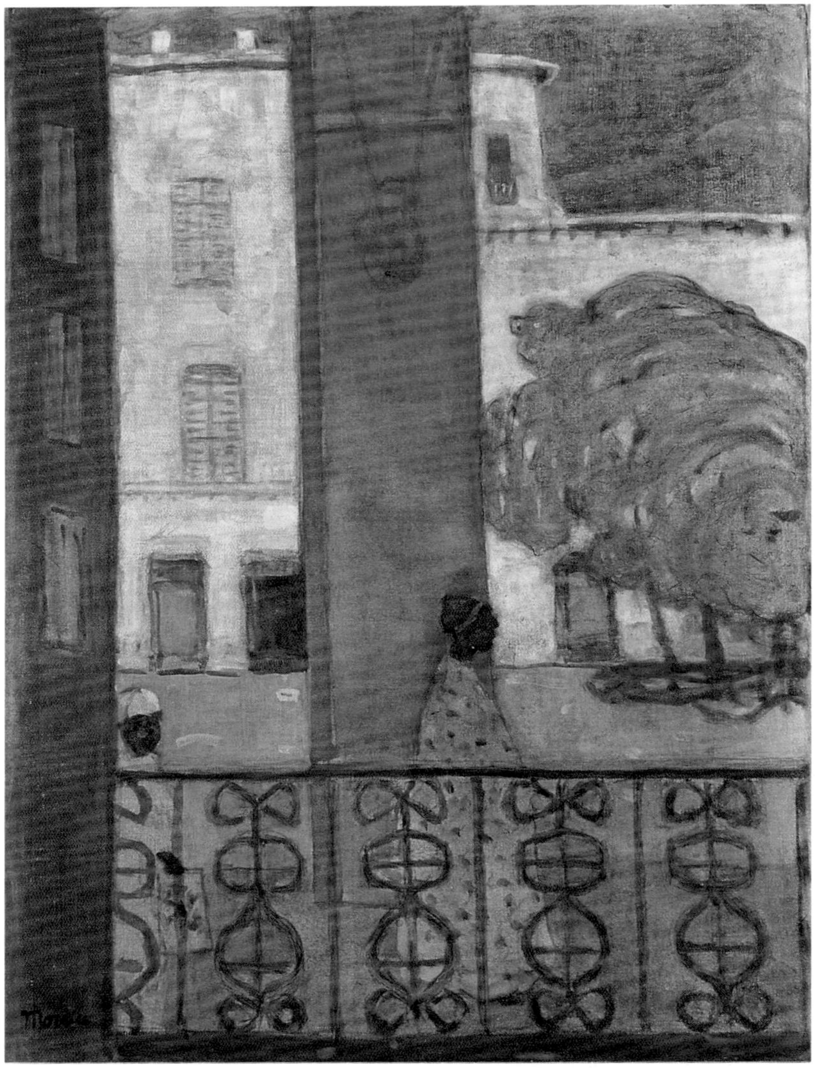

Fig. 76b
Scene in Havana, c. 1915, oil on canvas, 72.4 × 53.7 cm. Art Gallery of Ontario, Toronto. Purchased with the assistance of Wintario, 1977 (77/10).

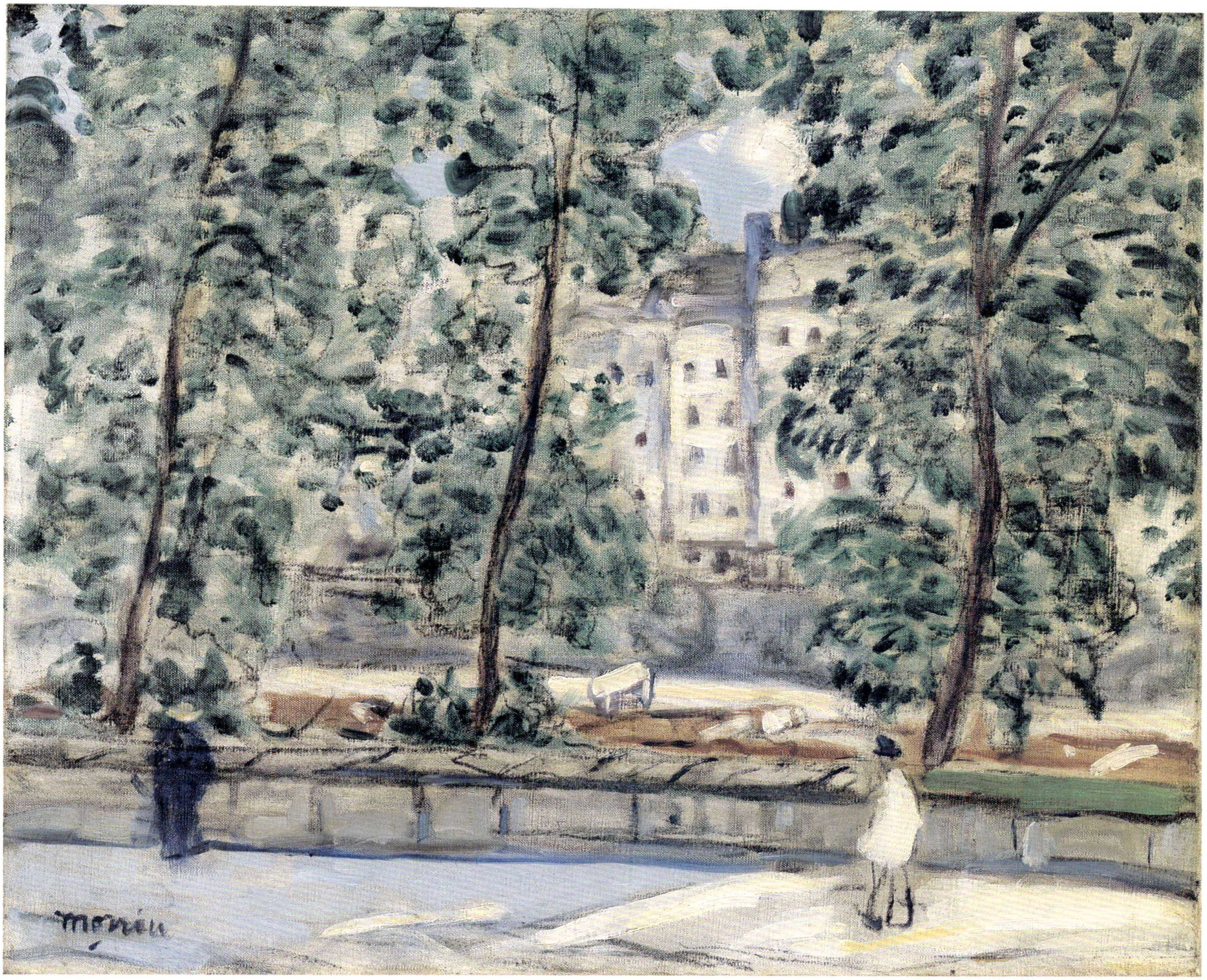

77

Spring, Quai des Grands-Augustins

c. 1915–16

Oil on canvas, 38.3 × 46 cm

Inscriptions: signed l.l., *Morrice*; stretcher: u.l. in blue pencil, *Morrice* [—], l.c. in graphite, *17¾ × 14½*, l.l. in graphite, *xx*, l.c. in red pencil, *–Spring in Paris–*, c.r. stamped, *8*; on crossbar, c. in graphite, *2*, c. stamped, *MODÈLE DÉPOSÉ / B*, in graphite, *0/2808*; back of frame: u.r. in graphite, *Cat #38 / Nat Gallery 1937*

Provenance: Estate of the artist; Galeries Simonson, Paris, by 1927;[1] W. Scott & Sons, Montreal, by 1932;[2] F.J. Campbell, Montreal, by 1936.[3] Dr. G.H. Henderson, Halifax; G. Blair Laing, Toronto, c. 1978.

30481

Little is known of Morrice's activities after his return from Cuba in the spring of 1915. In May he was visited by Roger Fry, whom he had met the previous fall in London.[4] He travelled to Toulouse, Bayonne, and Carcasson in August,[5] but after that there is no further trace of his comings and goings until November 1917. At some point during that interval he was forced to leave his old studio at 45 Quai des Grands-Augustins and move to 23 Quai de la Tournelle, a material improvement in his living conditions to which he apparently never fully adapted.[6]

In the same sketchbook that Morrice used in London and Cuba are two drawings (figs. 77a and 77b) that show his continuing interest in bookstalls and in the view from his studio. In the lower-left corner of the view of the Seine there is a note to himself, "higher," and indeed in the painting he has raised the trees within the picture frame, providing a glimpse of the buildings through the green foliage.

This springtime view of the Quai des Grands-Augustins and a related work of the same view in autumn (fig. 77c) may be the last scenes that Morrice painted from his old studio. There is a lightness of touch and a freedom of handling that set these works apart from the very structured *Café el Pasaje* (cat. no. 76). The foliage is thinly brushed and the cool-white and pink-blue foreground is freely drawn. No preliminary painted study was necessary: he has treated the canvas as if it were an enlarged sketch, drawn with a thin black brush instead of graphite. At the age of fifty Morrice here achieved the perfect translation of the freedom of the sketch into a canvas.

1. Loaned by M. Simonson to Paris 1927, no. 171, as *La Seine à Paris* (confirmed by installation views).
2. Montreal 1932, no. 23, as *Paris, Spring View from Studio.*
3. Buchanan 1936a, p. 169.
4. Buchanan 1936a, p. 124; Denys Sutton, ed., *Letters of Roger Fry* (London: Chatto & Windus, 1972), vol. 2, p. 385.
5. Letter from Morrice to Newton MacTavish, 13 September [1915], MacTavish Papers.
6. Ciolkowska 1925b, p. 52. We know that Morrice was on the Quai de la Tournelle by 16 November 1917 (letter from Edmond Dyonnet to Eric Brown, 16 November 1917, Archives, National Gallery of Canada, file 7.1–Art & Artists). One view of the Quai de la Tournelle is known from its reproduction in Paris 1926, no. 49, confirming that these canvases depict the Quai des Grands-Augustins.

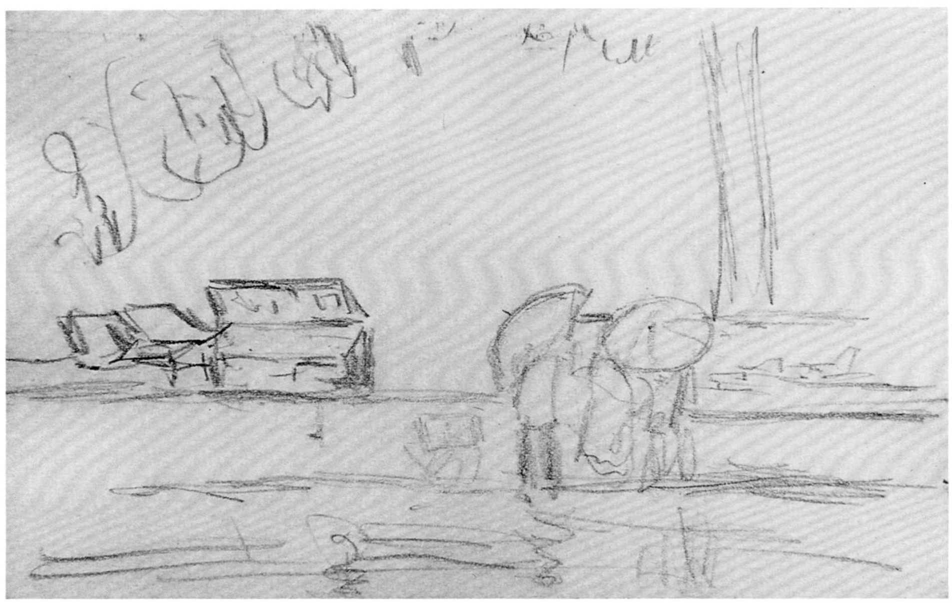

Fig. 77a
Sketchbook 10, p. 12r, c. 1915, graphite on wove paper, 10.7 × 16.5 cm. Montreal Museum of Fine Arts. Gift of David R. Morrice, 1973 (Dr.1973.33).

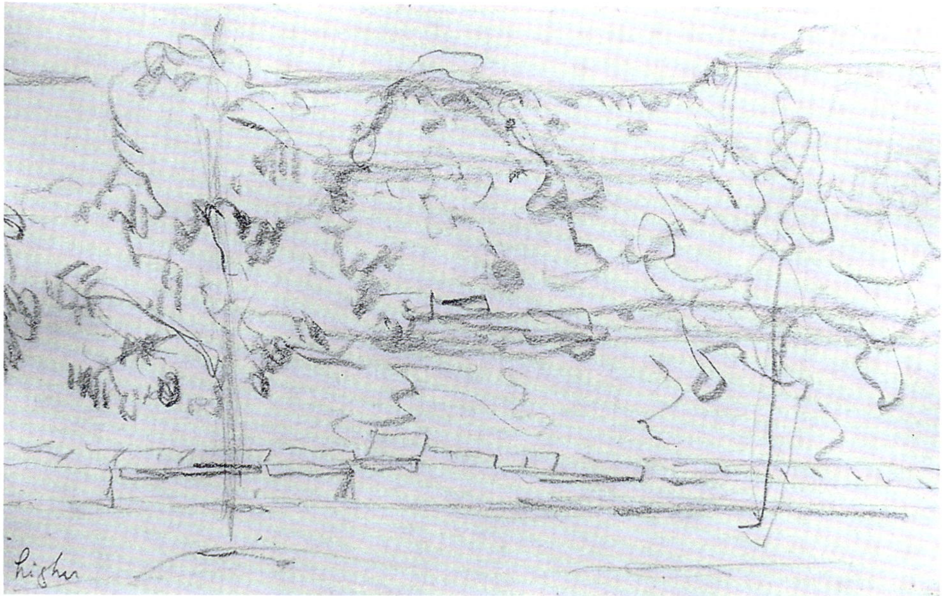

Fig. 77b
Sketchbook 10, p. 44r, c. 1915, graphite on wove paper, 10.7 × 16.5 cm. Montreal Museum of Fine Arts. Gift of David R. Morrice, 1973 (Dr.1973.33).

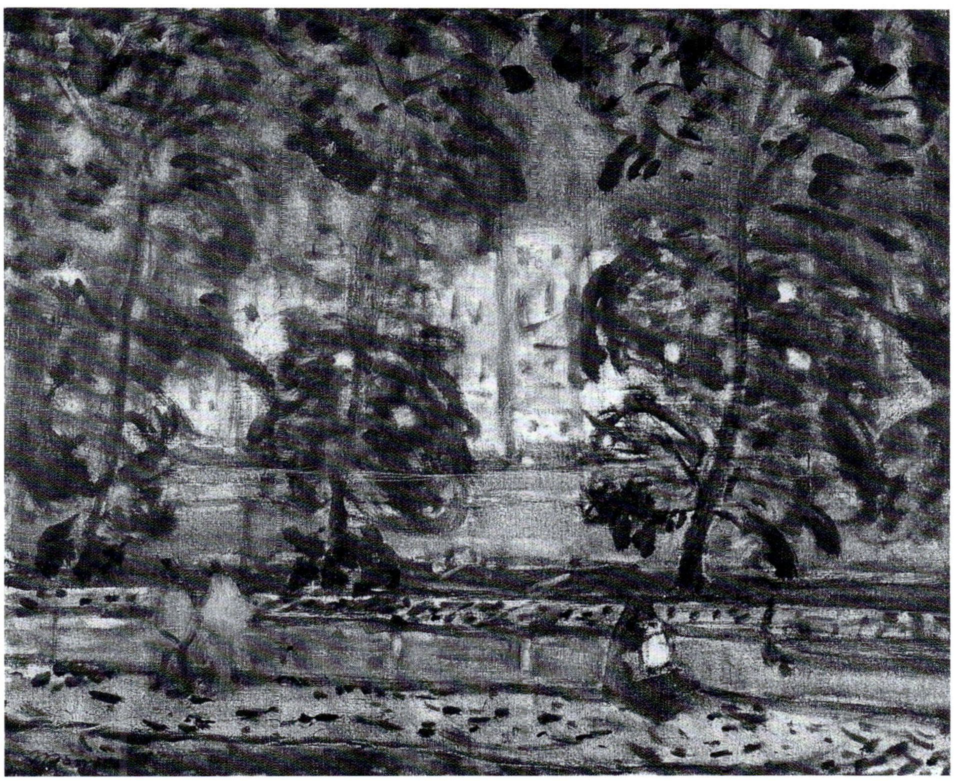

Fig. 77c
Autumn, Quai des Grands-Augustins, c. 1915–16, oil on canvas, 38.3 × 46 cm. Present location unknown.

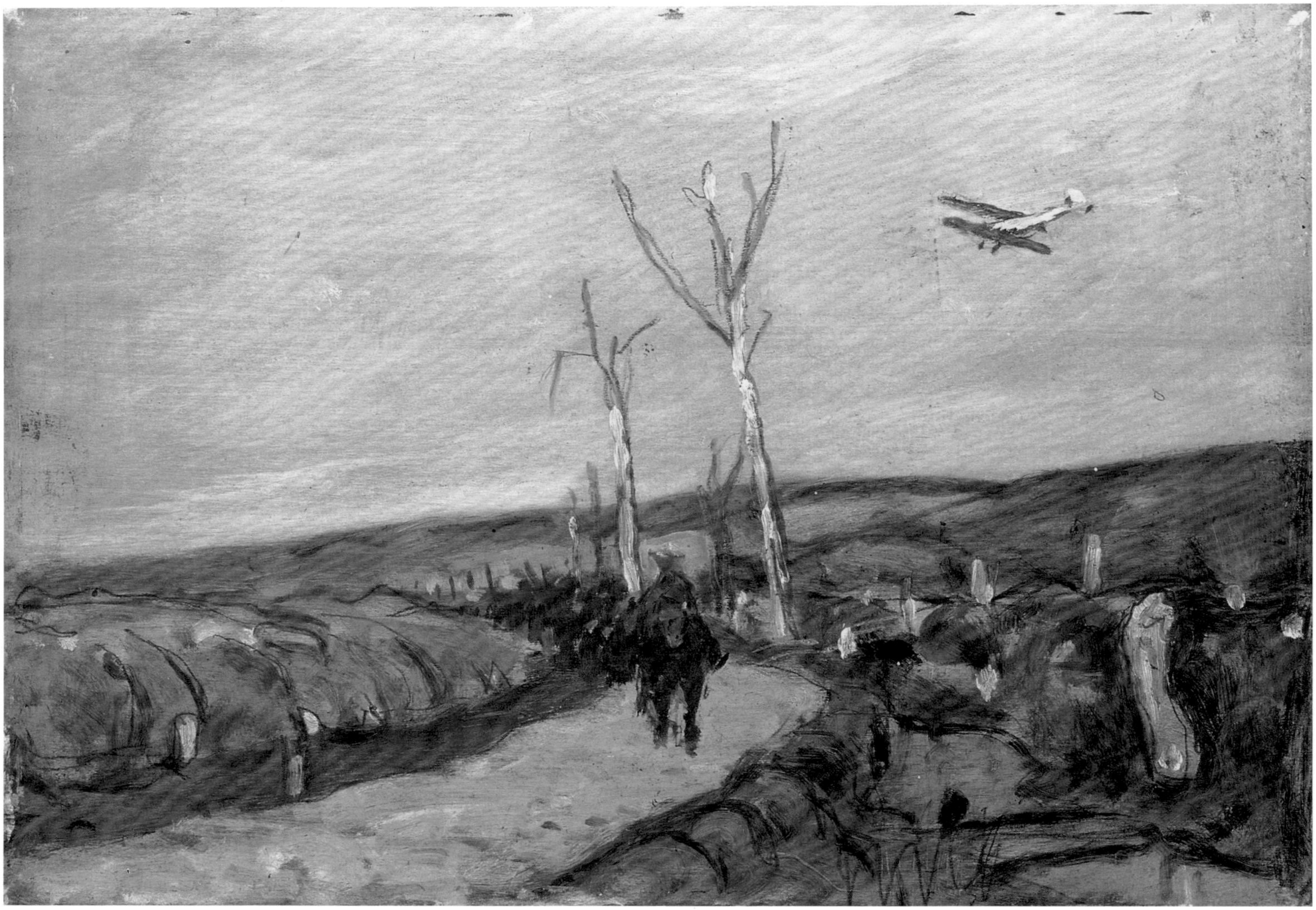

78

Study for "At the Front"

1918

Oil and graphite on wood, 23.5 × 33 cm

Inscriptions: verso: u.l. in graphite, *Brooke Claxton*, in graphite (artist's hand), *Route / La Chapelle*, c. stamped, *STUDIO / J.W. MORRICE*, c.r. in black ink, *This is the work of J W Morrice / received by us from his studio after his death / Signed / W. Scott & Sons*; back of frame: u.r. in graphite, *Claxton*

Labels: partly torn, typed, *MORRICE EXHIBITION / ARTIST: MORRICE / TITLE: STUDY FOR 'AT THE FRONT' /* [—] *MRS. BROOKE CLAXTON, ROCKCLIFFE*; typed, *ARTIST: J.W. MORRICE / TITLE: A SKETCH AT THE BATTLE- / FRONT / FROM: MRS. BROOKE CLAXTON / RO 179-5-70*; MMFA 1965, no. 123; in blue ballpoint pen, *A SKETCH / AT THE / BATTLE-FRONT*; stamped, *MAY 1987*, in blue ballpoint pen, *508-1*

Provenance: Estate of the artist; W. Scott & Sons, Montreal; Brooke Claxton, Montreal, by 1936;[1] Mrs. Brooke Claxton, Ottawa; by descent to a member of the Claxton family (sold, Joyner Fine Art Inc., Toronto, 20 May 1987, lot 77); G. Blair Laing Ltd., Toronto, 1987.

30437

In November 1917 Lord Beaverbrook contacted Morrice on behalf of the Canadian War Records Office to commission from him a painting as part of the decorations for the new House of Commons in Ottawa. The painting was to be titled *Winter in France (Troops Marching)* and was to measure nine by twelve feet. Works were also commissioned from the British artists George Clausen, John Lavery, Alfred Munnings, and Algernon Talmage. The subjects of the paintings and their dimensions were established with a view to their arrangement in pairs or sets of equal sizes and of compatible subjects.[2] Morrice left for the front in February 1918, visiting the site of the battle at Vimy and possibly also Ablain St-Nazaire, Lorette, Liévin, and Albert.[3] According to Morrice's inscription on the back, this oil sketch shows troops marching on the Cambrai Road near Chapel Hill. After making his sketches Morrice went to Concarneau to paint the commissioned canvas in a studio there.[4]

A smaller canvas (fig. 78a) was painted from this sketch in which the patterning of colour areas is more emphatic, especially in the water in the trench and the light on the hillside. The subdued tones of the sketch have been modified to portray a bright summer landscape with a dark cloud at the upper left. Treated in a very different manner is a companion view (fig. 78b) showing the troops in a winter landscape marching in the direction of a windmill and followed by a mounted rider, with airplanes flying overhead and gun smoke on the horizon. These two canvases, realized in an interim size, were perhaps meant to be shown to Beaverbrook and to P.G. Konody, his art advisor, for approval before being enlarged. The initial intent must have been to realize the two as a complementary pair – troops marching to battle under a sombre grey winter sky, and troops returning in the sunlight of summer. Morrice did paint a nine-by-twelve-foot canvas of the winter landscape that he donated to the Canadian War Memorials.[5]

As early as 1936 this sketch was in the collection of Brooke Claxton, who was to become the minister of national defence from 1946 to 1954, and it remained in his family until it was acquired by Blair Laing in 1987.

1. Buchanan 1936a, p. 170.
2. Letter from Beaverbrook to Sir Edmund Walker, 4 July 1918, Archives, National Gallery of Canada, file 5.41–Miscellaneous Correspondence re War Art.
3. Sketchbook 22 (Montreal Museum of Fine Arts, Dr.1973.45), pp. 8r, 75v, and inside back cover; Buchanan 1936a, p. 126.
4. Buchanan 1936a, p. 128, n. 1.
5. *Canadian War Records Office: Report Submitted by Lord Beaverbrook to the Honourable Sir Edward Kemp, dated 31 August 1919*, Appendix 2, Archives, National Gallery of Canada, file 5.41–Miscellaneous Correspondence re War Art. The painting (together with the other large commissioned canvases) was not included in any of the post-war exhibitions of the Canadian War Memorials, most likely because of its size. See Cloutier 1985, p. 228. Now titled *Canadians in the Snow*, it is in the Canadian War Museum, Ottawa (8949).

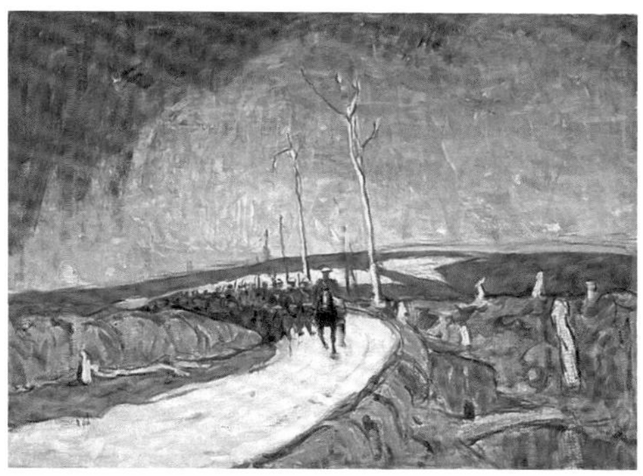

Fig. 78a
At the Front, 1918, oil on canvas, 60.5 × 81.6 cm. National Gallery of Canada (6357).

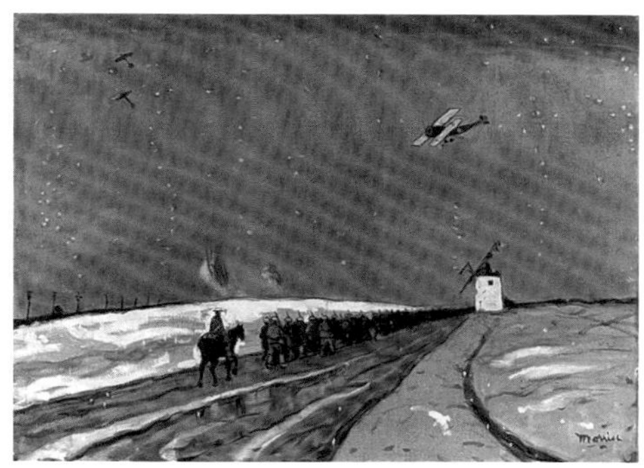

Fig. 78b
Canadian Troops at the Front, 1918, oil on canvas, 60 × 81 cm. Montreal Museum of Fine Arts. Gift of the artist's estate, 1925 (925.332).

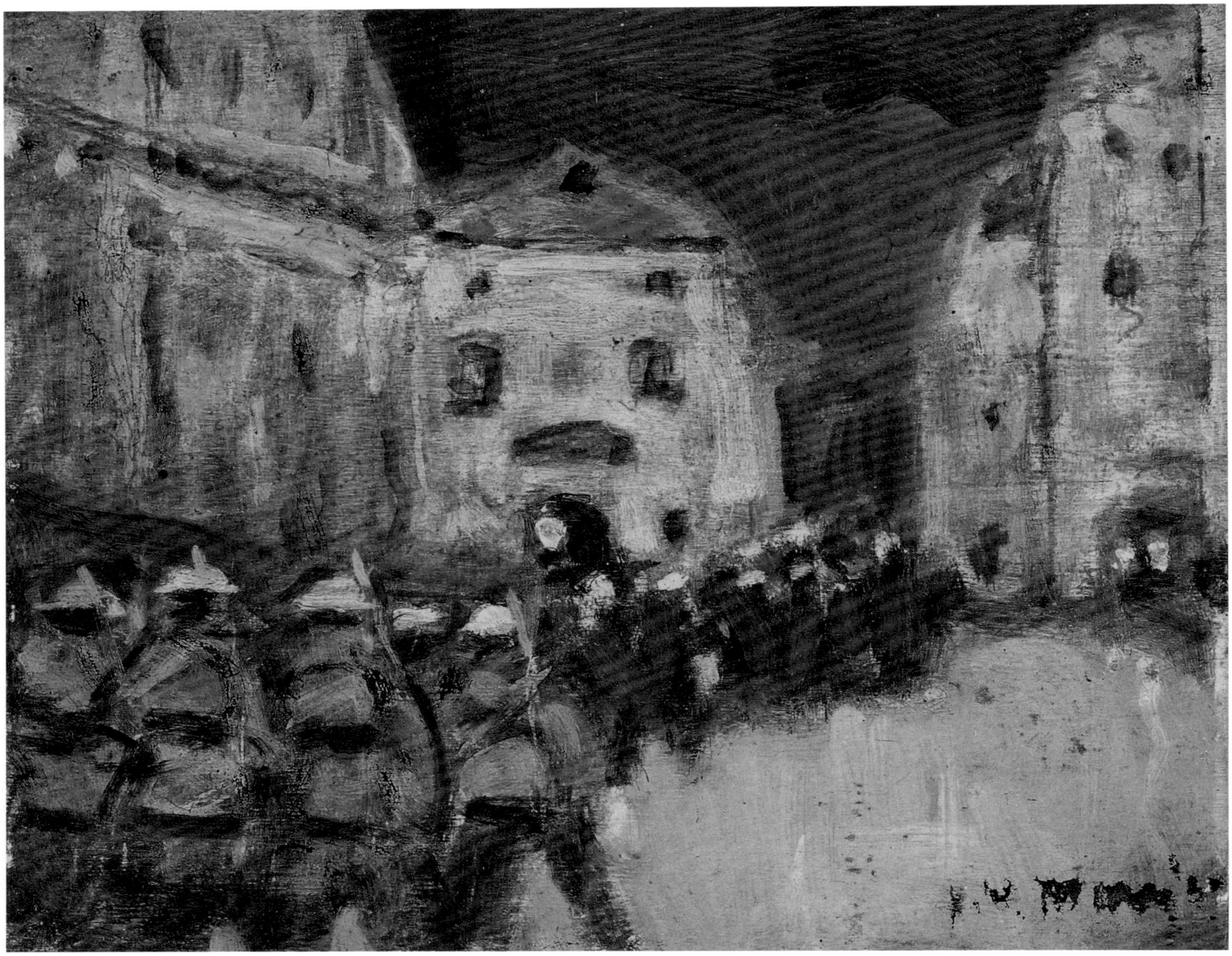

79

Soldiers in France

1918

Oil and graphite on wood, 13.4 × 16.8 cm

Inscriptions: signed l.r., *J.W. Morrice*; verso: u.c. in graphite, *1071*, u.r. in blue ink, *46396*, c. stamped, STUDIO / J.W. MORRICE; back of frame: u.l. in graphite, *From Collection / of Mrs James Law / Montreal*

Labels: in blue ballpoint pen, *86-15 / CDN SOLDIERS / AT ROUEN*

Provenance: Estate of the artist. Mrs. James Law, Montreal. Mrs. Ward C. Pitfield, Montreal (sold, Joyner Fine Art Inc., Toronto, 1 December 1986, lot 28); G. Blair Laing Ltd., Toronto, 1986.

30436

Handled very differently than the foregoing study is this roughly sketched oil of troops marching through a French town. The flat blue sky, grey street with lights reflecting on it, and hauntingly drawn buildings create an almost hallucinatory effect.

When acquired by Blair Laing from the collection of Mrs. Ward C. Pitfield in 1986, this work was titled *Germans Entering Rouen* – possibly a misreading of the soldiers' bayonets for the spikes of German helmets.

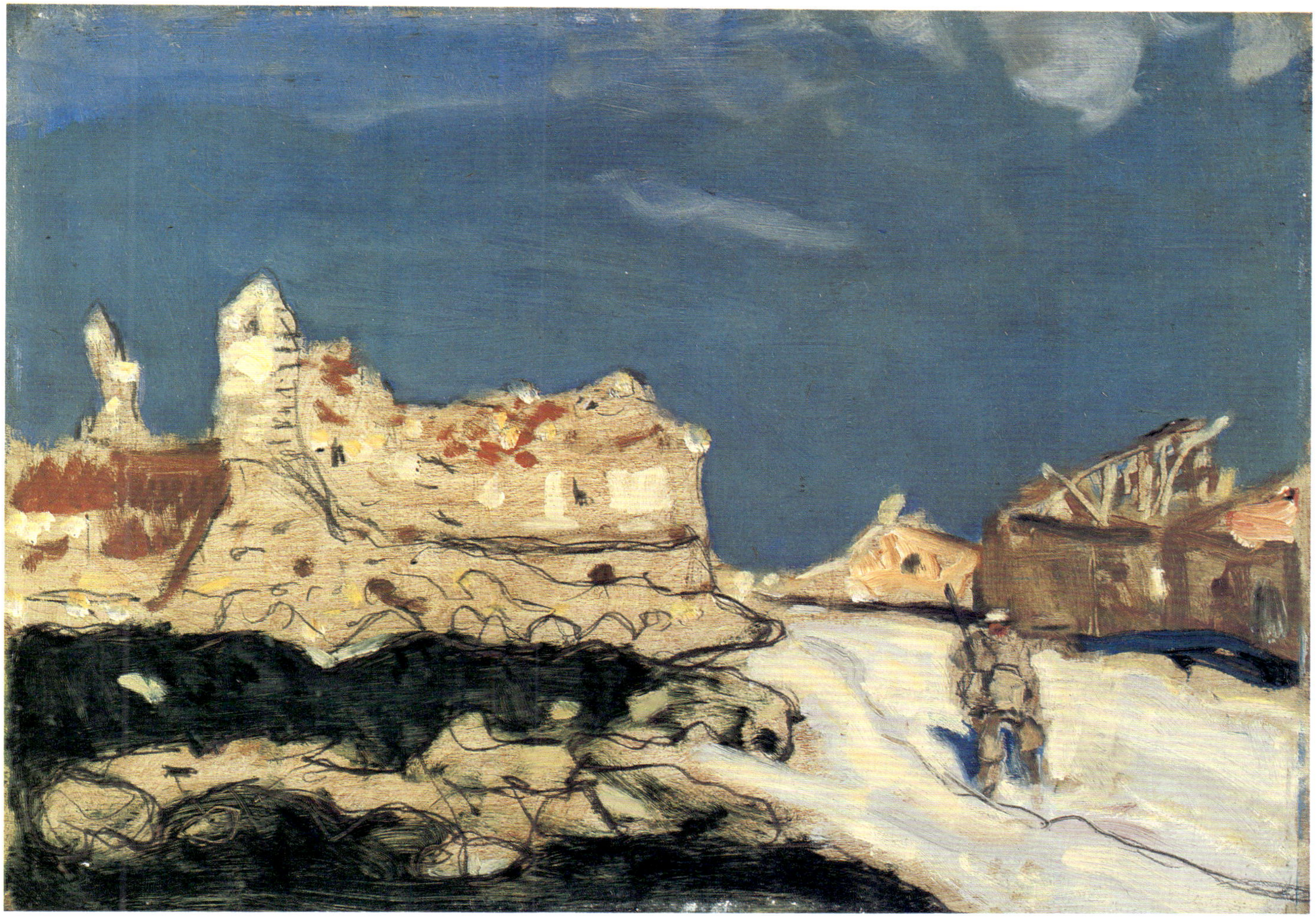

80

War Scene

1918

Oil and graphite on wood, 23.5 × 33 cm

Inscriptions: verso: u.c. in black ink (Joseph Shima's hand?), *"War Scene, in Flanders" / by James W. Morrice, R.C.A.*, u.l. in green pencil, *M204*, in brown ink, *0/3226*; back of frame: u.c. in graphite, *War Scene in Flanders*

Labels: typed, THE / NATIONAL GALLERY OF CANADA OTTAWA / *Paintings in Ottawa Collections* / OHMS *April 9, 1959. / Name Eugene M. Henry / Address 228 Lisgar Rd., Rockcliffe / Title Flanders – World War I / J.W. Morrice RCA / Value $900.00*; OKanada, no. 45; in blue ink, *81-5* / *WAR SCENE / FLANDERS 1918*

Provenance: W. Scott & Sons, Montreal;[1] Continental Galleries of Fine Art, Montreal. Eugene Henry, Ottawa; by descent to a member of the Henry family; G. Blair Laing Ltd., Toronto, 1981.

30422

Of the war sketches by Morrice in the Blair Laing collection, this one is certainly the finest. The flat-blue sky and dense dark-green grass frame a ruined building that is drawn on the bare wood with a fluid line and merely touched with a bit of red and yellow. Morrice has further emphasized the line by drawing with the dark graphite into the paint and with the end of his brush into the wet paint at the right. A solitary soldier walks on the white and grey road – a haunting image of beauty in the ruins. Painted on a panel of the same size as *Study for "Environs of Tangiers"* (cat. no. 67), this oil has all the sophistication and elegance of the artist's pre-war sketches.

1. "Phases of Art of J.W. Morrice on View at Scott's Galleries," *The Gazette* (Montreal), 4 February 1939.

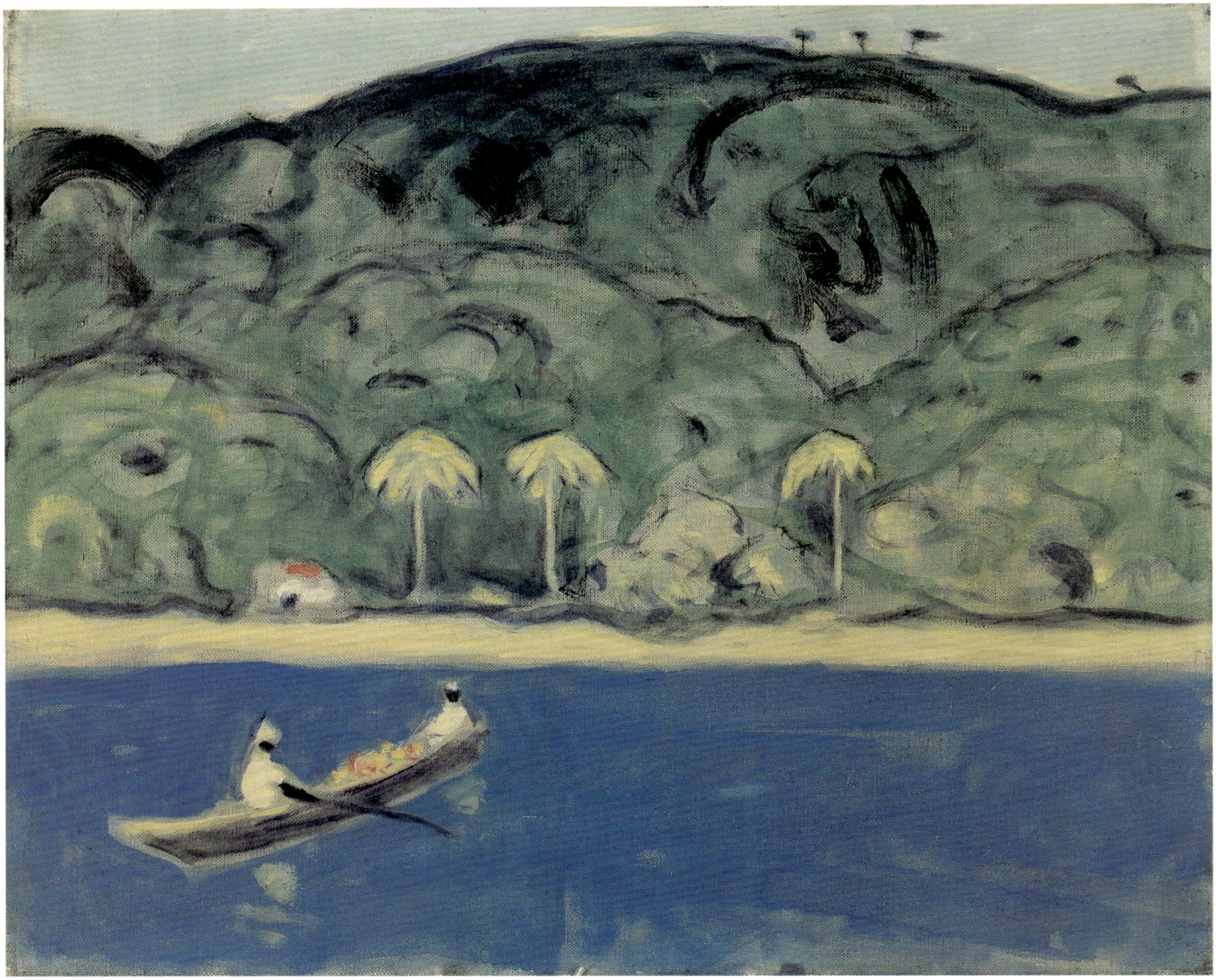

81

Fruit Boat, Trinidad

c. 1921

Oil on canvas, 38.3 × 46.5 cm

Inscriptions: stretcher: u.l. in brown ink, *IN TRINIDAD*, u.r. in brown ink, *From the Studio of J.W. Morrice / J C Heaton*; on crossbar, u.c. in graphite, *M235*

Labels: partly torn, typed, [—] Catherine St. West, MONTREAL / ARTIST *James W. Morrice*; partly torn, in blue ink, *GBL / FRUIT BOAT / TRIN*[I]*DAD*; in graphite, ***#20***

Provenance: Estate of the artist; W. Scott & Sons, Montreal. Continental Galleries of Fine Art, Montreal, by 1949;[1] Lawrence M. Hart, Montreal, by 1953.[2] G. Blair Laing, Toronto, 1963.

30459

In late 1920 Morrice returned to Canada for the first time in six years. By early January 1921 he had left for Trinidad.[3] Painting at Macqueripe Bay and Las Cuevas,[4] he was especially attracted to the beaches and the lushly verdant hills. Two preparatory drawings for this canvas (figs. 81a and 81b) were made in Trinidad, one a rough idea and the second a compositional sketch. In the canvas, the building evident in the second drawing has become just a dot of white and red in a natural paradise of deep-blue water, rich-green hills topped by a few lone palms, and a soft-blue sky. The hill is drawn with a dark line over a thin, transparent green and then brushed with darker greens to give the impression of lights and shadows. All is serene and glowing with colour, as the fruit-laden canoe is rowed from shore.

1. "Art," *The Gazette* (Montreal), 21 March 1949.
2. Loaned by Lawrence M. Hart to Toronto 1953, no. 28, as *Trinidad* (confirmed by installation photographs).
3. Elizabeth Cadiz Topp, *Endless Summer: Canadian Artists in the Caribbean* (Kleinburg: McMichael Canadian Art Collection, 1988), pp. 16, 19–20. Morrice had left Montreal by 3 January 1921; see letter from W. Scott & Sons to J.W. Beatty, Pittsburgh, Carnegie Institute Papers, Archives of American Art, Washington, D.C., microfilm 38, file 405. Buchanan (1936a, p. 131) states that Morrice also spent time in Jamaica during this trip, but that claim is disproven by the information published by Topp.
4. Conversation with G.H. Tyler, Vancouver, 29 June 1977. Mr. Tyler had been an inspector for the Royal Bank of Canada and met Morrice in Trinidad. See also Dorais 1985b, p. 21.

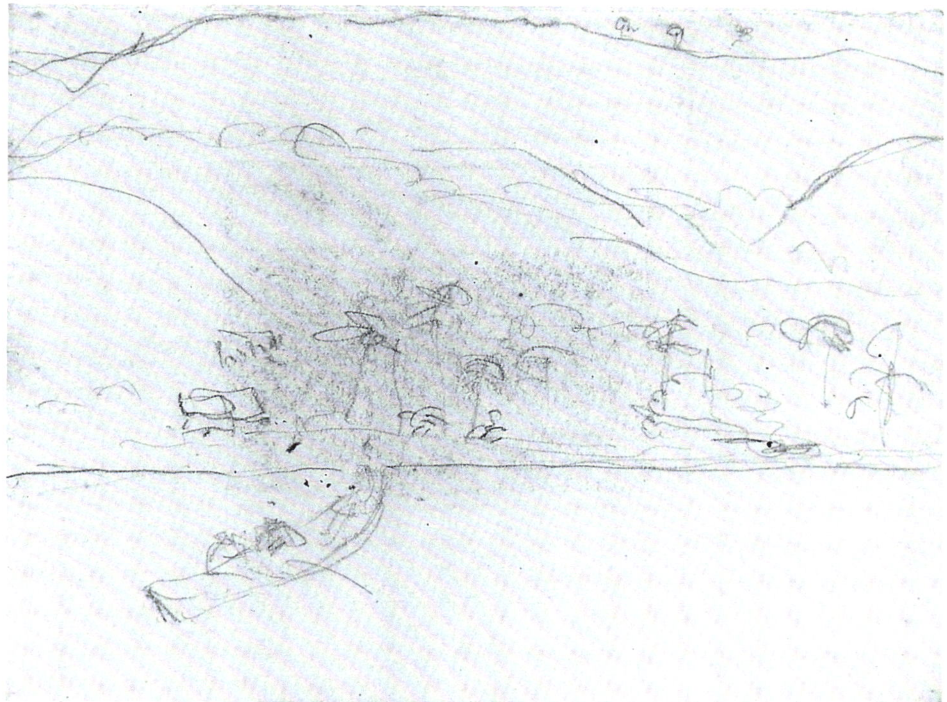

Fig. 81a
Sketchbook 21, p. 40r, 1921, graphite on wove paper, 12.6 × 16.5 cm. Montreal Museum of Fine Arts. Gift of David R. Morrice, 1973 (Dr.1973.44).

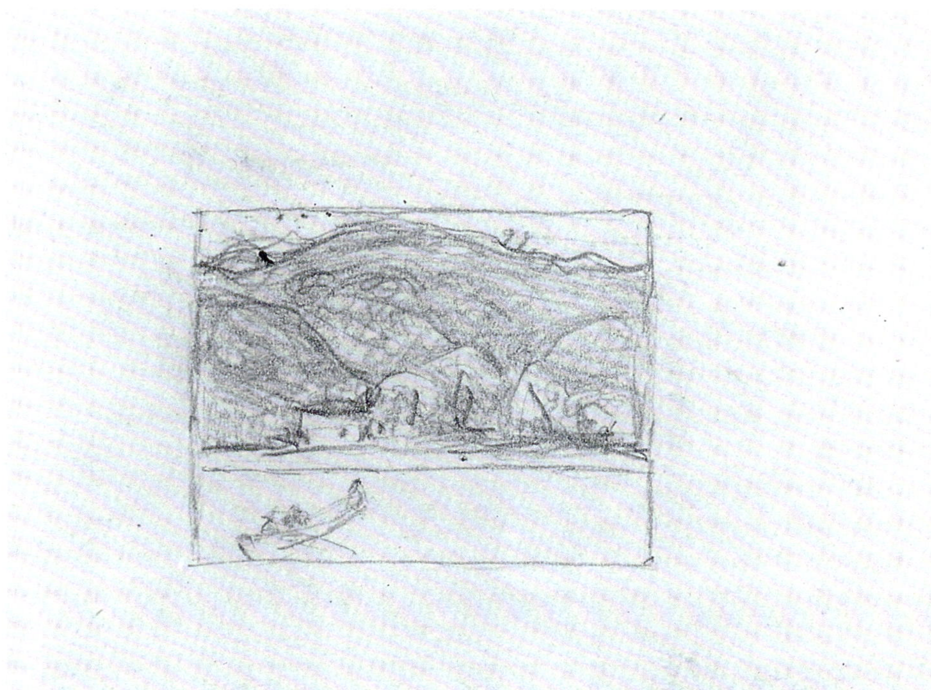

Fig. 81b
Study for "Fruit Boat, Trinidad", 1921, graphite on wove paper (p. 39v detached from Sketchbook 21), 12.6 × 16.5 cm. Montreal Museum of Fine Arts. Bequest of David R. Morrice, 1978 (Dr.1981.14v).

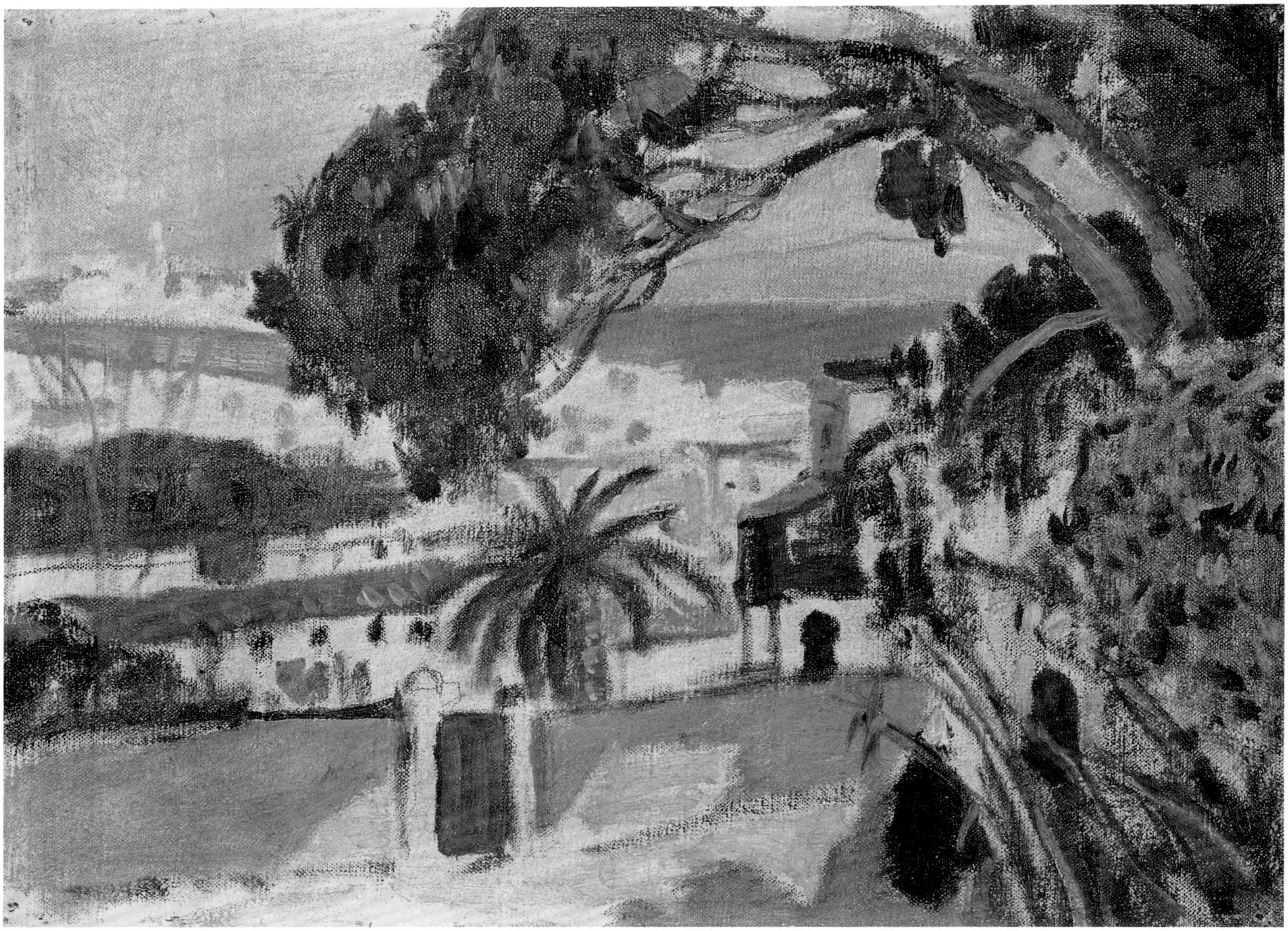

82

In Tangiers

c. 1912–22

Oil on canvas mounted on wood-pulp board, 24 × 31.7 cm

Inscriptions: verso: c.l. stamped, *STUDIO / J.W. MORRICE*, u.c. in black ink (Joseph Shima's hand), *"In Tangiers" / by James W. Morrice, R.C.A.*

Labels: in blue ballpoint pen, CONTINENTAL GALLERIES / OF FINE ART / 1310 ST. CATHERINE W. MONTREAL, PLateau 1072, *Property of Mrs. V. Lafontaine*

Provenance: Estate of the artist. Vilma Lafontaine, Montreal; G. Blair Laing, Toronto, 1966.

30461

From the 1890s on, Morrice almost always painted his oil sketches on wood panels,[1] but either just before or soon after the First World War he returned to canvas supports. In the Montreal Museum of Fine Arts there is a canvas sketch of the bay of Tangiers (fig. 82a) that is related in composition to, but not the actual study for, Morrice's 1912 Salon d'Automne canvas *Tanger, la plage*.[2] It is possible that *In Tangiers* and the canvas sketch in Montreal were painted after the war, though we have no documentation confirming that Morrice returned to Tangiers after 1913. Tack holes are visible in the corners of both these oil sketches where Morrice fixed the canvas to a secondary support for painting.

In subject and colour, *In Tangiers* bears certain similarities to the problematically titled *Monastery Gate, Cuba* (cat. no. 74); in its texture and paint application it is comparable to the unfinished canvas sketch of Algiers in the Mackenzie Art Gallery (fig. 83a). In the present work Morrice has reinforced the lines of the overhanging branches in black and has highlighted the foliage with touches of black and brown. The construction of forms is somewhat tentative; it is as if he were working toward a new visual language through his understanding of the work of Cezanne, whom he greatly admired. "Fine work, almost criminally fine," he remarked about Cézanne. "I once disliked some of his pictures. I now like them all. His is the savage work that one would expect to come from America – but it is always France that produces anything emphatic in art."[3]

1. *Pont St-Michel* (cat. no. 35) is on a wood-pulp board, as is an oil sketch titled *Portail d'église*, in the Mackenzie Art Gallery, Regina (78-4).
2. Musée du Québec, Quebec City (34-467P), reproduced in Cloutier 1985, p. 211. The study (oil and graphite on wood, 23.5 × 33 cm) was with the Dominion Gallery, Montreal, in 1958, and is reproduced in *Canadian Art* XV:4 (November 1958), p. 313.
3. Letter from Morrice to Edmund Morris, 30 January [1910], Morris Papers.

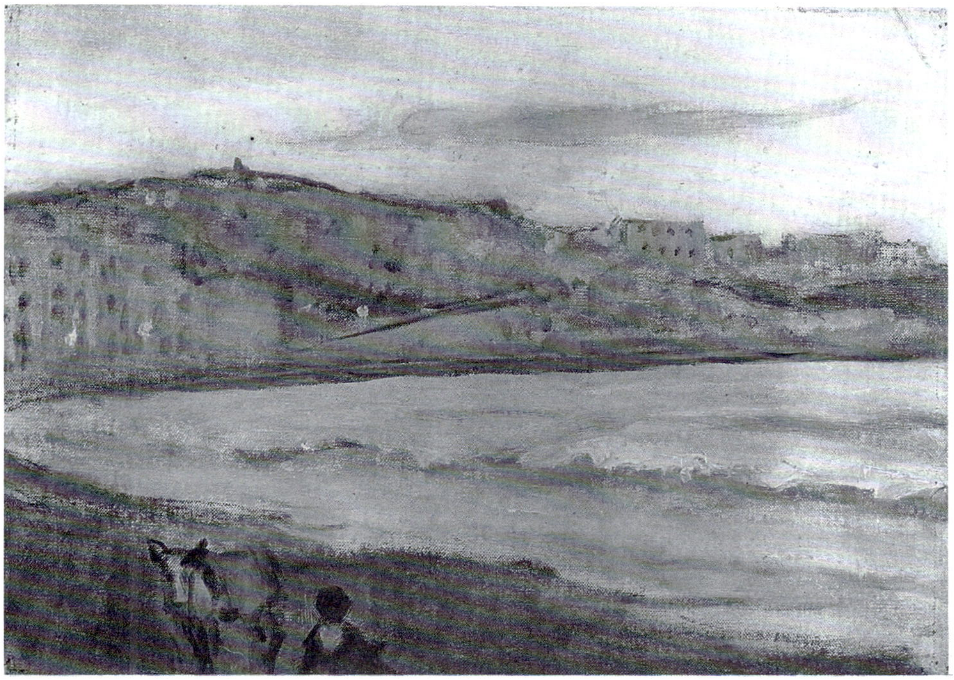

Fig. 82a
Tangiers, c. 1912–22, oil on canvas, 23 × 31.2 cm. Montreal Museum of Fine Arts. Bequest of F. Eleanore Morrice, 1981 (1981.50).

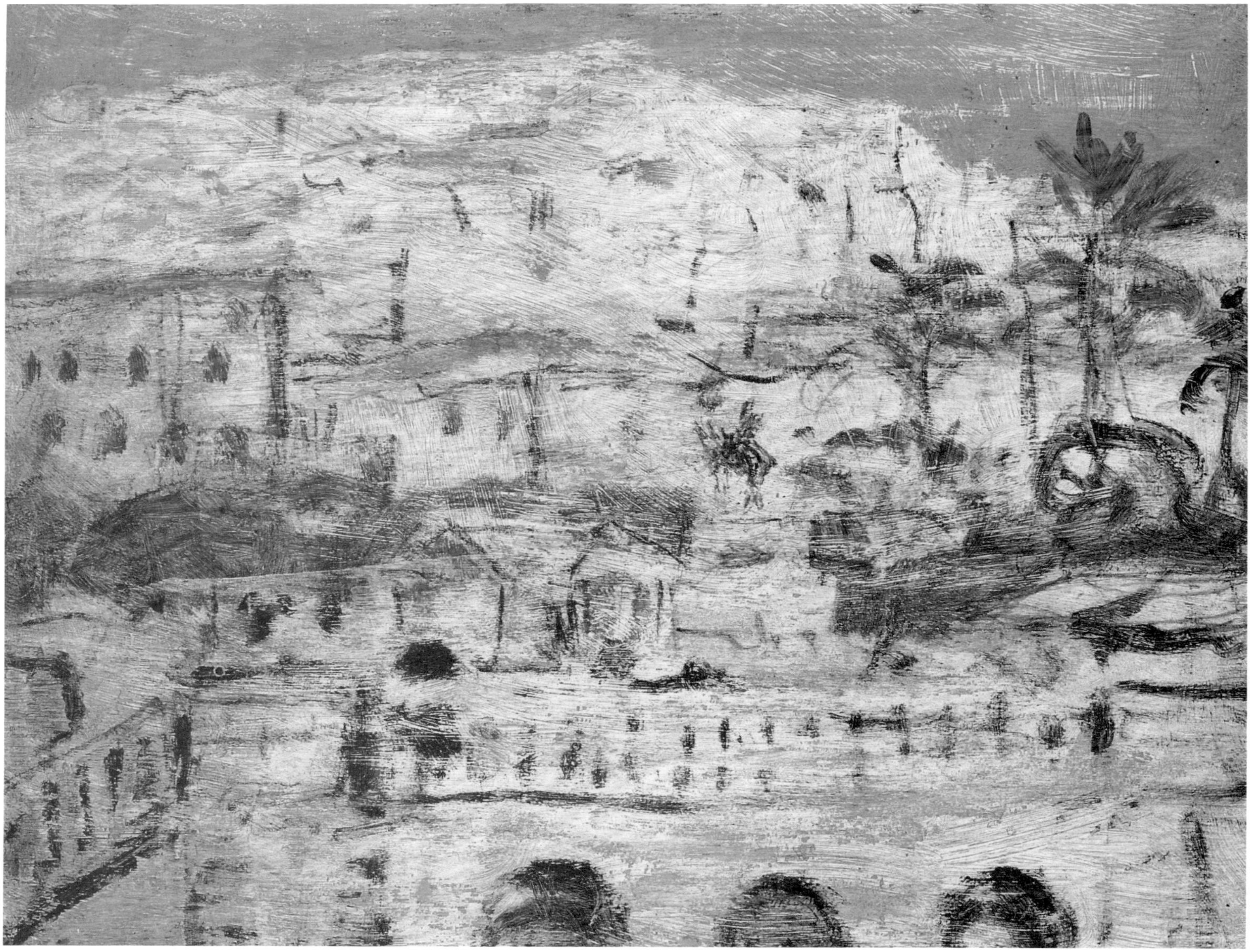

83

Algiers

c. 1922

Oil and graphite on wood, 12.9 × 16.3 cm

Inscriptions: verso: u.l. in graphite, *85.00*, u.c. in graphite, "*Algiers*", u.r. in graphite, *Tan*[—], c. stamped, *STUDIO / J.W. MORRICE*, in stamp in graphite, *307*

Provenance: Estate of the artist. Continental Galleries of Fine Art, Montreal; Lawrence T. Porter, St. Andrew's East, Quebec; G. Blair Laing, Toronto, c. 1980.

30456

After the war Morrice's wanderings became even more frenetic than before. He visited Cagnes (where he purchased a house for Léa Cadoret),[1] Monte Carlo, Marseilles, Nice, Dieppe, Boulogne, Majorca, Corsica, Bastia, Biskra, and Algiers.[2] His preference in the end was for Algiers, and a number of his last major canvases depict this port city.

In an unfinished canvas sketch in the Mackenzie Art Gallery (fig. 83a)[3] Morrice presents a panoramic view of Algiers, with large imposing buildings surmounting the arcaded port. In this small sketch on wood the terraced arches define the foreground, with the hills, villas, and palm trees fleetingly suggested. Black paint and graphite define the main forms, a blue sky crowns the hill, and a thin coat of blue has been brushed over much of the lower portion of the panel, unifying the composition.

Donald Buchanan describes in some detail the hardships of Morrice's last few years – his alcoholism and ill health, his hospitalization, his search for cures.[4] On 18 December 1923 Morrice wrote to Léa Cadoret from Tunis: "Arrived this morning. The weather is good. Hotter than in Nice. Don't forget letters at Lloyd's Bank. Address for now is 'Poste Restante.' Yours Morrice."[5] In January he made a last trip to Palermo, Sicily, before returning once again to Tunis.[6]

It was during that same month that Homer Saint-Gaudens, Director of Fine Arts at the Carnegie Institute, happened to write to Morrice in Paris: ". . . anxious to have painting from you but unfortunately I hear you are in Nice or Algiers or some happy place where the weather is dry and the sun is brighter."[7] The letter, having been forwarded to Tunis, was returned to its sender. Morrice had died in Tunis on 23 January 1924.

1. Buchanan 1936a, pp. 136–37; Laing 1984, pp. 138–42.
2. Sketchbook 21 (Montreal Museum of Fine Arts, Dr.1973.44) contains many drawings and inscriptions that enable us to document Morrice's travels in 1921 and 1922; it includes as well drawings of Trinidad. See also the letter from William Brymner to Maurice Cullen, 23 February 1922, typed transcript, Archives, National Gallery of Canada.
3. A preparatory drawing for *Port of Algiers* is in Sketchbook 21, p. 19r.
4. Buchanan 1936a, pp. 133–40.
5. Quoted in Johnston 1968, p. 457, n. 8.
6. Postcard from Morrice (in Palermo) to Brymner (in Menton, France), 14 January (postmarked 14 January 1924), photocopy in Blair Laing's notes on Morrice, Archives, National Gallery of Canada.
7. Letter from Saint-Gaudens to Morrice, 15 January 1924, Carnegie Institute Papers, Archives of American Art, Washington, D.C., microfilm 46 (1923–24), file 600.

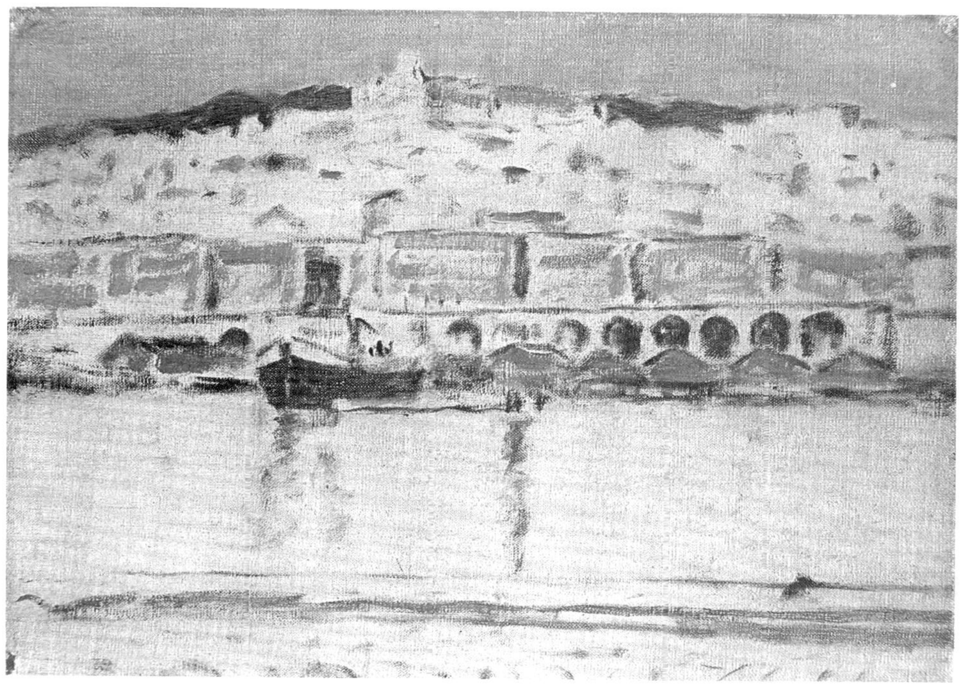

Fig. 83a
Port of Algiers, c. 1922, oil on canvas, 24.7 × 32.4 cm. Mackenzie Art Gallery, Regina, University of Regina Collection. Bequest of William R. Tobin, 1978 (78-3).

Selected Bibliography

AYRE, ROBERT. "A Distinguished Exhibition Affirms Genius of James Wilson Morrice." *The Gazette* (Montreal), 27 February 1937.

AYRE, ROBERT. "J.W. Morrice Pictures at Scott's 'One of Greatest of Our Painters'." *The Standard* (Montreal), 28 January 1939.

BAZIN, JULES. "Hommage à James Wilson Morrice 1865–1924." *Vie des Arts* 40 (Autumn 1965), pp. 15–24.

BELL, CLIVE. *Old Friends Personal Recollections.* London: Chatto & Windus, 1956.

BENNETT, ARNOLD. *Buried Alive.* London: Chapman and Hall Ltd., 1908.

BENNETT, ARNOLD. "Evening with Exiles." In *Paris Nights*, pp. 21–37. London: Hodder and Stoughton, 1913.

BENNETT, ARNOLD. *The Journals of Arnold Bennett 1869–1928.* New York: The Viking Press, 1933.

BENNET, ARNOLD. *The Journals.* Edited by Frank Swinnerton. Harmondsworth: Penguin Books, 1971.

BORGMEYER, C.L. "The Master Impressionists." *The Fine Arts Journal* (Chicago), XXVIII:6 (June 1913), pp. 322–54.

BROOKE, JANET M. "James Wilson Morrice." In *The Art of Connoisseurship* (exhibition catalogue), pp. 113–21. Montreal: Montreal Museum of Fine Arts, 1978.

BUCHANAN, DONALD W. *James Wilson Morrice: A Biography.* Toronto: The Ryerson Press, 1936. [Cited as Buchanan 1936a.]

BUCHANAN, DONALD W. "James Wilson Morrice." *The University of Toronto Quarterly* V:2 (January 1936), pp. 216–27.

BUCHANAN, DONALD W. "James Wilson Morrice." *Saturday Night* LI:14 (8 February 1936), p. 9.

BUCHANAN, DONALD W. "A Canadian in St. Malo." *Queen's Quarterly* XLIII:3 (Autumn 1936), pp. 298–300.

BUCHANAN, DONALD W. "World of Art." *Saturday Night* LIII:11 (15 January 1938), p. 6.

BUCHANAN, DONALD W. "The Gentle and the Austere: A Comparison in Landscape Painting." *The University of Toronto Quarterly* XI:1 (October 1941), pp. 72–77.

BUCHANAN, DONALD W. *James Wilson Morrice.* Toronto: The Ryerson Press, 1947.

BUCHANAN, DONALD W. "The Sketchbooks of James Wilson Morrice." *Canadian Art* X:3 (Spring 1953), pp. 107–09.

BUCHANAN, DONALD W. "James Wilson Morrice – Painter of Quebec and the World." *The Educational Record of the Province of Quebec* LXXX:3 (July–September 1954), pp. 163–69.

BURGOYNE, ST. GEORGE. "Phases of Art of J.W. Morrice on View at Scott's Galleries." *The Gazette* (Montreal), 28 January 1939.

CHARLESWORTH, HECTOR. "The Late James Wilson Morrice." *Saturday Night* XXXIX:12 (9 February 1924), p. 3.

CIOLKOWSKA, H.S. "James Wilson Morrice." *L'Art et les Artistes* 62 (December 1925), pp. 90–94.

CIOLKOWSKA, MURIEL. "James Wilson Morrice, peintre canadien et peintre du Canada." *France-Canada*, supplement to *La Canadienne* XI:5 (May 1913), pp. 55–57.

CIOLKOWSKA, MURIEL. "A Canadian Painter: James Wilson Morrice." *The Studio* LIX:245 (August 1913), pp. 176–83. [Cited as Ciolkowska 1913b.]

CIOLKOWSKA, MURIEL. "Memories of Morrice." *The Canadian Forum* VI (November 1925), pp. 52–53. [Cited as Ciolkowska 1925b.]

CLERMONT, GHISLAIN. "Morrice et la critique." *Revue de l'Université de Moncton* XV:2–3 (April–December 1982), pp. 35–48.

CLOUTIER, NICOLE. "Canadian Painting and Decorative Arts." In *A Montreal Collection: Gift from Eleanore and David Morrice* (exhibition catalogue), pp. 15–46. Montreal: Montreal Museum of Fine Arts, 1983.

CLOUTIER, NICOLE. *James Wilson Morrice 1865–1924* (exhibition catalogue). Montreal: Montreal Museum of Fine Arts, 1985.

CLOUTIER, NICOLE. "Deux tableaux de James Wilson Morrice dans la collection Morozov." *The Journal of Canadian Art History* IX:1 (1986), pp. 81–88.

CLOUTIER, NICOLE. "Short Note: Morrice 1912." *The Journal of Canadian Art History* X:2 (1987), pp. 153–60.

Cowart, Jack, and Pierre Schneider, John Elderfield, Albert Kostenevich, and Laura Coyle. *Matisse in Morocco: The Paintings and Drawings 1912–1913* (exhibition catalogue). Washington, D.C: National Gallery of Art, 1990.

Crowley, Aleister. *The Confessions of Aleister Crowley: An Autohagiography.* Edited by John Symonds and Kenneth Grant. London: Cape, 1969; Bantam, 1971.

Crowley, Aleister. *Snowdrops from a Curate's Garden.* Chicago: The Teitan Press, 1986.

Dorais, Lucie. "Deux moments dans la vie et l'oeuvre de James Wilson Morrice." In *Bulletin 30/1977*, pp. 19–35. Ottawa: National Gallery of Canada, 1978.

Dorais, Lucie. *James Wilson Morrice: Les années de formation.* Master's thesis, Université de Montréal, 1980.

Dorais, Lucie. "Morrice and the Human Figure." In Cloutier 1985, pp. 63–72. [Cited as Dorais 1985a.]

Dorais, Lucie. *J.W. Morrice.* Ottawa: National Gallery of Canada, 1985. [Cited as Dorais 1985b.]

Éthier-Blais, Jean. "James Wilson Morrice." *Vie des Arts* 73 (Winter 1973–74), pp. 41–44.

"Fine Paintings Shown in Heaton Collection." *The Gazette* (Montreal), 22 October 1949.

Fromuth, Charles H., Journals (mnc 2796). Library of Congress, Washington, D.C.

Gillson, A.H.S.. "James W. Morrice – Canadian Painter." *The Canadian Forum* v:57 (June 1925), pp. 271–73.

Hedges, Doris E. "The Art of James Wilson Morrice." *The Bridle and Golfer* (April 1932), pp. 22–23, 50.

Henri, Robert. Diaries. Collection of Janet LeClair. Microfilms 885 and 886. Archives of American Art, Washington, D.C.

Henri, Robert. Papers. Beinecke Rare Book and Manuscript Library, Yale University, New Haven, Connecticut.

Hill, Charles C. *Exploring the Collections: James Wilson Morrice (1865–1924).* Ottawa: National Gallery of Canada, 1977.

Hill, Charles C. "Morrice at Montreal." *RACAR* xiii:1 (1986), pp. 52–59.

Homer, William Innes. *Robert Henri and His Circle.* New York: Hacker Art Books, 1988.

Hunter, E. Robert. *Masterpieces of Twentieth-Century Canadian Painting* (exhibition catalogue). West Palm Beach, Florida: The Norton Gallery and School of Art, 1984.

Ingram, W.H. "Canadian Artists Abroad." *The Canadian Magazine* xxviii:3 (January 1907), pp. 218–22.

Johnston, W.R. *James Wilson Morrice 1865–1924* (exhibition catalogue). Montreal: Montreal Museum of Fine Arts, 1965.

Johnston, W.R. "James Wilson Morrice: A Canadian Abroad." *Apollo* lxxxvii:76 (June 1968), pp. 452–57.

Laing, G. Blair. *Memoirs of an Art Dealer.* Toronto: McClelland and Stewart, 1979.

Laing, G. Blair. *Memoirs of an Art Dealer 2.* Toronto: McClelland and Stewart, 1983.

Laing, G. Blair. *Morrice: A Great Canadian Artist Rediscovered.* Toronto: McClelland and Stewart, 1984.

Langdale, Cecily. *Charles Conder, Robert Henri, James Morrice, Maurice Prendergast: The Formative Years, Paris, 1890s* (exhibition catalogue). New York: Davis & Long Co., 1975.

Leblond, Marius-Ary. *Peintres de races.* Brussels: G. Van Oest & Cie., 1909; Geneva/Paris: Éditions Slatkine, 1981.

Lyman, John. "Morrice, the Master Incognito." *The Montrealer*, 15 January 1937, pp. 18–20.

Lyman, John. "Art World." *Saturday Night* lii:18 (6 March 1937), p. 10. [Cited as Lyman 1937b.]

Lyman, John. "Morrice – The Shadow and the Substance." *The Montrealer*, 15 March 1937, pp. 22–23. [Cited as Lyman 1937c.]

Lyman, John. "Morrice Retrospective." *The Montrealer*, 15 February 1938, pp. 18–20.

Lyman, John. "Mr. Gagnon on Morrice." *The Montrealer*, 1 March 1938, p. 21.

Lyman, John. "In the Galleries." *The Montrealer*, 1 February 1939.

Lyman, John. *Morrice.* Montreal: L'Arbre, 1945.

Lyman, John. *Inédits de John Lyman.* Edited by Hedwige Asselin. Montreal: Bibliothèque Nationale du Québec, 1980.

McTavish, David. *Canadian Artists in Venice* (exhibition catalogue). Kingston: Agnes Etherington Art Centre, 1984.

MacTavish, Newton. Papers. Canadiana Collections, North York Public Library, Toronto.

Malkin, Peter. *James Wilson Morrice 1865–1924* (exhibition catalogue, introduction by Denys Sutton). Vancouver Art Gallery, 1977.

Maugham, Somerset. *The Magician*. 1908. London: William Heinemann Ltd., 1956 (includes "Fragment of Autobiography").

Moisan, Micheline. "Prints and Drawings." In *A Montreal Collection: Gift from Eleanore and David Morrice* (exhibition catalogue), pp. 49–89. Montreal: Montreal Museum of Fine Arts, 1983.

Montreal, Art Association of Montreal. *Memorial Exhibition of Paintings by the Late James W. Morrice, R.C.A.* (exhibition catalogue). 1925.

Montreal, Fraser Bros. Ltd. *Art Auction: The Entire Stock of Messrs. W. Scott & Sons* (auction catalogue). 1–9 April 1938.

Montreal, W. Scott & Sons. *James Wilson Morrice: Exhibition of Paintings* (exhibition catalogue). 1932.

Montreal, W. Scott & Sons. *Exhibition of Paintings by J.W. Morrice*. 1937. Mimeographed checklist.

"Morrice as Painter Analyzed by Gagnon." *The Gazette* (Montreal), 12 February 1938.

Morris, Edmund. Papers, including records of the Canadian Art Club. E.P. Taylor Reference Library, Art Gallery of Ontario, Toronto.

Murray, Joan. *Impressionism in Canada* (exhibition catalogue). Toronto: Art Gallery of Ontario, 1973.

Neve, Christopher. "A Canadian Nomad in Search of a Style." *Country Life* CXXXXIII:3720 (20 June 1968), pp. 1680–81.

O'Brian, John. "Morrice-O'Conor, Gauguin, Bonnard et Vuillard." *Revue de l'Université de Moncton* XV:2–3 (April–December 1982), pp. 9–34.

O'Brian, John. "James Wilson Morrice: His Relationship with the Avant-Garde in France." In *OKanada (Original Texts for German-Language Catalogue)*, pp. 57–62. Ottawa: The Canada Council, [1985]. German text, with illustrations, in *OKanada* (exhibition catalogue), pp. 62–69. Berlin: Akademie der Künste, 1982. [Cited as O'Brian 1982b.]

O'Brian, John. "Morrice's Pleasures (1900–1914)." In Cloutier 1985, pp. 89–97.

Ostiguy, Jean-René. "The Sketch-Books of James Wilson Morrice." *Apollo* CIII:171 (May 1976), pp. 424–27.

Ottawa, National Gallery of Canada. *Souvenir Catalogue: The Imperial Economic Conference* (exhibition catalogue). 1932.

Ottawa, National Gallery of Canada. *James Wilson Morrice, R.C.A., 1865–1924: Memorial Exhibition* (exhibition catalogue). 1937.

Paris, Galeries Simonson. *Catalogue des Tableaux et Études par James-Wilson Morrice* (exhibition catalogue, preface by Armand Dayot). 1926.

Paris, Musée du Jeu de Paume. *Exposition d'art canadien* (exhibition catalogue). 1927.

Paris, Société du Salon d'automne. *Catalogue. Salon d'automne. Exposition rétrospective d'oeuvres de sociétaires du Salon d'automne décédés depuis le dernier salon* (exhibition catalogue). 1924.

Pennell, Joseph. Papers (S79-35857). Library of Congress, Washington, D.C.

Pepper, Kathleen Daly. *James Wilson Morrice*. Toronto: Clarke, Irwin & Company Ltd., 1966.

Reid, Dennis. *James Wilson Morrice 1865–1924* (exhibition catalogue, introduction by Denys Sutton). Bath: Holburne of Menstrie Museum, 1968.

Stevenson, O.J. *A People's Best*. Toronto: Musson Book Co. Ltd., 1927.

Szylinger, Irene. "A Brief Analysis of the Watercolours." In Cloutier 1985, pp. 79–88.

Tally, M.K. *Robert Henry Logan (1874–1942)* (exhibition catalogue). New York: Davis & Long Co., 1980.

Thomson, Eileen B. "James Wilson Morrice." *The Canadian Forum* XII:141 (June 1932), pp. 336–39.

Toronto, Art Gallery of Toronto. *Catalogue of Inaugural Exhibition* (exhibition catalogue). 1926.

Toronto, Art Gallery of Toronto. *Exhibition of Paintings by James Wilson Morrice* (exhibition catalogue). 1932.

Toronto, Art Gallery of Toronto. *Royal Canadian Academy of Arts: Memorial Section, Paintings and Drawings by J.W. Morrice, R.C.A., 1865–1924* (exhibition catalogue). 1953.

Toronto, Mellors Fine Arts Ltd., *James Wilson Morrice: Exhibition of Paintings* (exhibition catalogue). 1934.

Vauxcelles, Louis. "The Art of J.W. Morrice." *The Canadian Magazine* XXXIV:2 (December 1909), pp. 169–76.

Viau, Guy. "Morrice." *Le Quartier Latin* XXVI:11 (17 December 1943), p. 11.

Watson Art Galleries, Montreal. Papers, including ledgers and inventory books, 1911–58. Archives, National Gallery of Canada.

Watson, William R. "J.W. Morrice, R.C.A.." *The Gazette* (Montreal), 27 July 1932.

Watson, William R. *Retrospective: Recollections of a Montreal Art Dealer*. Toronto: University of Toronto Press, 1974.

Photograph Credits

Photographs have been provided by the owners or custodians of the works reproduced, except for the following (all indicated by figure number):

Art Gallery of Ontario, E.P. Taylor Reference Library, Toronto, 3 (Introduction)

J.-L. Boutillier, Amiens, 5 (Introduction)

Miller Comstock / © 1989 Yousuf Karsh, front flap

Dalhousie Art Gallery, Halifax, 6b

Galerie Dominion, Montreal, 72b

Sherman Hines, Toronto, 4 (Introduction)

Joyner Fine Art Inc., Toronto, 16a

G. Blair Laing Ltd., Toronto, 7a, 60a

Montreal Museum of Fine Arts, frontispiece (copy photo), 1a, 18b (copy photo), 30b, 33c

National Library of Canada, Ottawa, 33a (copy photo, 17565)

National Gallery of Canada, 1 (Introduction), 9 (Introduction), 10a (Thomas Moore Photography, Toronto), 17a, 18a, 24a, 30a, 30c, 31a, 32a, 39b, 43b, 46b, 47a, 47b, 51a, 59b, 63a, 66a, 75b

Notman Photographic Archives, McCord Museum of Canadian History, Montreal, 67a, 77c

Southern Alberta Art Gallery, Lethbridge, 64b